# Testimonials for

# Trauma and Well-being Among Legal Professionals

'Throughout the book, Dawn D'Amico raises the pivotal issues that plagued law students and lawyers. Readers will learn about these issues through a variety of compelling approaches. They also will learn about secondary trauma and its effects. The case studies show the patterns of behavior that lead to Judge and lawyer dysfunction and suggest ways to prevent maladaptive behaviors from consuming our lives. Readers also will appreciate a series of reflection and writing exercises that can increase resilience, if completed."

- *G. Andrew H. Benjamin, JD, PhD, ABPP, University of Washington, School of Law and Department of Psychology, Web site: https://washington.academia.edu/GAndrewHBenjamin*

"Trauma and Well-Being Among Legal Professionals takes an unapologetic and refreshing deep dive into the realities of the emotional costs and burdens that we often carry in silence. It provides expert, valuable, and practical information as well as real stories that help to normalize the conversation.

Our mental health is a topic that needs to be openly discussed, clearly understood, and effectively addressed for meaningful support, education and change to occur. Thank you, Dawn, for shining the light and holding the space for the legal profession to grow in awareness, take courage to disclose and overcome barriers that truly hold us back.

This is a must read for every law student, judicial member, and practitioner."

- *Lara Wentworth, Lawyer, Performance and wellness advocate and coach for lawyers. www.larawentworth.com.au*

"The recent book by Dr Dawn D'Amico, *Trauma and Well-Being Among Legal Professionals,* is an important initiative in shining the light on the real challenge presented by secondary trauma experienced by judges, lawyers, and other professionals engaged in dealing with disputes, especially in family separations and divorce."

- *Retired Judge Rob Murfitt, New Zealand Family Court*

"A long-overdue book, tackling an important but painful aspect of legal work that's been too-long ignored. Invaluable."

- *Will Meyerhofer, Psychotherapist, former Attorney and Author of* Way Worse Than Being a Dentist: The Lawyer's Quest for Meaning.

# Trauma and Well-Being Among Legal Professionals

## By

## Dawn D'Amico
LCSW, PhD, CFCM

**Summerland Publishing**
Offices in Salt Lake City, UT and Summerland, CA
www.summerlandpublishing.com
Email: summerlandpublishing@gmail.com

Printed in the United States of America.

ISBN #: 978-1-7329072-8-7

Library of Congress #2021904405

# Acknowledgments

Over the course of three years, I want to thank all of the legal professionals around the world who were open and willing to tackle this subject with me during your hectic days and nights.

I want to give a special thank you to Dr. Michelle Sharpe, JD, PhD for all of her support, knowledge, and expertise.

Attorney Daniel Lukasik, thank you for all of your never-ending encouragement, understanding and support.

Andy Benjamin, JD, PhD, thank you for your truly dedicated help and inspiration.

Thank you to all of the Champions of Disclosure. You amaze me.

Thank you, Agatha Petrulis for getting the ball rolling with the creation of the very first survey and the use of your hands-on tools and your patience.

Thank you, Ed Cohen of the U.S. Judicial College and Melissa Perkin of the New Zealand Bar Association for understanding the importance of this work and helping to move it forward.

Thank you to Attorney Paul Bucher, for introducing me years ago, to this unique part of the law.

Thank you to Madeline Lebiecki, student intern, for all of your work and enthusiasm.

And thank you to Jolinda at Summerland Publishing for your patience and support.

Thank you to Michael for your nonstop encouragement, support and enthusiasm. You helped me to find my way and to stay focused.

Finally, to all the contributors to whom have shared their stories and expertise, thank you for sharing your wisdom.

# Dedication

*To*

Agatha, Michael and Mom and Dad.

And to Shamie, in your memory.

# Trauma and Well-Being in the Legal Profession

Welcome, this book is intended for lawyers, legal associations, and law students to provide a touchstone for health and well-being as well as insight into secondary trauma and other mental health concerns that may arise within legal practice.

Readers will be introduced to trauma, well-being, coping, and resiliency and will be provided with tools to measure personal health and to help create, motivate, and sustain well-being. Readers will also learn about the outcomes of pressure and stress in the legal profession through case studies and literature reviews. The book will explore the cross-cultural effects of healthy and unhealthy ways of coping, including alcohol and other drug use and abuse issues. Mental health issues such as anxiety, depression, and suicide will be covered, and readers will be exposed to the concept of secondary trauma as it relates to the practice of law. We will also look at the results of case studies and interviews from individuals around the globe. Finally, readers will learn from "Champions of Disclosure," self-identified people who share their stories of struggle, coping, and success, as well as one institution that worked to improve the lives of its members.

What is so important about learning more about health and well-being? You made it to this point, right? You must be doing something OK. So have the many other legal professionals before you. Still, there seems to be something inherent in the work, culture, and formal learning processes of law that cause distress for many. We will be attempting to change this by implementing personal and group tools.

Along with others, this book continues to work for an international recognition and discussion of health, including mental health, and well-being among legal professionals and students. It aims to confront the myth that lawyers, barristers, and judges, as well as law students, are immune to the effects of secondary trauma and other mental health effects of stress-filled schooling and jobs. After demonstrating how secondary trauma and other mental health issues affect careers, we will look at how to identify the symptoms and provide self-care solutions.

Listings of resources and statistics are also provided, as are real-life, self-identified, first person narratives.

Readers, you may wonder what drove me to write this book. I have been in private practice as a psychotherapist for over 25 years. During that time, I served as a preferred provider for family court, juvenile court, and the Wisconsin Addictions Resource Council, and I have worked extensively in criminal court. Since about 2013, I have worked on numerous paedophilia cases, both with victims and perpetrators. As I did so, I noticed that I was beginning to experience symptoms of secondary trauma, and it because particularly apparent to me after one particularly egregious case, in which an infant was sexually assaulted.

This case became all-consuming, and I started to have feelings of sadness and fear. I kept having intrusive thoughts and I could not stop questioning how this even happened. I became more fearful for children in general. I remember going to a movie and instead of seeing happy, carefree children in the lobby, I began wondering how many of them had been assaulted, and how many would be in the future.

My world view was beginning to change. No longer did I feel free to walk around alone, for fear for my safety. I also became increasingly concerned about my family. I wondered if I would be able to play with the free abandon that I used to with my niece's children without continually being concerned about what could happen to them. I began to question how anyone could bring a child into this dangerous world.

As a therapist, I am trained to know what to look for and what to do next. I recognized my own symptoms. I met with colleagues and worked my way through the scenarios and the feelings I was having. I began to be more aware of my own self-care practices, including coping and self-soothing methods. My coping had shifted from good self-care to keeping busy, putting my nose to the grindstone, and pushing through. After all, there were so many people who all needed help! At times, I would reflect and evaluate, but not as often as I had previously.

To respond to this, I reinvigorated my exercise routine and started swimming two to three times per week in addition to my walking and weightlifting. The swimming was pure joy, and I looked forward to it. In the past, I simply did not make time for the drive to the pool. I also made time to make sure that I was eating homemade, nutritious, delicious, hot meals. I made these meals because I loved myself and I was keenly aware that what I put into my body affected my emotional state. In short, I did an overhaul and returned to the healthy behaviors in place before the secondary trauma symptoms.

At that point, I looked around me. I began to wonder what my friends and colleagues, who are mostly all legal professionals, are doing to protect themselves from secondary trauma and related issues. But they weren't doing anything. In fact, secondary trauma was simply not talked about. I thought maybe this is just an issue within my own friends and colleagues. I started to read more and talk with more legal professionals on the matter and found more of the same. No one was talking. Finally, I thought maybe this is just a U.S. phenomenon. I started reading about other countries and talking with leaders around the globe and I found that not only is secondary trauma an issue, but so are a host of other mental health and behavioral issues.

Of course, some work has been done, by courageous and passionate people in the countries I have studied, which are primarily the United States, the United Kingdom, Australia, Canada, and New Zealand. Those I spoke to were so supportive of me in writing this book. I cannot believe how many people truly care about this issue, each other, and the profession in general. I wanted to bring this work together in an effort to inform legal professionals, organizations and students. Like most mental health issues, secondary trauma tends to be highly stigmatized around the world. I decided that I would devote part of my time here in attempting to relieve some of the anguish and distress among legal professionals and among law students by writing this book. It's my hope that it encourages discussion, de-stigmatization, and action.

This is a labor of love, which arose from concern for the well-being of my friends, colleagues, and the issue of suffering in general. There is a global effort to end stigma, but we are a long way from there.

## What to Expect

Each chapter starts with a quote. Within some chapters you will find interviews with legal professionals and experts and the results of survey responses. You will meet Champions of Disclosure; individuals who have shared their name, position, and personal story of their experience with chapter content. Each chapter ends with discussion questions.

Well, let's get you started. We are on the way.

# Table of Contents

# Chapter 1 Abstract: Introduction to Trauma

In this chapter, we will introduce the concept of secondary trauma. We will briefly review the myriad of terms used globally and often interchangeably with secondary trauma, exploring how some differ in meaning and how some may overlap. It is important to come to a common understanding so that appropriate language can be used, and everyone understands what we are communicating, rather than what we have now, which is a confusion of terms and symptoms which ultimately make it very difficult to share, destigmatize and get help. We will ultimately come to a useful and intuitive understanding of secondary trauma based on a variety of resources, as well as input from pioneers in the field. Finally, we will briefly explore other types of trauma to better understand our various types of exposures.

We will be exposed to true accounts of secondary trauma and other trauma from our Champions of Disclosure, individuals sharing stories of how secondary trauma or other mental health issues occurred and how they attempted to cope in both healthy and, in some cases, unhealthy ways. Our Champions of Disclosure serve to demonstrate that secondary trauma and other mental health issues are real issues for legal professionals and students that must be acknowledged and accepted and ultimately tended to in thoughtful, healthy, and productive ways.

# Chapter 1: Introduction to Trauma

"I've also seen the maligned forgive, and the sun rise. I've marvelled at the color of a peacock and the intricacies of a fly's wings and a person's smile. At the miracle of a gentle touch or the kind nod of the head. All the while racing around the Sun at more than 65,000 mph, while our solar system circles the entire of our galaxy at more than 500,000 mph. Perhaps the word miraculous could be used for just about everything. Even seemingly horrible things. Maybe there's intelligence to it all."[1]

I love this quote by Andrew Bloomfield's book *Call of the Cats*. In your work life and school life, you will be exposed to cases, narratives, process, and perhaps even media that could be deemed egregious or "horrible," but there is a way through to the other side. Remember to look around you on the journey and see the beauty in your work, in your study, and in the people and living creatures around you.

## Section 1: Secondary Trauma

Definitions and terms used for secondary trauma vary across the globe as well as within countries. Secondary trauma, secondary traumatic stress, vicarious trauma, vicarious traumatic stress, and indirect trauma are all used interchangeably; and post-traumatic stress and compassion fatigue may be sprinkled in as a part of the generalized discussion on secondary trauma. Not only is there difficulty in agreeing on a common name; there is also difficulty in coming to a common definition across the globe. The definition of primary trauma also is shifting. Globally, we are seeing primary trauma described as not just exposure to life-or-death events but including the removal of the parent or child from the home, exposure to child pornography, and more. Although the exact use of terms varies, there is an agreement that the impact of any kind of trauma is real, costly, and pervasive. In this book, secondary trauma will be defined as the trauma response that one experiences from another individual's trauma experience or trauma narrative. Secondary trauma among legal professionals will be defined as an exposure to an event such as a client's narrative, photos, videos, etc., that causes ongoing distress symptoms in the individual, resulting in physical, behavioral and/or emotional symptoms. Secondary trauma can occur with one exposure to an event, or over time through an accumulation of exposures.

Little is taught about secondary trauma, and few studies exist on this subject within the legal profession. The work by Andrew Levin and others on secondary trauma among attorneys in the Wisconsin State Public Defender's Office is the largest study on secondary trauma to date. Attorneys in this study had significantly higher levels of secondary traumatic stress, post-traumatic stress disorder, depression, and burn out compared with administrative support staff. The attorneys also had longer work hours and greater contact with clients who had experienced trauma.[2]

---

1 Call of the Cats. Copyright © 2016 by Andrew Bloomfield. Reprinted with permission by New World Library, Novato, CA. www.newworldlibrary.com

2 Levin, Andrew P., and Scott Greisberg. 2003. Vicarious Trauma in Attorneys, 24 Pace Law

The study found that State Public Defender Attorneys reported significantly higher levels of compassion fatigue, depression, PTSD, functional impairment, and burnout than administrative support staff and the general population. In addition, caseload and exposure to other's trauma were found to be related to symptoms of compassion fatigue while history of personal trauma, office size, gender, age, or number of years on the job did not affect compassion fatigue levels.[3]

Of particular interest to law students and legal professionals is Tehila Sagy's work. Sagy discusses that when a listener believes a narrative, there exists a heightened emotional impact, regardless of the legal outcome. She points out that listening to and eliciting detailed narratives can cause an emotional impact, especially when the narratives are reoccurring, without a time to process in between. This can be a cumulative effect. Sagy contends that this response is barely acknowledged as an issue, let alone a source of concern. Sagy further contends that the risk of secondary trauma is significant.[4]

Secondary trauma occurs across cultures, gender, and age. It should be noted at this point that other occupations that frequently come into contact with clients' trauma stories, such as counselors, psychotherapists, social workers, and psychologists, have specific training as part of the curriculum, as well as continuing education on how to address the risks of secondary trauma. They learn basic coping methods, and debriefing—basically how to remain healthy while listening to unhealthy real-life stories.

Legal professionals, unless they take a specific continuing legal education class or attend a seminar focusing on these issues, have not had this training. The lack of education has caused a huge gap in resiliency, the ability to get back to a healthy state after exposure to stressors. In addition, this gap may have helped to fuel fears of discussion or lack of discussion, and the stigma associated with appearing to have problems of secondary trauma. This trend is changing, as you are reading this book.

For legal professionals, exposure to detailed accounts, photographs, audio, and videos of traumatic events, listening to clients' trauma stories/narratives, preparing cases, reading trauma stories, and hearing testimony as well as other evidence that affected others is a daily occurrence. These exposures have caused secondary trauma among many in the legal community, including lawyers, barristers, judges, clerks, legal assistants, and jurors.[5]

In most countries, the mental health awareness training that legal professionals receive is limited or non-existent. Secondary trauma is by no means limited to professionals; students also experience it under similar circumstances. This may be particularly true for students who are in clinical programs with clients. This is an area for further reflection and assessment for individual students.

---

[3] Molvig, Dianna. 2011. "The Toll of Trauma." WisBar, December 1. https://www.wisbar.org/newspublications/wisconsinlawyer/pages/article.aspx?volume=84&issue=12&articleid=2356. Reprinted with permission of the December 2011 Wisconsin Lawyer, the official publication of the State Bar of Wisconsin, Wisconsin, USA.

[4] Sagy, Tehila. 2006. "Even Heroes Need to Talk: Psycho-Legal Soft Spots in the Field of Asylum Lawyering." bepress Legal Series. Working Paper 1014. (March 1). https://law.bepress.com/expresso/eps/1014.

[5] Wood Smith, Deborah. 2017. "Secondary or Vicarious Trauma Among Judges and Court Personnel." Secondary or Vicarious Trauma Among Judges and Court Personnel. The National Center for State Courts. Accessed December 2, 2019. https://www.ncsc.org/microsites/trends/home/Monthly-Trends-Articles/2017/Secondary-or-Vicarious-Trauma-Among-Judges-and-Court-Personnel.aspx.

---

In study after study, we see the phenomenon of secondary trauma. It becomes apparent that the ways in which legal professionals engage in the narratives of victims and the information they are exposed to, can take a psychological toll. These studies highlight the urgent need to promote an individual and organizational understanding of secondary trauma and learn the skills necessary to cope with trauma narratives. This is a crucial aspect to maintaining the health and well-being of those affected.

According to the Center for Substance Abuse Treatment, symptoms of secondary trauma include the following:

- Physical distress
- Sleep disturbance and nightmares,
- Headaches
- Stomach pain
- Fatigue
- Startle reaction
- Emotional distress
- Intrusive thoughts
- Irritability
- Anger
- Hypervigilance
- Avoidance of things or people that are reminders of the event
- Strained relationships with family and friends
- Changes in parenting, such as being overprotective
- Cognitive changes
- Negative thinking and a tendency to become upset about everything
- Doubts about whether the world is a safe place
- Inability to focus[6]

As we have seen, the research tends be focused on groups such as health care providers and not individuals in the legal profession. "Historically, the research on secondary or vicarious trauma focused on professions such as nurses, emergency responders, therapists, and other helping professions who were repeatedly exposed to the traumatic events that affected the people they were helping. the fifth edition of the Diagnostic and Statistics Manual (DSM-5) was released in May 2013 and for the first time included vicarious trauma defined as 'repeated or extreme exposure to details of the event(s).' Exposure through pictures or media to someone else's trauma did not qualify unless it was related to work. This is what happens in court every day. The repeated exposure to detailed accounts, pictures, and videos of traumatic events that affected someone else is a daily occurrence for judges and other court personnel. Trial judges, to some degree, are isolated as they must make their rulings and decisions individually without the ability to discuss ongoing cases. In addition, legal and judicial training do not typically focus

---

[6] Center for Substance Abuse Treatment (US). 1970. "Understanding the Impact of Trauma." Trauma-Informed Care in Behavioral Health Services. U.S. National Library of Medicine, January 1, 1970. https://www.ncbi.nlm.nih.gov/books/NBK207191/.

on how one feels. Judges and lawyers as a group are known to be at high risk for depression and substance abuse. In 2003, 105 judges working in criminal, family, and juvenile court completed surveys on trauma while attending various judicial conferences. Based on the responses, 63% reported symptoms of work-related vicarious trauma."[7] We will be reviewing additional studies to support this notion below.

Another definition of vicarious trauma is by Donald C. Murray, QC, and Johnette M. Royer: "It [vicarious trauma] appears to be best understood as an effect. The effect is a disruption of an ordinary level of the psychological and emotional functioning of a helping professional. The disruption has a negative effect on the professional's competence in performing professional tasks. This disruption seems to be caused by a professionally obligated involvement with traumatic events, or a professionally obligated close contact with persons who have been involved in traumatic events. If left unmanaged, vicarious trauma reduces the helping value that the professional relationship is supposed to have for the client. The kind of traumatic event required would appear to be an event that resulted in physical or psychological distress to a person, which is outside ordinary human and community experience."[8]

Vicarious Trauma and secondary trauma are frequently used interchangeably. Please note we will be using the term "secondary trauma" and the corresponding definition that you reviewed earlier throughout the remainder of the text.

Our first Champion of Disclosure, David Heilpern, is a judge and author. He is the author of a major study of sexual assault in prisons and is an advocate of prison and law reform. In 1998, he became one of the youngest magistrates in New South Wales, Australia. In 2004, he was named as Southern Cross University's Alumnus of the Decade.

---

[7] Wood Smith, Deborah. 2017. "Secondary or Vicarious Trauma Among Judges and Court Personnel." Secondary or Vicarious Trauma Among Judges and Court Personnel. The National Center for State Courts. Accessed December 2, 2019. https://www.ncsc.org/microsites/trends/home/Monthly-Trends-Articles/2017/Secondary-or-Vicarious-Trauma-Among-Judges-and-Court-Personnel.aspx.

[8] Murray, Donald C., Q.C., and Johnette M. Royer. 2003. Vicarious Traumatization: The Corrosive Consequences of Law Practice for Criminal Justice and Family Law Practitioners. http://norestdefence.com/wp-content/uploads/2020/01/Vicarious-Traum%E2%80%A6AP-edited.pdf

**Section 1.1: Champions of Disclosure:**

**Judge David Heilpern, Australia: Lifting the Judicial Veil--My Story**

I wish to preface this tale by paying tribute to the others in the court process who suffer direct trauma as a result of crime. First and foremost are the victims. Victims of sexual assault, domestic violence, robbery, and the like suffer firsthand trauma that is tragic and deep. Seeing them bravely confront their tormentors and give evidence is a humbling experience, and I pay homage to them. Secondly, I'd like to note that first responders, such as the police, who have to deal day in and day out with the violence, death, and despair that they see often struggle with trauma. I appreciate that their experience is much more direct and immediate than the perspective of the bench. Thirdly, I acknowledge the trauma encountered and experienced by the legal practitioners on both sides of the adversarial system. They often live, breathe, and eat their cases, striving for justice by representing the accused or the Crown.

I have been a magistrate for twenty-on years. As this book is being published in the United States, it is helpful if I explain the nature of that work, as "magistrate" denotes different roles in various jurisdictions. The Local Court is the lowest rung in the hierarchy of criminal courts in New South Wales, and has an extraordinarily broad jurisdiction covering traffic, family, domestic violence, children's, civil, coronial, environmental, and administrative law. We are busy, with many list days having over a hundred matters, and we have ever-increasingly serious criminal matters before us as the pressure from higher courts inevitably works its way down. We can imprison for up to five years. However, all criminal matters commence in our court, and 96% of all matters are finalized in our court.

So, we manage murder, sexual assault, and drug offenses of enormous complexity and seriousness in addition to the detritus typical of courts at the bottom of the rung. A colleague once described sitting in our court like having your mouth over a fire hydrant, another as putting a Band-Aid on a gaping wound. The best descriptor of magistrates in our court is "harried," a beautiful onomatopoeic word that perfectly encapsulates that frazzled blurry feeling in the midst of a long list.

Here is a little bit about me. I do not drink, and I am a committed meditator and yoga practitioner. I took my lay Buddhist vows a decade ago. Prior to that, I was a criminal lawyer and an academic. I represented those charged with child sexual assault, murder, and serious domestic violence. I taught mainly criminal law and cowrote a leading casebook, which meant reading copious transcripts and judgments of a violent nature. I researched and published papers and a book on the sexual assault of prisoners—primarily by interviewing victims and perpetrators. I thought I had a pretty good amount of distance from my work, in the sense that while it occasionally upset me, it did not stay with me too often in my personal life.

About fourteen years ago, I was sitting in a series of cases involving child pornography in Batemans Bay. In those days, it was always necessary for the court to view the pictures and videos to determine the seriousness of the charges—fortunately that is far less common today due to computer classification. As is regularly the case, the charges included thousands and sometimes tens of thousands of images and hundreds of videos. I will not re-traumatize all of us or re-victimize the victims by describing the images except to repeat something that the chief magistrate wrote in the case of Police v Power [2007] NSWLC 1 at 36:

*To see the pale death of innocence and trust in the eyes of so many young children is to bemoan the capacity for some members of the human race to descend into the dark and depraved side of the human condition.*

I dealt with over a dozen of these cases within a couple of months. I started dreaming of these children and the torment perpetrated upon them. I would wake up in the witching hour screaming, sweating, and panicked. I thought it would pass, but it did not. I was scared about going to sleep, and that fear was well placed. I began thrashing around in my sleep, making it impossible for my wife to remain in bed with me for fear of getting struck.

After weeks of this, I sought professional help and was referred to a trauma psychologist who engaged in some talk therapy by way of debriefing. I also informed the chief magistrate of my difficulties and asked his permission to avoid such cases for a time. He was extremely sympathetic, and my colleagues from other circuits carried the load for that time. The relief from the nightmares was immediate and dramatic. "Cured!" I thought.

In the intervening years, and up to the present, my involvement in judicial education increased, and I became a lead trainer of new magistrates in Australia and the Pacific. One of the sessions I ran, and still run, is on mental health, and I would use my Batemans Bay experience as a salutary lesson.

Some ten years later, I had a bad six months on my current circuit. Over all of that time, I dealt with a child sexual assault case which the sentencing judge accurately described as the "worst of the worst." She sentenced the father to 48 years of imprisonment and the mother to 12 years: this is probably all I need to say about the horrors that were perpetrated on this poor child. I had to deal with bail applications, contested interim apprehended violence orders, committal hearings, and subpoena issues, all of which required reading and making determinations on the evidence. My grandchildren had been born around that time, and I think I was in, as we on the North Coast of New South Wales would say, a "heart-opened" state. I now know that empathy is a key determinant of vicarious trauma. I now know that empathy is not static—it fluctuates with time. I think I was particularly empathetic at that time.

During this period, the crystal methamphetamine problem was escalating in my area, and there were four violent incidents inside the court, including a young addicted man who jumped out of the dock, fought his way out of the courtroom, and jumped over the front balcony, breaking his spine. I dealt with two juveniles from the far west of New South Wales who, having been bailed out that very night, held a toddler at knifepoint while they raped his mother, a nurse. And I dealt with another horrible case of child pornography in which I had to watch a video which involved binding, gagging, suspending upside down, and violating a conscious two-year-old.

That week, a friend died in a freak surfing accident, and at the funeral I was very messy. I was particularly nervous for my own and my family's safety. I now see this as hypervigilance. I found making hard decisions in court really painful. Actually, physically painful—my head would hurt (just like Winnie the Pooh) when trying to decide whether to imprison someone, or refuse them bail, or admit evidence. A good night's sleep had become a distant memory. I would wake myself up screaming.

My family and friends had been concerned about me for some time. They encouraged me to take some time off work and to seek help. I stubbornly refused.

In retrospect, of course, this stubbornness was completely unreasonable. I would like to try to explain it though without excusing it. Firstly, my reaction seemed so pathetic in comparison to the victims. I thought what a "sook" [cry-baby] I was. I saw victims work their way out of psychiatric care and through university with flying colors, the calm determination of domestic violence victims, and the shaking voices of police officers in coronial matters, and I was thinking that my reactions were just so much "weak little me, me, me." Second-hand trauma just seemed so, well, second-hand. Secondly, up to that point, in my entire working life I had rarely had a single sick day. This was a question of pride, and I saw it as part of my reputation as a reliable, dependable rural magistrate. After all, if the magistrate gets sick at short notice literally hundreds can be inconvenienced, hearings that have been waiting with defendants in custody and witnesses from interstate may have to wait another six months. I think that one of the symptoms of trauma is catastrophizing, and another is an inflated sense of irreplaceability. Thirdly, there were the usual reasons people don't want to admit to mental fragility, especially men.

After probably three months of bleakness, I took the "advice" of my GP and took a couple of weeks off. (Advice is in inverted commas because she was utterly insistent. I wrote a letter to the Deputy Chief Magistrate responsible for leave and spilt the beans on my state of mind. She was a friend and colleague of many years standing and to this day I cannot believe how hard this letter was to write. It was achingly difficult, and I can honestly say it was the hardest letter I have written in my life. Crazy but true.

I went on a Buddhist retreat with a long-term teacher, at Chenrezig on the Sunshine Coast. This was an icebreaker and over the period of the next few months I progressively improved. I do not wish to be prescriptive on treatment, as I'm sure different processes work for different people. I started with talk-based therapy (good, but sometimes re-traumatizing), tried medication (a nice mental holiday, but didn't last), and then EMDR (eye movement desensitization and reprocessing), which was brilliant. If someone had once told me that wiggling fingers in front of the eyes could actually work, I would have laughed out loud. I do not mean to belittle EMDR. It has truly been a wonderfully helpful treatment for me. I did nine sessions with a terrifically skilled psychologist, and from the outset felt a lifting of anguish.

During this time the support of my colleagues and the chief and deputy chief magistrates was magnificent. Calls, emails, and check-ins were almost (but not quite) overwhelming. I am fortunate indeed that the New South Wales bench is collegiate and supportive. This is no accidental development. As the chief magistrate has often noted, the strength of the bench, in the end, comes down to the health of the people who sit on it.

Apart from the two weeks at Chenrezig and normal leave, I returned work while getting better. I approach my ability to cope with traumatic cases with a mixture of confidence and trepidation. Did it affect my ability to competently do my job during my darkest days? It is difficult to tell. Certainly, there was no rash of appeals from my decisions or criticisms by higher courts. There were no complaints to the Judicial Commission. I probably consulted more with my colleagues on harder cases to check that I was on the right path, and perhaps I was gruffer than usual with lawyers whom I perceived as incompetent or worse.

After the EMDR, I viewed my mind as a big sponge when dealing with traumatic cases. It sucks up some of that trauma vicariously, and I became watchful to ensure that the sponge did not get too full. I became determined that I would not hesitate to seek help should the sponge feel close to full, and I was certainly better placed to watch for the signs given my experience.

It was certainly not my intention to become some sort of poster child for vicarious trauma or PTSD and the judiciary. However, neither could I remain silent. I became convinced that it was time to lift the veil for the benefit of the judiciary, but also for the system of justice itself—and that the community is best served by recognizing and acknowledging this issue, rather than hiding it.

And so, in this spirit, I decided to give a lecture. I delivered the Tristan Jepsom Memorial Lecture in October 2017. I spoke of dealing with nests of child pornography, of the impact of a particular case of horrific child abuse, and I spoke of the heart-opening experience of having grandchildren and how this impacted my struggle to deal with cases involving children of the same age. I then detailed how this affected my sleep, my mood, and my self-confidence, and the pain I inflicted on those around me. I then explored my pathway to wellness through treatment for vicarious trauma.

Tristan Jepson Memorial lectures had been delivered many times before, and the impact within the profession had been significant, but had not generated extensive publicity. I had thought that my little speech might be of interest to a select few involved in judicial education and management and would otherwise pass somewhat unnoticed. How wrong I was. To my surprise, my paper really hit a nerve, with an article on the front page of *The Sydney Morning Herald* kicking things off. Things snowballed, and articles referring to my paper and speech appeared thousands of times in the media and journals around the world.

I received thousands of emails of support from judicial officers from everywhere: the Americas, the Pacific, Africa, and the United Kingdom, some pouring out their own horrific experiences on the bench—just what I needed! Not. But I dutifully replied personally to each one and realized that I had scratched a sore that now bled.

I would like to share one account from a judge in an African country:

In my country the virgin rape myth is alive and well. It is considered that one can be cleansed and cured of HIV-AIDS by raping a virgin female infant. Further, we deal with cases of horrific female genital mutilation regularly. This takes an intolerable toll on the sanity of us judges, and it is not unusual to see physical and mental self-harm, including alcohol abuse to try to cope.

I received invitations from around the world to do media and address conferences, and I rejected all except one. First, I felt that I needed to exercise some self-preservation and protect myself from raking over the same old coals. Second, I felt like I had said it all in my paper and lecture in 2017: what more could I add? Finally, I did not speak out to make myself the self-appointed guru of vicarious trauma for judicial officers. Grandfathering and keeping bees are much more my scene.

I did accept an invitation to the Philippines after receiving a heartfelt email from a judge there. I started my paper in Manila with the following scene:

You are sitting in court hearing a child sex case. The alleged victim is aged eight, a cheeky smart, chatty child who runs through her early evidence with ease. The prosecutor asks her familiar questions: What year are you in at school, what is your favorite TV show, do you play sport? She reminds you of your daughter, or niece, or yourself at that age. You warm to her.

Then she gets to the hard part. The part where she has to describe what brings her to court. And she cracks. Her little face drops, the tears come, but she bravely tells her story of abuse—embarrassed, ashamed, but determined. It is heartbreaking.

And what do you do? You the judge. You ignore every single human impulse you feel. You do not cry, you do not hug the child, you do not jump over the bench and beat the defendant, you do not hold her hand. You sit, stoically mute. You force yourself to evaluate, to test, to assess that evidence. You will have to objectively judge this little girl, and the path of her life will undoubtedly be altered by whatever you decide—to believe her or doubt her.

And after the case you leave the bench and speak to no-one. And likely when you go home, you want to avoid spreading the stain of the case to your loved ones, and to relive it by the retelling.

And tomorrow, in the next case, you do it all over again.

To undertake this seemingly impossible theater, where you show no emotion whatsoever, you do all the tricks you have mastered over the years: you pull up your armor, you focus on your breathing, you are hearing without really listening, taking notes almost like an automaton. You harden your heart. For if you do not, you are afraid it might burst.

But this armoring up, this hardening of the heart, comes at a great personal and psychological cost for many. It is completely unnatural in every way. And that psychological cost is what I want to talk with you about today. The price of stoicism.

Barristers and solicitors had also contacted me on my speech. Hundreds of them. I could not respond to all of them, so had a stock thank-you response instead. However, I was deeply shocked and saddened when an old colleague from my defense-lawyer days appeared as counsel before me in court and asked me to declare myself unfit to hear a case and to disqualify myself as a result of my speech and disclosures. Whilst all sexual assaults are serious, this allegation involved a single incident of touching and was thus at the very low end of the scale. If I had disqualified myself, or declared myself unfit, then my career would have been terminal.

Further, what of other judicial officers who wanted to speak out about their own frailties or traumas or personal history—were they forever to be condemned to silence? It brought home to me the risks of speaking out, and reminded me of why sitting judicial officers, as opposed to retired ones, seldom spoke of such matters.

I researched the issue extensively and could find no precedent in which a judicial officer had dealt with an issue of unfitness—the application was unique and challenging. I rejected the applications of counsel and wrote a detailed judgment as to the reasons. Essentially, I found there was a presumption of fitness, and unless counsel had evidence to rebut that presumption, then the status quo remained. I also found that my lecture and associated media reporting was not evidence of unfitness. On later consideration, perhaps a history of self-reflection and disclosure is greater evidence of fitness than silence and mystery. I also found that there was no perception of bias, as my paper and speech showed no favoritism toward either side in a criminal trial.

I was personally devastated and outraged by this application, reactions that I buried with some degree of honorable professionalism. But of course, other traumatic experiences have continued. A close colleague committed suicide. There have been three death threats against me or my family with associated court cases and applications. I refused bail to a defendant who was shot dead an hour later by guards when he was taken to the hospital for treatment. I still hear horrible and distressing cases. The difference is that I seek help when needed. And I know the end is nigh.

Having given this issue some thought over the last few years, it seems that there are some issues that require addressing. First, modern technology has made the trauma much more "in your face." I can read a violent scene in a book and be unaffected, but a movie is far more challenging. Real violence is now captured on CCTV, smartphones, in-car-videos, and body-worn cameras. When I started in this job, some form of graphic video or photographic evidence was a rarity. Now there are few cases without it. I have put in place protocols to protect myself and my staff as much as possible. Our coronial files have the on-scene photographs in a sealed envelope. I resist observing child pornography videos and having them played in open court is a very last resort. Similarly, once tendered, photographs of wounds are sealed to avoid accidental exposure.

Second, I suspect that judges who sit without juries are particularly vulnerable. In our court there is no jury, so we alone must determine guilt or innocence, largely based on the evidence of the victim and the defendant. That means we have to assess the truthfulness of the witnesses very carefully. This involves, to some extent, getting inside the head of both. Often that is a very frightening place. Did the victim really get touched like that? Did the defendant really believe the victim was consenting? Is the inconsistency of the victim's first complaint and evidence today suggestive of fabrication? Is a person of such fine character really likely to have done such an abhorrent thing?

These are tough questions to answer, and for a conscientious judicial officer require a determined focus and concentration. My hypothesis is that this level of absorption makes vicarious trauma unsurprising. We cannot just listen dispassionately to the evidence; we have to digest and ruminate on each morsel and literally judge the people before us. This is a level of intimacy, for want of a better word, that perhaps fills the sponge more rapidly than one would expect.

Third, the relationship between decision fatigue and vicarious trauma is, as far as I can tell, completely unresearched. However, in my view, there is a fair chance that each exponentially affects the other. In the local court, on my current circuit I have four list days per week. Most of those involve over 100 cases. On average, I will have over fifteen people in custody, and deal with around eight bail applications every list day. I will have fifteen to twenty coronial matters on the boil, inevitably involving gore and grief. Some days I will come home and be asked some innocuous question involving choice– "what would you like to eat?" for example—and I will respond that if I have to make one more decision I will actually just dissolve. I suggest that this pressure, felt at all levels of the judiciary to some extent, is poisonous to maintaining a vicarious trauma shield.

Fourth, throughout our education, our practice, and our role as a judicial officer we are taught to suppress our emotions in a quest for apparent objectivity. It is perhaps time to recognize that the expression of emotion is not the opposite of administering justice. I have laughed on the bench, and I have teared up on the bench. This is neither good nor bad. It just is, and part of recognizing that judicial officers are humans, not automatons. I have learned that to suppress emotion every day is a recipe for mental health fragility.

Finally, it is essential to recognize the inherent loneliness of the job. I have worked in both the city and the country, and in both places the job can feel exceptionally lonely, despite the collegiate nature of the bench. There are real limits on your social life, and in particular the mates and friends from the legal profession are likely to give you some distance. Many judicial officers work in single courts and are away from loved ones for days or weeks at a time. There is little opportunity for the kind of informal talk therapy or debriefing that can empty the sponge in that scenario.

Chief Justice James Spigelman wrote:

*There is a loneliness about it . . . and that's what really got to Jeff. He started drinking alone. It was a huge personal tragedy and I actually attribute it to the loneliness of being a judge. He had a predilection, and the loneliness of the job tilted him into this world that he couldn't escape from.*

I am in the twilight of my career as a full-time judicial officer as I write these words, and this experience of speaking out on vicarious trauma has been an enormously valuable one for me personally. Hopefully, it has encouraged others to recognize issues and improve their own mental health without shame or derision. I remain convinced that the judiciary, and thus the administration of justice, is best served by a recognition that we judges are merely mortal people trying to do a difficult job in accordance with our oath of office and with a commitment to addressing our own mental well-being.

These musings are not intended to be a final word on these issues. I hope that they engender debate, and that my personal experience is useful in formulating approaches in protecting the law's most precious assets—its people.

Judge David Heilpern has so kindly shared his experience of secondary trauma with us for you to better understand its meaning, how it works, and what to do with it. Judge Heilpern's story is one of understanding, action, and commitment. He works to help destigmatize these issues by teaching others through his own story that secondary trauma is real, and how he was able to cope with it and maintain health.

To better understand Secondary Trauma, I have created the Secondary Trauma Spiral.

# Secondary Trauma Spiral

"I notice..."

Questioning institution/feelings or thoughts of institutional betrayal

Oversimplification of social world – seeing things as only black or white

Thoughts of leaving the population or profession

Shift in level of confidence in professional life- "I am not as good as I used to be."

Thoughts of the world as an unjust or a dangerous place

Thoughts that people can't be trusted

Hypervigilance

Changes in behavior towards children/ family

Avoidance of situations which are reminders of event or narrative

Fearing for safety of family and significant others

**Shift in World View**

Fearing for safety of self

Being argumentative

Gambling

Increased alcohol use

Drug use

Dreams/ nightmares of event or narrative

Memory issues

**Physical & Emotional Symptoms**

Changes in respiration- breathing fast, shallow breathing, or holding of breath

Headaches/ Migraines

Change in heart rate

Nausea, diarrhea

Difficulty separating work life from personal life

Ruminating and/or racing thoughts

Difficulty falling asleep and/or staying asleep

Shame

**Ongoing Distress**

Others have noticed a change in emotional state

Remembering images of event or parts of narrative/ flashback

Post-Traumatic Shame

Shutting down/ isolating one's self

Loss of appetite

Fatigue

Being easily startled

Sadness/ Depression

Anxiety/ nervousness

Tensing of the body- clenching hands into fists, clenching jaw, etc.

**Initial Reactions**

Feelings of anger, fear, irritability, loss

Shock

Possible memory of personal trauma (childhood or adult)

**Secondary Trauma Exposure**

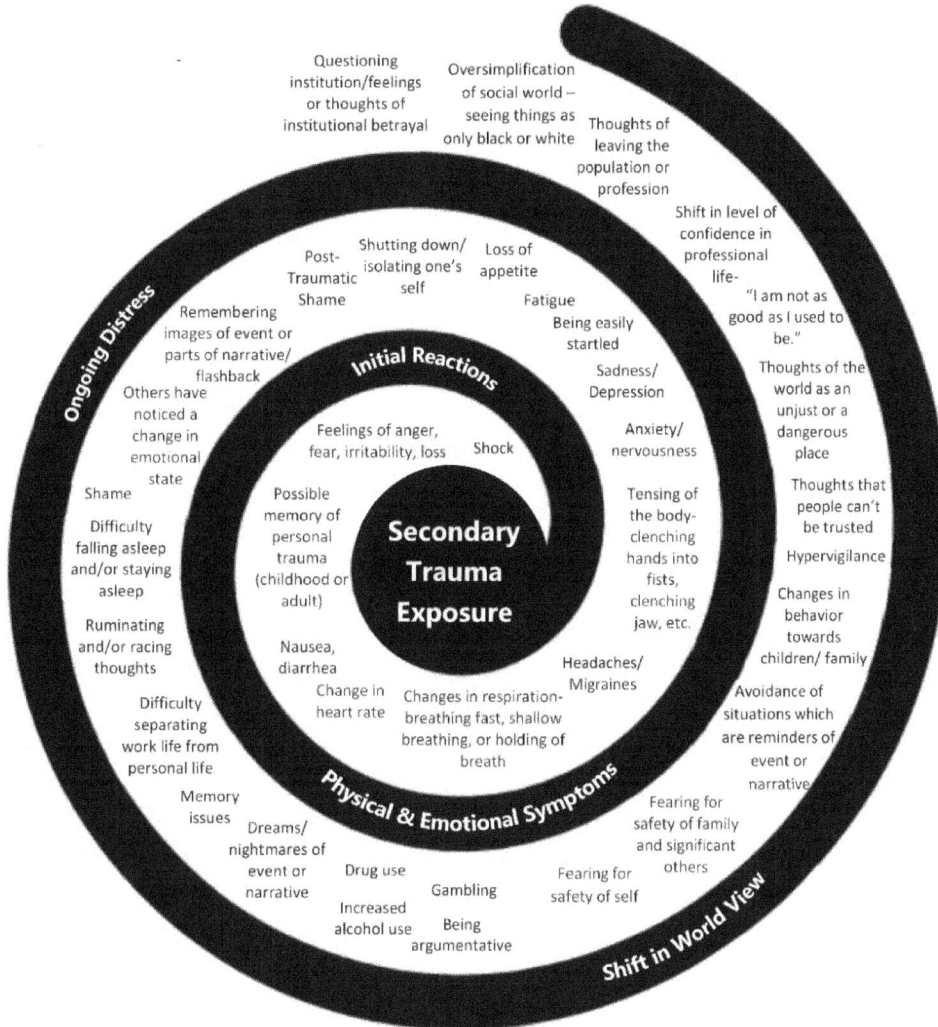

The Secondary Trauma Spiral is a personal, nondiagnostic tool which you can use to quickly determine how many symptoms you are experiencing. You may find yourself having a cluster of symptoms, or symptoms throughout the Spiral. As with any other condition that persists and causes suffering, seek the help of a mental health provider as needed. You can start anywhere on the Spiral. Some individuals, due to the number of trauma narratives they are exposed to, no longer recognize the narratives as potentially traumatic. You may find yourself identifying with aspects on the outermost regions of the Spiral first. Move around the Spiral and check off what you are noticing about yourself. Use the Spiral to touch base with yourself from time to time, then use tools found in Chapter 6 to help you cope.

## Champion of Disclosure:

## Judge Robert Murfitt -New Zealand

My perspective on secondary (or vicarious) trauma comes after serving for 15 years as a judge in the Family Court division of the District Court of New Zealand, as well as sitting in the Youth Court and general summary criminal court jurisdictions. In New Zealand District Court is the primary jurisdiction, disposing of over 90% of the litigation here, including crime, family, and relationship breakdown (including domestic violence, children's care disputes, property division, child support and maintenance), property disputes (civil and also in relation to testamentary disputes), as well as mental health committal hearings, youth crime and child welfare matters.

I sat as a judge for seven years from 2004 in New Plymouth, a city of 60,000 in a province with a population of 100,000, as one of two judges (the other dealing with jury trial crime and general summary crime). Since late 2010, I sat in Christchurch for eight years, until I retired in January 2019.

In New Zealand, as in the United Kingdom, Australia, Canada, and most other jurisdictions based on the English Common Law heritage, Judges are not elected (as they are in the U.S.), but are appointed and are not removable except for gross misconduct or function loss (and generally by action of the legislature). This is to protect the independence of the judiciary.

Prior to my appointment in 2004, I operated as a lawyer specializing in family law disputes for about 20 years. A significant part of my work involved representing children in post-separation disputes between parents, and children who had often suffered family abuse. In the criminal jurisdiction I was involved in several murder trials and cases involving sexual assaults.

Judges and trial advocates are exposed daily to detailed accounts of humans being brutal (at worst) to being unkind (at the least) to each other. Lawyers receive instructions from their clients in office interviews, and set out the stories in affidavits, and are regularly active in court while the contestants exchange their versions of the truth. Judges read the documentary accounts and hear the witnesses tell their stories.

Inevitably, there is a toll taken on the emotional resilience of the professional by this constant exposure to other people's dysfunctional lives, and professionals need to be aware of the risks to their own psychological (or even mental) health.

In addition, underfunding of the justice sector has added pressures on those judges who are conscientious and want to do a good job for the public who appear before them. In this country, a previous government reduced the number of active District Court judges from 178 to 160, as a cost-cutting exercise. The delays in administration of justice grew and grew, to the frustration of the judges, the staff, the profession, and the public. Child custody disputes commonly took two years or more to reach a conclusion, and the litigation stress on families was enormous. Simple defended criminal cases often took a year to reach a hearing, with witnesses' memories failing and people's lives put on hold for so long. Fortunately, the current government is in the process of restoring the numbers of lost judges.

Before I retired, I saw colleagues gradually sapped of energy and their faith in human nature, to the point where some have come to hate the job, and many have become cynical. A few have (in my opinion) lost the ability to manage the workload and deal with members of the public with respect and calmness.

One female judge has something of a reputation for abusing counsel, and even witnesses, and even exploding in irrational rage at her own colleagues. I am sure her behavior is an example of succumbing to the vicarious trauma described above, the exposure to the trauma of others, and the frustrations caused by an inefficient system.

In her case, the stress also made the workplace a most uncomfortable place for other colleagues, and so there was an on flow of the stress affecting her to affect others.

Indeed, some judges achieve some relief from the stresses of the day by unloading on their colleagues during adjournments and lunch breaks (usually the story of the bad case of the morning). Of course, every colleague has their own share of a stressful day to absorb, and the "downloaders" are often viewed with dread as they enter the room.

Our life-partners are also one of the options for a download of daily stresses for a judge or lawyer. They too have their own daily difficulties in these days of two working spouses (or partners), and they can be a forgotten casualty in the landscape of people affected by vicarious trauma through the courts. The downstream effects of work life stress may emerge as a tertiary trauma.

I have spoken to law students at Canterbury University as a visiting lecturer on family law as a career. In that, I encouraged them to avoid taking this career as "therapy" for their own life experiences, because they need to retain objectivity and calm to deal with the sometimes-horrible people they will encounter in their work. They need to have a healthy balance between their work life and personal life, including a circle of friends who are not lawyers, good hobbies or sports, and cultural lives. They need good holidays as a break from the pressures of a stressful career and take those opportunities to really unwind.

For myself, a sideline interest in writing children's storybooks has been a healthy distraction from work-life pressures. I know of other judges in New Zealand who find the same sort of release by writing poetry (in the case of John Adams, who wrote *Briefcase* and *Rumpelstiltskin Blues*), or writing a science fiction novel, or directing a movie (for instance, Judge Rosemary Riddell's *The Insatiable Moon*). Others run marathons or find pleasure in sailing or other sports.

have seen it written that family law careers invoke the same vulnerability to secondary trauma as a career in the fire service, police, or emergency wards does, because professionals are likewise exposed to gruesome or traumatic events. The burnout factor in police is a notorious truth. Judges and lawyers are no less at risk of early burnout.

Judge Murfitt has generously shared his secondary trauma experience. We can see through his story the tremendous daily, ongoing emotional strain that legal professionals undertake. This strain as Judge Murfitt states can lead to a decrease in emotional resiliency or the ability to regain our previous emotional state. He has compared the burn out risk of legal professionals to other professional groups such as police officers, fire services and emergency services. Through his story we can see the importance of rest, fun, and creativity. We have learned how he and other legal professionals cope in fun, healthy and often creative ways.

## Section 2: Compassion Fatigue

"Compassion Fatigue is the negative aspect of helping those who experience traumatic stress and suffering. There are two parts to compassion fatigue: burnout and secondary trauma."[9]

"Burnout occurs in organizations typified by high demands and low personal rewards, and it is the increased workload and institutional stress, (not trauma), that serve as the precipitating factors."[10]

Compassion Fatigue is the "emotional and physical impact of working in these circumstances without time or ability to regenerate, relax or decompress."[11]

According to the American Institute of Stress, symptoms of compassion fatigue include the following:

- "affects many dimensions of your well-being
- nervous system arousal (sleep disturbance)
- emotional intensity increases
- cognitive ability decreases
- behavior and judgment impaired
- isolation and loss of morale
- depression and PTSD (potentiate)
- loss of self-worth and emotional modulation
- identity, worldview, and spirituality impacted
- beliefs and psychological needs-safety, trust, esteem, intimacy, and control
- loss of hope and meaning=existential despair
- anger toward perpetrators or causal events"[12]

---

[9] Figley, Charles R. 1995. Compassion Fatigue: Coping with Secondary Traumatic Stress Disorder in Those Who Treat the Traumatized. 1st ed. New York: Routledge.

[10] Middleton, Jennifer. 2015. "Addressing Secondary Trauma and Compassion Fatigue in Work with Older Veterans: An Ethical Imperative." Aging Life Care Association, Spring 2015. https://www.aginglifecarejournal.org/addressing-secondary-trauma-and-compassion-fatigue-in-work-with-older-veterans-an-ethical-imperative/. Journal of Aging Life Care, Spring 2015, used with permission from the Aging Life Care Association®, Tucson, AZ 85741, aginglifecare.org

[11] Figley, Charles R. 1995. Compassion Fatigue: Coping with Secondary Traumatic Stress Disorder in Those Who Treat the Traumatized. 1st ed. New York: Routledge.

[12] American Institute of Stress. 2017. https://www.stress.org/military/for-practitionersleaders/compassion-fatigue.

There are many symptoms and components of compassion fatigue. One does not have to experience all of these symptoms to have compassion fatigue.

It should be increasingly clear that the nature of the work and the information that is being shared can be emotionally impacting. As mammals, we are empathic creatures by nature, we must recognize and react to the psychological implications. According to Lewis, "Empathy is the pathway through which trauma is vicariously transferred."[13]

## Section 3: Post-Traumatic Stress Disorder

More confusion arises with post-traumatic stress disorder. Globally, we will see these terms being used interchangeably. I have included the definition of post-traumatic stress disorder to help to minimize this confusion.

The International Statistical Classification of Diseases and Health Related Disorders, World Health Organization, defines Post Traumatic Stress Disorder, also known as PTSD, as a "delayed or protracted response to a stressful event or situation of an exceptionally threatening or catastrophic nature, which is likely to cause pervasive distress in almost anyone."[14]

Please note again, the varying terminology. Symptoms of PTSD may include the following:

- flashbacks
- avoidance
- distress
- memory issues
- sleep changes
- anger or irritability
- difficulty concentrating
- hypervigilance
- startle response[15]

Other symptoms may include physical symptoms such as aches and pains, diarrhea, irregular heartbeat, headaches and emotional such as panic and fear, depression and behavioural such as drinking too much alcohol or using drugs.[16]

---

[13] Lewis, K.R., Lewis, L.S. & Garby, T.M. Surviving the Trenches: The Personal Impact of the Job on Probation Officers. Am J Crim Just 38, 67–84 (2013). https://doi.org/10.1007/s12103-012-9165-3

[14] World Health Organization. 2016. International Statistical Classification of Diseases and Related Health Problems. Geneva, Switzerland.

[15] World Health Organization. 2016. International Statistical Classification of Diseases and Related Health Problems. Geneva, Switzerland.

[16] Royal College of Psychiatrists. n.d. "Post-Traumatic Stress Disorder (PTSD)." Accessed April 6, 2020. https://www.rcpsych.ac.uk/mental-health/problems-disorders/post-traumatic-stress-disorder?searchTerms=PTSD.

According to the World Health Organization, a wide variety of experiences can elicit trauma and psychological reactions to it. Stressful events will vary greatly between individuals, and depend on a range of factors:

- characteristics of the stressor
- the individual's personal history of trauma and age
- individual resilience
- access to resources and support networks[17]

Another concept to consider is how organizational trauma and secondary trauma are intertwined. According to Pat Vivian and Shana Hormann, "Organizational trauma is a collective experience that overwhelms the organization's defensive and protective structures and leaves the entity temporarily vulnerable and helpless or permanently damaged."[18] Although rarely talked about, organizational trauma can affect any organization.

Organizations as well as individuals can be affected by secondary trauma. The psychiatrist Marilyn Kroplick states that organizations can also suffer from relationship issues such as PTSD. Organizations that work in stress-filled situations such as public defenders or nongovernmental organizations working on child abuse cases. Dr. Kroplick states that staff at the organization In Defense of Animals have experienced the trauma of toxic relationships in addition to the secondary trauma of witnessing animal abuse. She identifies these organizational wounds and creates plans to heal them. "With a focus on self-compassion and empathy for others, staff dynamics can be greatly improved." So many in the legal community try to convey themselves as rational and unemotional by suppressing their feelings in a misguided attempt to appear more "professional." Dr. Kroplick (2014) states, regarding her organization, that the "movement can't survive and make positive changes unless this suppression, or marginalization of emotional life is addressed."[19]

Primary trauma is important to know about because it is the trauma that the individual experiences directly. As we are human beings in addition to being professionals, some of us may have also experienced primary trauma. Memory and responses to our own primary trauma may be triggered when we work with a client who has suffered a similar trauma.

---

[17] World Health Organization. 2014. "WHO Releases Guidance on Mental Health Care after Trauma." World Health Organization, May 26, 2014. https://www.who.int/mediacentre/news/releases/2013/trauma_mental_health_20130806/en/.
[18] Vivian, Pat, and Shana Hormann. 2012. Organizational Trauma and Healing. Self-published, CreateSpace.
[19] Kroplick, Marilyn. 2014. "Organizational Trauma." In Defense of Animals USA, July 2, 2014. https://www.idausa.org/organizational-trauma/.

## Section 4: Primary Trauma

Just as we have seen with secondary trauma, primary trauma, often simply called trauma, also has multiple definitions. There have been efforts to consolidate and better define the definition of trauma on an international basis. However, there continues to exist inconsistency.

According to Wall, "Individual trauma results from an event, series of events or set of circumstances that is experienced by an individual as physically or emotionally harmful or life threatening and that has lasting adverse effects on the individual's functioning and mental, physical, social, emotional or spiritual well-being. (SAMHSA, 2014, p. 7)"[20]

"Traumatic events have been described as those that "overwhelm the ordinary human adaptations to life [and] … generally involve threats to life or bodily integrity, or a close personal encounter with violence and death" (Herman, 1992, p. 33)."[21]

The Australian Institute of Family Studies states that "traumatic events have been described as those that 'overwhelm the ordinary human adaptations to life [and] … generally involve threats to life or bodily integrity, or a close personal encounter with violence and death' (Herman, 1992, p. 33)."[22]

According to the Substance Abuse and Mental Health Services Administration of the United States, "Individual trauma results from an event, series of events, or set of circumstances that is experienced by an individual as physically or emotionally harmful or life threatening and that has lasting adverse effects on the individual's functioning and mental, physical, social, emotional or spiritual well-being.[23]

Although the definition of trauma is inconsistent, we do know that trauma events occur with frequency. According to van der Kolk, "One does not have to be a combat soldier or visit a refugee camp in Syria or the Congo to encounter trauma. Trauma happens to us, our friends, our families, and our neighbors. Research by the Centers for Disease Control and Prevention has shown that one in five Americans was sexually molested as a child; one in four was beaten by a parent to the point of a mark being left on their body; and one in three couples engage in physical violence. A quarter of us grew up with alcoholic relatives, and one out of eight witnessed their mother being beaten or hit."[24]

---

[20] Wall, L., Higgins, D., & Hunter, C. (2016). Trauma-informed care in child/family welfare services (CFCA Paper No. 37). Melbourne: Child Family Community Australia information exchange, Australian Institute of Family Studies. behalf of the Commonwealth of Australia, CC BY 4.0

[21] Wall, L., Higgins, D., & Hunter, C. (2016). Trauma-informed care in child/family welfare services (CFCA Paper No. 37). Melbourne: Child Family Community Australia information exchange, Australian Institute of Family Studies. behalf of the Commonwealth of Australia, CC BY 4.0

[22] Australian Institute of Family Studies. 2016. "Trauma Terminology." Child Family Community Australia, February 2016. https://aifs.gov.au/cfca/publications/trauma-informed-care-child-family-welfare-services/trauma-terminology. © Commonwealth of Australia 2016

[23] Substance Abuse and Mental Health Services Administration of the United States. n.d. "Trauma." Accessed December 3, 2019. https://www.integration.samhsa.gov/clinical-practice/trauma.

[24] van der Kolk, Bessel A. 2014. The Body Keeps the Score: Brain, Mind, and Body in the Healing

According to the World Health Organization (WHO); "Traumatic events and loss are common in people's lives. In a previous WHO study of 21 countries, more than 10% of respondents reported witnessing violence (21.8%) or experiencing interpersonal violence (18.8%), accidents (17.7%), exposure to war (16.2%) or trauma to a loved one (12.5%). An estimated 3.6% of the world's population has suffered from post-traumatic stress disorder (PTSD) in the previous year."[25]

As we have seen by the statistics, primary trauma can happen at any time, but often occurs in childhood. The effects of a primary trauma can impact our work and personal lives just as secondary trauma can. The need to help individuals who have been traumatized was so intense that in 2013, the World Health Organization extended its programming to include care for post-traumatic stress disorder, acute stress, and bereavement within its global programming.

- Signs and symptoms of a stress reaction to trauma
- Physical:
- nausea (feeling sick)
- upset stomach
- tremors (lips, hands)
- feeling uncoordinated
- profuse sweating
- diarrhea
- dizziness
- chest pain (should be checked at hospital)
- rapid heartbeat
- headaches
- sleep disturbances
- chills
- Cognitive:
- slow thinking
- difficulty making decisions
- difficulty with problem solving
- confusion
- disorientation (especially to time and place)
- difficulty calculating
- difficulty concentrating
- difficulty with remembering
- difficulty naming common objects
- seeing the event over and over
- hypervigilance
- Emotional:
- anxiety

---

of Trauma. New York: Viking.
[25] World Health Organization. 2014. "WHO Releases Guidance on Mental Health Care after Trauma." World Health Organization, May 26, 2014. https://www.who.int/mediacentre/news/releases/2013/trauma_mental_health_20130806/en/.

- fear
- guilt
- grief
- depression
- sadness
- feeling lost
- feeling abandoned
- feeling isolated
- worry about others
- anger
- irritability
- feeling numb, startled, shocked"[26]

The website recommends that if you continue to have distress to seek professional help, and also that partners, family and friends can help by those affected in these ways:

- believing them
- listening and allowing them the opportunity to talk about the event in their own time and in their own way
- not judging them
- spending time with them
- allowing them some private time
- reassuring them they are safe
- allowing them the opportunity to express their feelings
- not taking the person's anger and feelings personally
- helping with some tasks such as minding the children or cooking, if this is what they want
- not saying things such as "lucky it wasn't worse"—people who have experienced trauma are not consoled by statements like these[27]

## Section 5. Generational Trauma

For many, the least talked about and studied trauma is generational trauma. Generational trauma speaks to how trauma moves across generations. Generational trauma can be broken down into distinct parts: intragenerational trauma and intergenerational trauma.

---

[26] World Health Organization. 2014. "WHO Releases Guidance on Mental Health Care after Trauma." World Health Organization, May 26, 2014. https://www.who.int/mediacentre/news/releases/2013/trauma_mental_health_20130806/en/.
[27] World Health Organization. 2014. "WHO Releases Guidance on Mental Health Care after Trauma." World Health Organization, May 26, 2014. https://www.who.int/mediacentre/news/releases/2013/trauma_mental_health_20130806/en/.

These are some of the ways in which trauma can travel from one generation to another:

Environment Influences: "Parents with PTSD respond differently to their children resulting in greater disruptions in care and attachment. Mothers with PTSD are more likely to be both overprotective and reactive and as a result child may develop less-secure attachment."[28]

In Utero Influences: Research by Dr. Stacy Drury, a child psychiatrist at Tulane University, demonstrated that "a parasympathetic mediated biomarker of self-regulation, called Respiratory sinus arrhythmia, (RSA) [that] showed that infants' RSA is affected by mothers' life course experiences of stress… In utero, maternal stress has an almost immediate impact on fetal autonomic nervous system activity and maternal chronic stress and depression predict neonate autonomic nervous system activity. Both preconception and prenatal factors affect the autonomic nervous system and SRS's both within and across generations."[29]

"Besides the impact on mental well-being and behavior in the exposed individuals, it has been suggested that psychological trauma can affect the biology of the individuals, and even have biological and behavioral consequences on the offspring of exposed individuals." "Our review found an accumulating amount of evidence of an enduring effect of trauma exposure to be passed to offspring transgenerationally via the epigenetic inheritance mechanism of DNA methylation alterations and has the capacity to change the expression of genes and the metabolome."[30]

Transgenerational epigenetic transmission is defined as the transmission of genomic information (in this paper DNA methylation) from one generation to the next without changing the main structure of DNA (i.e., nucleotides sequence). [31]

## Section 5.1: Intragenerational Trauma

Intragenerational trauma is also known as family trauma. The trauma of a stillborn birth within a family can effect changes in remaining parent child relationships, sibling relationships and parental relationships. We can also expect that as adult children have children, in other words, the second generation moving into the third generation, we will see the effects of the trauma of the stillborn birth on the current mother to be. These effects may include the mother being worried about having her own stillborn birth, grandmother and grandfather being overly concerned about a stillborn birth, particularly, if this is the first birth.

---

[28] Schwartz, Arielle. 2017. "The Neurobiology of Transgenerational Trauma: Dr. Arielle Schwartz." December 20, 2017. https://drarielleschwartz.com/the-neurobiology-of-transgenerational-trauma-dr-arielle-schwartz/#.XeaUYOhKg2x.
[29] Gray SAO, CW Jones, KP Theall, E Glackin E, and SS Drury. 2017. "Thinking Across Generations: Unique Contributions of Maternal Early Life and Prenatal Stress to Infant Physiology." Journal of the American Academy of Child & Adolescent Psychiatry. https://www.ncbi.nlm.nih.gov/pubmed/29096774
[30] Youssef, Nagy A., Laura Lockwood, Shaoyong Su, Shaoyong, Guang Hao, and Bart P.F. Rutten. 2018. "The Effects of Trauma, with or without PTSD, on the Transgenerational DNA Methylation Alterations in Human Offsprings." Brain Sciences 8, no. 5: 83. https://www.ncbi.nlm.nih.gov/pmc/articles/PMC5977074.
[31] Youssef, Nagy A., Laura Lockwood, Shaoyong Su, Shaoyong, Guang Hao, and Bart P.F. Rutten. 2018. "The Effects of Trauma, with or without PTSD, on the Transgenerational DNA Methylation Alterations in Human Offsprings." Brain Sciences 8, no. 5: 83. https://www.ncbi.nlm.nih.gov/pmc/articles/PMC5977074.

## Section 5.2: Intergenerational Trauma

Intergenerational trauma, also known as transgenerational trauma, cultural trauma, or historical trauma, is another type of trauma and one which most people may be familiar with. Some examples of cultural trauma include the trauma that indigenous cultures have experienced and the trauma of the Holocaust.

"Trauma can be transferred from the first generation of survivors that have experienced (or witnessed) it directly in the past to the second and further generations of descendants of the survivors (Atkinson et al. 2010). Historical trauma is a type of trauma transmitted across generations (that is, intergenerational trauma). It is defined as the subjective experiencing and remembering of events in the mind of an individual or the life of a community, passed from adults to children in cyclic processes as 'cumulative emotional and psychological wounding' (Mu'id 2004: 9). Duran and Duran (1995) suggest that historical trauma can become normalized within a culture because it becomes embedded in the collective, cultural memory of a people and is passed on by the same mechanisms through which culture generally is transmitted. As Dr. Charles Nelson Perrurle Perkins AO (an Australian Aboriginal activist, football player and administrator) explained: 'we know we cannot live in the past but the past lives in us' (cited at the close of the motion picture One Night the Moon 2001)."[32]

According to a white paper written under the auspices of the National Child Traumatic Stress Network, "Research on intergenerational trauma and urban poverty has demonstrated that adults with histories of childhood abuse and exposure to family violence have problems with emotional regulation, aggression, social competence, and interpersonal relationships, leading to functional impairments in parenting which transmit to the next generation."[33]

Bree Buchanan, J.D., MSF, is senior advisor for Krill Strategies, and past director of the Texas Lawyers Assistance Program of the State Bar of Texas. She serves as cochair of the National Task Force on Lawyer Well-Being and as Chair of the ABA Commission on Lawyers Assistance Programs. Ms. Buchanan practiced in the public and private sector with a focus on representing both adult and child victims of family violence. She worked on public policy initiatives and systems change at both the State and Federal level as the Public Policy Director for the Texas Council on Family Violence and the National Domestic Violence Hotline. Ms. Buchanan was also appointed Clinical Professor and Co-Director of the Children's Rights Clinic at the University of Texas School of Law. She also graduated from Seminary of the Southwest where she received a master's degree in spiritual formation in 2018.

---

[32] Atkinson J 2013. Trauma-informed services and trauma-specific care for Indigenous Australian children. Resource sheet no. 21. Produced for the Closing the Gap Clearinghouse. Canberra: Australian Institute of Health and Welfare & Melbourne: Australian Institute of Family Studies. © Australian Institute of Health and Welfare 2013

[33] Collins, K., K. Connors, S. Davis, A. Donohue, S. Gardner, E. Goldblatt, A. Hayward, L. Kiser, F. Strieder, and E. Thompson. (2010). "Understanding the impact of trauma and urban poverty on family systems: Risks, resilience, and interventions." Baltimore, MD: Family Informed Trauma Treatment Center.

## Section 5.3: Champion of Disclosure

## Attorney Bree Buchanan

What role did generational trauma play in your life? When did you identify the issue of generational trauma?

My mother, born in 1928, was the only child of a father who, a former boxer, took his frustrations of the post-Depression era out on her and his wife. An alcoholic with a fierce temper, he beat either or both of them when drunk and, when sober, took in and cared for the homeless who came to their door. He also sexually abused my mother for years. Fortunately (that's her word), he died when she was 16. It's almost to be expected that my mother, in turn, suffered from terrible depression that cycled with episodes of extreme rage and aggression. When depressed, she would recede behind the locked door of her bedroom for days. When very young, this terrified me (also an only child) more than anything, as I feared she was dead, gone, or just not coming back. When angry (which I now know was likely the expression of her manic episodes), she would scream, cry, threaten to kill me and herself, and beat me with whatever object was in reach. Without exception, no one ever intervened, at least not that I witnessed. Not my father, my maternal grandmother, who lived with us, not a neighbor. Nor was there a response from the school when I tried to kill myself in middle school.

As a child and then teenager, I had no idea why my mother behaved the way she did. It wasn't until after my father died in 1987, during the summer following my first year in law school, that my mother opened up about the abuse she experienced at the hands of her father. This helped tremendously at the time, finally having some answer as to "why" these things happened. It did not go far, however, in soothing the extreme anxiety I experienced on a daily basis, nor the episodes of depression. Through therapy and self-reflection, I understood that these mental health problems plaguing my mother—and now me—had their etymology in my grandfather's abuse.

When did you first notice being triggered: in law school, in professional life, both?

In retrospect, I can now see that much of my experience in the legal profession has been rooted in a deep-seated drive to get help to those who had none. In law school, I participated in the Children's Rights Clinic, through which I was assigned to the district attorney's office to represent the state's child welfare office in their suits to remove and protect children from abusive parents. I took the Juvenile Justice Clinic course, which assigned me to representation of children who had committed minor offenses and had almost invariably been raised in impoverished and neglectful, if not abusive, circumstances. Fresh from law school, I went to work for the Legal Aid Society, where I alternated between representing adult victims of domestic violence and parents in the child protective services system. After eight years, I was exhausted from the vitriolic litigation and moved to working in the policy arena on national and statewide domestic violence initiatives.

Throughout, saving someone's life from violence and varied forms of abuse were the common theme. It wasn't until I returned to the Children's Rights Clinic as an adjunct professor that I finally I had insight into what would surely have been obvious to anyone from the outside looking in had they been given the information. That insight came about after watching multiple students become triggered and decompensate to varying degrees all of whom, I ultimately learned, had been exposed to some sort of adverse childhood experiences (a phrase I only learned of in the 1990s).

What role, if any, does secondary trauma play in your life? Did you experience it as a student of law or a professional? Can you give a brief example?

Like the term "adverse childhood experiences," secondary trauma was not a concept I identified until well into my legal career. That did not mean, however, that I was not affected by it. In the clinical programs working with neglected and abused children, I remember being strongly affected by the injustices perpetrated by the parents, as well as the state, both of whom had been charged with protection and both of whom regularly failed in their mission. My anger and alternating despair at the circumstances seemed disproportionate to the responses of other students, who seemed more able to maintain a professional distance. Because of my life experiences, the weight I bore in dealing with those cases far exceeded that borne by my fellow classmates. For me, I was much more susceptible to the effects of the injustices (secondary trauma) I witnessed in the clinical programs because of my similar experiences from childhood, a phenomenon borne out in research studies, and confirmed through my years of working with students in clinical legal programs.

I also experienced the effects of secondary trauma through my representation of victims of domestic violence. These cases did not have the same triggering impact as the ones involving child welfare, but the fact patterns, physical evidence of the effects of violence and, particularly, working with highly traumatized victims themselves, set me up for secondary PTSD or compassion fatigue. A precursor to this condition is burnout and, working for Legal Aid, the incessant flow of cases coupled with low levels of support, I was almost continuously in a state of burnout and overwhelmed. I found over those years that when I was particularly exhausted, perhaps because of a lengthy child custody trial or the like, I had very little ability to hold up internal boundaries and block out ruminations of the graphic evidence and fear of what the perpetrator may do to me or my family.

At this point in my life, I was able to employ more healthy coping mechanisms to deal with the extreme stress, which primarily involved exercise. I also made good use of psychotherapy, which was at the urging of my supervisor after several over-the-top emotional outbursts at the office. I struggled emotionally but had not yet been overwhelmed; it took the demise of my marriage to reach that point.

As we discussed, a common coping method is to reach for something socially acceptable and legal, can you explain the course of time and the story and the genetic predisposition?

In an attempt to cope with the painful feelings of anxiety, depression, anger, etc., I routinely turned to alcohol, the sanctioned go-to intoxicant for members of the legal profession. Like so many other law students, I binge drank but always was able to complete the tasks required. This seesaw pattern continued through my early days as a lawyer in my late twenties but changed once married and having a young child. This abatement in the progression of my drinking ceased as my marriage worsened. What was once two glasses of wine [a day] became two bottles of wine over the course of about a decade. Whenever I had the opportunity, through frightening risk-taking behavior, I added opioids to the mix, as they were a quick route to complete cessation of emotional pain. As I become more dependent upon wine to get me through the evenings, my ability to exercise became compromised. I avoided therapy as I was certain that any therapist would demand that I cut back on or cease my drinking. (Turns out, I was wrong about this.) The progressive nature of substance abuse for me, a person who is genetically predisposed towards addiction, meant that I reached the nadir of every alcoholic's misery where I felt that I would die if I kept drinking and would die if I stopped. By this time in my life, I had left the legal profession and had taken a position as executive director of a political organization. My husband left me during this time, but it wasn't until a series of events instigated by a couple of public drunken incidents that I lost my job. At this point, I was finally ready to get help.

What recommendations can you make from your personal experience in terms of healthy coping, as your story is truly one of coming to a healthy and safe place in your life.

Help for me came in many forms. As a drowning person grabs for any support to keep from going under, I reached out to friends, a mutual support group for people in recovery, a psychotherapist and a psychiatrist. I spent a year unemployed and tending to my recovery needs, during which time I went through a contested and most painful divorce involving my adolescent son. I had a small group of friends with whom I chose to be honest about my circumstances and who stayed close to make sure I was supported. My recovery group and my therapist helped me develop a new way of living that didn't involve alcohol. My psychiatrist helped me find medications that treated my depression and anxiety. I learned how to, and ultimately became a teacher of, meditation. I reconnected with spirituality and enrolled in seminary, earning a master's degree in spiritual formation. My greatest weakness became the prime qualification for working at a lawyer's assistance program, where I became the director after three years. This positioned me to begin work on national efforts to address lawyer impairment, all the while being informed by my life's experiences.

Knowing that you have co-chaired National Task Force on Lawyer Well-Being and are the co-author of the 2017 report on well-being, can you share what are the most important recommendations and findings that emerged?

The report was written by a small group of national legal organization representatives and researchers over the course of nine months in late 2016 and the first half of 2017. It was immediately endorsed by both the Conference of Chief Justices and the ABA and, to date, over 30 states have initiated bar- or court-led state-wide projects to promote lawyer well-being and prevent impairment. (see www.lawyer well-being.net for ongoing updates.)

As the report is intended to inspire systemic rather than individual change, it contains 44 recommendations to stakeholder groups in the legal profession. The most important of these, I believe, are at the outset, which charge all stakeholder groups, and especially the judiciary, with taking action to address the woeful state of lawyer well-being. (See Krill study of lawyers, and Organ study of law students, both in 2016). Every member of the profession is directed to make well-being an issue, and leaders of groups are called upon to serve as exemplars. Each state supreme court chief justice is encouraged to convene (or use their influence to get others to convene) a multi-stakeholder group to systemically address well-being for all members of the profession in their state.

All of the topics surrounding mental health are unfortunately still wrapped up in stigma. What would you recommend to law students or professionals who are struggling with these topics?

Special emphasis is given in the report to the role of stigma, as writers understood that fear was keeping legions of lawyers and law students from getting the help they needed. They feared being found out, believing that their reputations would be damaged, and their chance of success would be ruined once and for all if anyone learned that they had problems with depression, anxiety, substance abuse, or another behavioral health disorder.

Students and lawyers today must understand that the notion that one is weak and therefore unsuited to the legal profession because they experience behavioral health issues is outmoded and increasingly inaccurate. These problems should be avoided *when possible* through modifications in the profession's relationship with alcohol and with how it tends to and honors the humanity of its members. But ours is a highly stressful profession and that will not change. What needs to change is the willingness of those experiencing the most detrimental effects of this chronic stress to ask for and get help. They need to know that asking for help will not ruin their career and they need to know where to go for help. The willingness of employers and administrators to make behavioral health a topic of discussion is key, bringing what had formerly been reserved for hushed tones into the open. Making use of resources must be encouraged and supported, with transparent procedures and policies for how to do so. Finally, we must also become attuned to one another as we lawyers are a self-governing profession. By our very structure, we are our brothers' and sisters' keepers. As such, we must all learn how to know if someone is in distress, be aware of resources available and – most important – be willing to reach out and offer help.

## Section 6: Secondary Trauma Studies by Country:

## The United States, The United Kingdom, Australia, Canada, New Zealand

Secondary trauma is not a new phenomenon. The new phenomenon is the conversation surrounding it. I have talked with pockets of people from every country covered in this book and beyond; we can see that this issue is a profound and cross-cultural concern. Leaders are all around us, working diligently in their respective country. As we move through the book you will continue to see their work and encounter their stories. Below are studies from each country highlighting the issue of secondary trauma.

## Section 6.1: The United States

Jaffe et al. (Juvenile and Family Court Journal, Fall 2003) surveyed symptoms of secondary trauma in 105 judges from across the United States. They found that the majority of judges reported at least one symptom that they identified as a work-related vicarious trauma experience: including anger, anxiety, flashbacks, loss of faith in humanity, lack of empathy and a sense of isolation from others. [34]

Levin and Greisberg surveyed three different groups in New York: attorneys working with victims of domestic violence and with criminal defendants, mental health workers, and social services workers. They found that the attorneys demonstrated higher levels of secondary traumatic stress and burnout than the other groups, with higher levels of intrusive recollection of traumatic material, avoidance of reminders of the material and difficulties with sleep, irritability, and concentration. [35]

In a most recent United States Judicial College study of over 800 judges, almost half of the respondents reported having symptoms of secondary trauma due to their job. (The National Judicial College 2017).[36]

## Section 6.2: The United Kingdom

This information is currently unavailable in The United Kingdom. We can, however, extrapolate from the examples from the other countries.

## Section 6.3: Australia

Vrklevski and Franklin studied vicarious trauma in the Australian legal profession, comparing the "impact on criminal and non-criminal solicitors using a number of rating scales. They found that the level of vicarious trauma in criminal lawyers had higher levels of subjective distress, depression, stress, and cognitive changes in relation to safety and intimacy. Higher levels of avoidance, intrusions, and hypervigilance were also noted. Please note, all lawyers are subject to stress and may have distress responses."[37]

---

[34]Jaffe, Peter, Claire V. Crooks, Billie Lee Dunford-Jackson, and Judge Michael Town. 2003. "Vicarious Trauma in Judges: The Personal Challenge of Dispensing Justice." Juvenile and Family Court Journal. 54. 1 - 9. 10.1111/j.1755-6988.2003.tb00083.x.

[35] Levin, Andrew P., and Scott Greisberg. 2003. Vicarious Trauma in Attorneys, 24 Pace Law Review. 245 https://digitalcommons.pace.edu/plr/vol24/iss1/11

[36]National Judicial College, The. 2017. "Nearly Half of All Judges Have Suffered from This Condition." The National Judicial College, October 20, 2017. https://www.judges.org/nearly-half-judges-suffered-condition/. From the October 20, 2017 Judicial Edge Newsletter of The National Judicial College, Reno, Nevada. Used by permission.

[37] Vrklevski, Lila, and John Franklin. 2008. "Vicarious Trauma: The Impact on Solicitors of Exposure to Traumatic Material." Traumatology. 14. 106–118. 10.1177/1534765607309961.

## Section 6.4: Canada

In a 2003 study of Canadian Lawyers, 9% met the clinical threshold for PTSD, 23% psychological distress, and 23% unsatisfactory quality of life. Trauma-exposed lawyers were 2.62 times more likely to meet the probable PTSD threshold than the unexposed lawyers.[38]

## Section 6.5: New Zealand

There have been numerous articles in New Zealand surrounding the issue of secondary trauma among legal professionals. Many of these articles refer to previous studies and statistics from other countries. At the time of this writing, New Zealand statistics on secondary trauma among legal professionals are not available. However, we may be able to extrapolate that the experiences of legal professionals in New Zealand, maybe comparable to that of the experiences of secondary trauma in Australia and perhaps in all of the countries that we have cited.

---

[38] Leclerc, Marie-Eve, Jo-Anne Wemmers, and Alain Brunet. 2019. "The Unseen Cost of Justice: Post-Traumatic Stress Symptoms in Canadian Lawyers." Taylor & Francis, May 10, 2019. https://doi.org/10.1080/1068316X.2019.1611830.

## Discussion Questions

- What are the similarities between secondary trauma and PTSD?
- What are the different names for secondary trauma?
- What is secondary trauma?
- How does secondary trauma differ from burnout?
- What is compassion fatigue?
- What are the symptoms of compassion fatigue?
- What was the outcome of Margaret Pack's work in New Zealand?
- Review Levin and Greisberg's article (2003) and discuss their implications for family court and criminal court attorneys. Could Levin and Greisberg's implications be applied to other legal professionals such as judges, legal assistants and bailiffs? Who else could be affected?
- What is Sagy's main point?
- What was the most important concept that you learned from our Champions of Disclosure, Judge David Heilpern of Australia and Judge Robert Murfitt of New Zealand? How did they cope?
- What are the different types of trauma?
- What is generational trauma?
- How did our Champion of Disclosure Bree Buchanan ultimately cope with generational trauma?
- What was the most important aspect of each Champion of Disclosure's story that you could apply to your own practice in business or in school?
- Where are you on the Secondary Trauma Spiral?

# References

American Institute of Stress. 2017. https://www.stress.org/military/for-practitionersleaders/compassion-fatigue.

Atkinson J 2013. Trauma-informed services and trauma-specific care for Indigenous Australian children. Resource sheet no. 21. Produced for the Closing the Gap Clearinghouse. Canberra: Australian Institute of Health and Welfare & Melbourne: Australian Institute of Family Studies. © Australian Institute of Health and Welfare 2013

Australian Institute of Family Studies. 2016. "Trauma Terminology." Child Family Community Australia, February 2016. https://aifs.gov.au/cfca/publications/trauma-informed-care-child-family-welfare-services/trauma-terminology. © Commonwealth of Australia 2016

Center for Substance Abuse Treatment (US). 1970. "Understanding the Impact of Trauma." Trauma-Informed Care in Behavioral Health Services. U.S. National Library of Medicine, January 1, 1970. https://www.ncbi.nlm.nih.gov/books/NBK207191/.

Collins, K., K. Connors, S. Davis, A. Donohue, S. Gardner, E. Goldblatt, A. Hayward, L. Kiser, F. Strieder, and E. Thompson. (2010). "Understanding the impact of trauma and urban poverty on family systems: Risks, resilience, and interventions." Baltimore, MD: Family Informed Trauma Treatment Center.

Figley, Charles R. 1995. Compassion Fatigue: Coping with Secondary Traumatic Stress Disorder in Those Who Treat the Traumatized. 1st ed. New York: Routledge.

Gray SAO, CW Jones, KP Theall, E Glackin E, and SS Drury. 2017. "Thinking Across Generations: Unique Contributions of Maternal Early Life and Prenatal Stress to Infant Physiology." Journal of the American Academy of Child & Adolescent Psychiatry. https://www.ncbi.nlm.nih.gov/pubmed/29096774

Jaffe, Peter, Claire V. Crooks, Billie Lee Dunford-Jackson, and Judge Michael Town. 2003. "Vicarious Trauma in Judges: The Personal Challenge of Dispensing Justice." *Juvenile and Family Court Journal*. 54. 1 - 9. 10.1111/j.1755-6988.2003.tb00083.x.

Kroplick, Marilyn. 2014. "Organizational Trauma." In Defense of Animals USA, July 2, 2014. https://www.idausa.org/organizational-trauma/.

Leclerc, Marie-Eve, Jo-Anne Wemmers, and Alain Brunet. 2019. "The Unseen Cost of Justice: Post-Traumatic Stress Symptoms in Canadian Lawyers." Taylor & Francis, May 10, 2019. https://doi.org/10.1080/1068316X.2019.1611830.

Levin, A., A. Besser, L. Albert, D. Smith, and Y. Neria. 2012. "The effect of attorneys' work with trauma-exposed clients on PTSD symptoms, depression, and functional impairment: A cross-lagged longitudinal study." *Law and Human Behavior, 36*(6), 538–547. https://doi.org/10.1037/h0093993

Levin, Andrew P., and Scott Greisberg. 2003. *Vicarious Trauma in Attorneys*, 24 Pace Law Review. 245 https://digitalcommons.pace.edu/plr/vol24/iss1/11

Lewis, K.R., Lewis, L.S. & Garby, T.M. Surviving the Trenches: The Personal Impact of the Job on Probation Officers. *Am J Crim Just* 38, 67–84 (2013). https://doi.org/10.1007/s12103-012-9165-3

Middleton, Jennifer. 2015. "Addressing Secondary Trauma and Compassion Fatigue in Work with Older Veterans: An Ethical Imperative." Aging Life Care Association, Spring 2015. https://www.aginglifecarejournal.org/addressing-secondary-trauma-and-compassion-fatigue-in-work-with-older-veterans-an-ethical-imperative/. Journal of Aging Life Care, Spring 2015, used with permission from the Aging Life Care Association®, Tucson, AZ 85741, aginglifecare.org

Molvig, Dianna. 2011. "The Toll of Trauma." WisBar, December 1. https://www.wisbar.org/newspublications/wisconsinlawyer/pages/article.aspx?volume=84&issue=12&articleid=2356. Reprinted with permission of the December 2011 *Wisconsin Lawyer,* the official publication of the State Bar of Wisconsin, Wisconsin, USA.

Murray, Donald C., Q.C., and Johnette M. Royer. 2003. *Vicarious Traumatization: The Corrosive Consequences of Law Practice for Criminal Justice and Family Law Practitioners.* http://norestdefence.com/wp-content/uploads/2020/01/Vicarious-Traum%E2%80%A6AP-edited.pdf

National Judicial College, The. 2017. "Nearly Half of All Judges Have Suffered from This Condition." The National Judicial College, October 20, 2017. https://www.judges.org/nearly-half-judges-suffered-condition/. From the October 20, 2017 Judicial Edge Newsletter of The National Judicial College, Reno, Nevada. Used by permission.

Royal College of Psychiatrists. n.d. "Post-Traumatic Stress Disorder (PTSD)." Accessed April 6, 2020. https://www.rcpsych.ac.uk/mental-health/problems-disorders/post-traumatic-stress-disorder?searchTerms=PTSD.

Sagy, Tehila. 2006. "Even Heroes Need to Talk: Psycho-Legal Soft Spots in the Field of Asylum Lawyering." *bepress Legal Series*. Working Paper 1014. (March 1). https://law.bepress.com/expresso/eps/1014.

Schwartz, Arielle. 2017. "The Neurobiology of Transgenerational Trauma: Dr. Arielle Schwartz." December 20, 2017. https://drarielleschwartz.com/the-neurobiology-of-transgenerational-trauma-dr-arielle-schwartz/#.XeaUYOhKg2x.

Substance Abuse and Mental Health Services Administration of the United States. n.d. "Trauma." Accessed December 3, 2019. https://www.integration.samhsa.gov/clinical-practice/trauma.

van der Kolk, Bessel A. 2014. The Body Keeps the Score: Brain, Mind, and Body in the Healing *of Trauma*. New York: Viking.

Vivian, Pat, and Shana Hormann. 2012. *Organizational Trauma and Healing*. Self-published, CreateSpace.

Vrklevski, Lila, and John Franklin. 2008. "Vicarious Trauma: The Impact on Solicitors of Exposure to Traumatic Material." *Traumatology*. 14. 106–118. 10.1177/1534765607309961.

Wall, L., Higgins, D., & Hunter, C. (2016). *Trauma-informed care in child/family welfare services* (CFCA Paper No. 37). Melbourne: Child Family Community Australia information exchange, Australian Institute of Family Studies. behalf of the Commonwealth of Australia, CC BY 4.0

Wood Smith, Deborah. 2017. "Secondary or Vicarious Trauma Among Judges and Court Personnel." Secondary or Vicarious Trauma Among Judges and Court Personnel. The National Center for State Courts. Accessed December 2, 2019. https://www.ncsc.org/microsites/trends/home/Monthly-Trends-Articles/2017/Secondary-or-Vicarious-Trauma-Among-Judges-and-Court-Personnel.aspx.

World Health Organization. 2014. "WHO Releases Guidance on Mental Health Care after Trauma." World Health Organization, May 26, 2014. https://www.who.int/mediacentre/news/releases/2013/trauma_mental_health_20130806/en/.

World Health Organization. 2016. International Statistical Classification of Diseases and Related Health Problems. Geneva, Switzerland.

Youssef, Nagy A., Laura Lockwood, Shaoyong Su, Shaoyong, Guang Hao, and Bart P.F. Rutten. 2018. "The Effects of Trauma, with or without PTSD, on the Transgenerational DNA Methylation

Alterations in Human Offsprings." *Brain Sciences* 8, no. 5: 83.
https://www.ncbi.nlm.nih.gov/pmc/articles/PMC5977074.

# Chapter 2 Abstract: Stress and Other Mental Health Issues

In this chapter, we will examine stress and a number of mental health issues that commonly affect legal professionals and students, including depression, anxiety, alcohol and other substance abuse, and suicide. These topics like, secondary trauma also can have a great impact on the legal professional's mental health. Taken together with secondary trauma, legal professionals need to be aware of these issues and take care of themselves. Each topic will be reviewed utilizing research specific to the United States, the United Kingdom, Australia, Canada, and New Zealand. We will also be highlighting the major studies, including the 2016 American Bar Association and Hazelden Betty Ford Study and the 2009 study from the Brain & Mind Research Institute, Australia. We will look at the available statistics for each issue, so that we have a beginning understanding of the prevalence of these issues. By demonstrating the commonality of these issues, we hope to break down some of the stigma. We will also provide a country-by-country list of resources to help address these mental health issues, including specific responses to suicidal ideation, a crucial issue. Finally, we will learn from Champions of Disclosure, individuals who share how they encountered the various mental health concerns and what actions they engaged in to obtain help and in some instances to learn to continue managing and living with their ongoing mental health concern.

# Chapter 2: Stress and Other Mental Health Issues

"Lawyers affect more of the public and private decision-making that occurs in the country, more than any other group. If one-third of the active practicing bar is significantly impacted by affective disorder or AODA it affects their decision-making, and that is an issue."[39] Professor G. Andrew H. Benjamin.

In the following sections you will find information from studies for each country. It should be noted that we will be looking at the most recent data available, and that not all countries have research available, especially as it pertains to law students. The countries themselves use data from other countries regularly in articles to demonstrate that what occurs in one country is most likely occurring in their home country as well. In other words, the profession is already generalizing, and there is beginning to be a global recognition that these issues impact everyone. I see over and over again in my research references to the 2016 report "The Prevalence of Substance Use and Other Mental Health Concerns Among American Attorneys,"[40] published in the *Journal of Addiction Medicine* with the support of the Hazelden Betty Ford Foundation and The American Bar Association. This study, along with "Courting the Blues,"[41] a study from Sydney's Brain & Mind Research Institute, were key studies that dispersed information about the problems of mental health and addiction widely. They became thought about, discussed, and hopefully accepted.

## Section 1: Stress

Everyone can identify with stress. Stress is the response to conditions in our lives which cause worry or concern. We may notice both an emotional as well as a physical response to stress.

Stress has been a part of culture for a long time. We tend to think of stress only in recent terms and how it affects us. As technology became more complex, with "motorcars" and telephones, our grandparents and great-grandparents talked about the complexity of modern life and the stress which it created. As we began to move around with cars, then airplanes and landline telephones, to handheld phones and the internet; we had the ability to be constantly connected and in nonstop production. This nonstop production can lead to chronic stress.

---

[39] Beck, Connie J. A., Bruce D. Sales, and G. Andrew H. Benjamin. 1995. "Lawyer Distress: Alcohol-Related Problems and Other Psychological Concerns among a Sample of Practicing Lawyers." Journal of Law and Health 10:1 (199596): 10.

[40] Krill, Patrick, Ryan Johnson, and Linda Albert. 2016. "The Prevalence of Substance Use and Other Mental Health Concerns Among American Attorneys." *Journal of Addiction Medicine* 10: 46–52. 10.1097/ADM.0000000000000182.

[41] Kelk, NJ, Luscombe, GM, Medlow, S, Hickie, IB (2009) Courting the blues: Attitudes towards depression in Australian law students and lawyers, BMRI Monograph 2009-1, Sydney: Brain & Mind Research Institute.

"When cortisol levels are chronically elevated it can cause permanent changes in the brain and gene expression."[42]

"Stress becomes trauma when the intensity of frightening events becomes unmanageable to the point of threatening physical and psychological integrity."[43]

We will examine three types of stress:

"Acute stress: A very short-term type of stress that can either be positive or more distressing. This is the type of stress we most often encounter in day-to-day life.

Episodic acute stress: Acute stress that seems to run rampant and be a way of life, creating a life of relative chaos.

Chronic stress: Stress that seems never-ending and inescapable, like the stress of a bad marriage or an extremely taxing job. Chronic stress can also stem from traumatic experiences and childhood trauma."[44]

Stress has wide-reaching effects on the body. It affects the musculoskeletal system: our muscles tense up and if we are in a chronic state of tension this may trigger other reactions in the body, including stress-related disorders.

Stress affects the respiratory system and can present as shortness of breath and rapid breathing. Psychological stressors can make pre-existing health conditions (such as asthma) worse.

Stress affects the endocrine system, which turns on the production of steroid hormones called glucocorticoids. These include the "stress hormone," cortisol.

Stress affects the gastrointestinal system and can cause stomach discomfort. Stress can have effects on the esophagus, causing difficulty in swallowing, and in the bowels, causing diarrhea or constipation.

Stress affects the male reproduction system and can have an impact on sexual desire, reproduction and diseases of the reproductive system. Stress affects the female reproductive system and can have an impact on menstruation, sexual desire, pregnancy, premenstrual syndrome, menopause and diseases of the reproductive system.

---

[42] Kuehn, Bridget M. 2015. "Reducing Toxic Stress in Childhood." SAMHSA. https://www.samhsa.gov/homelessness-programs-resources/hpr-resources/reducing-toxic-stress-childhood.

[43] Lieberman and Van Horn, Psychotherapy with Infants and Young Children: Repairing the Effects of Stress and Trauma on Early Attachment, Guilford, 2008

[44] Scott, Elizabeth. "How Is Stress Affecting My Health?" Verywell Mind. Verywell Mind, July 17, 2019. https://www.verywellmind.com/stress-and-health-3145086.

A healthy stress system turns on when we need it and turns off when we don't: this is essential to ensure our survival. Chronic stress, on the other hand, doesn't turn off, and this affects the brain: including memory, selective attention, self-control, and the ability to turn off the stress response.

One representation of stress appears in Angus Lyon's book *A Lawyer's Guide to Well-Being and Managing Stress*. Lyon describes the Stress Sequence in terms of a ball with four colors.

"The yellow zone represents insufficient pressure, which can lead to boredom, rigidity, monotony, clock-watching, or 'under stress.'

The green zone represents appropriate pressure, which brings with it the opportunity of creativity, aliveness, productivity, profitability, resilience, and prehabilitation (Prehabilitation is the work that can be done on the front end which sustains health and well-being.)

The red zone represents excessive pressure leading to high anxiety, exhaustion, irritability, self-medication through alcohol or drugs, breakdowns in relationships ('over stress') which leads to the blue zone, which represents the blues, burnout, depression, mental illness, the need for prescription medication, therapy, and 'rehab.'"[45]

Stress in general helps to motivate us to reach our goals, but too much stress, or stress without breaks or periods of recovery, can interfere with our coping abilities and ultimately, create health issues.

Dr. Ahmed Tawakol, a cardiologist at Massachusetts General Hospital and Harvard Medical School, conducted a study with 293 participants, with no prior history of heart disease. The study was conducted for over three-year period to see how stress affected their health. The results of the study found that people had more activity in regions of the brain that which were involved in memory and they were also at a higher risk for stroke, heart attack and heart disease.[46]

Again, stop, pause, and think, there is clearly evidence of a higher risk for major health issues due to stress. This should be a wake-up call to motivate you to take care of yourself when it comes to stress.

## Section 1.1: United States

Stress is tied in with substance use. For many, substance use becomes a way of coping. The largest study on this issue to date, "The Prevalence of Substance Use and Other Mental Health Concerns Among American Attorneys," a study by Patrick Krill, Ryan Johnson, and Linda Albert, found that "28% of lawyers have depression at some level, and 19% have symptoms of anxiety."[47]

---

[45] Lyon, Angus. 2015. *A Lawyer's Guide to Wellbeing and Managing Stress*. London: Ark Group.
[46] Relation between resting amygdalar activity and cardiovascular events: a longitudinal and cohort study. *Br Dent J* **222,** 170 (2017). https://doi.org/10.1038/sj.bdj.2017.119
[47] Krill, Patrick, Ryan Johnson, and Linda Albert. 2016. "The Prevalence of Substance Use and Other Mental Health Concerns Among American Attorneys." Journal of Addiction Medicine 10: 46–52. 10.1097/ADM.0000000000000182.

The Dave Nee Foundation (n.d.) found that "depression and anxiety is cited by 26% of all lawyers who seek counseling."[48]

Nearly all (96%) law students experience stress, compared to 70% in medical students, and 43% in graduate students. Entering law school, law students have a psychological profile similar to that of the general public, but after law school, 20 to 40% suffer from different forms of psychological dysfunction. Psychological distress, dissatisfaction, and substance abuse that begin in law school follow many graduates into practice.[49]

According to Professor G. Andrew H. Benjamin, several studies have shown that up to 40% of law students have failed to cope effectively with the stressors of law school. A longitudinal study found that 32% of law students suffered from depression within their first year of law school, and by the third year of law school, 40% suffered from depression.[50]

In a study by Krystia Reed, Brian H. Bornstein, Andrew B. Jeon, and Lindsey E. Wylie, law students experienced high levels of psychological distress. About one in ten participants from all classes reported experiencing high levels of symptoms for depression, anxiety, and stress, with 13.2% of participants having scores that placed them above the "normal" range for the anxiety subscale, 11.4% on the stress subscale, and 9.6% on the depression subscale.[51]

## Section 1.2: The United Kingdom

According to the statistics published by the Health and Safety Executive, from 2014 to 2017, legal professionals come in third on a list of the most stressful jobs in the UK, on the basis of work-related stress, depression, or anxiety. In the past three years, 3,010 of every 100,000 workers in the legal profession have reported feeling stress, depression, or anxiety. The main causes of these issues were workload, tight deadlines, and pressure or responsibility.[52]

In 2019, attorney Kayleigh Leonie prepared a survey for third-year students on behalf of the Junior Lawyers' Division of The Law Society of England and Wales (JLD) to ascertain the levels of negative stress and mental ill-health experienced by junior lawyers. The 2019 survey produced 1,803 responses compared to the previous year's 959. "The survey found that 93.5% of respondents had experienced stress in their role in the last month with almost a quarter (24.8%) of those respondents experiencing severe/extreme levels of stress. It is concerning (albeit understandable given the connection between mental and physical ill-health) that 34.5% of respondents stated that work-related stress also had a negative impact on their physical health (physically sick and chest pains). It is

---

[48] Dave Nee Foundation. n.d. "Lawyers & Depression." Accessed December 12, 2019.
http://www.daveneefoundation.org/scholarship/lawyers-and-depression/.
[49] Dave Nee Foundation. n.d. "Lawyers & Depression." Accessed December 12, 2019.
[50] Benjamin, G. Andrew H. 2008. "Reclaim Your Practice, Reclaim Your Life." Trial, December 2008. https://ssrn.com/abstract=1344655
[51] Reed, Krystia, Brian H. Bornstein, Andrew B. Jeon, and Lindsey E. Wylie. 2016. "Problem signs in law school: Fostering attorney well-being early in professional training." International Journal of Law and Psychiatry 47. 10.1016/j.ijlp.2016.02.019.
[52] Health and Safety Executive. 2019. Work-related stress, anxiety or depression statistics in Great Britain, 2019. October 30, 2019. http://www.hse.gov.uk/statistics/causdis/stress.pdf.

extremely concerning that 1 in 15 junior lawyers (6.4%) have experienced suicidal thoughts, in the month leading up to taking the survey.

In relation to mental ill-health, around half (48%) of respondents stated that they had experienced mental ill-health concerns (whether formally diagnosed or not) in the last month.[53] This is a substantial increase on the 38% reported in the 2018 survey. Only around one-fifth (19.3%) of those respondents experiencing mental ill-heath indicated their employer was aware. Nearly two-fifths (38%) of respondents were unaware of any organizations that could help if they wanted to discuss stress or mental ill-health at work.

We can compare the results of the 2019 survey with the that of the 2018 survey and see the ongoing issue of stress. The 2018 survey results of the Junior Lawyers Division showed that over 82% of respondents reported either regularly or occasionally feeling stressed in the month before completing the survey, with 26% of those individuals being severely/extremely stressed. [54]

The major stressors for the junior lawyers were high workload, client demands/expectations, lack of support, and ineffective management. 83% of respondents said that their firm could do more to support stress at work. To that end, The Junior Lawyers Division (JLD) released guidance for employers in February 2018 that encourage businesses to destigmatize mental health and wellness issues.[55]

## Section 1.3: Australia

There have been several studies in Australia looking into the well-being of law students and practitioners. The most widely publicized of these was "Courting the Blues" released by the Brain & Mind Research Institute. After surveying 741 students, 924 solicitors and 756 barristers, the institute found that 31% of the solicitors and 16.7% of the barristers suffered from high or very high distress levels "severe enough to warrant clinical assessment," compared to 13% in the general population. [56]

A study by Natalie Skead and Shane L. Rogers, "Stress, Anxiety and Depression in Law Students: How Student Behaviours Affect Student Well-Being," examined whatthe relationship between mental health in law students and student behaviors. Though much research has been conducted by law schools, this relationship has not been clearly explored. In 2013, the authors undertook an empirical study at the University of Western Australia involving over 500 law and psychology students. The study suggests that time spent in social activity is important for health and well-being. In addition, the students' perception of the quality of the time spent correlates with lower levels of stress, anxiety, and depression. Thus, it is important for students to engage in activities with friends, family, and partners. It should be noted that online activity, such as social media and university related activities, were not rated

---

[53] Junior Lawyers Division of the Law Society of England and Wales. April 2019. Resilience and Wellbeing Survey 2019 Survey Report.
[54] Junior Lawyers Division of the Law Society of England and Wales. April 2018. Resilience and Wellbeing Survey 2018 Survey Report.
[55] Junior Lawyers Division of the Law Society of England and Wales. April 2018. Resilience and Wellbeing Survey 2018 Survey Report.
[56] Kelk, NJ, Luscombe, GM, Medlow, S, Hickie, IB (2009) Courting the blues: Attitudes towards depression in Australian law students and lawyers, BMRI Monograph 2009-1, Sydney: Brain & Mind Research Institute

as particularly enjoyable or relaxing. The more students are able to engage in personal relationships; the more balanced and happier they seemed to be.[57]

Also found in the "Courting the Blues" Study, over 35% of Australian law students were found to experience high or very high levels of "psychological distress," compared with 13% of the general population within the same age range. Beginning in the first semester of their studies, law students experience stress, anxiety, and depression at rates higher than their peers who do not study law, including those studying in other professional degree programs.[58]

This is of particular interest, since it implies that something changes for this particular group of students. The study also suggests that this group of individuals may be more prone to depression. Another important factor that the study addresses is the role of the student. What are students doing to combat stress? Are they personally engaging in behaviors that promote health and well-being? Are they taking personal responsibility for choices and making positive lifestyle changes to accommodate the stressors of the law school experience? These are questions that you can also be asking yourself.

## Section 1.4: Canada

Though we may not have the current in-country study to review, we can generalize from other country's studies to legal professionals and law students in Canada.

## Section 1.5: New Zealand

In New Zealand, 162 people responded to a New Zealand Law Society (2014) survey question. Of those who responded to the question, "as a lawyer, what is your biggest concern? What keeps you awake at night?" 24% said workload was the greatest stressor, followed by the 16% who said the possibility of making mistakes weighed on their minds, 9% were feeling the effects of the changes to the Family Court, and 10% of respondents were worried about practice performance and their careers respectively.[59]

In June 2013, the New Zealand Law Students' Association (NZLSA) conducted a survey of New Zealand law students about their mental health and well-being. Over 60% of New Zealand law students attribute high stress levels to their studies, and a quarter report developing a clinical mental health disorder since beginning their legal education: "Of those, 1 in 6 affected students believe their law studies were a direct cause of their illness, and a further half of affected students cite being a law student as a contributing factor. The disorders recorded include depression, anxiety, eating disorders and OCD."[60]

---

[57]Skead, Natalie, and Shane L. Rogers. 2014. "Stress, Anxiety and Depression in Law Students: How Student Behaviours Affect Student Wellbeing." Monash University Law Review 40, no. 2:1–24.

[58] Kelk, NJ, Luscombe, GM, Medlow, S, Hickie, IB (2009) Courting the blues: Attitudes towards depression in Australian law students and lawyers, BMRI Monograph 2009-1, Sydney: Brain & Mind Research Institute

[59] New Zealand Law Society. 2014. "It's a Stressful Profession." *LawTalk* 855. November 21, 2014. https://www.lawsociety.org.nz/lawtalk/lawtalk-archives/issue-855/its-a-stressful-profession.

[60] NZLSA. n.d. "Mental Health and Wellness." NZLSA. Accessed December 12, 2019. http://www.nzlsa.co.nz/mental-health-and-wellness/.

## Section 1.6: Case Studies

I had the opportunity to interview Professor Colin James, a contributing editor of the book *Promoting Law Student and Lawyer Well-Being in Australia and Beyond*. Dr. James has also published papers on professional identity in law students and academic integrity in legal education. Professor James thought the biggest challenges that law students face are those of perfectionism, procrastination, temptation to cheat, guilt from cheating and not showing weakness. He also noted a lack of taking care of self physically, anxiety about reputation, fitting in, and job outlooks as additional challenges.

## Interview with Professor Colin James

What are the biggest mental health challenges that law students face?

- Perfectionism: stress from performing at a high level
- Procrastination: "I always work better under pressure, so I'll wait until last minute"
- In L1: being good enough in a competitive class
- Temptations to cheat, plagiarize, engaging an essay mill, and anxiety about getting caught
- Guilt from cheating
- Not showing weakness
- Anxiety about reputation if not performing extremely well
- Effects of poor sleep, diet, fitness and reduced supportive connections
- [Worrying about] being "cool" or attractive enough to be accepted and connected with important others
- Time management: most need to earn a living while studying full-time.

Nearing the end of law school: stress on getting a job when there are so many graduates and so few positions available. Then if missing out on a law job, coping with "second-best" alternatives, such as public service etc.

What comments do you have regarding ethical dilemmas, if any, that students and professionals face when their own moral or value base is challenged by the work that they do?

Professor James stated that ethical dilemmas for students include the duty to the court over their idea of justice and being willing to adopt commercial law priorities such as time billing targets, tax minimizing cases, etc., to work at the big firms.

The ethical challenges that lawyers face include meeting time-billing targets including rounding up, fudging times spent on files, etc. doing work they feel ethically uncomfortable about, tolerating bulling of themselves or others and overlooking conflict of interest issues to not to lose a client.

In what scenarios if any, are values suppressed and what are the outcomes when one suppresses their core values?

Everyone else is doing it (e.g., rounding up hours in this workplace), so it must be OK.

If I don't take this (dodgy or conflicted) client, someone else will, so it may as well be me.

Magical thinking: If I don't get caught, it's OK, and since I didn't get caught it must be right.

The rule needs to be changed, so until it is changed it must be OK for me to ignore it.

Breaching ethical rules involves "emotional labor," which is often subconscious or partially under the surface and can accumulate in ways we don't notice until we suffer some kind of breakdown, exhaustion, or collapse we didn't see coming.

The thin edge of the wedge—often allowing our self to breach in one way, makes it easier to justify other breaches and other types of breach, which can have a snowballing effect, leading to significant errors in time.

What does the role of secondary trauma stress (STS) and stress itself play in the lives of law students?

Not much role of STS with law students studying from books, but ordinary direct stress can be significant. . . . Students in law clinics or on placements in workplaces may be exposed to traumatic situations or events, or traumatized clients or witnesses–and since they are young are likely to be more impacted and damaged by it. In any case, it is very important to educate law students about STS and VT [vicarious trauma] theory, its frequency in legal practice, its damaging effects, and strategies for protection—because many will be exposed to the trauma of others, some as a regular part of their job. They need to get over any stigma against mental health issues ASAP. [It's best] if they know about VT before applying for the job; and if they end up in a job with traumatic exposure [that they know] how to cope and look after themselves and their colleagues.

Is secondary trauma and ways of coping with secondary trauma part of the curriculum in law school in Australia?

No.

How do we overcome stigmas associated with basic issues of stress and secondary trauma as well as mental illness so that law students and professionals can get help earlier to cope better and stop suffering and to prevent suicide?

Make sure the policy is "Are you OK?" not "Toughen up, Princess"—i.e., [there should be] a policy of care and compassion for staff that is informed about the reality of VT in legal practice.

In law schools and as continuing professional development in legal practice - Psychological education as soon as possible. Teach VT theory, evidence of commonality, symptoms and effects, treatments and protective actions.

Regular staff meetings—have someone give a mini-presentation on latest research or cases, and have experienced staff discuss their experience and how they have learned to cope.

Make sure there is no "hidden" stigma, or discrimination, at any level—including laughing at someone who is different or any "jokes" by emails etc. Have a culture that does not tolerate crap.

Professor James pointed out that perfectionism and procrastination are areas where students struggle. Students have tremendous stressors placed on them both externally as well as internally. Part of those struggles include ethical dilemmas that students face as they move through the practice of law. As Professor James notes, stigma about mental health issues, including stress, must be addressed throughout student and professional life.

## Section 1.7: Champions of Disclosure

### *Christopher R. Foley*

Judge Christopher R. Foley is a judge for the Milwaukee County Circuit Court in Wisconsin, United States. He was appointed to the bench in 1985 to fill the position of his retiring father, Judge Leander J. Foley Jr.

Thoughts from Judge Foley on anxiety:

Children's court for me has been my main focus as a judge. Issues that we see are abuse, neglect, and termination of parental rights and adoption. The dilemma for judges engaged in that type of work is that you can't be good at that work unless you give a damn about what happens to them [the children].

They, the parents, the children, the lawyers, and if you don't care they know it within fifteen seconds and if you do care about these children in a personal way you do a little more dying every day then you normally would. The hurdles that these children face are so daunting and overwhelming that a lot of them are not going to succeed [and instead] end up in prison and dead. It takes a toll and learning to manage it takes time. I manage it in standard ways and somewhat unique ways. [I] exercise bicycle and walk "grand-dogs" routinely. I am a fairly devout religious person. I don't do a lot of praying on individual cases, but I do pray about being a good judge and keeping my balance.

I succeeded my father as a judge, and Dad has been gone for 20 some years and Mom twenty years and I do a lot of talking to them. On a limited basis, I talk with Deb (my wife) about it, and that is hard too.

The way I deal with . . . within the limits of ethical obligations, I love to engage with the kids outside of the courtroom. I can't do that with all of the kids. One grabs my heart or attention and I help get them over the hump. I was so frustrated with one child in children's court [when] four days turned into fourteen days, and that is one of the ways that I deal with it, and that can backfire too. I had two children that I ended up speaking at their funerals. Having them come to their home, going to their birthday parties, and athletic events.

I do unhealthy stuff too, brooding; I get into that mindset on occasion without noticing and the people who notice it are my staff, and then they hit me with a quip [like] "you need a bike ride," and it gets me focused on [health]. Children's court is one thing; I have consciously chosen to never do a criminal calendar. That level of violence and sexual assault and victimization, I literally don't think I would be capable of doing that. I have consciously dodged it for all thirty years.

People need, as they chose their career paths in legal field, to be very conscious of what you do, anticipate what you can handle and what you can't. If you wade into a field where you are incapable of handling the emotional fallout you are headed for real problems.

As Judge Foley has shown us, it is difficult to do good work unless you genuinely care about the people that you are working with. When we genuinely care, we are affected by what happened and what will happen to the individuals we work with. It is critical that we determine ways of coping that are healthy and that we can use on a regular basis. Make these coping methods unique to you, so that you will actually use them.

### *Will Meyerhofer*

Will Meyerhofer holds a B.A., magna cum laude, from Harvard University, a Juris Doctor from the New York University School of Law, and a Master of Social Work from the Hunter College School of Social Work. Will has written the books *Life is a Brief Opportunity for Joy, Way Worse Than Being a Dentist (The Lawyer's Quest for Meaning), Bad Therapist: A Romance,* and *Still Way Worse Than Being a Dentist.*

Will also writes a regular column for AboveTheLaw.com. In addition to his writing, Will works as a psychotherapist in private practice.

What was role did stress play for you in your professional life as an attorney and also as a student, if any?

Student life in law school, at least for me, was rather relaxed, actually, once I got past the first semester and learned I was doing fine and could ignore my classmates' stressing out over exams and so forth. In the law firm, I was in a constant state of stress—anxious and depressed that I always seemed to be failing at whatever task they assigned me, and that the workflow was so unpredictable—it would suddenly stop, and then, without warning, I'd be buried, working days, nights, and weekends with no end in sight. I never seemed to be able to relax, or to catch up, or to please anyone I worked for. And at some point, I realized I was pretending to be someone I wasn't, just because I felt I had to succeed in this profession, but I was essentially only in it for prestige and money—I didn't really care for the work or care about what I was doing. That was an enormous stressor, since I was over 30 and in debt from school loans and really had no Plan B.

What is the impact you see of stress on the lawyers and law students you work with?

I see a lot of burnout from lawyers who never seem to get a vacation. I see a lot of anxiety among lawyers who worry constantly that they're going to make a mistake and that if they do, instead of support, they'll be thrown under the bus in this endlessly competitive field, where not only the judges and opposing counsel can seem like adversaries, but so can your own clients and even colleagues at your own firm.

What are some of your recommendations for coping with stress?

I'm not really the yoga and wellness type: I'm a vegetarian and a weightlifter, so I believe in fitness, but I think there are limits on the usefulness of lecturing lawyers on wellness when they're stuck working crazy eighty-hour weeks and have no time to sleep. Sure, they should eat more kale and meditate, I suppose, but that's probably not the big issue here. My approach is psychoeducation: to increase an awareness of what they're experiencing and affirm that it really is happening and is happening to other lawyers too. Just getting lawyers to trust one another enough to share their honest experiences can make an enormous difference. Awareness, especially of one's own situation and authentic self, tends to create change all by itself.

As Will Meyerhofer pointed out it took the stress of working long hours, with few breaks and without seeing an end; for him to recognize this work was not for him. Now serving lawyers as a psychotherapist, he sees the same stressors in other people. In addition, he notes that among lawyers there is rarely support or comradery for each other, but instead here is a sense of fear. As Will points out, it is important to recognize the commonality of these feelings.

### *Jerome Doraisamy*

Jerome is a lecturer at the University of Western Australia Law School, a writer, and a former lawyer. He has written the *Wellness Doctrines for Law Students and Young Lawyer*s and *The Wellness Doctrines for High School Students*. He is also a senior writer for *Lawyers Weekly*. He is on the board of the Minds Count Foundation, which works to bring mental health initiatives to the legal profession.

Is your health history public?

Yes, public in that I've published two books about it. In a nutshell, I had a major breakdown in my final year of law school. Which meant that I wouldn't have been able to take up a graduate position with a law firm I thought I was going to have, which really derailed the career in that sense. And so, I had an approximate 18 months of severe clinical depression and anxiety, which resulted in one period of hospitalization. The biggest contributing factor was that I had pushed myself to the limit for too long. With the study schedule, with work in a law firm, with volunteering activities, with not sleeping enough, not prioritizing health and happiness as much as I should have been, it eventually culminated in a big breakdown at a music festival in rural Australia when I was with a bunch of my old school friends. So with [that] 18-month time of ill health that I had meant I couldn't work for a long time and finally when I was about to go back to work it was to my old law school in Sydney to do some teaching and research work, because that was an environment in which I felt comfortable so that seemed like a good place to start my post-graduate career

I'm wondering [since] a couple of the areas [you] were working on in the book is stress, anxiety, and depression, can you talk at all about the influence of stress and how that contributed either to the breakdown or to you writing the books?

Sure, so I think that when it comes to stress, one of the primary reasons I had stress was because I became so consumed by the competitive, perfectionist nature of the legal educational environment. Law school really breeds those type A personalities that can't accept anything less than 100% or being Number 1, and that's something that you put your mind to, and because I was already predisposed to such competitive streaks it was easy for me to fall into those kinds of traps and because I'd also grown up achieving everything I wanted to achieve, the idea of failure was a foreign thing and therefore a very scary thing. And so I ended up just putting so much pressure and stress on myself to be the best, and then I'm sure that the issues are similar in the States, but there are so many law graduates but then very few jobs with top-tier firms and law schools, and the legal profession generally haven't done a very good job of advertising the different options that are available vocationally, so students think that going into the big commercial firms is their only option. So, you've got that very sheltered impression of what you can actually do with a law degree. And so that creates a lot of status anxiety, and then of course you have to factor in the volume of work required in law school. The fact [is] that you're being trained to think in a pessimistic fashion, because you always have to look for the flaws, mistakes, worst-case scenario in any given problem, and so you have this pessimistic attitude to work that kind of bleeds over into your personal life. There's a lot of law students or young lawyers who will self-medicate with alcohol or with drugs, [or who] have disordered their eating patterns to match their study habits. It's a whole cocktail of issues that contribute to that stress.

Did you have any of those issues associated with the alcohol or drug use while you were coping?

Not drugs. With alcohol, I guess the idea of going to social events and being able to let your hair down was something that was pretty common. It would never have been a crutch for me, but that was seen as being the way to unwind or destress.

I know there's been a lot of talk about that recently, and I know especially in the U.S. we are trying to kind of limit [that], especially in law schools, trying to teach them other ways of engaging each other (outside of the school scenario) that are alcohol free.

Yeah, that's really important, and also getting students into good eating habits. You should have a look at the research I did last year with the University of Western Australia, which examined the rates of disordered eating among lawyers and law students in Australia, which hasn't been done before.

That showed that too many lawyers and law students are eating lunch at their desk or skipping meals, eating at the wrong time of day, snacking rather than having proper meals, and the cumulative impact of eating in such a way and not have the standard three square meals a day is correspondingly, people who display those behaviors will also have higher levels of stress, anxiety, and depression.

What percentage of people did you have respond?

We surveyed about 600 lawyers and law students across Australia, and about 30% of lawyers say that they rely on caffeine every single day to get through. 75% of lawyers have had to skip a meal in the last month. About 20% of lawyers say that they have eating, weight, and shape concerns to a level of clinical significance. About 48% say they have eating, weight, and shape concerns through a level of eating disturbance. Not quite a disorder, but it's having a cumulative negative impact on their holistic wellness They were quite shocking finds.

So, as I was thinking about our discussion and some of the background here, can you tell us also Jerome, as you were going through this . . . you were quite into your studies by that point, correct?

I was in my final year and that's why it kind of moved the career off track because I was in the middle of the summer clerkship at one of the big law firms and as a result of my ill health and being unable to perform at the level that would have been expected I was not kept on as a graduate, which really rocked my confidence. Which not only felt like the first time in my life that I had every really failed at something, but also felt like I was being punished for being unwell. So that created a lot of resentment, and even though people tell you it's important to speak up, by speaking up I shot myself in the foot.

You didn't really receive a lot of support then when you spoke up?

Not from this law firm, no. But then from family and friends and from mentors back at university and some professional mentors I did receive a lot of good support, which was incredibly helpful.

You said when you went to the music fest, you noticed that this just happened or you just crumbled at the music festival, you had your breakdown there—did you notice as you were going along to that point, could you discern unhealthy coping skills or you were just ploughing through and you couldn't really notice that or help it?

Yeah, I wasn't very self-aware at the time. Which is obviously hugely problematic in hindsight, as it wasn't until I had a breakdown that I appreciated what some of the issues I was going through were. but then once I did recognize them, once I did have a breakdown, I was very proactive about trying to put in place the solutions and strategies I thought were going to help. I was going to see a counselor and starting to eat right and move back home to see my parents, [a] whole range of things I thought would be really helpful, and I thought if I got on the front foot, I would be able to work through all of the issues.

That's wonderful. It's quite amazing that when you were suffering from the depression especially that you were able to think clearly enough to be able to be solution-focused.

Well I think it was probably also partly the competitiveness kicking in. thinking if I do x, y, z to look after myself, then everything will get better. And it didn't quite work out like that, so I had to reframe my thinking, but certainly it was helpful to try to put in place all the different things that I thought were going to work to feel better in the long run.

Yes, I understand. So, do you remember what your unhealthy coping was versus your new healthy coping and how you did reframe things?

I don't think necessarily that I had things that were specifically unhealthful, but it was specifically a matter of having cut out or having neglected the things that were going to be helpful for me. I didn't have the right balance. I had stopped playing teams sports, and stopped reading books, and going for walks, and listening to music, and doing the things that have always been very helpful for me. So, it was a matter of reengaging with those activities so that I could strive for the right balance and I could have more joy and meaning in my daily and weekly schedule and have more fun as well. By rediscovering those things, I was about to kind of get back on track.

I think that's very interesting; the issue of competitiveness and I get it how it stays in there. How were you able to do what I'm calling work-life balance with that competitive edge still there? How do you maintain that?

In the end, I decided that it was incumbent on me to prioritize health and happiness above all else, because I decided that I wasn't going to be a productive, successful lawyer unless I was first a healthy, happy person. I decided that one couldn't exist without the other. Because I had already recognized that I was predisposed to certain health problems, and it was going to be really important for me to remain constantly vigilant of looking out for myself, and if something wasn't making my happy or fulfilled in the workplace, then it wasn't going to be something worthwhile.

Very good. That's a very sophisticated way of looking at things.

Well, it took a breakdown and a bad period of ill health to recognize that, but I got there in the end.

Wonderful, and was that the motivation for the Wellness Doctrines?

Partly, but also because when I did go back to my old law school to do some teaching and research work, I witnessed new law students coming through the ranks with the same issues, so it struck me as a very cyclical process and it didn't appear that enough was being done about it, and that made me rather upset . . . I had a long think about what I could potentially do to help and I decided against doing a charity, because there was already an established charity for depression in law in Australia, and I didn't want to compete with that, but I realized that there was no central resource for which young lawyers and law students could refer to if and when they were having any problem . . . so I decided to write that central resource, which ultimately became the form of a self- help book.

That was a positive and healthy way of copying. And then you decided to do it for high school students as well?

Yeah, I did. So that one got published just under eighteen months ago, and it was just another interest area of mine . . . Obviously I've been through high school as well as law school, and so it just seemed like a natural thing to do and do the book for lawyers, that's really been successful for me.

Do you find that now when you are going back to the school or teaching, you are continuing to find this cyclical process with the new students that are coming in?

Yeah, to an extent, but they're also much more aware of the issues and more likely to put in place certain activities to look after themselves. I mean they're still working very hard academically, but simultaneously they're also looking to do a number of things to take care of themselves, so that's a step in the right direction.

What would you say to students right now who are struggling with stress and anxiety and depression and who are really concerned about the issue of stigma and the issue of competition? We keep hearing over and over again people saying that they are reluctant to talk about it because they're worried that they'll be seen in an unfavorable light.

I guess it would be important to recognize that you don't have to speak to your boss about such issues if you don't want to. There's a million and one people in your life with whom you can have a private, confidential conversation with if you need to do that, so that would be your mates, your parents, your partners, your siblings, your mentors, your lecturers at university. You don't have to risk having some kind of negative professional outcome by talking to the partner at the law firm or anything like that. Just be strategic about whom you talk to.

And for the students who are still in law school, what do you think about that? Who do you think would be good resources?

I think if you're a first- or second-year student, it's really important to speak to some of the students in their final year. I think it's important to identify which academics will be willing to have a chat. There are of course the career counselors on campus as well, but sometimes they may not be as specifically tailored to the needs of your educational strain and so again it can be really important to find somebody who understands you a bit better. So, yeah, there are people on campus but there's also people in your personal life too, and they're more often than not going to be best placed to assist.

I see a lot of people in my own practice where the stress has gone unabated for so long and it's at such a moderate to severe level without ceasing that eventually it does move into anxiety, and then the anxiety moves into depression. Do you think that was the pathway that you kind of found yourself in?

I think the depression probably came first, and then the anxiety kind of crept in and I think it was probably lying underneath the surface for a bit longer and I just didn't realize it, but it's easily to hypothesize in hindsight.

What about the issue of stigma associated with talking about these things? So many people are concerned about the stigma. I sometimes think, are we really going into 2021, with the stigma surrounding so much of this?

My general impression is that we've come a long way in the last 10–15 years toward addressing this issues, but also we've got a very long way to go, and there's a lot we can be proud of in what we've achieved in the last 10–15 years of raising awareness and trying to get people more comfortable talking, but we also have to recognize that there's still so many workplace issues that haven't been properly addressed that can impact upon wellness, like the disordered eating that I was mentioning before, like sexual harassment and misconduct, like cultural issues, like bullying, leadership limitations. There's a lot of things that still impact upon wellness and are unrelated in a sense to someone's individual health, and so it's really important that we recognize all of those issues and be able to address each and every one of them.

Where are you now? I know you're writing for *Lawyers Weekly*. What else are you doing?

Yeah, well, I've got a couple of different paths. I'm obviously doing the writing for *Lawyers Weekly* from 9–5, but outside of that I do lot of lectures and workshops for law firms, universities, and high schools around the country about mental health issues and how to look after yourself. I am a lecturer with the University of Western Australia. I'm also a board director for a not-for-profit in Australia, for Minds Count.

It sounds like you're coping really well and are doing really well.

Yeah, absolutely. I mean I recognize that I have to be constantly vigilant about looking after myself, but yeah, I'm enjoying my day-to-day work and enjoying life so yeah, on the right track.

When you say "constantly vigilant" is that so you don't have another occurrence of major depression?

Essentially, yes.

Jerome has demonstrated that our initial course may change. There exist numerous areas in the law in which you can use your education, skills, and creativity to create new possibilities.

Both Jerome and Will have demonstrated this courage, flexibility, and ultimately success.

As you have seen, stress affects everyone, taking a psychological and physical toll. Examine the role of stress in your life and take measured steps to help mitigate its influences. The Champions of Disclosure demonstrate the broad effects of stress and ways that they have discovered to manage their stress. Many tools for coping with stress are listed in the Methods Section of this book. It is essential to use healthy coping techniques and techniques that work for you as an individual.

## Section 2: Depression and Anxiety

The World Health Organization defines depression and anxiety disorders in this way:

"Depressive disorders are characterized by sadness, loss of interest or pleasure, feelings of guilt or low self- worth, disturbed sleep or appetite, feelings of tiredness, and poor concentration. Depression can be long lasting or recurrent, substantially impairing an individual's ability to function at work or school or cope with daily life. At its most severe, depression can lead to suicide. Depressive disorders include two main sub-categories: major depressive disorder / depressive episode, which involves symptoms such as depressed mood, loss of interest and enjoyment, and decreased energy; depending on the number and severity of symptoms, a depressive episode can be categorized as mild, moderate, or severe; and dysthymia, a persistent or chronic form of mild depression; the symptoms of dysthymia are similar to depressive episode but tend to be less intense and last longer."[61]

Anxiety disorders cover a group of disorders characterized by anxiety and fear. Some of the disorders in this group include Generalized Anxiety Disorder (GAD), panic disorder, phobias, social anxiety disorder, obsessive-compulsive disorder (OCD), and post-traumatic stress disorder (PTSD). These disorders can range in severity and typically are chronic.

More than 300 million people have depression. And the number keeps rising, with an increase worldwide of 18% between 2005 and 2015. People with depression most often also have anxiety. Worldwide it is estimated that 264 million people have anxiety disorders. As with depression, anxiety disorders are also growing, with an increase of 14.9% between 2005 and 2015.[62]

Depression has the potential to affect physical structures in the brain and literally decrease some of the areas of the brain. The volume of the brain can actually decrease.[63]

Finally, widespread reductions in grey matter volume can occur in the brain with depression.[64]

### Section 2.1: The United States

As the Dave Nee Foundation, notes, we have seen chronic stress can trigger the onset of depression. Lawyers are frequently the most depressed occupation in the United States. They suffer from depression 3.6 times more than non-lawyers. More than a quarter of lawyers seeking counseling cite

[61] World Health Organization. 2017. *Depression and Other Common Mental Disorders: Global Health Estimates*. Geneva: World Health Organization. https://eac.eu.com/newsletter/booklets/who%20mental%20disorders.pdf.

[62] World Health Organization. 2017. *Depression and Other Common Mental Disorders: Global Health Estimates*. Geneva: World Health Organization. https://eac.eu.com/newsletter/booklets/who%20mental%20disorders.pdf.

[63] Yüksel, Dilara, Jennifer Engelen, Verena Schuster, Bruno Dietsche, Carsten Konrad, Andreas Jansen, Udo Dannlowski, Tilo Kircher, and Axel Krug. 2018. "Longitudinal brain volume changes in major depressive disorder." *Journal of Neural Transmission* 125: 1433–47. https://doi.org/10.1007/s00702-018-1919-8.

[64] Grieve, Stuart M., Mayuresh S. Korgaonkar, Stephen H. Koslow, Evian Gordon and Leanne Maree Williams. 2013. "Widespread reductions in gray matter volume in depression." *NeuroImage: Clinical* 3: 332–39. https://doi.org/10.1016/j.nicl.2013.08.016.

depression and anxiety as what brought them in for help. 15% of those with depression commit suicide and lawyers rank the fifth in incidence in suicide by occupation. [65]

One study found that 44% of law students meet the criteria for clinically significant levels of psychological distress including stress, anxiety, and depression.[66]

## Section 2.2: The United Kingdom

In general, work life can be stressful. According to a survey completed by Deloitte-UK, a third of the UK workforce experiences anxiety, depression, or stress, according to a survey of employees in junior and senior roles. A survey found two in five (39%) of employees said they had taken time off work or reduced their responsibilities due to their health. And nearly a quarter, 23%, said they do not think their organization takes employee well-being seriously. However, of those who had taken time off work for health reasons, 39% said they did not feel comfortable telling their employer about the issue. Could this be another demonstration of the continuing influence of stigma surrounding taking care of one's mental health? If all workers are affected, we know lawyers are too.[67]

Reluctance to talk about mental health issues is pervasive, as we have seen. Richard Collier, Professor of Law at Newcastle University, has posited several important questions on "the law's well-being problem." Our discussion covered such topics as standards of emotional competence in legal practice, the place of emotion in the traditional university law degree, what it means to learn to "think like a lawyer," and the issues surrounding transition from legal education into a career in law and "how well-being and mental health agendas are central to ensuring lawyers 'thrive from the start.'"

## Section 2.3: Australia

A 2016 study by Grace Maguire and Mitchell Byrne of the University of Wollongong speculated that the lack of support for secondary trauma initiatives in the legal profession has led to higher levels of symptoms, particularly depression, anxiety, and stress. The study found that legal professionals had even higher rates of these issues than mental health professionals who frequently work with trauma survivors.

Maguire and Byrne noted that support services for professionals who may be exposed to trauma victims have traditionally been only for the helping professions, such as mental health workers and social workers. While barristers also constitute a helping profession, there has been limited study in Australia on this issue. This study greatly helped to undermine the stigma of mental health concerns by

---

[65] Dave Nee Foundation. n.d. "Lawyers & Depression." Accessed December 12, 2019. http://www.daveneefoundation.org/scholarship/lawyers-and-depression/.

[66] Peterson, Todd D., and Elizabeth W. Peterson. 2009. "Stemming the Tide of Law Student Depression: What Law Schools Need To Learn from the Science of Positive Psychology. *Yale Journal of Health Policy, Law, and Ethics* 9, issue 2. https://digitalcommons.law.yale.edu/yjhple/vol9/iss2/2

[67] DELOITTE

noting that the study attributed the greater vulnerability of lawyers to organizational issues and not individual personality characteristics. [68]

*Under the Radar: The Mental Health of Australian University Students* examined 2015 statistics, showing that out of 1.4 million Australia students, one in four will experience mental health issues in any one year. The research suggested that students do not disclose or seek support for mental health issues due to stigma and the lack of understanding among academic or administrative staff about these conditions.[69]

In a study conducted by the University of Sydney's Brain & Mind Research Institute, 74.9% of law students stated that they, or someone close to them, had experienced depression. Of these students, 46.9% had personally experienced depression. Disproportionately high levels of depression don't end at graduation, either.[70]

According to work done by Molly Townes O'Brien, Stephen Tang, and Kath Hall at Australian National University, first-year law school students may experience negative changes in thinking styles, stress levels, and satisfaction with life. The authors examined the underlying foundations of the legal curriculum, including the competitive, adversarial and emotionally detached concepts, which may negatively impact student well-being. [71]

## Section 2.4: Canada

"52% of practicing lawyers describe themselves as dissatisfied. Certainly, the problem is not financial. As of 1999, associates at top firms could earn up to $200,000 per year just starting out, and lawyers long ago surpassed doctors as the highest-paid professionals. In addition to being disenchanted, lawyers are in remarkably poor mental health. They are at much greater risk than the general population for depression."

"They are the best-paid professionals, and yet they are disproportionately unhappy and unhealthy. And lawyers know it; many are retiring early or leaving the profession altogether."[72]

Another study, by Megan Seto, looked at self-reports of depression from lawyers. They ranged from 3.5%–37%, depending on the measurements used.[73]

[68] Maguire, Grace, and Mitchell K. Byrne. 2017. "The Law Is Not as Blind as It Seems: Relative Rates of Vicarious Trauma among Lawyers and Mental Health Professionals."
[69] *Under the Radar: The Mental Health of Australian University Students.* Parkville: ORYGEN - The National Centre of Excellence in Youth Mental Health., 2017. Reproduced with the permission of Orygen, Australia.
[70] Kelk, NJ, Luscombe, GM, Medlow, S, Hickie, IB (2009) Courting the blues: Attitudes towards depression in Australian law students and lawyers, BMRI Monograph 2009-1, Sydney: Brain & Mind Research Institute.
[71] Townes O'Brien, Molly, Stephen Tan, and Kath Hall. 2011. "No time to lose: Negative impact on law student wellbeing may begin in year one." The International Journal of the First Year in Higher Education 2, no. 2 (July 30, 2011): 49–60. https://doi.org/10.5204/intjfyhe.v2i2.84.
[72] Seligman, Martin E. P. 2016. "Why Are Lawyers So Unhappy?" Lawyers With Depression, September 20, 2016. http://www.lawyerswithdepression.com/articles/why-are-lawyers-so-unhappy/.
[73] Seto, Megan. 2012. "Killing Ourselves: Depression as an Institutional, Workplace and Professionalism Problem," 2:2 online: OWOJ Leg Stud 5

Finally, a 2012 "Survey of Lawyers on Wellness Issues," conducted by Ipsos Reid and commissioned by the Canadian Bar Association, found that close to 50% of lawyers have suffered from some sort of anxiety.[74]

## Section 2.5: New Zealand

According to an article from the New Zealand Law Society, lawyers have higher rates of physical and psychological issues, as well as substance abuse issues.[75]

As reported by Harmer, the 400 New Zealand lawyers who participated in The Well-Being 360 Health Assessment had on average "twice the rate of poor mental health" fewer of them had "good social and work well-being."[76]

The 2013 survey from the New Zealand Law Students Association (NZLSA) found that 27% of respondents had developed a clinical mental health problem since being in law school. Some of the mental health problems included depression, anxiety, eating disorders, OCD, bipolar disorder, panic attacks, self-harm and insomnia; 63.5 of survey respondents reported high levels of stress. Reasons for stress included high expectations for top grades (selected by 89% of students), pressures of finding a job after law school, the number of readings, the amount of time that had to be dedicated to study, and the pressures exerted by other law students (selected by 51% of students). 55% of those surveyed reported feelings of depression.[77]

In another study, "The Making of Lawyers: Expectations and Experiences of Second Year New Zealand Law Students," 227 students expressed how satisfied they were with their law school experience. Three in five (60%) of students reported feeling satisfied or very satisfied, 30% were neutral, and 7% reported feeling dissatisfied or very dissatisfied.[78]

## Section 2.6: Case Studies

Amir H. Rezvani, Ph.D. is a Professor of Psychiatry and Behavioral Sciences, Professor of Psychology and Neuroscience, and Associate Director, Addiction Division, at the Department of Psychiatry and Behavioral Sciences at Duke University Medical Center. He spoke about the biology of depression.

---

[74] Ipsos Reid. 2012. "Survey of Lawyers on Wellness Issues." Commissioned by the Canadian Bar Association. https://www.cba.org/Sections/Wellness-Subcommittee/Resources/Research

[75] New Zealand Law Society. 2014. "It's a Stressful Profession." *LawTalk* 855. November 21, 2014. https://www.lawsociety.org.nz/lawtalk/lawtalk-archives/issue-855/its-a-stressful-profession.

[76] NZLSA. n.d. "Mental Health and Wellness." NZLSA. Accessed December 12, 2019. http://www.nzlsa.co.nz/mental-health-and-wellness/.

[77] NZLSA. n.d. "Mental Health and Wellness." NZLSA. Accessed December 12, 2019. http://www.nzlsa.co.nz/mental-health-and-wellness/.

[78] Taylor, Lynne, Ursula Cheer, Natalie Baird, John Caldwell, and Debra Wilson. 2016. "The Making of Lawyers: Expectations and Experiences of Second Year New Zealand Law Students." University of Canterbury, February 2016. https://www.canterbury.ac.nz/media/documents/research/S11503-The-Making-of-Lawyers.pdf.

## *Amir H. Rezvani, Ph.D.*

Depression is a major health issue affecting millions of people worldwide. The incidence of depression is about 15–20% of the population. Bipolar depression, on the other hand, is rare; only 1% of the population suffer from it. Depression is more common in women. Depression is a chronic mental disease that does not discriminate. One historic example is our beloved 16th president, Abraham Lincoln, who suffered from clinical depression at various times throughout his life. According to his biographers, he often wept in public. His episodes of depression were so severe that he even could not show up at his own wedding, leaving his bride and the guests waiting for him.

Major depression has several severe long-lasting debilitating symptoms that can significantly affect daily activities. It can cause decreased energy, restlessness, difficulty sleeping or oversleeping, thoughts of death or suicide, irritability, pessimism, anxiety, feeling restless and anhedonia (the inability to experience pleasure). However, not everyone who is depressed experiences all of these symptoms. Both the frequency and the severity of these symptoms as well as how long they last vary in different individuals under different circumstances. Both family studies and identical and fraternal twin studies support the involvement of genetic factors in manifestation of depression.

Heritability of depression has been reported to be around 0.37. Concordance rate of depression in identical twins is about 69%, while this concordance rate in fraternal twins is about 13%. The fact that the concordance rate of depression in identical twins is not 100%, even though they have an identical genome, suggests that environmental or other factors also play a major role in depression. Thus, although genetics play a role in expression of depression, other factors such as unwanted life events, PTSD, anxiety and other brain illnesses such as addiction to drugs of abuse might lead to the development of depression. Current findings suggest that depression can be caused by a combination of genetic, environmental, and psychological factors. It is interesting to mention that among Americans who born before 1905 only 1% developed depression by age 75, whereas among those born since 1955, 6% experienced depression symptoms by age 24. Environmental factors and a modern stressful lifestyle may have contributed to this phenomenon, as stress-induced hormonal changes have a significant effect on initiation of depression.

Depression is a treatable brain disease and has to be addressed as a brain disease. An occasional bad mood or feeling is not considered depression. True depression goes beyond the natural sad reaction to an unwanted event and situation. Depression is the result of a significant change in brain anatomy and functions that lasts for at least several months or in some people for years.

In addition to major depression or dysthymia, which lasts at least two years, there are other forms of depression such as postpartum depression, psychotic depression, and seasonal affective disorder (SAD). The mood of people with seasonal affective disorder rise and falls with change in seasons. Most individuals with SAD are more depressed during the fall and winter, when there is less natural light. It has been suggested that the lower serotonin level in winter contributes to SAD. A treatment for SAD is phototherapy, exposing the patient to bright light for a couple of hours a day. Most patients with SAD are women.

Another form of depression is postpartum depression. Women with postpartum depression experience major depression after delivery. Postpartum depression is different from the so-called baby blues, which is mild and disappears after two to three weeks. The cause of postpartum depression is a major drop in the levels of estrogen and progesterone hormones after delivery. Changes in hormones produced by the thyroid gland may also contribute to postpartum depression. Sleep deprivation, change in pre-delivery routine lifestyle, anxiety, and being overwhelmed with a new lifestyle may also contribute to postpartum depression. Postpartum depression is not limited to mothers only. Fathers can also experience this problem. This is called paternal postpartum depression and is caused by being overwhelmed with new tasks, anxiety, change in sleep pattern and lifestyle, and financial struggle. Postpartum depression in one of the partners may also contribute to other partner's depression.

According to the Diagnosis and Statistical Manual of Mental Disorders, there are two types of depression: major depression or unipolar depression, and bipolar disorder or bipolar depression.

Several hypotheses have been suggested for major depression. The most known is the monoamine hypothesis. According to this, depression is the result of a monoamine (serotonin and norepinephrine in this case) deficiency in the brain. It has been shown that drugs that increase these neurotransmitters in the synapse are effective in the treatment of depression. This can be accomplished by increasing the release of these neurotransmitters into synaptic cleft by stimulating specific neurons or by blocking reuptake of these neurotransmitters into the neuron or preventing their metabolism or breakdown in the synapse. The end results are an elevation of these neurotransmitters in the synaptic cleft. For example, fluoxetine (the generic name for Prozac) is a serotonin reuptake inhibitor, which by blocking reuptake of serotonin into the serotonergic neurons elevates the level of serotine in the synapse, leading to the reduction of a depressive mood. Another group of drugs, called tricyclics, are used for the treatment of depression, and are believed to increase both serotonin and norepinephrine in certain areas of the brain. However, not all patients with depression respond to antidepressant drugs such as Prozac or tricyclics, suggesting the involvement of others neuronal systems in depression. It is important to remember that these neurotransmitters do not work in isolation, but instead they are parts of a complex network of constantly interaction neuronal system.

Depression is usually treated with medications, psychotherapy (cognitive-behavioral therapy (CBT), interpersonal therapy (IPT), and problem-solving therapy) or a combination of these treatments. The combination of medication and psychotherapy usually leads to much better outcomes. Brain electrical stimulation (transcranial magnetic stimulation, TMS or deep brain stimulation) has recently been shown to be effective in treating depression in some individuals. The earlier the treatment begins the better. When it comes to depression, it is critical to educate the public and try to remove the stigma. Unfortunately, in some culture's depression is still seen as a sign of those with weak willpower. Patients have to be educated and constantly reminded that to be affected by depression is not their fault and is not a sign of weak willpower, but it is a treatable brain disease.

Amir explained the various types of depression and the neurobiology pertaining to each, as well as different types of effective treatments. Depression is a real, treatable brain disease and not a sign that someone is weak.

## <u>Section 2.7: Champions of Disclosure</u>

### <u>*Joseph Milowic III*</u>

Attorney Joseph Milowic III is a partner at Quinn Emanuel Urquhart & Sullivan, LLP in New York City, he was selected as a Global Fellow by the Federal Circuit Bar Association and named "Super Lawyer" by his peers in the specialty of Intellectual Property. He is also a Founder of the Lawyers Depression Project (LDP.) In our discussions, Joseph shared that his depression ultimately inspired him to create the Lawyers Depression Project. He has graciously shared his story, which was previously published in the National Law Journal. https://www.law.com/nationallawjournal/2018/03/28/quinn-emanuel-partner-suffers-from-depression-and-he-wants-everyone-to-know/

My name is Joe Milowic. I am a partner at Quinn Emanuel Urquhart & Sullivan. And I suffer from depression.

A prominent Johns Hopkins study found that lawyers are more likely to suffer from depression than any other profession. The Centers for Disease Control and Prevention (CDC) reported that lawyers have higher rates of suicide than all but three professions (dentists, pharmacists, and doctors).

So, naturally, the legal profession is buzzing about what to do about this serious problem; well, not quite. To say there is a "stigma" associated with discussing mental illness in the legal profession, where mental acumen directly correlates with your livelihood, is an understatement.

For a long time, I did not feel comfortable admitting this to my colleagues for fear of being perceived as incapable or unproductive. But it is my truth. It is an illness like any other illness, and it deserves to be recognized and treated as such without fear of stigmatization.

I had my initial diagnosis of major depression over a decade ago. I went to my primary care physician complaining of exhaustion and lack of energy. I had no idea what was wrong with me, and neither did my doctor. She diagnosed me with prehypertension, put me on a low-carb diet, and referred me to a diabetes specialist.

I monitored my blood glucose levels strictly, but the lethargy and lack of energy and motivation only seemed to get worse. I was dwelling on my thoughts, consumed by an endless loop of anxiety and negativity. I was losing weight and losing interest in everything. I questioned the purpose of my work and even life. What was the point of it all? Why spend so many hours working at a job that seems so pointless?

I remember suffering from terrible anxiety (I didn't know what it was called at the time) and I would go out running to try to shake it. One night while running around a track outside my apartment, I was so besieged by thoughts that everything was meaningless that I fell to my knees and screamed to make the thoughts stop.

I was convinced there was no point to my job and that it was contributing to my illness. It actually made a lot of sense. So, I decided that I would quit my job and find something else. I didn't know what, but I knew I could not do this job anymore because it was making me sick.

I sent an email to the diabetes specialist telling him that I'd decided to leave my job because it lacked meaning for me and was making me sick (though I noted that *everything* seemed to lack meaning for me). It was a cry for help. I was lost. Fortunately, he recognized the symptoms and referred me to a psychiatrist, who quickly diagnosed me with major depression. I was enrolled in an experimental study for a new drug called Lexapro. After a few weeks I began to feel better.

I found meaning in things again—the beauty in a smile, a butterfly or a bird flying by, a good book, a job well done. It was obvious from outside depression that I had been ill. I realized too why depression is so dangerous—when your mind is ill, you can actually believe there is no point to anything, including living. And unfortunately, sometimes, when you don't realize you're sick the results can be tragic, particularly for those we leave behind.

My first bout of depression was over ten years ago. The doctor warned that depression often comes back later in life and can be even worse the next time. Over the years, I've battled it off and on, in what I would describe as cycles of high productivity and occasional ruts that I just need to work through. During the ruts, I lose motivation, and need to remind myself that it is only temporary—it is an illness and that life is not in fact pointless.

Until recently, I never mentioned my struggles with mental illness to anyone outside of my family and close friends. As a young associate, I was worried people would be less likely to entrust me with important matters if they knew that I sometimes go through periods where I lose motivation and focus. So, I said nothing.

I put financial security above the possibility that speaking up could alert a young attorney unknowingly suffering from depression that what he is suffering through is an illness that is treatable. I feel bad for staying quiet for so long—but I also believe that speaking out now as a partner at Quinn Emanuel could be more impactful. The fact is we should be talking about this, because you can succeed in Big Law, and at a top law firm, even if you suffer from depression. I'm writing this in hopes that someone who is unknowingly suffering from depression, like I was, will read this and get help.

To associates: please remember that while our cases are extremely important to us, you need to prioritize your health. Be efficient, avoid all-nighters, exercise regularly (meditation and yoga can be helpful), learn to say no when you have too much on your plate, and take care of yourself.

I want to thank John Quinn and my colleagues at Quinn Emanuel for supporting me in speaking out about mental illness.

It is easy for us to see the ravages that depression creates thanks Joseph's story. It took great courage to share his story and truly be a role model for others and emphasize the fast that yes, depression is very hard, but it's also treatable.

As we have seen, anxiety and depression are real health issues that require a response, treatment, and care. The first step of course is being able to step over the hurdle of stigma, which we will be addressing in Chapter 4. Once we have accepted that something is wrong, getting help can be another struggle. There are many systems in place, in every country we examined. It all starts with a phone call and developing rapport with someone you trust. There are many health care providers available; keep looking until you find one that you feel comfortable with and can talk to openly. You can get the best and most effective help you can.

## Champion of Disclosure

### *Daniel Lukasik*

Attorney Daniel Lukasik is the creator of the website lawyerswithdepression.com. He is a prolific writer, presenter, and advocate for mental health. He's also Director of Workplace Well-Being for the Mental Health Association in Buffalo, New York.

You have struggled with major depression for a long time. How did the depression evolve?

I was diagnosed when I was 40 years old. Now, I am 58, so almost a third of my lifetime I have been living with depression. So, over the course of time it has changed a lot, both the nature of the illness, the symptoms, and the kind of treatment and self-care I have been using to recover.

Did you know what it was when you were initially getting depressed in your forties?

I didn't at the time. I was the managing partner of my litigation firm here in Buffalo. And I always, like most lawyers, go through certain periods of time of high stress, but was always able to rebound from them. Over the course of time and up until that point I had gone to therapy for different segments of time, related to stress management issues but also run-of-the-mill things: psychological issues, relationships . . . and I thought at first when I turned forty that was what it was. You know, stress management, sleep difficulties, burnout, but it wasn't that because some other symptoms manifested themselves, such as lack of concentration, my sleep became very fragmented, and the other big one was that I was sad all of the time . . . and that was a big one for me as it was unusual for me and it went on for months.

I understand, it is very interesting because a lot of people do not recognize it as being depression. They see it as being stress issues.

Now in retrospect, and I understand from talking to so many lawyers and other people just with depression, it manifests differently for men and women. I don't know if that it is cultural or whatever, but women are more tearful, emotional, and men seem to manifest it more as irritability and anger. For me it was never anger or irritability, which maybe I am the exception because of my family history with anger. For me, I think I became more and more isolated and inward with my symptoms. It became more and more difficult to manage and more and more isolating.

Do you feel like you were using isolation as a way of coping?

I think so. And it was also just a way of hoping that it would all going away. It took a tremendous amount of energy to put up a front that everything was OK, even though the depression got worse and worse over time. I had very low energy, so I didn't feel like being in groups or socializing. So, I would go to a coffee shop, Starbucks, and be by myself. And I didn't talk about it because I didn't think anybody would understand.

Yes, that is a really big issue, people getting it. How did people understand? How did you kind of break that?

I guess, like for many people, maybe this is a common thing and maybe we have to keep this in the context that it was twenty years ago and a lot of things have changed in the last twenty years in terms of public knowledge and mood disorders and also stigma. I think it also lessened. But when I was first diagnosed, I didn't understand it or know how to articulate it. So, it was difficult for other people to understand it, or they wouldn't identify it as depression. They would see the symptoms like sleeplessness or other things . . . I think most people thought it was burnout or stress.

But the first person to understand it was my psychologist, and he was the one who said he recognized the symptoms. He recognized that it had been going on too long and resulting in impairment. And that is when he called it depression and he referred me to a psychiatrist. And of course, the psychiatrist understood exactly what was going on and that is when I received a formal diagnosis. So that was the first time that people took what I was experiencing and made a diagnosis out of it. So that was the first group of people and I think the next group of people would be family and friends and then beyond that other businesspeople: lawyers, judges, people like that.

How long do you think, Dan, that it took between the time you were starting to feel the distress and the time that you were actually diagnosed?

That is a good question. Rough estimate, I would say, about three months. I think the slide had begun before that, but it wasn't a rapid slide. It was like, almost like you are going down a decline and it is icy and you are sliding and you are trying to grip onto something and I was trying to do that too, but it just, over time it escalated to the point where I could not function anymore. I think that is where the rubber meets the road for a lot of people. Not feeling as much motivation or passion as I had before the major symptoms.

You mentioned the role of stigma. And that is something that I wanted to talk with you about. It seems like it has changed from twenty years ago, people know more. Do you think people are accepting more, particularly in the law?

I think what I have noticed is a couple of things. First, I gave a speech at Harvard Law School, and students came up to me afterward and said they themselves did not have a problem identifying themselves as people who have depression, and they didn't have a problem sharing it among their peers. Those are things that are different than twenty years ago.

They did not have a problem in any way, sharing it at work. I think the battleground is and should be focused in the workplace. That is a lot of the work that I have done in the last ten years, in the workplace. Because we spend so much of our time, more than the average person in the workplace and it is already a stressful place, and if it is a place that you cannot discuss this issue or get the help that you need. It's only begun to compound the problem and that has been my experience and I think that is the national movement that we see with the number of wellness and well-being programs that followed the two major studies that came out in 2016 and the national task force of 2017.

Dan, how are you coping with the reoccurring depression? A lot of people think depression is a one-time thing and they don't realize that even when you're on medication the depression can come back. So, the medication isn't a cure.

Well, I think that is the most difficult part of the whole deal. The first time I was diagnosed it was pretty awful, but there was an expectation that it would end and it wouldn't come back, and I remember my psychiatrist so vividly saying what is the goal here, like there is an end point, and he said complete remission. So, I thought, great. I am going to be on the medication, I am going to do therapy and just like you would have any other kind of illness, but that did not happen, not by a long stretch. And I think that over the last twenty years I have had several episodes of reoccurrence, sometimes more profound than others. But I think I have a lot of more self-management tools now, and insight into the cause and triggers and I am much more willing to ask for and talk to other people. So even though the reoccurrences still come, I think they tend to be shorter in length and not as deep, so I am not really impaired as I was in that first major episode. That is now, but over the twenty-year period there where periods where the depression was not well managed, and I did have the impairment.

At that time, you were still having the impairment? What was the obstacle that you faced? Was it going back to get help again, or what was the actual obstacle to getting help during the reoccurrence.

I think one of the obstacles was myself; in the sense that I did not want to go back or feel or admit that I had lost and that I had not defeated depression. I wanted to proceed as if I had recovered and everything was OK and everything was not OK. When I hit my first reoccurrence and I think also the expectations of my fellow lawyers and partners in my firm, because I was the leader of the firm and there were certainly expectations that that was over and done with that depression thing and get your back on the horse, you are earning money again. You are running the firm. They did not want to go through that again . . . you mentioned barrier and I think that is an accurate way of putting it. [Given]the rigors and demands of the profession, there is little time left over, and I mean crumbs of time, to do things like exercise or meditate or eat well so that was another major barrier.

That leads to another question. How do you do the balance of work and life, now that you have a little bit more time and you are learning more self-care tools.

I think that really some of it is a deep, deep recognition and understanding that depression can kill you. It is a serious, serious condition. It can threaten you livelihood and as a consequence the impairments both at home and at work place, so that you realize when you think of work life balance and we think of that in terms of contentment, happiness and maybe stress and think that as it gets more serious and has more gravity to it, when we think about depression. And so, for me the equation in my head is not that, oh this would be nice if I took more time for self-care but I don't. Now I know that I must. It is not like I can kick it to the bottom of the priority list. Now it is at the top of the priority list. So, it might involve something that I do not take a traditional lunch where I go to lunch with other people and I just talk socially, it might involve getting to bed earlier and missing a Netflix episode so there are usually choices of some kind involved. I almost thought that depression is very disempowering, we have no choices, we are kind of crushed by it. But I think recovery is about getting healthy and staying healthy and I think that is recovery is about choices and I think that is empowering.

Yes, that is a great way of saying it, Dan. You do have choices and you are making them so that you have a healthy lifestyle.

I now know that there is a consequence and I have to give it a lot of weight. If I eat a bowl of ice-cream versus a bowl of yogurt, that my mood is going to suffer. These things all seem like they are so isolated, but they are cumulative, and they are linked together: diet, exercise, and sleep. So I really have to address all of them and I really appreciate that because I do want to be healthy, I don't want to fall back into depression, and I realize when I do not take care of myself that is exactly what happens.

When you were in your more difficult states or even in the beginning when you didn't know what it was; the depression, did you ever contemplate suicide?

I think that happened during periods of the more serious reoccurrences. Not so much during the first major episode, where I was just in the process of being diagnosed, because I think I was still hopeful that I would get better and still hopeful the medication would help, it just needed time. So, I think at the time I did not feel that way. I knew I wanted the pain to stop and I wanted to feel better, but I did not feel suicidal. That came later, when I went through periods of increasing significant reoccurrences of the depression. There is a profound sense of hopelessness when that happens, because you feel you know that you are giving it everything that I've got and I am trying. I do not want to go back into a depression and here it comes. It is like looking over the horizon on a sunny day and you see the storm clouds rolling in and you know you're in trouble. And you don't know how long it will last, and you don't know the depth of it. In the earlier years my self-management tools I had at the time failed me, so I really tried to ride it out and I did it, because I am still here..

But those were very, very difficult things. And I had a recent one in August that lasted about three weeks. I tried my self-management skills, [but] there is a limit to any one of these things. Eventually I went to my psychiatrist, and he added a medication, Abilify, onto my regular two medications and it got me out of what my brain was in.

That is great self-care. Now you can kind of see it coming on and you can get help.

Yes, and when I think about it, and when I try to help other people and by helping other people, I help myself. I think we all need a toolbox of sorts, with different tools in the box, and that we can reach for at different times. And at different times, different tools will be more effective than others. Sometimes if it is a deeper depression, not incapacitating, [then] deeper therapy might not be helpful. Maybe on that particular day or time, blasting through a hard exercise program would help. Other days it is a support group. So, we need different tools at different times. Not one tool, I think, but it is the accumulation of working with all of these tools that I think helps us recover.

And what flexibility in how much you have learned about yourself in what you need at the moment, whether if it is exercise or individual therapy or group or if it is another tool. What kind of outside support do you have?

I created the [Erie County Bar Association Depression Support Group for Lawyers]. That was twelve years ago. It was a weekly group and it is still going strong today. It is a confidential setting, so that's a big one. [We] start like clockwork and we end like clockwork. Some people have friendships outside of the group and some people don't, and you know over the last twelve years probably a couple hundred lawyers have come through the group.

Even during the difficult times, you have created some important and helpful things.

I created something that I thought I would want, and I asked my psychiatrist about twelve years ago, I had read something about support groups and [asked him if there were any he could] recommend, and he said I really can't, Dan, there isn't something like that for someone like you. And it made me really sad and also really angry, so I created this support group. And that is important, and the other thing that is important to me is the website that I created twelve years ago, Lawyers with Depression. That is a great source of interaction for me with people all around the world, including with you, Dawn. I have conversations with people around the world. It is meaningful to me and encouraging to me and it is an outlet for me to make meaning out of my experiences. There are all kinds of experiences in life, and I have learned too that I am not my depression. It is a part of my life, and I talk about all kinds of other things: stress, meaning, purpose, life events, my parents passing away. That's another important outlet that I have . . .

I might interview a neuropsychologist from Berkeley, and then interview a Jewish rabbi from Long Island, and they all have different life experiences with [depression], and they all have a different perspective on it. I think taking these perspectives, it is almost like a collage: when you look at it, it gives you a broader, maybe richer understanding too. I think this can be about suffering in anyway. You know depression is a form of suffering, [but] there is the potential to make you a deeper and more compassionate person, and it also has the protential to make you a harder, more bitter resentful person. You and I have known both kind of groups, and I have been through those experiences myself where I have felt both ways. I have a pretty positive outlook on it now. I believe and I did for many years. But it is a challenge, because those negative thoughts can creep in, and you think why me, or why do I have to go through this again, or this isn't fair but those things are not very productive, those thoughts and emotions, I am pretty good at cutting them off pretty quick if they come up. because they are just not going to take me where I want to go.

It is great that you can recognize that because a lot of people don't.

It has taken years, probably years.

I believe that, Dan. My other questions were what advice would you give others who are currently suffering with depression and the stigma surrounding it?

Get the help, I think the first thing to do is of course get help, because a lot of people think they can manage it themselves, or they self-diagnose [and] talk to their friends, and they think that suffices. But people who have never been through depression really have no reference point for what it is. That has been my experience. They think of it as sadness or burnout, but they don't think of it as an illness. So, I think getting help with it. I think the best first step is a therapist to sift out and see if this is truly a mental health condition, is it clinical depression or just as likely, is it sadness, the stress of life's problems. And try to unpack what is going on. And if need be a referral to a psychiatrist or I know that 80% of antidepressants are prescribed by family physicians. So, a lot of people began their journey not where I began but talking to their own family doctor, who's also trained to diagnose depression..

So, there are different ways for people to get help. And I think what they have to overcome is the stigma. . . Years ago, when I first underwent it, people felt more license to say negative things out loud: "What the hell is wrong with you?" But I don't think people say that anymore. I think if they think it to just kind of move away from a person or isolate if they feel that way. But I think more important is the self-stigma. That I think is more devastating. Where people give up, they don't want to get help. They think this is just the way life is. I have heard a lot of people say that I think getting help and getting educated in the form of websites, books, and tools. So, there is lots of stuff available for people to get help.

Self-stigma is a really important concept. Did you feel like you dealt with self-stigma as well?

Oh yes, I think part of the vicious circle of depressive thinking are the ruminations, the negative thinking, the self -accusations, the low self-esteem, and then looking back on it, seeing the connection between my thinking and my mood disorder. I am actually manufacturing, in a way, my own depression. And I think that helps me say I have choices here, and I have thoughts that are either going to produce or inflame my depression, and these thoughts will tend not to. And it took a long time [to realize], but I think seeing even your thinking is a choice.

Attorney Daniel Lukasik's tenacity to get better and get through depression with each new episode is courageous. Dan has also been innovative with the creation of Lawyerswithdepression.com over ten years ago. He continues to bring up-to-date information to the legal community from many different professional viewpoints.

# Section 3: Alcohol and Other Drug Abuse (AODA)

Professor G. Andrew H. Benjamin noted "lawyers affect more of the public and private decision-making that occurs in the country, more than any other group. If one-third of the active practicing bar is significantly impacted by affective disorder or AODA it affects their decision-making, and that is an issue."

Alcohol or drug/substance abuse is a worldwide issue. According to statistics from the World Health Organization, alcohol is the world's third highest risk factor for disease and disability. Alcohol is a causal factor in 60 diseases and a component cause in 200 other diseases. In 2016, the use of alcohol resulted in some 3 million deaths (5.3% of all deaths) worldwide. Death resulting from alcohol consumption is higher than that caused by diseases such as tuberculosis, HIV/AIDS and diabetes. Alcohol is associated with many serious societal issues including violence, child neglect and abuse and absenteeism in the workplace. The world's highest levels of alcohol consumption are found in high-income countries. The highest rates of consumption are in western and eastern Europe. Of interest, in 2016 more than half (57%, or 3.1 billion people) of the global population aged 15 years and over had abstained from drinking alcohol in the previous 12 months. While 2.3 billion people are current drinkers. Alcohol consumption among current drinkers over 15 years of age rose from 5.5 liters of pure alcohol in 2005 to 6.4 liters in 2010 and remained at the level of 6.4 liters in 2016.[79]

In 2016, it was estimated that 275 million people or 5.6% used illicit drugs, such as cannabis, amphetamines, opioids, and cocaine, in 2016 which translates into an annual prevalence of illicit drug use of 5.6%. Cannabis is most used drug with 192 million users. 31 million people suffer from drug use disorders. Finally, it is estimated that almost 11 million people inject drugs.

These are truly eye-opening facts. This is going on worldwide, so why would you think you are immune, or that you can handle it better than others? Let's find out more about what the studies are showing us.

## Section 3.1: United States

According to a report commissioned by the ABA and the Hazelden Betty Ford Foundation, "substance abuse among lawyers is rampant. While 10% of the general adult population is alcohol-dependent, among lawyers practicing from 2-20 years, the number jumps to 18%. For those practicing more than 20 years, the number is 25%. Many of these individuals are both depressed and chemically dependent." [80]

Furthermore, the study found that more than a fifth of licensed, employed attorneys in the U.S. consume alcohol at levels consistent with problem drinking. That compares with 12 % of a broad sample

---

[79] Global status report on alcohol and health 2018. Geneva: World Health Organization; 2018. Licence: CC BY-NC-SA 3.0 IGO
[80] Krill, Patrick, Ryan Johnson, and Linda Albert. 2016. "The Prevalence of Substance Use and Other Mental Health Concerns Among American Attorneys." Journal of Addiction Medicine 10: 46–52. 10.1097/ADM.0000000000000182.

of highly educated workers across various professions. The study also found that 28 % of attorneys struggle with some level of depression, and 19 % show symptoms of anxiety.[81]

According to work published by Beck, Sales, and Benjamin "Lawyer Distress: Alcohol-Related Problems and Other Psychological Concerns Among a Sample of Practicing Lawyers," two-thirds of the actively practicing lawyers had sufficient negative consequences associated with their alcohol abuse that they exceeded the clinical cut-offs for problem drinkers, (based upon the Michigan Alcohol Screening Test). The report notes that lawyers are particularly subject to psychological distress, which result in unhealthy ways of coping and impairment. This is a larger concern for society, as many lawyers are elected officials, policy advisors, and advocates of public and private interests.

The report also found that while 9% of adults in the United States meet the criteria for alcohol abuse or dependency, for lawyers in Washington the percentage doubled, with 18% of them problem drinkers.[82]

## Section 3.2: United Kingdom

Though we may not have the current in-country study to review, we can generalize from other country's studies to legal professionals and law students in the United Kingdom.

## Section 3.3: Australia

According to a 2014 report in the *University of New South Wales Law Journal*, "Lawyering Stress and Work Culture," 32 % of the 1,000 lawyers studied were problem drinkers. The study also linked regular alcohol consumption to more serious depression, anxiety and stress symptoms.[83]

For the study *Courting the Blues,* the University of Sydney's Brain & Mind Research Institute surveyed almost 2,500 professionals and law students from thirteen law schools. The results showed that 41 % of law students, 31 % of solicitors, and 19 % of barristers suffer from psychological distress severe enough to justify clinical assessment.[84]

The study also showed that law students tended not to know the most commonly identified symptoms of depression. They were also found to be the least likely of the surveyed groups to seek help for depression; 38% of students stated that they would not seek any treatment, as compared to 31% of solicitors and 21% of barristers claiming they wouldn't seek additional help. Additionally, it was found that alcoholism and drug use is higher among lawyers than any other profession, and that substance abuse is a contributing factor for up to 80% of all complaints levelled against practitioners.

---

[81] Krill, Patrick, Ryan Johnson, and Linda Albert. 2016. "The Prevalence of Substance Use and Other Mental Health Concerns Among American Attorneys." *Journal of Addiction Medicine* 10: 46–52. 10.1097/ADM.0000000000000182.

[82] Beck, Connie J. A., Bruce D. Sales, and G. Andrew H. Benjamin. 1995. "Lawyer Distress: Alcohol-Related Problems and Other Psychological Concerns among a Sample of Practicing Lawyers." Journal of Law and Health 10:1 (199596): 10.

[83] Chan, Janet, Suzanne Poynton, and Jasmine Bruce. 2014. "Lawyering Stress and Work Culture: An Australian Study." 37(3) *University of New South Wales Law Journal* 1062.

[84] Kelk, NJ, Luscombe, GM, Medlow, S, Hickie, IB (2009) Courting the blues: Attitudes towards depression in Australian law students and lawyers, BMRI Monograph 2009-1, Sydney: Brain & Mind Research Institute.

## Section 3.4: Canada

"Roughly 9% of the calls to the Ontario Lawyers' Assistance Program relate to alcohol dependency," and roughly 20 to 25% of legal professionals have alcoholic tendencies." In 2004, 63 % of the calls placed to provincial Lawyer Assistance Programs concerned mental concerned mental illness or psychological difficulties.[85]

## Section 3.5: New Zealand

Though we may not have the current in-country study to review, we can generalize from other country's studies to legal professionals and law students in New Zealand.

## Section 3.6: Case Studies

### *Terry Harrell*

Terry Harrel is the Executive Director of the Indiana Judges & Lawyers Assistance Program (JLAP); she worked first as a lawyer then transitioned into clinical work. She is a licensed clinical addictions counselor and has a nationally recognized master addiction counselor certification. She serves on many national committees for lawyer assistance programs, is a member of the Indiana State Bar Association (ISBA) and is a past Chair of the Professional Legal Education Admission and Development Section (PLEADS) and the Wellness Committee.

Since the major and historical American Bar Association Study of 2016, the Prevalence of Substance Use and other Mental Health Concerns Among American Attorneys, have you seen any real movement for change at a ground level, such as in firms or in law schools?

It has been my experience from talking to people not only in the U.S. but also in the UK, Australia, Canada, and New Zealand that firms are signing charters for health and well-being, and there is talk in schools at the first-year intro, but not much else is occurring; no real action.

I believe that a lot is happening both in firms and particularly in law firms. Over a hundred legal employers have taken the Pledge to Well-Being started by the ABA Working Group to Advance Well-Being in the Legal Profession. Last February we held a workshop. In August we will have a telephone call for pledge signatories to exchange ideas, successes, and challenges. At the first of the year we will be asking the signatories in a formal way what they have done. So far, we have had law firms, two large corporations with large in-house departments, and a good number of law schools sign the pledge. Firms are beginning to hire wellness directors. Robin Belleau is the new Director of Well-Being at Kirkland and Ellis. Right now, bar associations, law firms, law schools, and in-house lawyer groups are eager for CLE [continuing legal education] presentations on well-being. That door has flown open. Bar

---

[85] Kelly, Owen. 2014. "Lawyers and Anxiety: Three Case Studies." The Canadian Bar Association, August 21, 2014.
    https://www.cba.org/Publications-Resources/CBA-Practice-Link/Work-Life-Balance/2010/Lawyers-and-Anxiety-Three-Case-Studies.

associations are creating well-being committees. Florida has a relatively new program. Indiana and Tennessee have had wellness committees at the state bar for a long time.

I did not see a question on the issue of secondary trauma in the study. Did I miss that or was it not included? And if it was not included, do you know why?

I do not believe secondary trauma was included. (Kind of funny as Linda and I were both doing a ton of presentations on secondary trauma at the time.) . . . I'm guessing they thought substance use disorder, depression, and anxiety was plenty for one study, but I don't know how that decision was made.

Do you see secondary trauma a significant issue for law students and legal professionals and why?

Absolutely. Lawyers frequently see people who have been through or are going through "bad stuff," and the lawyer has a responsibility to do something for the client. They hear these horrible stories. And, unlike first responders or emergency medical folks, they work with these facts, they often work with these facts and these people for extended periods of time—months and years..

And they have very little time to recover from one case to the next. Little time for recovery, rejuvenation, and positive activities to balance all the bad stuff they see and hear. (Think about a big murder or injury case, where the lawyer deals with horrible photos over several years. Here's the story, develops the story, delivers it ...) I think it also bothers lawyers when they see people who have so many problems, and whether they can fix their legal problems or not, they certainly can't fix all their problems. Sometimes you feel like you fixed the smallest problem.

As stigma has always been an issue with regard to mental illness across the globe, do you think the tide is changing at all with legal professionals and students?

I do, particularly with the younger lawyers and law students. My hope is that telling your lunch buddies that you are headed to your therapy appointment or to see your psychiatrist will someday be viewed the same as telling them you are heading to the dentist or your allergist appointment. I think the younger generations will push this. They are much more open about mental health. And we have a good number of established lawyers speaking out about their own experiences. I'm sure Bree told you about the anti-stigma podcasts CoLAP [the Commission on Lawyer Assistance Programs] is working on. And in every state the lawyer assistance programs have brave volunteers who are willing to tell their story. It really helps people let go of their preconceived ideas about mental illness and substance use.

What do you believe is the current most pressing and important issue that legal professionals and legal students need to face in terms of health and well-being? (This may be different for professionals versus law students). What are the best methods for coping with the above-named issues?

Oh, Dawn ... that last question is a book unto itself. So is the first, really. I think educating law students and lawyers about suicide is probably top of my list. This is not because it is the largest issue but because we don't get second and third chances at this one. When it comes up you have to take immediate action. With other issues you can spend more time gathering resources and advice before acting. We need to figure out how to provide everyone with good health insurance, including true solo [practitioners]. As a profession we need to change our attitudes toward alcohol. I'm not advocating abstinence from alcohol for everyone. But if should not be normal or funny for a lawyer to be unable to walk to his or her hotel room at the end of an evening with legal colleagues. That should raise concern for the person. And it should be comfortable to drink or not drink at social events. The emphasis on drinking needs to be dialled down. And lawyers need to find work that is meaningful. That is different for everyone, but if you find your work meaningful and you think what you are doing is contributing to the good in some way, you are more resilient and more able to cope with the annoying, frustrating components of your work. Or the long hours ….

Maybe we need better career counseling as law students and lawyers. Working with a therapist or life coach to increase one's resilience should be viewed as a proactive, positive thing to be doing. I think we're getting there, but it does require a shift from thinking about seeking therapy as a sign of weakness to a sign of strength or wisdom.

Attorney and counselor Terry Harrell is a leader of change in the United States. Her leadership roles have allowed her to have a global view of what is happening on this forefront. Let us try to take up her thought of making a mental health appointment as natural as making a dental appointment; no shame, just self-care.

### *Derek LaCroix*

Derek LaCroix is the Executive Director of the Lawyers Assistance Program of British Columbia, Canada. He has served on committees with the Canadian Bar Association and the American Bar Association, and he was a commissioner of the Commission on Lawyer Assistance Programs (CoLAP) and the Chair of the annual CoLAP conference for several years.

What do you see as the most pressing mental health concern facing lawyers today?

The resistance to seeking help. This has a number of causes, two of which are: (personal) lack of clarity about purpose and values, with a strong emphasis on extrinsic values and a concurrent loss of focus on intrinsic values, and (systemic) stigma. The idea that lawyers don't have problems and need to tough it out. That any mental health issue is a sign of weakness to be taken advantage of.

In the 2016 American Bar Association and Hazelden Betty Ford study that we discussed; many lawyers skipped the question on drug use entirely. There has been much conjecture as to the reason for the skip. However, I am wondering if you are finding more lawyers being open in your region to talk about AODA [alcohol and other drug abuse] issues, particularly drugs?

My clients are fairly open with me about drugs, because we are highly confidential. Mostly they will talk about cocaine, often in combination with alcohol. I do have a few who are or were using heroin or other opioids (but not many). Since the legalization of marijuana, I have had several who are now talking to me about that problem. Some speak about the problem with prescription drugs, notably benzos and amphetamines.

What role does stigma play in seeking for mental health issues?

It is pervasive. There are two kinds [The first] I call positive stigma, that is the idea that the ideal lawyers can work and work and push and push and just keep going, that some overwork and fatigue is good. And [the second kind of stigma are the] negative stereotypes that addicts and people with mood disorders are broken and fundamentally flawed and will always be suspect. They fear admitting and getting help for the problem will be career limiting, (e.g., not get hired, not making partner, not becoming a judge). This is quite pervasive.

What would you recommend for law students who are struggling with mental health or AODA issues?

Get help. Call the LAPBC; we are completely confidential and can help in multiple ways and will do it with their careers in mind.

Derek LaCroix has shared with us the profound resistance for seeking help that he has encountered through his work. He has also shared with us how the concerns of values and stigma continue to play a role in this issue.

## Section 3.7: Champions of Disclosure

### *Lisa Hanna*

Lisa Hanna is a criminal defense attorney, author, and speaker. She has graciously been willing to share her story from addiction and incarceration, to practicing law.

When it comes down to it, we all suffer from the same disease, whether it is opioid use, meth use, it's a disorder, and it takes the same healing for all of us to get through it. Making yourself unique or distinguishing yourself from the misdeeds of others or making yours out to be worse than mine [to] glorify your addiction, either way it's unhealthy, because we need to recognize we all have the same foundation. Whatever our rock bottom was, [we need to] be humble enough to recognize that whatever the next addict's problem was, from our perspective we are all hoping for the same relief.

When did you realize you were an addict?

It is kind of embarrassing now. I was probably incarcerated for a couple of years before I would call myself an addict, and you know the first step is to say I am powerless over whatever, and your life has become unmanageable. And here I am at the beginning of a twenty-year federal prison sentence and not recognizing that as unmanageable. So, it took a while for me. And when I do my lead, I always give props to people who got clean on the outside, because I was locked up, but I still had access to drugs and alcohol because that is how the system is. But I chose for reasons good to me to avoid all that; I would get in trouble, I would be shipped and be behind the fence and be far from home and already in the federal system I was already far enough from home so on the outside if you are just doing your outpatient thing or the court has you go to meetings, that is amazing to me. So, [September 24th] was my twentieth recovery anniversary . . . so I posted on Facebook "Twenty years in recovery today, a shoutout to the FBI and federal marshals . . . for helping me to kickstart that journey." It did, because I had to go through detox and that part was hard because I was in county jail, but then I was without drugs and then I had to choose what it is like on the outside not to do that, not to go there. So, I was always afraid to come home. I had always planned to move to Indianapolis and that did not work out and I ended up coming back to where I was from, and I was so worried that I would end up with the people I would use with before and didn't give myself credit for being as strong as I became going through that I guess because I am not hanging around with any of those people, I promise. How long you're in that using cycle you come to believe that those people are your friends, and they care about you and now my people outside of my co-workers and family are people from recovery. [They] are the people who I hang out with. I am not trying to go hang out in bars . . . for my twentieth anniversary I went out with my boss and his wife. I was in law school when my son passed away, and then I started drinking and then I moved to San Francisco and started using meth. I was diagnosed with MDD (major depressive disorder) only during my addiction and while I was incarcerated—not until after my son died, [during] the last seven months of law school.

I received a medical malpractice settlement for over a third of a million dollars, and I know at that point people pretended to care about me [but really, they cared about] how much my money could buy drugs. Nobody at that point in my life would have been, "We need to get you to rehab," or "We need to get you to a counselor." I was already locked up for a while and finally surrendered that I am powerless and need help and sought out meetings. I think most every state has a JLAP or something like that, and even when you fill out a bar application the questions have changed, I applied to Indiana in 2016, and the questions were basically, "Have you ever used any kind of drug, and if you did, what was it?".

And now when I passed, and I was allowed to take it in 2018. the questions have evolved into, "Have you ever used anything that would currently impair your ability to practice law?" So, it is definitely evolving, people are recognizing that it is an illness, a disorder that can be treated. We don't have to all be shunned and kicked out of the practice. It is sad, because there are so many attorneys who are practicing alcoholics but also drug addicts, especially the older-school guys who have been in practice for a long time. I believe they believe that there is such a stigma that they are really reluctant to reach out to a JLAP, and it is sad, because JLAP would hook them up with a monitor who would be able to help them and genuinely care about them and help them in some kind of recovery. I think mental health now has even less stigma than substance use disorder . . . There still are the narrow-minded or cavemen . . . I do quite a lot of family law [and] you get these guys who say, "She is crazy and she has been treated for this and that" and I just have to let them vent, because I have been treated too and because of the grace of God have come out the other side, so to judge someone, especially if they are undergoing treatment and sticking to their medication plan, God bless them. I love my job, and we do deal with criminal law and people who are facing time, and the gift that I have with my experience is to be able to counsel people through the various plea offers and risk assessment as far as going to trial and been trail or jury trial and how to deal with it. And my experience in dealing with every kind of experience on earth. Helps me to navigate counsel and clients and the people on the other side.

I was self-medicating, no question, first with alcohol to numb everything and then with the meth, because I had myself so down with everything and I liked the upper kind of high better then depressing myself further, and that is pretty much what I stuck with.

You have talked a lot about the reception that you have received from people in the legal community. You are accepted and encouraged—even by the person who prosecuted you. What is the environment like now for people with addiction issues? And people with mental health issues?

I had a federal prosecutor [who was] my old boss, and I thought nothing good can come from this, but they have championed me from when I got out and I just . . . keep doing the next right thing, as they say. But I am fortunate that I don't have a desire to use or drink, I honestly don't, and I didn't ever think about it even when I lost my parents. I didn't ever think 'I need a drink.' Now I think 'I need a meeting.' My brother got in trouble recently, and it was a very stressful thing and omigod, I love my brother so much and that night I had to be at a meeting. That is a lot better than getting drunk, what is that going to fix? At least at a meeting your people will help you process something.

What is the key to your emotional stability?

The meetings and the people at the meetings are key to my emotional stability as well. If something feels really haywire to me, [the people are the meetings are] who I am going to reach out to. . . at the same time part of what I learned in rehab was keeping a balance in my life.

How do you achieve life balance?

Being back with my family is what I mean by understanding the consequences, because I am so blessed that my siblings trusted me to be around their grandchildren when I got out, because all they knew of me was phone calls and visits for fifteen years, and they did. You know, my nieces and nephews were all heartbroken when I left, so for them to turn around and let their kids get attached to me not knowing what was going to happen to me, so I know the consequences, that is what I mean by that. Yes, a lot of times from my experience with the women I was locked up with, if it was a second or subsequent incarceration, they probably don't have family to go back to. That is why I say I understand the consequences, because I put my family through hell. Could I reasonably expect them to stand by me if I decided I was going to pick up and use again? I don't think so. Yes, it wasn't that easy when I got out. I was afraid of being around people I had used with before. I was really nervous, but the first thing I remember doing when I got out of the halfway house was going to an NA meeting and meeting my friend Sam; the people that I have met there and know there are part of my foundation. If there is someone that you know there and are uncomfortable with, then find another meeting: many towns have meetings in several different places or several different times of day. I live in a little town and we have 8 am meetings, noon meetings, 6 pm meetings every day, and that is just NA. AA has at least two meetings a day. Yes, so . . . that person you are uncomfortable around will not be at all of the meetings—or go to the town six miles over: they will take you. We have to ask for some stuff, and it is hard if you are proud, and it is our pride that leads us to use in the first place and keep everything in and not ask for help. Pride is a hard thing to recover from, but with any part of re-entry you have to figure out where the resources are and ask for them: ask to participate in those programs.

I addressed that in the JLAP presentation where I talked about [how] we are lawyers. We are educated . . . and how do you slink off to an AA meeting because you do not want anyone to know. . . This Sunday I will start going to meetings where I practice—I am not going to hide from my community, I don't have anything to be ashamed of. I am in recovery and that is where my people are and that is where my people will be. But we discussed how lawyers feel like they hold themselves to a higher standard and maybe think that others have higher or unrealistic expectations of themselves so they cannot admit that which they see as a weakness and so what's funny is that in Fort Wayne, Indiana, there is an attorney-in-recovery meeting, and they are huge and it is every day at noon, and it is amazing because they all turn up and they say, "Hey, I am Sam and I am an addict," or, "Hi, I am Chris and I am an alcoholic." It's an all-inclusive twelve-step group, and nobody is ashamed to be there, go there, or be seen there. It is amazing. Attorneys in Recovery. My boss that I skipped out on when I got in trouble when I was using meth. No, [we don't have anything to be ashamed of] at all. I like to do Pilates—I taught Pilates for ten years while I was locked up—so for me that gets my feel-good brain chemicals going and helps to give me some inner peace. As far as other coping skills, The Serenity Prayer. if anything starts to get under my skin, whether silently or audibly I say The Serenity Prayer and just [take] deep breaths or . . . a walk to get away from whatever the situation is to be able to think clearly and process it. I always love a [what] gratitude meeting does—I just have that in my spirit . . . I had so little, even [a] lack of, human contact for so long that I am grateful just to go to a meeting just to get the hugs at the end. I am always grateful to my family for including me. I am grateful to my boyfriend for teaching me how to live in the 21st century, because I left in '99 and got out in '15 and so he pretty much had a blob of clay to work with—don't even get me started on the GPS thing, just everything he had to teach me so I am grateful to him for a lot of things. I am grateful to my boss and JLAP and all of the people who have supported me and my career and my mission to practice law when I got out. People who gave me jobs to practice in their law offices and knew I had a felony and had been in prison and everything and gave me a chance just . . . it is endless. Yes.

Attorney Lisa Hanna has experienced a myriad of issues surrounding her addiction, from loss of her freedom through incarceration, to coming to the realization that she was an addict while incarcerated, to getting treatment while incarcerated and now actively working as an attorney and coming full circle to give back, which is a tradition of Narcotics Anonymous and the other anonymous groups. Lisa gives back though her numerous and heartfelt public speaking events, which I encourage you to attend.

As we have seen, alcohol and other drug issues are of great concern. There is a cross-cultural trend emerging of recognizing and talking about the issues of rampant alcohol usage and other drug usage in legal circles. However, again we see the issue of different types of stigma playing a role in people hesitating or outright not obtaining help. Every country we have focused on provides alcohol and drug awareness, and counselling service resources. As with mental health issues, AODA issues require us to take the first step and seek help.

# Section 4: Suicide

I have had an overwhelming number of requests to talk about suicide in this book. This request has come from students and professionals alike. We have seen so many articles on suicide of professionals and law students all over the world. People wonder why it is happening and what we can do. We need to find answers, and quickly.

In this section you will read about Champions of Disclosure and their stories about suicide. I thank them for sharing this part of their life experience. Don't you wish we could just talk openly, and we didn't have to be brave about it? Why can't we make it easier and more acceptable to seek mental health assistance, as we do if we break a leg or need insulin? These Champions, like their counterparts in other chapters of the book, are leading the way and making a difference in our discussion and our culture. They are demonstrating that lawyers can have mental health issues, learn how to manage the issues, and be successful in their lives.

As I am writing this book, another lawyer committed suicide. We can only imagine what he was going through, and now what his family is going through. And here I am yet again, rewriting. Just this month a second-year law student committed suicide. This is an ongoing, pervasive issue that we must address swiftly.

I had conversations with family members of a lawyer who committed suicide, and I can't begin to describe the loss and the unknowingness of family members surrounding their loved one's state of mind or mental health in general. It seems like, for some of the individuals, intense stress becomes normalized. It may become normalized for the entire social system of that individual. What a loss, that can't be described. Legal professionals and law students are intelligent, articulate, well-educated individuals who want to make a difference in the world. Somewhere along the line something goes very wrong, and it is very difficult to talk about it or reach out.

First, let us remember suicidal ideation, which is thinking about or planning suicide, the result of a number of issues rather than just a person's occupation. Of course, we know that the legal profession and law school are highly stressful. We also know in general that high levels of mental distress that is not managed can lead to anxiety and depression and to suicidal ideation and or behavior.

According to the World Health Organization almost 800,000 people die to suicide yearly and many more people attempt suicide. Suicide is the second leading cause of death among 15 to 29-year-olds. Attorneys rank 4th in suicide by occupation.

In addition, The World Health Organization notes that one of the obstacles to prevention is stigma. "Stigma, particularly surrounding mental disorders and suicide means many people thinking of taking their own life or who have attempted suicide are not seeking help and are therefore not getting the help they need. The prevention of suicide has not been adequately addressed due to a lack of awareness of suicide as a major public health problem and the taboo in many societies to openly discuss it. To date, only a few countries have included suicide prevention among their health priorities and only 38 countries report having a national suicide prevention strategy."[86]

"Because of their experience with the law, most attorneys have lost their rose-colored glasses some time ago. (Or else they never had them and chose the law as a career because it suited their personality). Attorneys know that life is hard and doesn't play fair. They're trained to look for every conceivable thing that could go wrong in any scenario, and they rarely are able to leave that attitude at the office. They see the worst in people (sometimes they see the best, but that's rare). They tend to be strivers and individualists, not wanting to rely on others for support. They have high expectations of success, but they often find that when they've attained success, they have no one to play with, and have forgotten how to enjoy themselves anyway. All this makes it hard for attorneys to get help with their depression. They tend not to recognize it as such; they just think its stress, or burn out, or life. They don't expect that anyone is going to be able to help."[87]

According to the World Health Organization (2006) "Worker suicide is complex and involves individual vulnerabilities, stressful working conditions and living conditions. Stress factors which contribute to stress on the job include lack of time, uncontrollable work schedules, background distractions, strife caused by poor employee relations, bullying or harassment, lack of space, general uncertainty, and a push to do more with less."[88]

Additionally, post-traumatic stress disorder has been shown to be a factor in suicide, as well as accumulation of trauma or secondary trauma[89]

- Workplace warning signs:
- Being very happy after a period of depression
- Acting more aggressive or stressed out than usual (e.g. lashing out at people)
- Commenting on being tired all the time, being noticeably fatigued
- Commenting about being a burden to others (e.g. "Everyone would be better off if I wasn't here")
- Not showing up for work as often or being absent for periods of time (absenteeism)
- Not being as productive as usual, being un-motivated (presenteeism).
- Some warning signs require more immediate action than others. If someone is exhibiting the following warning signs, call the emergency number for the country you are in:
- Talking about wanting to die or to kill oneself; and

---

[86] World Health Organization. 2019. "Suicide." September 2, 2019. https://www.who.int/news-room/fact-sheets/detail/suicide.

[87] Samra, Joti, Dan Bilsker, and Simon Fraser. 2019. "Coping With Suicidal Thoughts." The LifeLine Canada Foundation, February 26, 2019. https://thelifelinecanada.ca/help/coping-with-suicidal-thoughts/.

[88] World Health Organization. (2006). Preventing suicide: a resource at work. World Health Organization. https://apps.who.int/iris/handle/10665/43502

[89] Panagioti, Maria, Patricia Gooding, and Nichola Tarrier. 2012. "A meta-analysis of the association between posttraumatic stress disorder and suicidality: The role of comorbid depression." *Comprehensive Psychiatry*. 53. 915-30. 10.1016/j.comppsych.2012.02.009.

- Looking for a way to kill oneself or already having a plan.[90]

Other advice, from the LifeLine Canada Foundation:

"Connect with others: If you are worried that you may lose control or do something to hurt yourself, tell someone. Make sure you are around someone you trust. If you live alone, ask a friend or family member to stay with you. If you don't know anyone or can't reach friends or family members, call your local crisis line.

Keep your home safe by getting rid of ways to hurt yourself.

Develop a safety plan. Keep this plan somewhere you can see or find easily. Write down the steps you will take to keep yourself safe (see the following example). Follow the steps. If you follow these steps and still do not feel safe, call a crisis line, get yourself to a hospital emergency room or call the emergency number for the country you are in.[91]

## Safety Plan:

If you have thoughts of hurting yourself, start at Step 1. Go through each step until you are safe. Remember: Suicidal thoughts can be very strong. It may seem they will last forever. With support and time, these thoughts will usually pass. When they pass, you can put energy into sorting out problems that have contributed to your feelings. Since it can be hard to focus and think clearly when you feel suicidal, please copy this and put in places where you can easily find it and use it.

- Remind myself of my reasons for living
- Call a friend or family member
- Call a health care provider
- Call my local crisis line
- Go somewhere I am safe
- Go to the Emergency Room

If you feel that you can't get to the hospital safely, call the emergency number for your country. They will send someone to transport you safely."

As we have seen, the rates of suicide continue to grow. Brave individuals have shared their stories regarding suicide, and the roads which have taken them there. The stories are heart-wrenching and bring out concern and compassion. The stories from our Champions of Disclosure are also victorious. Their stories are of great courage and strength. With that being said, let us really begin to take hold of the issues that lead to suicidal thoughts and seek safety and treatment for ourselves and others as we encounter this mental health scourge.

---

[90] Centre for Suicide Prevention. (2017). *The workplace and suicide prevention.* accessed June 11, 2020, https://www.suicideinfo.ca/resource/workplace-suicide-prevention/.

[91] Samra, Joti, Dan Bilsker, and Simon Fraser. 2019. "Coping With Suicidal Thoughts." The LifeLine Canada Foundation, February 26, 2019. https://thelifelinecanada.ca/help/coping-with-suicidal-thoughts/.

There is a continued need for research on the prevalence of suicide among legal professionals and law students. The following information includes emergency telephone numbers and/or suicide prevention hotlines by country.

## Section 4.1: United States

- United States 911
- Or Suicide Prevention Hotline 1-800-273-8255
- Section 4.2: United Kingdom
- United Kingdom 999
- Samaritans Hotline: +44 (0) 8457 90 90 90 (UK - local rate)
- Hotline: +44 (0) 8457 90 91 92 (UK minicom)
- Hotline: 1850 60 90 90 (ROI - local rate)
- Hotline: 1850 60 90 91 (ROI minicom)
- Section 4.3: Australia
- Australia 000
- Lifeline Australia - 13 11 14 - Crisis Support and Suicide Prevention
- Section 4.4: Canada
- Canada 911
- Tollfree 833 456 4566
- Section 4.5: New Zealand
- New Zealand – 111
- Quick links
- Lifeline 24/7 Helpline: 0800 543 354 (24 hrs.)
- Depression Helpline: 0800 111 757 (24hrs)
- If you, or someone you know, is thinking about suicide call the 24-hour Suicide Crisis Line 0508 TAUTOKO (0508 82 88 65).48:1

## Section 4.2: Case Studies

### *Alan Berman, Ph.D.*

Interview with Dr. Alan Berman, psychiatrist and former Executive Director and President of the American Association of Suicidology.

Is everyone susceptible to suicide?

For the most part, a susceptibility to suicide is equivalent to diathesis—a vulnerability that makes stressful events more distressful and impactful. This vulnerability might be created by one's genetics (family history of suicide or psychopathology) or biochemistry (e.g., inflammatory markers, bipolar disorder) or by traumatic events in childhood (e.g., sexual abuse). Add in developmental factors, such as other mental disorders that may further weaken one's ability to cope, then a significant loss or threat or intimate partner problem or job or financial stress, or legal issues, then you have a much more potentially lethal mix of vulnerability and stress, hence susceptibility.

---

How do we overcome stigmas associated with mental illness so that people can get help earlier to prevent suicide?

I don't have the answer for this. For years, we stressed a greater societal openness about suicide and mental illness, talking about it, educating the public about it, etc., and now that that has begun, suicide rates have risen versus fallen. Someone much smarter than I am will eventually figure this out.

What are the best things to do if you think someone is suicidal?

Stay attached in a supportive manner and get them to a competent, trained mental health provider, consistently reassuring them, not with pablum, but with realistic examples of how things can and do change with time, how most all problems are solvable with a "two heads are better than one" mindset, and that nobody needs to bear the burdens of whatever alone; and that while history can't be changed, one's ability to cope better and find meaning and value are learnable.

What group of people are most likely to reach out for help?

Women (versus men).

What do you think about the way suicide impacts professions and is there a difference in the rate of suicide by types of work or depression?

There are epidemiologic studies accessible on the Internet regarding suicide and occupations or professions.

The more socially isolating the profession, the higher the rate; the more one has access to means, the higher the rate. The more an occupation is comprised of males, the higher the rate so what's new in this?

What steps should one take if they are feeling suicidal themselves?

Get them to help—seek a referral to someone trained in working with suicidal issues. Do not drink.

Dr. Berman shared that anyone can be susceptible to suicide. He also provided us with factors that may be associated with an increased risk for suicide. Dr. Berman shared a critical first step; when someone feels suicidal is to seek help and stay attached and supportive to the individual. If you feel suicidal, seek help immediately and do not drink. Finally, Dr. Berman commented on characteristics of certain professions that may make them susceptible to suicide.

## **Section 4.3: Champions of Disclosure**

### *Brian Clarke*

Judge Clarke an Administrative Judge with the United States Equal Opportunity Employment Commission. He was in practice for eleven years and served seven years as a full-time law professor.

Thank you for taking the time for this conversation Brian. So, there are so many issues of stress and stigma where would you like to start?

You know you have sort of a number of different sets of expectations; so, your legal work expectation, billable hours, collections, or even on a smaller firm scale and probably more appropriate scale, doing a good job for your clients. Which in and of itself is a lot, because depending on your practice you're dealing with a lot of [reluctance in clients] . . . maybe in one situation that I've ever been able to come up with is someone really happy and excited to hire a lawyer. The only circumstance I could ever come up with is adopting a child. That's the only one I've ever been able to come up with..

Otherwise, you are hiring a lawyer because you're in trouble with the law, you've been charged with a crime rightly or wrongly, you've been sued in civil court, you're getting divorced, you're thinking about dying, so you get a will drawn up. There's nothing and even on the business side you're trying to get a deal done, trying to buy a business . . . You know [a lawyer's] a necessary evil rather than something you're just pumped to do. You start off in any legal representation, legal relationship in sort of a negative footing . . . this is not something I want to do. I'm coming to you because I have to, not because I want to. And generally speaking, the whole representation, kind of the whole environment, just sort of has that negativity surrounding it. So just that in and of itself is a lot, and then you layer on sort of the business expectations if your firm of any real size, you know, the civic expectation and then of course you have the other the sort of social expectation of whether it's just going out and schmoozing with clients, you know, taking clients to play golf on the weekends . . . joining the country club, living in the right neighborhood, having the right car, all sort of cultural and social [expectations] that all Americans have an unhealthy obsession with..

I think that's an issue when we think about intrinsic versus extrinsic values. [When] people come into law school it seems with these positive intrinsic values; social justice, wanting to do the right thing, and I'm reading about the top students in law school has changed from intrinsic values to extrinsic values.

When I do talk, a standard piece of my presentation in 2014 Mindy Kaling, who's a comedian actress, was asked to speak as part of Harvard's commencement speech she said, in this class at Harvard there are like five Rhodes Scholars, ten Fulbright Scholars, five members of the Peace Core students, who before they arrived here started their own non-profits, were committed to making the world a better place. Now with your coveted Harvard law degree in hand, many of you will go onto the noblest of pursuits, such as helping a telecoms company buy an internet service. You will defend BP from birds, you will spend many hours arguing that no, in fact the well water was polluted well before fracking occurred. So, she really hit on [the fact] that so many people come into law school wanting to make the world a better place. [But they] come out and the focus is on money and it's the extra money being the one sort of extrinsic [value.] But then prestige, power those stuff as well, I'm going to go to the biggest, fanciest law firm that will hire me with the most possible money, well what if the work is terrible? Oh, I don't care. I'll get through it, for that it's worth it. But I mean no, what happened to being proud of what you do? I mean in a meaningful personal way—you're in fact making the world a better place rather than an objectively worse place.

And I mean one of the things especially with the law right now is [that] legal education has become profoundly expensive.

So, for my personal situations it was sort of the confluence of all different sets of expectations and it really sort of came to a head with me when my second child was born, because then I'm trying to be super-lawyer over here and I was doing a great job at the law firm. I was on half a dozen not-for-profit boards and being the president of a couple of them at like twenty-eight, and then you know I have one kid and my wife, who was the public defender. After our first kid was born, she stayed home, so I'm the sole bread winner and then I have another kid and for me it all just started manifesting as guilt.

I read that, yes. Please tell me about that, Brian.

. . . I was guilty all the time because I had so many balls in the air that something was going to get neglected, you know, there was just too much to do. And . . . when I was at work, I was guilty that I wasn't at home helping with my toddler and infant because that's tough, you know. [When I] was at home I was guilty that I wasn't at work, billing more hours when I was at work or at home I was constantly guilty that I [wasn't giving enough time to[ the non-profits that I was supposed to be working [for] and I think it was probably anxiety before it was guilt because the law, in addition to everything else, is extraordinarily unforgiving. You make a single mistake, and it's not like a doctor, we don't make a mistake, and somebody dies. We make a mistake, and it may cost someone some money or some extra attorney fees, but even still one mistake can injure a career, and lawyers do not forgive each other; judges are very unforgiving and the whole idea of, we're all human, we all make mistakes, it is just not a thing, there's almost no tolerance for mistakes, and this is true in litigation. Obviously when you're dealing with a court you know your opponent is just waiting for you to make a mistake. Even the tiniest mistake to jump on it and gain an advantage, this is true on the transactional side where the lawyer on the other side of the deal or lawyers on the other side of the deal are, you know, as a way to make themselves look better to their client are hunting for any, even the most inconsequential, mistake. Like a friend who accidentally repeated the word "the" in the middle of a 50-page single-spaced deal document and absolutely got ripped not only by the other side but by her own side for a single very human typographical error that had no impact on anything. And the fact that anyone would even still remember that ten years later, and I mean this one, it's not traumatizing to me. but [in my] second year of practice, I was representing a big company second chair, I was not lead attorney on it but I and in a brief that we sent . . . I misused "principal" instead of "principle" . . . it might have even been an autocorrect thing I just didn't catch. Every time I see that client, he mentioned it 20 years late.

The client?

Yeah, I mean the in-house attorney [at] a big energy company . . . he still raises it twenty years later. I mean raises it sort of jokingly, but still the fact that you remember that—that's what you remember about me, not the wonderful legal work I did for you. You remember my misuse of one word in one brief in one case.

And Brian, was that supposed to be humiliating? What's the purpose of doing that, I don't understand?

Other than, you know, just as the only legitimate purpose for any rational human is just to be like, "Oh, hey, there's a typo, let's fix it, or "Yeah, sorry," and it's not like this particular in-house lawyer was a huge jerk or anything, he wasn't. He was really good to work for, but at the same time, I just think it's indicative of the culture, this like forced expectation of utter perfection at all times. And I mean, when I talk about this stuff, perfectionism is something I always hit on because we're constantly, if we expect ourselves to be perfect, we're always going to fail, because perfection is of course unobtainable. And so sort of back to my own personal situation, I expected perfection of myself at work at home in the community, and it was impossible and eventually after living with constant raging anxiety, fear of making some mistake, then it started whatever, causing changes in brain chemistry or whatever it is, and really before I even knew it I was just profoundly depressed. . . I of course hid it very successfully for a long time, and I mean not only at work but at home so eventually all of my energy went to appearing fine, sort of maintaining the facade of normalcy and not only of competence but of extreme competence, and so it all sort of came crashing down. My wife we were on our way back from a doctor's appointment with one of the kids and . . . I was just a zombie, you know, completely flat. I was just trying to survive, and she [just asked] fairly innocuously, "Are you okay?" and my response was, "I just don't think I can do this anymore," and she said what, take time off to take the kids to the doctor? And I was like, no, life, living. I think I'm done with that, and you know that was probably the first time that I had actively admitted to myself what was wrong. But when I said that I sort of let go of the facade and it just sort of crashed down.

Judge Brian Clark gave us a great example of how lawyers and judges are affected by the notion of perfectionism and how individuals can get so caught up in expectations in personal life and public life there really does not exist a balance or downtime. One feels like a gerbil on a wheel, spinning from one event to another and worrying about the events that are not being attended to at a given time. As Judge Clark points out, this kind of belief system and the behaviors attached to these beliefs are not realistic and cannot be sustained.

## Champion of Disclosure Orlando Da Silva

Attorney Orlando Da Silva is Chief Administrator and Chief Executive Officer of the Administrative Tribunals Support Services of Canada. He is the former President of the Ontario Bar Association, with over 16,000 members, and was a Crown Counsel with the Ontario Ministry of the Attorney General. Between 2016 and the end of 2019, Orlando was a criminal prosecutor and, subsequently, a senior prosecutor with the Serious Fraud Office of Ontario. He has been working for many years on the destigmatization of mental health issues. Attorney Da Silva was named by *Canadian Lawyer* magazine one of the "Top 25 Most Influential Lawyers in Canada," he is the recipient of the Law Society of Ontario Law Society Medal and was nominated by CBC Metro Morning as Torontonian of the Year. In 2017, the Ontario Bar Association bestowed its highest honor, the Distinguished Service Award, on Da Silva. And in 2018, the Ontario Bar Association, Public Law Section, gave him the Tom Marshall Award of Excellence for Public Sector Lawyers.

Orlando, thank you so much for sharing your thoughts and story with us today. What are your thoughts on secondary trauma, an issue that people are just not talking about?

Yes, you are right, we don't hear a lot about secondary trauma. The trauma that arises out of seeing traumatic evidence, photographs, or a client's narrative. I have heard it also [called] vicarious post-traumatic stress.

Yes, that is another term that can be used as well. There are so many terms it can get very confusing. I don't think from what I have seen . . . we are not seeing this in any format being talked about in law school or continuing legal education.

Now if you want me to, I can launch into what I am thinking; I am happy to do that. I will get into secondary trauma, but before I do I have personally suffered from major depressive disorder since I was about nine years old, and disclosed it for the first time when I became president of the Ontario Bar Association some six years after a suicide attempt. I made mental health the core of my mandate for my one-year term. It gave me a platform where I could do some good with an audience that was larger than I expected I would ever have again. I gave an interview to the *Toronto Star*, which I believe has the largest circulation in the country, and they put my story on the front page of its edition. So, everyone learned, including my own family for the first time in a circulation of some 800,000 people that I suffer from this condition, and it had been longstanding and that I had a near-death experience. I had consumed about 180 sleeping pills with two bottles of wine. I learned many years later that the lethal dose for someone my size was about 30 tablets. So, it was through luck and probably the grace of God that I survived, and I kept all of that secret until I started my term in August of 2014, and that quickly led to an invitation to speak to government lawyers, which then resulted in another 200 invitations over the next five years, and many invitations to speak to the press. . . through the process of being open about my own condition and started a conversation in the legal community when I learned a lot about what was happening among lawyers and paralegals. Long story short After each one of these speeches I would be approached in long lineups of people telling me their own stories, but also approached hundreds of thousands of emails and social media telling me their stories. And their stories were about themselves having depression generally from a predisposition, maybe a genetic disposition but also the perfectionism, [the] competition extremely long hours and living a life in which you learn you are living in conflict . . . lawyers have told me that they are in conflict with everybody. That is to say their opposing counsel, their client, their partners in their firms, their partners at home, and to be successful they have to give up a lot of things that keep them balanced and happy, which is hobbies and downtime and things like that. Now [about] that predisposition to depression . . . according to John Hopkins University, lawyers are 3.6 times more likely to suffer from depression then the rest of society, who themselves are vulnerable: [about]one in five. More recent statistics have come out in the American Bar Association, so that is the baseline.

Now if you add to that the unique circumstances of criminal lawyers, prosecutors, and defense, who are exposed to traumatic evidence, whether it is pictures, oral testimony, videotape testimony, or audio recordings, it ups the ante quite a bit. Criminal lawyers probably [are more at risk] than civil, and I have some direct experience because I have done both and I am currently a criminal lawyer prosecuting, and they may complain about inability to admit that the evidence affects them because when they do, stigma and generalizations being what they are, people can conclude (and by people I mean more specifically their managers) that they are not strong enough to do these cases. So, they are taken off the big cases and put on smaller cases or they are taken off of trials and put on case management, so they are afraid to speak up. Second, when they do speak up the resources aren't there to help them: you have things like employee assistance plans where you can call and talk with therapists, [but] they are short term. You can talk three or four times and then you are on your own. So I have developed a community of people, and I say that loosely . . . former prosecutors who have left the business because they can no longer manage the stress of one long trial after another and being understaffed and exposed to traumatic evidence. The tragedy is that it is not hidden. Just in 2018, I believe since July of 2018, there have been two suicides in the criminal law division in Ontario, which has 800 lawyers. Family members approached me, and I did not even know there had been suicides despite my outspoken views on these things. I did not know about it until a family member took me out to lunch and asked [me about] the meaning of her death. How can we give her death meaning? What can you do in the criminal law division to give her death meaning? So, I try to advocate within our own ministry within the attorney general, like the Department of Justice in the United States, I suppose, and trying to help my colleagues navigate through the stresses and stigmas that come from seeking help. I remind them that [among] those who get help . . . there are some statistics that show they 80% recover.

Yes, those are good statistics. Orlando, this goes back to core idea of stigma and having difficultly normalizing the idea that these kinds of cases can affect people. In my practice, my training that is part of what we learned. We learned how to take care of ourselves, how to process things. We learned that in our formal training.

Yes, there is no such formal training in law.

So, what do you think individuals can do?

. . . I have a friend that was the head of psychiatry at the University of Toronto and is currently the Chair of Psychiatry at Mount Sinai Hospital he said that the best way to help people who are suffering from depression and anxiety, [which is] better than any medication or talk therapy, is share their own experience. S, I have developed a speaker's bureau of people who are willing to share their stories and who will talk to other lawyers in the ministry and across Canada. The appetite for this kind of thing astonishes me. I think it was January 10th I put out a tweet that said I was going to the University of Calgary and the University of Vancouver to talk about depression, and success, despite depression. Does anyone else want to hear about it? And within five days I was invited to thirteen other law schools stretching between the Atlantic Ocean and the Pacific Ocean. And it is amazing: the students especially are desperate to hear about this stuff. You know they are stressed out; they have high debt; they don't know if they are going to get a job and [they have their] student loans. They want to know that despite their depression they can still have a full and rewarding life. So that is the core part of the solution to me, is to get us talking about this stuff very early on before it is becomes an irreparable problem like it is among those who have quit the law or quit criminal prosecutions or defense. They, because of the stigma, the negative consequences to their career whenever they wait so long their careers are not salvageable, and I want to prevent that . . having the conversation, the easy way is to have it occur very early on, and without career consequences.

Yes, you said that people are afraid to talk about things because they may be taken off of the case by their manager. Is there anything that can be done in terms of that scenario; where people can be better educated as part of continuing education for attorneys or something where that could be taken care of?

Yes, I would love to see education. I am not sure where the best place would be, it might be right in law schools' part of criminal law curriculum, it could be part of licensing with the Criminal Law Society: before you become licensed to practice law you have to take some of these classes. Failing that it would become part of the employer's responsibility, but there has to be some training somewhere. And I think the earlier the better. Especially when it comes to being exposed to, using your example, sources of secondary trauma and what you should be doing because of your personality or predisposition you can make this early on before it negatively affects your career. So in that scenario it makes sense to me to have it taught in law school, but regardless if you are in criminal prosecution or defense and perhaps struggling with this . . . art of my volunteer work is to speak to senior management, the Minister of Justice Deputy, and say, you should be thinking of these things in terms of rotations. Crown attorneys, prosecuting attorneys in Canada, they rotate out of a child pornography group and into a fraud group or a case management group every few months so that they have a break, and the break is their hope. Almost everyone can tough out something for a little while if they know there is an end in sight. If we have this kind of rotations the pressure will come off.

That makes sense; just having the conversation, but then being able to take the next step. I think you are right, the EAPS [employee assistance programs] are so limited, and then what?

That is right. And often they do not turn to an EAP until far along in the deterioration of their mental health. What we need is early intervention, and if you normalize the discussion you make it safe . . . it is not a career limiting move. You can call the EAP, you may never need to call in a sick day, it is just part of water cooler talk. "I saw some awful evidence," and someone pats you on the back and says, "I know, I have been there," luckily, we are going to be rotating out to something less. If that is the situation created in the next five years or so we have done something good. That will be more important than any case that I have ever been on.

You will be affecting thousands of people and many generations. I really hope that goes through. It is an absolutely brilliant idea. I am not finding a lot of people, Orlando, who are practicing and still talking about this.

No, there isn't. There are some who are talking but who are not practicing. They are not listened to as much as those who continue to strive and practice.

I am wondering if you think that is because people are demeaning them with stigma?

I think that is true. They want to listen to people who are making it in the law. Their mind has given so they want to hear from people who have succeeded and know that they can succeed too.

I was talking to another lawyer, from a big firm in the U.S. He was telling me it is virtually impossible to say anything. He is suffering, but he is getting help. He said if he would state anything then his colleagues would see him as weak and even within his own firm the competition is so intense that he felt as though he couldn't reveal it.

I would echo that, if I was still in private practice in the firm I started out at and spent eleven years at. I made partner in that firm. If I said anything then [or] even today . . . my career would start a downward trajectory. I have no doubt about being in public practice [protecting] protects me.

How does that protect you versus being in private practice?

[In] private practice if your client finds out that you have something like depression or anxiety, they are going to conclude that you are weak or at least not strong enough to fight causes that they are not strong enough to fight on their own. And if you had a choice between someone you thought was weak and someone you thought was strong, who are you going to give the file to?

I get it. It is not just the clients; it is going back to the managers again.

Yes, and managers have some role in who they assign to files, or who they bring onto files and who they may pass over you if they think they are not doing you any favors by putting you on something that is stressful and high-risk. They are wrong because in my journey some of the strongest people I have ever known were people who suffer from depression and anxiety. They carry it over them like rolling it up the mountain knowing that if they relax just a little bit it is going to roll over the top of them.

People who suffer from anxiety and depression and many of the stigmatized illnesses are incredibly strong if they are able to continue to move forward on a daily basis.

I agree, and if anyone knows my highly publicized experience with depression, if they underestimate me, well better for me.

Sometimes in my field we use self-disclosure, as part of normalizing for people that we are working with, but that is really not something that plays a part in the legal profession I don't think.

I agree with you.

You also brought up the paralegals and those are people who are not even thought about in terms of these issues.

No, but they are as human as the rest of us. They experience the same things. You know it is the people who assist lawyers to the clerks who organize the traumatic evidence, and anyone exposed to it the whole justice sector needs help. First responders, police, judges, juries anyone exposed to this stuff. Many of them are suffering.

Thank you, Orlando for sharing your story and being a Champion of Disclosure.

Orlando has continued to advance in his profession while dealing with depression most of his life. He has helped many people through his willingness to share his story and be an advocate for mental health issues and self-care.

## Discussion Questions

- Which study or statistic did you find most surprising? Why?
- What are the three different types of stress? Which type of stress do you feel most commonly?
- How can stress affect the brain?
- What are the potential effects of depression on the brain?
- What were the results of the Brain & Mind Research Institute of the survey of 2,500 professionals and law students from thirteen law schools?
- There have been a number of studies on changes that occur for students within their study of law. What were the findings of Professor Benjamin's study?
- Who is least likely to seek help with depression, men or women?
- How can you take more personal responsibility for choices and making positive lifestyle changes to accommodate the stressors of the law school experience or professional life experience?
- What does the United Nations tell us about alcoholism?
- What is the leading cause of illness and disability globally?
- How much alcohol does the United Nations tell us is consumed annually by individuals?
- According to Derek LaCroix, what is the most pressing issue facing the legal profession today?
- What did you find most compelling about the Lisa Hanna's experience? What role did her peers play in her recovery?
- What are the warning signs of suicide?
- According to Dr. Berman, what are the issues that can weaken coping abilities?
- What should you do if someone you know feels suicidal?
- According the World Health Organization, how many people commit suicide every year?
- What is one of the biggest challenges or obstacles facing suicide prevention?
- What did you learn from Judge Brian Clark about suicide?
- What did you learn from Orlando DaSilva about suicide?

# References

Beck, Connie J. A., Bruce D. Sales, and G. Andrew H. Benjamin. 1995. "Lawyer Distress: Alcohol-Related Problems and Other Psychological Concerns among a Sample of Practicing Lawyers." Journal of Law and Health 10:1 (199596): 10.

Benjamin, G. Andrew H. 2008. "Reclaim Your Practice, Reclaim Your Life." *Trial*, December 2008. https://ssrn.com/abstract=1344655

Chan, Janet, Suzanne Poynton, and Jasmine Bruce. 2014. "Lawyering Stress and Work Culture: An Australian Study." 37(3) *University of New South Wales Law Journal* 1062.

Dan. "Can We Undo Lawyer Depression? A Psychologist Weighs In." Lawyers With Depression, August 27, 2019. http://www.lawyerswithdepression.com/articles/can-we-undo-lawyer-depression-a-psychologist-weighs-in/.

Dave Nee Foundation. n.d. "Lawyers & Depression." Accessed December 12, 2019. http://www.daveneefoundation.org/scholarship/lawyers-and-depression/.

*Global Status Report on Alcohol and Health*. Geneva: World Health Organization, 2011.

Grieve, Stuart M., Mayuresh S. Korgaonkar, Stephen H. Koslow, Evian Gordon and Leanne Maree Williams. 2013. "Widespread reductions in gray matter volume in depression." *NeuroImage: Clinical* 3: 332–39. https://doi.org/10.1016/j.nicl.2013.08.016.

Harmer, Sarah. 2017. "How healthy are New Zealand Lawyers?" New Zealand Law Society, June 2, 2017. https://www.lawsociety.org.nz/practice-resources/research-and-insight/practice-trends-and-statistics/how-healthy-are-new-zealand-lawyers.

Health and Safety Executive. 2019. *Work-related stress, anxiety or depression statistics in Great Britain, 2019*. October 30, 2019. http://www.hse.gov.uk/statistics/causdis/stress.pdf. Contains public sector information published by the Health and Safety Executive and licensed under the Open Government License

Ipsos Reid. 2012. "Survey of Lawyers on Wellness Issues." Commissioned by the Canadian Bar Association. https://www.cba.org/Sections/Wellness-Subcommittee/Resources/Research

Junior Lawyers Division. April 2019. Resilience and Wellbeing Survey 2019 Survey Report.

Junior Lawyers Division. April 2018. Resilience and Wellbeing Survey 2018 Survey Report.

Kelk, NJ, Luscombe, GM, Medlow, S, Hickie, IB (2009) Courting the blues: Attitudes towards depression in Australian law students and lawyers, BMRI Monograph 2009-1, Sydney: Brain & Mind Research Institute.

Kelly, Owen. 2014. "Lawyers and Anxiety: Three Case Studies." The Canadian Bar Association, August 21, 2014. https://www.cba.org/Publications-Resources/CBA-Practice-Link/Work-Life-Balance/2010/Lawyers-and-Anxiety-Three-Case-Studies.

Krill, Patrick, Ryan Johnson, and Linda Albert. 2016. "The Prevalence of Substance Use and Other Mental Health Concerns Among American Attorneys." *Journal of Addiction Medicine* 10: 46–52. 10.1097/ADM.0000000000000182.

Kuehn, Bridget M. 2015. "Reducing Toxic Stress in Childhood." SAMHSA. https://www.samhsa.gov/homelessness-programs-resources/hpr-resources/reducing-toxic-stress-childhood.

Lyon, Angus. 2015. A Lawyer's Guide to Wellbeing and Managing Stress. London: Ark Group.

Maguire, Grace, and Mitchell K. Byrne. 2017. "The Law Is Not as Blind as It Seems: Relative Rates of Vicarious Trauma among Lawyers and Mental Health Professionals." *Psychiatry, Psychology and Law*. 24, no. 2: 233–43. https://doi.org/10.1080/13218719.2016.1220037.

"New Research Suggests Solicitors in England and Wales Have Poorer..." LawCare, February 6, 2020. https://www.lawcare.org.uk/news/new-research-suggests-solicitors-in-england-and-wales-have-poorer-well-being-than-the-general-population.

New Zealand Law Society. 2014. "It's a Stressful Profession." *LawTalk* 855. November 21, 2014. https://www.lawsociety.org.nz/lawtalk/lawtalk-archives/issue-855/its-a-stressful-profession.

NZLSA. n.d. "Mental Health and Wellness." NZLSA. Accessed December 12, 2019. http://www.nzlsa.co.nz/mental-health-and-wellness/.

Panagioti, Maria, Patricia Gooding, and Nichola Tarrier. 2012. "A meta-analysis of the association between posttraumatic stress disorder and suicidality: The role of comorbid depression." *Comprehensive Psychiatry*. 53. 915-30. 10.1016/j.comppsych.2012.02.009.

Peterson, Todd D., and Elizabeth W. Peterson. 2009. "Stemming the Tide of Law Student Depression: What Law Schools Need To Learn from the Science of Positive Psychology. *Yale Journal of Health Policy, Law, and Ethics* 9, issue 2. https://digitalcommons.law.yale.edu/yjhple/vol9/iss2/2

Reed, Krystia, Brian H. Bornstein, Andrew B. Jeon, and Lindsey E. Wylie. 2016. "Problem signs in law school: Fostering attorney well-being early in professional training." *International Journal of Law and Psychiatry* 47. 10.1016/j.ijlp.2016.02.019.

Samra, Joti, Dan Bilsker, and Simon Fraser. 2019. "Coping With Suicidal Thoughts." The LifeLine Canada Foundation, February 26, 2019. https://thelifelinecanada.ca/help/coping-with-suicidal-thoughts/.

Scott, Elizabeth. "How Is Stress Affecting My Health?" Verywell Mind. Verywell Mind, July 17, 2019. https://www.verywellmind.com/stress-and-health-3145086.

Seligman, Martin E. P. 2016. "Why Are Lawyers So Unhappy?" Lawyers With Depression, September 20, 2016. http://www.lawyerswithdepression.com/articles/why-are-lawyers-so-unhappy/.

Seto, Megan. 2012. "Killing Ourselves: Depression as an Institutional, Workplace and Professionalism Problem," 2:2 online: OWOJ Leg Stud 5

Skead, Natalie, and Shane L. Rogers. 2014. "Stress, Anxiety and Depression in Law Students: How Student Behaviours Affect Student Wellbeing." *Monash University Law Review* 40, no. 2:1–24.

Taylor, Lynne, Ursula Cheer, Natalie Baird, John Caldwell, and Debra Wilson. 2016. "The Making of Lawyers: Expectations and Experiences of Second Year New Zealand Law Students." University of Canterbury, February 2016. https://www.canterbury.ac.nz/media/documents/research/S11503-The-Making-of-Lawyers.pdf.

Townes O'Brien, Molly, Stephen Tan, and Kath Hall. 2011. "No time to lose: Negative impact on law student wellbeing may begin in year one." *The International Journal of the First Year in Higher Education* 2, no. 2 (July 30, 2011): 49–60. https://doi.org/10.5204/intjfyhe.v2i2.84.

*Under the Radar: The Mental Health of Australian University Students*. Parkville: ORYGEN - The National Centre of Excellence in Youth Mental Health., 2017.

Wood Smith, Deborah. 2017. "Secondary or Vicarious Trauma Among Judges and Court Personnel." National Center for State Courts. https://www.ncsc.org/sitecore/content/microsites/trends/home/Monthly-Trends-Articles/2017/Secondary-or-Vicarious-Trauma-Among-Judges-and-Court-Personnel.aspx.

World Drug Report 2018 (United Nations publication, Sales No. E.18.XI.9).

World Health Organization. 2017. *Depression and Other Common Mental Disorders: Global Health Estimates*. Geneva: World Health Organization. https://eac.eu.com/newsletter/booklets/who%20mental%20disorders.pdf.

World Health Organization. (2006). Preventing suicide: a resource at work. World Health Organization. https://apps.who.int/iris/handle/10665/43502

World Health Organization. 2019. "Suicide." September 2, 2019. https://www.who.int/news-room/fact-sheets/detail/suicide.

Yüksel, Dilara, Jennifer Engelen, Verena Schuster, Bruno Dietsche, Carsten Konrad, Andreas Jansen, Udo Dannlowski, Tilo Kircher, and Axel Krug. 2018. "Longitudinal brain volume changes in major depressive disorder." *Journal of Neural Transmission* 125: 1433–47. https://doi.org/10.1007/s00702-018-1919-8.

# Chapter 3 Abstract: Bullying and Sexual Harassment

This chapter explores bullying and sexual harassment, both of which are coming into the spotlight as more studies show their frequency and impact. We will explore bullying through the eyes of Dr. Michelle Sharpe. We will also learn that bullying and sexual harassment can occur together. We will review the most recent study from the International Bar Association to see how prevalent sexual harassment is. We will also learn from leaders and pioneers on what to do next: what to do if you or someone else is being bullied or sexually harassed and how to determine if your own conduct might be bullying or sexual harassment. Finally, we will learn from Champions of Disclosure who provide their own accounts of being bullied and sexually harassed, and how they were able to heal and move forward.

# Chapter 3: Bullying and Sexual Harassment

## Section 1: Bullying, Harassment, and Incivility

Bullying, (nonsexual) harassment and incivility is common in the legal profession. Common but not acceptable, since the administration of justice depends heavily on the civility of lawyers and judges and other decision-makers. In the following pages I will attempt to define and identify behaviors commonly associated with bullying, harassment and incivility. But note that although there are some common themes, there is no consensus on what is or what amounts to bullying, harassment, or incivility. I will briefly explore the prevalence of inappropriate conduct in the legal profession and the harm it causes before addressing the thorny issue of how to respond. I think it is important to not simply focus on the target of the inappropriate conduct but to also take a look at bystanders and perpetrators. What can, or must, you do when you witness inappropriate conduct? How can you identify and change your own inappropriate conduct?

Before we begin, there are two things I must make clear.

First, time and space did not allow for a detailed examination of the law in each jurisdiction and the resources available to complainants. What follows is a broad outline of potential ramifications for inappropriate conduct in each jurisdiction. I hope that this might shine a small light on avenues for support and legal responses to inappropriate conduct and provide a starting point for readers to conduct their own research into local laws.

Second, no mistake or failing warrants bullying, harassment or incivility. Legal practice is often stressful, and lawyers are characteristically both perfectionists and pessimists (Daicoff 2004). But nothing justifies inappropriate conduct. Indeed, both lawyers and judges have an ethical obligation to act civilly, irrespective of whatever kind of provocation they may be met with. If you are the target of inappropriate conduct, you should not blame yourself. If you are, or think you might be, the perpetrator, avoid rationalizing or excusing your conduct by blaming your target for some perceived shortcoming.

### Section 1.1: What is bullying, harassment, and incivility?

Bullying, harassment, and incivility are terms that are often used interchangeably, but which may be used to describe different kinds of conduct or denote the severity of conduct. As a starting point it is useful to consider how these terms are defined in the jurisdictions canvassed by this text.

The terms "bullying" and "harassment" are typically defined as repeated, unreasonable behavior by an individual or a group toward another that is victimizing, humiliating, intimidating or threatening.

Some behaviors typically associated with bullying include exclusion, verbal taunts, belittling, yelling, giving highly critical and unnecessary comments and even throwing objects.[92]

In all the jurisdictions covered here, professional conduct rules (and in some jurisdictions in the United States, the oath of admission) require lawyers to act "civilly" or with "courtesy." But these terms are not defined in the rules, and no consensus exists as to their meaning. Civility has been described as including common courtesy, professionalism, dignity, and kindness. Some specific behaviors identified with civility include, for example, timeliness, accurate representation of law and facts, adherence to undertakings, and punctuality. Conversely, behaviors which have been identified as uncivil include, for example, behavior that is hostile or aggressive, using offensive or intimidatory language, making statements during proceedings that are disrespectful, or making allegations of dishonesty or impropriety.[93]

### Section 1.2: How widespread is bullying, harassment, or incivility in the legal profession?

The results of a global survey undertaken by the International Bar Association suggest that bullying, harassment, and incivility are endemic in the legal profession One in two female respondents, and one in three male respondents reported that they had been affected by bullying. Most respondents (65%) identified the perpetrator as a supervisor or senior colleague. But for those respondents practicing as either criminal lawyers or barristers/trial attorneys, judges were said to be responsible for bullying conduct (44% and 50% respectively).[94]

Victoria, Australia's Legal Services Commissioner, Fiona McLeay, is acutely aware of the structures within the legal profession that allow for and even incentivize, bullying. She is also advocating for change.

### Champion of Disclosure: Commissioner Fiona McLeay – AN ADVOCATE FOR DISCLOSURE AND CHANGE

In September 2017, Ms. McLeay was appointed Victoria's Legal Services Commissioner (LSC), an independent regulator of legal services. The LSC's role includes handling complaints about lawyers and assisting lawyers in acting ethically. I spoke with Ms. McLeay in December 2019 about bullying in legal practice. She said that her office had undertaken some research into well-being in the legal profession in an effort to understand why poor well-being was tolerated. From that research she was struck by respondents' stories of bullying and the profound impact that the conduct had on them. The junior lawyers who were mentored by bullying lawyers sometimes acted unethically, and some junior lawyers were even bullied into unethical conduct by supervisors. Ms. McLeay observed that, ultimately, it was in the interests of everyone, both lawyers and clients, to have a "healthy profession" in which

[92] Omari, Maryam, and Megan Paull. 2013. "'Shut up and bill': Workplace bullying challenges for the legal profession." *International Journal of the Legal Profession* 20, issue 2 (2):141–160. https://doi.org/10.1080/09695958.2013.874350.
[93] Baron, Paula, and Lillian Corbin. 2015. "Robust communications or incivility – where do we draw the line?" *Legal Ethics* 18 (1): 123).
[94] Pender, Kieran. 2019. *Us Too? Bullying and Sexual Harassment in the Legal Profession.* International Bar Association.

lawyers can enjoy a satisfying and sustainable career: lawyers are better able to communicate with each other, better able to resolve clients' problems and better able to serve the administration of justice. But Ms. McLeay noted that lawyers were often reluctant to complain about bullying. Instead, bullying was often accepted as a "rite of passage." In respect of the few complaints that were brought, Ms. McLeay found that lawyers tended to justify their conduct by pointing to the adversarial nature of the legal system or quibbling over whether their conduct fell squarely within legal definitions of bullying.

Ms. McLeay asks lawyers this: "What sort of profession do you want to be a part of? What sort of legacy do you want to leave?"

## Section 1.3: What are the adverse consequences of bullying, harassment, or incivility?

Civility is essential in the administration of justice. In Australia, Canada, New Zealand, United Kingdom and the United States, justice is administered through an adversarial system. The personal autonomy of litigants is a defining feature of this adversarial system. Litigants determine the issues in dispute and adduce evidence in a hearing. And civility is, essentially, concerned with respect for the personal autonomy of others.[95]

To this it can be added that without civility there can be no professional dialogue between, and among, legal practitioners and decision-makers. Professional dialogue is essential for the efficient resolution of disputes. A lack of civility also diminishes respect for the work of our courts and tribunals.
Lord Justice Singleton also observed that:

…a member of the Bar is a helper in the administration of justice. He [or she] is there to help the judge and, when there is a jury, to help the jury, to arrive at a proper result in the dispute between the parties … Continuous bickering becomes a burden for everyone in court—for judge and for jury—and it is almost impossible for justice to be done if that goes. (*Beevis v Dawson* [1957] 1 QB 195 at 201).

"The Health Risks of Bullying for the Victim
The effects of workplace bullying don't end when you leave the office. Being a victim of bullying can cause physical and psychological health problems, including:

- Stress
- Anxiety
- Panic attacks
- Trouble sleeping
- Higher blood pressure
- Ulcers
- Bullying Affects Job Performance

---

[95] Sharpe, Michelle. "The Importance of Civility" *Law Institute Journal* Vol 93 No. 6, June 2019, pages 29-33

Bullied workers can't perform their jobs to the best of their ability. Performance issues include:

Having trouble making decisions
An incapacity to work or concentrate
A loss of self-esteem
Lower productivity"[96]

## Section 1.4: What can I do if I am the target of bullying, harassment, or incivility?

Do not blame yourself. Whatever you think you may or may not have done, you are not responsible for the inappropriate conduct of another. No error or failing on your part justifies bullying, harassment, or incivility. Given the adverse health effects of bullying outlined above, seek out support as soon as practicable. For many lawyers, a trusted colleague is a good place to start. Speaking with a colleague provides an opportunity to unload negative emotions that may have arisen as a consequence of the bullying or uncivil conduct. And comfort can often be found in camaraderie. Indeed, by speaking with a colleague, you may quickly learn that the conduct that you have experienced is not at all uncommon and even, perhaps, that the perpetrator has a reputation for acting inappropriately. Most jurisdictions, and some employers, have assistance programs in place which, among other things, provide free counseling services. Information about the availability of these services can be provided by your law society or your employer. If you are concerned about the confidentiality of these services, then seeking assistance from your local general health practitioner might be a better option.

With the support of a colleague or health professional, you may be able to more clearly assess the bullying or uncivil conduct and whether or how to respond. The options open to you in responding to bullying or uncivil conduct will depend on whether the perpetrator of the conduct is a fellow lawyer or a judge or other decision-maker.

## Section 1.5: Incivility by decision-makers

The rule of law requires the impartial application of the law by judges. Impartiality is the "idea that judges will base their decisions on the law and facts: not on any predilections towards one of the litigants."[97]

First, it may be that the decision-maker's bullying or uncivil conduct gives rise to an apprehension of bias. An apprehension of bias exists if a fair-minded lay observer might reasonably apprehend that the judge might not bring an impartial mind to the resolution of the question the judge is required to decide. In these circumstances an application may be made for the decision-maker to disqualify him or herself from determining a matter. You should note that any such application should be brought *before* any decision is handed down. Waiting until a decision is handed down before

---

[96] Gordon, Sherri. "How Workplace Bullying Negatively Affects the Victim and Profits." Verywell Mind. Verywell Mind, March 10, 2020. https://www.verywellmind.com/what-are-the-effects-of-workplace-bullying-460628.
[97] Larkins, Christopher M. 'Judicial Independence and Democratization: A Theoretical and Conceptual Analysis" (1996) 44 *American Journal of Comparative Law* 605 at 609).

complaining about apprehended bias deprives the decision-maker of the opportunity to dispel any apprehension at the time it might be said to arise.

Second, it may be that the decision-maker's bullying or uncivil conduct has deprived the parties of procedural fairness. In these circumstances, an appeal may be brought to set aside the decision. See, for example the Australian decision of *Kuek v Wade & Magistrates Court of Victoria* [2017] VSCA 329. In that case the Victorian Court of Appeal set aside a magistrate's decision after finding, among other things, that the magistrate had behaved in a non-judicial (but *not* bullying) manner by ignoring the parties' pleadings, re-defining the issues in the proceeding and discouraging a litigant from adducing any further evidence on an issue that the magistrate had deemed irrelevant.

Third, you may wish to make a complaint about the decision-maker's conduct. You could complain directly to the chief justice or head of the jurisdiction in which you appeared. Some courts have published statements to signal their disapproval of bullying conduct and outline how a complaint may be received. Alternatively, you may consider making a complaint to your law society, which may raise the matter on your behalf. Some law societies have published protocols for the handling of complaints and advice about how to manage bullying conduct by decision makers. See, for example, in the United Kingdom, the Bar Council Guide "Advice to the Bar about bullying by judges." There may also be an independent body in your jurisdiction that has been established specifically for the purpose of handling complaints about decision-makers. Your law society, or an internet search, should be able to provide you with the necessary information about the existence of such an organization or commissioner, and how a complaint may be made. It is entirely a matter for you whether to make a complaint. The International Bar Association's research into bullying and incivility found that only 57% of respondents complained about bullying[98] (though not just bullying from just decision-makers). One of the reasons cited by respondents for not making a complaint about bullying conduct was the fear of repercussions. But you may wish to consider how reporting uncivil or bullying conduct may contribute to cultural change within the legal profession and assist in improving the delivery of justice. In some jurisdictions law societies or bar associations also allow for complaints to be made anonymously.

## Section 1.6: Incivility by lawyers

For most lawyers (those not practicing in criminal law or as barristers/trial attorneys), bullying conduct is most likely to come from a fellow lawyer, according to the International Bar Association's survey on bullying.[99] A trusted senior colleague may be willing to assist you by providing advice on how to manage the conduct or by interceding on your behalf. Many employers and law societies also have procedures in place for managing complaints about inappropriate workplace behavior. In navigating these options, or as a matter of last resort, you should be aware that incivility or bullying by lawyers may also result in disciplinary action.

Parliaments in all jurisdictions covered in this text have enacted legislation addressing workplace bullying. Workplace bullying is in some jurisdictions also prohibited under the professional conduct

---

[98] Pender, Kieran. 2019. *Us Too? Bullying and Sexual Harassment in the Legal Profession*. International Bar Association.
[99] Pender, Kieran. 2019. *Us Too? Bullying and Sexual Harassment in the Legal Profession*. International Bar Association.

rules. But professional conduct rules in all jurisdictions require practitioners to be civil or courteous in all dealings in legal practice (and especially in court). Baron and Corbin identify a number of principles relevant to determining whether conduct is uncivil, in breach of the professional conduct rules. The first among these principles is whether the conduct is likely to bring the profession into disrepute. The chief purpose of the professional conduct rules is to protect the reputation of the profession so that the public may have confidence in the provision of legal services. It follows that simple discourtesy will not attract any disciplinary sanction. But note that lawyers may be held to a higher standard of courtesy than the general public. Certain conduct by a lay person may be just rude, but the same conduct by a lawyer in legal practice may be dishonorable. Seniority is also relevant in any assessment of the lawyer's conduct. Other principles identified by Baron and Corbin in determining whether uncivil conduct may be sanctioned include whether the conduct is repeated and persistent and in the case of discourteous communications whether the statements may be true or amount to fair comment.[100] In Canada, Justice Moldaver observed that:

> …trials are not—nor are they meant to be—tea parties. A lawyer's duty to act with civility does not exist in a vacuum. Rather, it exists in concert with a series of professional obligations that both constrain and compel a lawyer's behaviour. Care must be taken to ensure that free expression, resolute advocacy and the right of an accused to make full answer and defence are not sacrificed at the altar of civility (*Groia v Law Society of Upper Canada* [2018] 1 S.C.R. 772 at [3]).

It should be noted that Canada enacted a Charter of Rights and Freedoms that explicitly guarantees freedom of expression. Not all jurisdictions enjoy the same kind of free-speech protection. But, in any event, Justice Moldaver's observation that a lawyer's ethical duty of civility is a duty that is balanced with, or qualified by, other ethical duties, is an observation that can be made in any jurisdiction. Conversely, it may also mean that incivility may breach ethical duties other than the duty to act with courtesy. For example, in all jurisdictions, lawyers have an ethical duty to act in the best interests of the client. Uncivil conduct may breach this duty. In Australia, the chief justice of the New South Wales Supreme Court, Justice Bergin, observed in *Knight v Carter* [2015] NSWSC 609 at [27]:

> …*it is part of the role of the legal practitioner in such cases to assist the client by endeavoring to take some heat out of the dispute rather than writing provocative letters …The Court expects that solicitors will behave professionally and bring an objective approach to their clients' problems so that the clients may understand the parameters of the dispute more realistically.*

Relatedly, the professional conduct rules in all jurisdictions require lawyers to not act in ways that undermine the administration of justice. Courts of superior jurisdiction also have an inherent jurisdiction to regulate conduct occurring within the court room and punish contempt. Lesser courts and tribunals may also be empowered by legislation to punish contempt. Words or conduct may amount to contempt in the face of the court if they are of a kind that would tend to interfere with the administration of justice. Such conduct would include, wilfully insulting a judge because such an insult "necessarily

---

[100] Baron, Paula, and Lillian Corbin. 2015. "Robust communications or incivility – where do we draw the line?" *Legal Ethics* 18 (1): 123).

interrupts the course of a trial and tends to divert attention from the issues to be determined" (see the Australian High Court case of *Lewis v Ogden* (1984) 153 CLR 682 at 688).

### Section 1.7: What can I do when I see bullying, harassment, or incivility?

As a bystander you can do more than watch: you can discourage inappropriate conduct and lessen the negative impact of such conduct. As the incident unfolds before you there may be some scope for you to challenge, dissuade, or distract the perpetrator from engaging in the inappropriate conduct. Whether and how you can do this will of course depend on the circumstances, in particular whether the incident occurs in or out of court and whether the perpetrator is a lawyer, a more senior lawyer to you, or a judge/decision-maker. But at the very least it is important that you do not behave in any way that might suggest to the perpetrator or target that you think the behavior is justified or amusing. To behave in this way is to encourage the perpetrator and deepen the target's shame. It also signals to others that you consider that this is an acceptable way to behave in the circumstances and that you are helping make this the standard for the legal profession in your jurisdiction.

After the incident, you can speak with the target. You can share your disapproval of the perpetrator's conduct and offer your support. It has always been my experience that lawyers typically feel very awkward about talking to colleagues on matters concerning inappropriate conduct and mental health. It doesn't form part of our law school training (though it probably should). In the end, there is no magic formula that needs to be said. All you have to do is to express empathy and a willingness to assist in an authentic way. You should also be aware that you may be required by the professional conduct rules in your jurisdiction to report misconduct by a fellow lawyer.

### Section 1.8: How do I know if my conduct may amount to bullying, harassment, or incivility and what can I do about it?

There are a number of "red flags" that may alert you to the possibility that your conduct may be inappropriate. A red flag should go up if you recognize any of the following:

- You appear to repeatedly upset someone around you. That is, someone regularly appears shocked, tearful or angry after exchanges with you
- You often find it difficult to understand and share other people's feelings
- You frequently get aggressive or passive-aggressive
- You feel most comfortable in the company of insecure people. And you make yourself feel better by unsettling people
- You often spread rumors about people
- You misuse your power or position to undermine others[101]

It is often difficult to objectively review one's own behavior. Speak with a colleague. Ask if your interaction with a person or a group of people is appropriate or even the best way to respond in a given situation. Be curious. Are there more effective ways to manage your workplace relationships or

---

[101] Gautier, Chantal. 2018. "Are You a Bully? Here's How to Tell." *The Conversation*, November 1, 2018. This article is republished from https://theconversation.com The Conversation under a Creative Commons license

recurring workplace challenges? Even if your conduct falls short of bullying or incivility, there are always ways to improve dealings with people to create a more pleasant and effective workplace. Make some enquiries about the availability of programs in your home jurisdiction to hone your people skills. There may be a person or a group of people who have made, or continue to make, mistakes or who do not perform at the standard you expect. But while you have no control over the conduct of others, you have complete control over our own conduct, and how you respond to others. And as outlined above, the delivery of justice and the reputation of the legal profession depends upon lawyers and judges/decision-makers acting with civility. Indeed, incivility may have severe adverse repercussions not just for the consumers of legal services and the well-being of others but also for you, professionally and personally.

As noted above, research also suggests that people who engage in inappropriate behavior typically have low levels of well-being. Honestly consider your current situation. Are you finding it difficult to manage work stress? Do you feel overwhelmed by feelings of powerlessness? Does work seem pointless and unfulfilling? Speak with those closest to you at home and at work. Do you seem unhappy? Are you difficult to be with? It may be time to seek out professional help from a counsellor or psychologist. You may be reluctant to seek professional help. And you would not be alone. One Australian study, for example, found that lawyers reported a reluctance to seek help if experiencing depression (Kelk et al. 2009). Consider, though, the costs to you and those closest to you if you don't access help. Not only will you continue to suffer, but it is likely, that you will also be undermining the well-being of those at work and at home. And, to quote Fiona McLeay, "What sort of profession do you want to be a part of? What sort of legacy do you want to leave?

### Section 1.9: Conclusion

Bullying and uncivil conduct is endemic in the legal profession. And it is not a problem for targets alone. It could adversely affect the well-being of bystanders and it is often symptomatic of the poor well-being of perpetrators. Any rewards that perpetrators might perceive to be theirs by engaging in inappropriate conduct are either illusory or pale in comparison to what such behavior may cost them—personally and professionally. Ultimately, though, uncivil conduct can undermine the administration of justice to the detriment of consumers of legal services and the wider community. Whether you are a target or a bystander, you are not powerless to respond effectively to uncivil or bullying conduct. Indeed, it might be said you have an ethical duty to act.

## Section 2: Sexual Harassment

Sexual harassment is widespread, cross-cultural, and pervasive. It does not recognize socioeconomic or professional boundaries. The number of articles and studies on sexual harassment is a testament to the need for continued work and concern on this issue.

Sexual harassment can be defined as unwanted verbal or physical behaviours of a sexual nature particularly from a person of power to a person of lesser power such as a boss to an employee or a teacher to a student. Its first known use was in 1971.

Sexual harassment as defined by the United Nations within the context of work as "any unwelcome sexual advance, request for sexual favor, verbal or physical conduct or gesture of a sexual nature, or any other behavior of a sexual nature that might reasonably be expected or be perceived to cause offence or humiliation to another person."[102]

The United Nations has created a document about sexual harassment to support policy makers, employers, and activists. It offers new guidance on policy and practice for sexual harassment and lists international standards and commitments against violence, discrimination against women and on human rights. The website, Towards an End to Sexual Harassment: The Urgency and Nature of Change in the era of #METOO is an additional excellent resource.

One only needs to read or watch the news to see examples of sexual harassment at all levels of society. The #MeToo movement, which started in 2006 as a grassroots organization to address the shortage of resources for survivors of sexual violence, has grown into an international community of survivors working together to help destigmatize the discussion and push to equalize the number of women in top tiered positions. A very public example of sexual harassment among legal professionals occurred in October 2019 when a United States Federal Court Judge was publicly reprimanded for sexual harassment.

Despite numerous laws and the flurry of activity, a great deal of work still needs to be done. Much is being talked about and indeed enacted into law. For example, in Australia, Attorney Fiona McLeod notes a profusion of laws, many of which are historical (2019).

In her lecture, McLeod stated, "Seventy years ago, the United Nations Declaration and the Declaration on Human Rights promised us equality. In that time, we have seen hundreds of conventions, treaties, resolutions, and dialogue. We have seen significant milestones with CEDAW (The Convention on the Elimination of all Forms of Discrimination Against Women), introduced into Australian. law in 1979 as the SDA, which prohibits discrimination, harassment, vilification"

"The law now recognizes that sexual harassment may include these kinds of unwelcome acts:

- Physical contact, touching, hugging, cornering, kissing
- Staring or leering
- Sexual gestures
- Suggestive sounds, comments or jests
- Intrusive questioning
- Requests or pressure for sexual acts
- Explicit comments and inappropriate advances in emails, messages and social media
- Sharing or threatening to share intimate images without consent"

---

[102] United Nations Population Fund. 2019. "Protection from Sexual Exploitation, Sexual Abuse and Sexual Harassment." December 20, 2019. https://www.unfpa.org/protection-sexual-exploitation-sexual-abuse-and-sexual-harassment.

## Section 2.1: The Gender Pay Gap

The gender pay gap is cross-cultural and historic in nature. It is a reflection of bias and discrimination against women. Sexual harassment can be an additional result of the gender pay gap because of the view that the less money you make, the less power you have, therefore making you seem weaker or easier to take advantage of. The gender pay gap not only represents a great loss of income over an individual's lifetime, it also represents true inequality; the same work for less pay. The issue of undervaluing women's work seems to continue unresolved, as you will see below.

Taking into consideration the number of laws and the historical nature of the laws, women still have a 147% wage gap to men even though for many years, law graduates and new admitted have been 50-60% female. Women make up around 25% partnerships and around 10% senior advocate. But where is the momentum behind these laws?

In the United States, studies have shown that wage gaps in the legal profession may be as high as 38.6%.[103]

"Among the AmLaw 200, women comprise only 4% of executive management overall; 19% of all equity partners; 23% of top governing committees; and 28% of promotion and compensation committees. And according to 2014 data released by the U.S. Census Bureau, full-time female lawyers earn 77% of what male lawyers do." (Cohen).

In the United Kingdom a study of 45 firms revealed that the average partner pay gap was, "16.8% with a median pay gap of 21.1%."[104]

"The Pay Gap Persists at All Job Levels. Gender differences in pay are especially pronounced in higher wage levels: 8% of women in-house counsels earn $180,000–$200,000 CAD, compared to 13% of men. 15% of women in-house counsels earn $200,000 CAD or more, compared to 26% of men. Among all types of law firms, Canadian women earned 93% of men's salaries across all stages of their careers in 2012. In the largest private firms, women earned 91% of men's salaries."[105]

---

[103] Monahan, Alison. 2019. "Understanding the Gender Wage Gap in the Legal Profession." The Balance Careers, updated May 5, 2019. https://www.thebalancecareers.com/understanding-the-gender-wage-gap-in-the-legal-profession-4000621.
[104] Willer, James. "The UK Gender Pay Gap 2018: What Do The Numbers Actually Tell Us?" Law.com, May 1, 2019. https://www.law.com/2019/05/01/the-uk-gender-pay-gap-2018-what-do-the-numbers-actually-tell-us/?slreturn=20191117132609.
[105] Catalyst. 2018. "Women in Law: Quick Take." Catalyst, October 2, 2018. https://www.catalyst.org/research/women-in-law/.

According to a study of law school graduates across Canada:

"Across all settings, women working full time are earning 93% of men's salaries. Women report median earnings of $75,000, compared to $80,500 for men. Men out-earn women in private law firms of all sizes, with the differences especially pronounced for those in solo practice; in the largest private firms (251+) women's earnings are 91% of men."[106]

A survey of 4000 New Zealanders found the largest pay gap was in the legal profession, with a median salary for men working of $128,250 compared with $66,454 for women—a staggering difference.[107]

## Section 2.2: Institutional Betrayal

In the mix, is the issue of institutional betrayal which refers to wrongdoings perpetrated by an institution upon individuals dependent on that institution, including failure to prevent or respond supportively to wrongdoings performed by individuals (e.g., sexual assault) that are committed within the context of the institution. Individuals feel betrayed by institutions when they fail to prevent sexual harassment and when they fail to respond to sexual harassment. Many institutions continue to turn a blind eye toward these behaviors. Some institutions have taken a more aggressive stance by mandating that employees cannot sue companies and institutions for sexual harassment, thereby denying victims recourse in this way.[108]

One possible response to Institutional Betrayal is Institutional Courage. "Institutional Courage is the antidote to institutional betrayal. It "includes institutional accountability and transparency. An example of this occurs when institutions conduct anonymous surveys of victimization within the institution: 'Enabling the methodical collection of data—and encouraging their transparent distribution and study—will signal to campus communities across the country that institutional betrayal can be replaced by institutional courage.'"[109]

Sexual harassment is a deeply pervasive and cross-cultural phenomenon. In what we consider modern times, with forward thinking and innovations in technology, we still have places where rape continues to be legal, women do not have rights to own property, drive, vote or even appear in public alone. In your own country, town, city, village what steps have you or your colleagues taken to help end sexual harassment? What real concrete steps have you taken in the past six months to a year to help change this issue?

---

[106] Dinovitzer, Ronit. 2015. *Law and Beyond: A National Study of Canadian Law Graduates*. May 27, 2015. http://dx.doi.org/10.2139/ssrn.2615062.

[107] Ryan, Holly. "Law Profession Has Widest Gender Pay Gap: YUDU Survey." NZ Herald. NZ Herald, July 2, 2018. https://www.nzherald.co.nz/business/news/article.cfm?c_id=3&objectid=12081261.

[108] Freyd, J.J. (2020). *Institutional Betrayal & Institutional Courage* Retrieved [*2/21/2020*] from https://dynamic.uoregon.edu/jjf/institutionalbetrayal/

[109] Freyd, J.J. (2020). *Institutional Betrayal & Institutional Courage* Retrieved [*2/21/2020*] from https://dynamic.uoregon.edu/jjf/institutionalbetrayal/

Many things can be done to continue to move forward in the change process. Again, this is a global issue and women taking on more leadership roles could be one answer, and equalizing pay rates, another. We need a global response, and we must come back to individual responsibility and accountability. Take action, respond, change the culture from inequality to equality and peaceful coexistence. Are you a part of the continuation of the current attitudes about sexual harassment by remaining silent? Can you act as an individual and move toward creating change? Can you organize people to act as change agents, as a group?

Keep in mind that sexual harassment can occur in any environment: work, school, at a coffee shop, anywhere. The harasser can have any number of kinds of relationships to the victim, including supervisor, teacher, peer, colleague.

### Section 2.3: Forms of Sexual Harassment

RAINN, the Rape, Abuse & Incest National Network, lists these as some of the forms of sexual harassment on its website:

- "Making conditions of employment or advancement dependent on sexual favors, either explicitly or implicitly.
- Physical acts of sexual assault.
- Requests for sexual favors.
- Verbal harassment of a sexual nature, including jokes referring to sexual acts or sexual orientation.
- Unwanted touching or physical contact.
- Unwelcome sexual advances.
- Discussing sexual relations/stories/fantasies at work, school, or in other inappropriate places.
- Feeling pressured to engage with someone sexually.
- Exposing oneself or performing sexual acts on oneself.
- Unwanted sexually explicit photos, emails, or text messages."[110]

But what is the difference between sexual harassment and sexual assault? What about sexual misconduct? RAINN, the largest anti-sexual violence organization in the United States.

Sexual harassment is a broad term, including many types of unwelcome verbal and physical sexual attention. Sexual assault refers to sexual contact or behavior, often physical, that occurs without the consent of the victim. Sexual harassment generally violates civil laws. You have a right to work or learn, without being harassed.

"Sexual misconduct is a non-legal term used informally to describe a broad range of behaviors that may or may not involve harassment. For example, some companies prohibit sexual relationships between co-workers, or between an employee and their boss, even if the relationship is consensual."[111]

---

[110] RAINN. n.d. "Sexual Harassment." Accessed December 17, 2019. https://www.rainn.org/articles/sexual-harassment.
[111] RAINN. n.d. "Sexual Harassment." Accessed December 17, 2019. https://www.rainn.org/articles/sexual-harassment.

## Section 2.4: Prevalence of Sexual Harassment

I was once again shocked and saddened when I spoke with female lawyers and students about bullying and sexual harassment. I found that bullying and sexual harassment are not only pervasive but, in some cases, expected as part of the profession. Since when is this OK? Some would argue that it has never changed, and this has always been the reality for women and sexual minorities. The people who are the harassers are supposed to be upholding the law. What has happened? Why is this persisting, especially among people who make the laws and should be enforcing the laws?

According to the most recent survey by the International Bar Association, one in three female attorneys has been sexually harassed. One in fourteen men reported sexual harassment. This is based on the online responses of 6,980 attorneys from 135 countries. According to the survey, the most common forms of sexual harassment were sexist comments, including inappropriate humor or jokes about sex or gender (67.9%); sexual or sexually suggestive comments, remarks or sounds (66.8%); being looked at in an inappropriate manner that made them feel uncomfortable (52.2%); and any inappropriate physical contact such as patting, pinching or brushing up against the body (48.6%), sexual propositions, invitations or other pressure for sex (24%); seriously inappropriate physical contact, for example, kissing, fondling or groping (21.6%); receiving sexually explicit content or propositions via email or social media (13%); implicit or explicit demands for sexual favors in exchange for employment or promotion (6.7%); and physical assault or rape (3.1%).[112]

The World Health Organization tells us much about sexual harassment. "Sexual violence, including sexual harassment, frequently occurs in institutions assumed to be 'safe,' such as schools, where perpetrators include peers and teachers. [Studies] have documented that substantial proportions of girl's report experiencing sexual harassment and abuse on the way to and from school, as well as on school and university premises, including classrooms, lavatories and dormitories, by peers and by teachers."[113]

The following provides rates of sexual harassment per location: "the highest prevalence of sexual harassment, at 30% on a gender-weighted basis. Africa (28%) and North America (28%) were both above the global mean of 22%, while Latin America (21%), Asia (20%), Scandinavia (20%) and Western Europe (19%) were all just below average. Eastern Europe had the lowest prevalence, at 13%. Female respondents from Africa had the highest prevalence (48%), just above female respondents from Oceania (47%) – see Figure 32. Among male respondents, those in Oceania and North America experienced the most sexual harassment (12%), while those in Western Europe experienced the least

[112] Pender, Kieran. 2019. *Us Too? Bullying and Sexual Harassment in the Legal Profession.* International Bar Association.
[113] World Health Organization and Pan American Health Organization. 2012."Understanding and addressing violence against women: intimate partner violence." World Health Organization. https://apps.who.int/iris/bitstream/handle/10665/77434/WHO_RHR_12.37_eng.pdf?sequence=1

(4%). Consistent with bullying, Africa had the largest gender disparity while Eastern Europe had the smallest gap."[114]

It is important to understand that sexual harassment is not limited to sexual behavior or behavior directed at a specific person. It can take the form of negative comments about women as a group.[115] Some of the possible effects of sexual harassment include emotional effects such as anger, fear, shame, betrayal, guilt, powerlessness, etc.; mental health effects such as anxiety, depression, panic attacks, Post Traumatic Stress Disorder, suicidal ideation, and substance use, etc; and physical effects, such as sleep and appetite disturbances, fatigue, etc. (RAINN n.d.)

"Sexual harassment often results in emotional and physical stress and stress-related mental and physical illnesses," wrote Shawn M. Burn in an article, "What Do Psychologists Say About Sexual Harassment?". She continued: "Research in the United States links sexual harassment to increased absenteeism, job turnover, transfer requests, and decreases in work motivation and productivity. Sexual harassers may be supervisors, peers, customers, or clients. Although men sometimes experience sexual harassment the vast majority of those who experience it are women. The Equal Employment Opportunity Commission in the United States estimates that between 25 and 50% of women have experienced sexual harassment in the workplace. When women are minorities, either statistically because there are few of them or because they are ethnic minorities, they are often at increased risk for sexual harassment."[116]

It is well known that sexual harassment is under reported. The reasons for underreporting include the following: lack of response, concern about revictimization through the court process, concern about how the individual who has been harassed will be perceived, and if the perception with have an impact on their career.

### Section 2.5: United States

It was only in 2016 that the American Bar Association adopted a model to prohibit and sanction sexist comments and conduct by lawyers.

In the United States between 24 and 35% of respondents reported being sexually harassed according to the International Bar Association study.[117]

[114] World Health Organization and Pan American Health Organization. 2012."Understanding and addressing violence against women: intimate partner violence." World Health Organization. https://apps.who.int/iris/bitstream/handle/10665/77434/WHO_RHR_12.37_eng.pdf?sequence=1
[115] World Health Organization and Pan American Health Organization. 2012."Understanding and addressing violence against women: intimate partner violence." World Health Organization. https://apps.who.int/iris/bitstream/handle/10665/77434/WHO_RHR_12.37_eng.pdf?sequence=1
[116] Burn, Shawn M. 2017. "What Do Psychologists Say About Sexual Harassment?" *Psychology Today*, Apr 29, 2017. https://www.psychologytoday.com/us/blog/presence-mind/201704/what-do-psychologists-say-about-sexual-harassment.
[117] Pender, Kieran. 2019. *Us Too? Bullying and Sexual Harassment in the Legal Profession.* International Bar Association.

In the United States sexual assault occurs every 92 seconds and 1 out of every 6 women and 1 in 33 men has been a victim of attempted or completed rape. It is estimated that 63,000 children were victims of sexual abuse from 2009-2013 according to Child Protective Services.

As we know, only a small percentage of incidents of sexual harassment and sexual assault are reported. Thus, we do not know the true scope of sexual harassment or sexual assault. For example, in the U.S. it's estimated that only 15.8 to 35% of all sexual assaults are reported to the police. U.S. Bureau of Justice Statistics, M. Planty and L. Langton, "Female Victims of Sexual Violence, 1994-2010," 2013; Wolitzky-Taylor et al.

## Section 2.6: United Kingdom

According to the International Bar Association findings, the frequency of sexual harassment among lawyers in the United Kingdom is close to the global average, with 38% of female and 6% of male respondents reporting they had been affected. Internationally, 37% of female respondents and 7% of male respondents had experienced sexual harassment during their career. (Pender 2019,[118] Bowcott 2019[119]).

Key statistics about sexual violence:

- In 2017, the United Kingdom's Office for National Statistics estimated:
- 20% of women and 4% of men have experienced some type of sexual assault since the age of 16, equivalent to 3.4 million female and 631,000 male victims.
- 3.1% of women (510,000) and 0.8% of men (138,000) aged 16 to 59 had experienced a sexual assault in the last year. [120]
- In January 2013, An Overview of Sexual Offending in England and Wales, the Ministry of Justice (MoJ), Office for National Statistics (ONS) and Home Office, revealed:
- Approximately 85,000 women and 12,000 men (aged 16 - 59) experience rape, attempted rape or sexual assault by penetration in England and Wales alone every year; that's roughly 11 of the most serious sexual offences (of adults alone) every hour.
- Only around 15% of those who experience sexual violence report to the police.
- Approximately 90% of those who are raped know the perpetrator prior to the offence.

---

[118] Pender, Kieran. 2019. *Us Too? Bullying and Sexual Harassment in the Legal Profession.* International Bar Association.
[119] Bowcott, Owen. 2019. "Bullying and Sexual Harassment Rife among Lawyers, Global Survey Finds." *The Guardian*, May 14, 2019. https://www.theguardian.com/law/2019/may/15/bullying-and-sexual-harassment-rife-among-lawyers-global-survey-finds.
[120] Office for National Statistics. 2017. "Crime in England and Wales: year ending March 2017." https://www.ons.gov.uk/releases/crimeinenglandandwalesyearendingmarch2017 Contains public sector information licensed under the Open Government Licence v3.0.

More key statistics (Rape Crisis England & Wales n.d):[121]

- 31% of young women aged 18-24 report having experienced sexual abuse in childhood
- Most women in the United Kingdom do not have access to a Rape Crisis Centre
- A third of people believe women who flirt are partially responsible for being raped
- Conviction rates for rape are far lower than other crimes, with only 5.7% of reported rape cases ending in a conviction for the perpetrator.

According to the Office for National Statistics, there was an increase of 0.7 percentage points in the proportion of adults in England and Wales who experienced sexual assaults in the year ending March 2018 (to 2.7%). These are the latest data available. In 2017, the same office estimated that 20% of women and 4% of men have experienced some type of sexual assault since the age of 16, equivalent to 3.4 million female and 631,000 male victims 3.1% of women (510,000) and 0.8% of men (138,000) aged 16 to 59 had experienced a sexual assault in the last year.[122]

In a 2013 report, An Overview of Sexual Offending in England and Wales, the Office for National Statistics (ONS) and Home Office, revealed that only around 15% of those who experience sexual violence report to the police.[123]

### Section 2.7: Australia

The International Bar Association found out of 1,000 lawyers, 37% had experienced harassment. More than 70% of female lawyers surveyed in New South Wales Australia reported being sexually harassed. 71% of the respondents reported that they have been sexually harassed at work and only 18% made a complaint to their employer.[124]

In a survey of 23,000 attorneys practicing in Victoria, Australia, 10% experienced sexual harassment. Two-thirds of the women experienced sexually harassing jokes, comments, leering, or staring; 15% experienced inappropriate touch or groping, or kissing. The perpetrators were overwhelmingly male, older, and in positions of power. When asked why they did not tell what happened, the majority of responses stated that they did not think anything would happen or be resolved, according to my conversation with Fiona McLeay, Board CEO and Commissioner of the Legal Services Board in Victoria.

---

[121] Rape Crisis England & Wales. n.d. "About sexual violence." Rape Crisis England & Wales. Accessed December 18, 2019. https://rapecrisis.org.uk/get-informed/about-sexual-violence/statistics-sexual-violence/.
[122] Office for National Statistics. 2019. "Crime in England and Wales: year ending December 2018." Office for National Statistics, April 25, 2019. https://www.ons.gov.uk/peoplepopulationandcommunity/crimeandjustice/bulletins/crimeinenglandandwales/yearendingdecember2018 Contains public sector information licensed under the Open Government Licence v3.0.
[123] Rape Crisis England & Wales. n.d. "About sexual violence." Rape Crisis England & Wales. Accessed December 18, 2019. https://rapecrisis.org.uk/get-informed/about-sexual-violence/statistics-sexual-violence/.
[124] Pender, Kieran. 2019. *Us Too? Bullying and Sexual Harassment in the Legal Profession.* International Bar Association.

Australian statistics on Sexual Assault:

- 17% of women and 4% of men experienced sexual assault since the age of 15
- 93% of offenders are male
- 1 in 6 reports to police of rape and less than 1 in 7 reports of incest or sexual penetration of a child result in prosecution
- Only about 17% of reported sexual offences result in a conviction, a figure consistent with data from other States and overseas
- 1 in 5 (1.7 million) women and 1 in 20 (428,000) men have been sexually assaulted and/or threatened since age 15
- 1 in 6 (1.5 million) women and 1 in 9 (992,000) men were physically and/or sexually abused before the age of 15
- 1 in 6 (1.6 million) women have experienced physical and/or sexual violence by a cohabiting partner since age 15

In Australia the number of sexual assault crimes continues to increase: In 2018 the number of victims recorded for Sexual assault increased for the seventh consecutive year to 26,312 victims nationally. This was an increase of 2% (475 victims) from 2017.[125]

In Australia, 1 in 2 women and 1 in 4 men have been sexually harassed since the age of 15. 1 in 5 women and 1 in 20 men have experienced sexual violence since age 15, according to the Australian Institute of Health and Welfare.[126]

## **Section 2.8: Canada**

In a 2018 Canadian Study, "five dimensions of gender-based violence are explored: unwanted sexual behavior while in public, unwanted sexual behavior online, unwanted sexual behavior in the workplace, sexual assault, and physical assault.

Women were more likely than men to have been sexually assaulted or have experienced unwanted sexual behavior in public, unwanted behavior online, or unwanted behavior in the workplace in the 12 months preceding the survey, and this was the case even when controlling for other factors. In contrast, men were more likely to have been physically assaulted.

Not only were women more likely to experience these behaviors, but the impact was also greater. Women were more likely than men to have changed their routines or behaviors and to have experienced negative emotional consequences. Women were also more likely to have talked to somebody about their experience following an incident of unwanted behavior or assault.

---

[125] Australian Institute of Health and Welfare 2018. Family, domestic and sexual violence in Australia 2018. Cat. no. FDV 2. Canberra: AIHW © Australian Institute of Health and Welfare 2018 under Creative Commons BY 3.0 (CC BY 3.0) license.
[126] Australian Institute of Health and Welfare 2018. Family, domestic and sexual violence in Australia 2018. Cat. no. FDV 2. Canberra: AIHW © Australian Institute of Health and Welfare 2018 under Creative Commons BY 3.0 (CC BY 3.0) license.

One in three (32%) women and one in eight (13%) men experienced unwanted sexual behavior in public. For both men and women, younger age and sexual orientation increased the odds of experiencing this behavior more than any other factor. More specifically, being younger and of a sexual orientation other than heterosexual was associated with much higher odds.

The most common types of unwanted sexual behavior experienced by women in public were unwanted sexual attention (25%), unwanted physical contact (17%), and unwanted comments about their sex or gender (12%). These were also the three most common types of behavior experienced by men, though at a considerably lower rate (each 6%).

One in five (18%) women experienced online harassment in the 12 months preceding the survey, slightly above the proportion of men (14%). Women were more likely than men to know the perpetrator.

Women (28%) were more likely than men (19%) to have taken measures such as blocking others online or deleting accounts to protect themselves from online harassment.

While men (56%) were slightly more likely than women (53%) to witness inappropriate sexual behavior in their workplaces, the opposite was true when it came to personally experiencing this type of behavior. Three in ten (29%) women were targeted by inappropriate sexual behavior in a work-related setting compared with 17% of men.

More than 11 million Canadians have been physically or sexually assaulted since the age of 15. This represents 39% of women and 35% of men 15 years of age and older in Canada, with the gender difference driven by a much higher prevalence of sexual assault among women than men (30% versus 8%).

Equal proportions of women (4%) and men (4%) were victims of violent crime in the 12 months preceding the survey, though the type of victimization differed as women were more likely to have been sexually assaulted (3% versus 1% of men) and men were more likely to have been physically assaulted (4% versus 2% of women).

The vast majority of incidents of violent crime did not come to the attention of police; 5% of women stated that police found out about the most serious incident of sexual assault they experienced, while 26% of women and 33% of men who were physically assaulted said likewise.

One in five victims of sexual assault—both women and men—felt blamed for their own victimization. Most commonly, the perpetrator or the victim's friends or family were the source of this feeling."[127]

---

[127] Cotter, Adam and Laura Savage. "Gender-based violence and unwanted sexual behavior in Canada, 2018: Initial findings from the Survey of Safety in Public and Private Spaces." Government of Canada, Statistics Canada, December 5, 2019. © Her Majesty the Queen in Right of Canada as represented by the Minister of Industry, 2018

In Canada, women were more likely to report sexual harassment in their workplace (4%) than men (less than 1%), according to data derived from the 2016 General Social Survey on Canadians at Work and Home.[128]

## Section 2.9: New Zealand

"It is estimated that 186,000 sexual offences were committed in 2013. No statistically significant change occurred between 2008 and 2013, a decrease occurred between 2005 (317,000) and 2013.

When we look at the percentage of New Zealanders who were victims of sexual violence, we found 2.1% of adults experienced one or more sexual offences in 2013. This decreased over time, from 3.9% in 2005 to 2.8% in 2008 and down to 2.1% in 2013.

Looking at sexual victimization by gender, we found that women (2.9%) were more likely than men (1.1%) to have experienced a sexual offence in 2013.

Overall, we found there were 5.2 sexual offences for every 100 adults in 2013" (New Zealand Ministry of Justice n.d.).

In New Zealand, 24% of women, and 6% of men, will experience sexual violence in their lifetime.[129]

Only 7% of sexual violence offences against adults are reported to New Zealand Police (New Zealand Crime and Safety Survey, Ministry of Justice, 2009 [not collated in 2014 survey]).

## Section 2.10: Case Studies

### *Catharine MacKinnon*

Professor Catharine MacKinnon is the Elizabeth A. Long Professor of Law at the University of Michigan Law School, and the James Barr Ames Visiting Professor of Law at Harvard Law School. She was the special gender adviser to the prosecutor of the International Criminal Court. She established the legal grounds for defining sexual harassment as sex discrimination, and the concept of "gender crime" through her work with the International Criminal Court.

In an email exchange with Professor MacKinnon, I shared my feelings of shock due to the results of the study by the International Bar Association, and in her response she wrote, "the class-based assumptions you mention are not generally borne out, in that the notion of 'empowered' based on a

---

[128] Hango, Darcy, and Melissa Moyser. "Harassment in Canadian Workplaces." Government of Canada, Statistics Canada, December 17, 2018. https://www150.statcan.gc.ca/n1/pub/75-006-x/2018001/article/54982-eng.htm. © Her Majesty the Queen in Right of Canada as represented by the Minister of Industry, 2018
[129] Sexual Abuse Prevention Network n.d. "Statistics." Accessed December 17, 2019. http://sexualabuseprevention.org.nz/who-we-are/statistics/.

profession being considered to have power does not keep women in that profession from being sexually harassed by more powerful men, and the idea that 'education' would minimize sexual harassment would be laughable if the reality were not so cruel. It is true that the rates of sexual harassment are even higher as one goes down the wage scale, which is not to say that elevated occupations are in any way exempt."

"Some two decades after the federal courts first recognized sexual harassment as a form of sex discrimination, debate still continues about what sexual harassment is, why it might be sex discrimination, and what law can and should do about it" (Siegel 2003).

## **Charlotte Proudman Interview**

Working in both law and academia, Dr. Proudman is an award-winning human rights barrister who fights for the rights of women and girls. She received her doctorate from King's College, Cambridge, and is a Junior Research Fellow at Queens' College, Cambridge. She has been called a "feminist barrister" and "#MeToo pioneer" by *Legal Cheek*. She was the winner of the Thomson Reuters 2018 legal debate arguing that quotas for women are the solution to gender equality in the workplace.

As a legal scholar and a woman what do you think about the current study from the International Lawyers Association [Pender 2019] that documented one in three women are being sexually harassed on the job?

In my view the statistics are just the tip of the iceberg, I suspect the actual number of women lawyers that experience sexual harassment is much higher. Whilst the ILA's study is important in drawing this issue to the attention of fellow lawyers, more needs to be done to change the cultural environment which has allowed sexual harassment to continue. There are too many surveys showing that sexual harassment is an issue within the law profession without focusing on proposals for change.

How can we improve the laws or the enactment of the laws that cover these crimes?

More needs to be done by professional regulatory bodies of lawyers to impose tough sanctions when lawyers engage in sexual misconduct. Case studies in the United Kingdom show that when barristers have been found to have engaged in sexual harassment or even assault, they have been permitted to continue practice (unchanged), having merely paid a menial fine. This sends out a message that sexual violence is tolerated by the law profession and allows perpetrators to continue such behavior with impunity. If tough sanctions are not imposed, it is unlikely women victims will go through the ordeal of making complaints. Arguably, lawyers that have been found to engage in wrongful behavior are not fit to practice; they are charged with upholding the law, setting an example; and yet their actions are bringing the law into disrepute. If a lawyer was racist, it is likely they would be reprimanded to the extent that they could lose their job, but when it comes to gender-based violence, it is not seen as serious.

Why haven't past solutions worked?

There have not been any decent solutions imposed that could possibly work. It has taken decades for lawyers to acknowledge that sexual harassment is rife in the profession. Only now are lawyers willing to acknowledge that there is a pressing issue. Now is the right time to consider solutions to change wrongful behavior.

What cultural changes need to take place within legal firms and in law school to help eradicate this issue?

We need gender parity at the top of the legal profession. We need to see 50% men and women partners in top firms and amongst the judiciary. Until we have gender parity there will continue to be a disproportionate balance of power skewed in favor of white, privileged men to the detriment of women, who remain a minority. When power is held by a minority it is more likely to be abused.

What else do you think can be done by current law students and future law students?

Law schools need to teach and inform students about the widespread nature of sexual harassment and assault in the legal profession. This is rarely taught, as such students begin their careers with no knowledge of the problem and believe that they are an isolated case or will consider leaving the profession. This is why the attrition rate for women barristers is high, partly because they experience sexual harassment and have no support offered to them. Both male and female students need to be aware of sexual harassment within the profession to prevent it from happening in the future.

## Sampling of results from the International Bar Association Study; Us Too? Bullying and Sexual Harassment in the Legal Profession.

Through my work on the board of the Mental Health Institute of Legal Professions, I have met many wonderful individuals. Among board members is Kieran Pender, who is a Senior Legal Advisor and Legal Policy & Research Unit for the International Bar Association. Kieran provided some of the anonymized examples of sexual harassment from the International Bar Association's Study, *Us Too? Bullying and Sexual Harassment in the Legal Profession*. Some of the results are as follows:[130]

*Being looked at in an inappropriate manner which made you feel uncomfortable*

'A number of male colleagues superior to me (including the partner I work for most) openly stare at my legs when I am wearing a skirt… It makes me feel uncomfortable and disrespected in my workplace… I have never reported this as I do not know how and fear it would not be taken seriously.' (Female, Germany, Law firm)

'I have been a trial attorney … for over 30 years. When I first started, it was common for male attorneys/judge/bailiffs and other court personnel to make sexual comments about a female attorney's attire, physical form, or mode of practicing law. That is SLOWLY changing.' (Female, United States of America, Law firm)

---

[130] Pender, Kieran. 2019. *Us Too? Bullying and Sexual Harassment in the Legal Profession*. International Bar Association.

'The owner of the law firm I worked for was 35 years older than me and repeatedly told me that female lawyers would only be successful if they were good looking, that female lawyers should only wear skirts (not pants) to work, that my education was a waste of time since I should be home and care for my children in the future and he also commented on my weight. It was a small firm of only 3 associates and in fear of bad references (and in the beginning of my career) I never reported this further.' (Female, Sweden, Law firm)

*Sexual or sexually suggestive comments, remarks or sounds*

'A member of the support staff suggested a threesome with himself, me and another colleague. 'You are so attractive. Both X and I should jump you at the same time." (Female, Sweden, Law firm)

'[M]en would tell sexist jokes or say sexually suggestive things while they were around me in a work environment, which was unprofessional, but I didn't realize it at the time that it was also sexual harassment. I[t] was so widely accepted it seemed normal to me.' (Female, United States of America, Government)

'I often received comments from my line manager that she wanted to 'f**k me'. Any conversation would seem to have a sexual reference in it.' (Male, United Kingdom, Barristers' Chambers)

'The comments were about me being 'sexy' and the partner saying stuff like 'I always look at you'. I find these comments highly inappropriate coming from a partner to a young associate. If another associate [said] the same thing it would be a lot easier to actually tell him/her off. The hierarchy plays an important role in sexual harassment.' (Female, Sweden, Law firm)

*Sexist comments, including inappropriate humor or jokes about sex or gender*

'After requesting that a sexual harassment policy be implemented, I experienced a huge backlash. Immediate increase in sexist comments, jokes and derogatory comments personally directed at me.' (Female, South Africa, Barristers' Chambers)

'Sexist comments are endemic … In addition to comments, men frequently interrupt women or disregard their opinions. If asked, they will not admit to it, but that is what happens in reality.' (Female, Brazil, Law firm)

'I have been subject to everyday sexism' throughout my legal career - I don't think anyone means any harm, but it is clear by their conduct that they view me differently because I am a woman. [For example] comments such as … 'can you come to lunch with X client - he likes a pretty face at the table' … 'you can't have an expenses card because you'll just spend all our money on shoes' and … 'you girls, you just need to have a bit of a wobbly every now and then, get it all out of your system, then you'll feel better'… [I]t's just exhausting feeling that you are constantly swimming against the tide.' (Female, Jersey, Corporation/Organisation)

*Receiving sexually explicit content or propositions via email or social media*

'The perpetrator sent me sexually explicit messages, photos and videos over a course of several months. I eventually reported it as I was concerned about him subjecting others to the same treatment who may be more vulnerable.' (Female, United Kingdom, Law firm)

'[E]mails of this nature appear to be sent … on the assumption by the sender that they are amusing or entertaining. One is made to feel that it would be 'prudish' to raise objection.' (Female, South Africa, Barristers' Chambers)

*Inappropriate physical contact, for example patting, pinching, brushing up against the body and any inappropriate touching or feeling*

'There was an after-work cocktail event which included retired lawyers and alumni of the firm. There was one particular retired partner who showed interest in me, and I was strongly encouraged to speak with him and 'make him feel welcome'. The uncomfortable situation escalated until he asked me to sit on his lap. The eye contact I received from superiors made it clear that I couldn't refuse.' (Female, Canada, Law firm)

'[A senior male lawyer] attempt[ed] to pull over my underwear, kiss my back, touched my body while I was … not sober. Some female attorney stopped his sexual misconduct … I was furious when I woke up … and said [to] him [not to] direct contacts to me anymore... I have never [forgotten] the trauma which he brought me.' (Female, Republic of Korea, Corporation/Organisation)

'Once, the managing partner left me alone with a senior lawyer the firm was courting, who ran his hands up my legs and tried to kiss me. I ran into the managing partner as I was running from the restaurant, and he suggested I should consider a relationship with this man.' (Female, Canada, Law firm)

*Implicit or Explicit demands for sexual favors in exchange for employment or promotion*

'I had a brief sexual relationship with my boss, which I terminated. After that, there were months of demands to resume the relationship, with both the implicit threat of termination and constant bullying and verbal harassment that only started after I ended the relationship.' (Female, United States of America, Other)

'The male bosses take advantage of young, temporary female employees, in need of work, and without professional experience. You cannot report, or they do not renew your position.' (Spanish, Female, Costa Rica, Government)

Implicit or explicit demands for sexual favours in exchange for work opportunity (i.e. to be involved in a matter)

'I was advised by the practice manager (female) that if I showed a sexual interest in my principal we'd get on very well and he'd be nicer to me.' (Female, United Kingdom, Other, Implicit or explicit demands for sexual favours in exchange for work opportunity)

'I was told because I was sexually harassed before on multiple occasions by multiple men, I was the problem.' (Female, Australia, Other)

'[O]ne of the Senior Partners ... offered to help me get a training contract at his firm, if I went to Casinos with him and agreed to get to know him better. I never reported it because it would have probably meant exclusion from the project and usually nothing happens to the Partner...' (Female, United Arab Emirates, Law firm)

*Sexual propositions, invitations or other pressure for sex*

'My boss ... resolved it by refusing all work from the same client, which was a wonderful solution and I felt protected and heard, but at another workplace (much bigger than the first and with a separate HR department) the perpetrator was a very influential person who would have had me fired... It contributed to me resigning not too long thereafter.' (Female, Namibia, Judiciary (including courts and tribunals))

*Serious inappropriate physical contact, for example kissing, fondling or groping*

'[A client] said I must see the view he had [from his hotel room] and after initially saying no thank you I eventually popped into his room 'just for a moment' to see the view. He then lunged. I moved away quickly and nothing terrible happened. Thankfully. I felt like an idiot. I thought his interest in me was professional. I felt horribly uncomfortable the next day in his team. I was worried it had ruined my career.' (Female, United Kingdom, Law firm)

'[A senior male colleague] started saying sexually suggestive things in reference to my breasts, and indicated he was going to perform a sex act on me, then spit on my chest to demonstrate what he was going to do... He made similar comments to another younger female colleague the same evening. We were both discouraged by others from officially reporting it, as it would 'ruin his life' or cause him to lose his job or get disbarred for something he did while drunk.' (Female, Canada, Law firm)

'[My line manager] tried to kiss me and put his hand on my leg / up my skirt. I pushed him away and he laughed. I did not report it as everyone knew he had wandering hands and I didn't see the point. He was popular and made money for the firm so I knew he would not be reprimanded but it would make life difficult for me to be seen as a troublemaker.' (Female, United Kingdom, Law firm)

'At an office party a female lawyer was intoxicated and approached me in a sexual manner, touching me in a sensual way and suggesting that we go home together... [I] repeatedly told her 'no'. She ignored this and put her hand on my crotch outside my pants. At this point I removed her hand and laughed it off whilst walking away. We have never spoken of the incident and have remained in contact

… I am absolutely convinced that she either does not remember the incident or believes she did nothing wrong, she was just being a little too persistent.' (Male, Sweden, Law firm)

*Physical assault or rape*

'When I wanted to go to my room [at a conference, a senior male colleague] followed me. I told him that I did not want him in my room. He kept asking, nagging until I let him in … After I fell asleep, he raped me.' (Female, Sweden, Law firm)

'[After I was sexually assaulted I] feared that his rank or reputation made me quite vulnerable to be attacked. My fear and disgust to remember this horrible event prevented me [from reporting it to the] bar association or police … He looked to attack female colleagues or juniors frequently. I should have stopped him.' (Female, Korea (Republic of), Corporation/Organisation)

'[I] was advised by my seniors and mentors not to become the 'poster child for sexual assault in the workplace' as this would seriously handicap my career.' (Female, Hong Kong, Law firm)

*Good News Stories*

'[I] went to my boss [about the inappropriate jokes made by a colleague], who gave me a professional and understanding meeting and then he later on reported the situation to the HR-department of the court. I was satisfied with male boss' action in the situation. My boss also talked to the perpetrator and informed him that his actions had not been liked by the court'. (Female, Sweden, Law Firm (judiciary at the time of the incident), Misuse of power or position)

'I spoke to the Supervisor about it and he was never inappropriate again. So just saw it as a one of incident … Once I explained that it should never happen again we had a good relationship.' (Female, Trinidad and Tobago, Law firm, Sexual or sexually suggestive comments, remarks or sounds)

'In my case I told my boss, who stepped over the line (on my 3rd day into my new job), that his behavior was out of line. He never did it again and it didn't have any consequences for me.' (Female, Norway, Law firm, Sexist comments, including inappropriate humour or jokes about sex or gender)

'[I]n the past 15 years, at least in my country, there has been an incredible advance (for the better) regarding these matters.' (Female, Chile, Law firm, Sexist comments, including inappropriate humour or jokes about sex or gender)

'I … did not report the incident for some time because I did not have faith in the firm to address the issue. There wasn't any transparency within the firm about how the incident would be handled and there were always rumours that people in a position of power would not be held accountable for their actions. However, once I finally reported the incident it was dealt with swiftly and my anonymity was protected within the firm.' (Female, Australia, Law firm, Receiving sexually explicit content or propositions via email or social media)

These stories are disturbing. Yet, it is through the efforts of individuals who are willing to share and organizations such as the International Bar Association who are willing to study these issues, that steps can be taken to implement additional measures that may lessen and eventually eradicate these issues.

## Section 2.11: Champions of Disclosure Fiona McCleod

Finding a Champion of Disclosure for this section on sexual harassment has been very difficult. I spoke with many women who have been sexually harassed, and with one exception, all were reluctant to come forward, due to the many reasons discussed earlier. For this reason, Attorney Fiona McLeod is a truly brave and real Champion.

Attorney McLeod has a long history of service, including chair of the Victorian Bar Council and president of the Australian Bar Association. She was appointed to the executive of the Law Council of Australia in 2014, serving as treasurer in 2015, president-elect in 2016 and president in 2017. She received the Australian Women Lawyers Award and is a fellow of the International Academy of Trial Lawyers and the Australian Academy of Law. She is a council member of the Commonwealth Lawyers Association, the Advisory Council of the University of Melbourne Law School, and the Victorian University Sir Zelman Cowan Centre.

Fiona thank you so much for helping with this very difficult issue. Where would you like to begin?

I've been on the end of numerous small incidents and, heard many more serious incidents so this, um, is just my disclosure of something that happened to me not too long ago. I was at a work function, it was a dinner, and it was a dinner of people who I knew fairly well. There were barristers I have been opposed to, or judges I have been in front of, and we are all from the same, uh, what we call "Clerking group." It was a list, so that means we had a person who runs our list for us, and we are all members, although we are all self- employed.

I had been [a member of the bar], I am trying to think of the timing now, I had been at the bar maybe, more than twenty years . . . so senior enough, and having had leadership positions where I'd been personally responsible for trying to change the culture around bullying and harassment. To try and reveal it. People were saying to me, "Well, you've done that now, so you can move on and there's nothing to see here."

So we are at this dinner—well, people had been saying that to me for a long time, and of course I knew [bullying and harassment] wasn't fixed, I just knew it wasn't acceptable—still not acceptable—for women to reveal that they'd been at the end of this behavior, and some young men too, because it . . . was seen as career-limiting to become a victim.

Yes, I understand. I have heard this frequently.

The culture was that somehow you were responsible, or if you weren't responsible, don't make a fuss, because then people would see you as a threat somehow. And that you should, you know, be a good girl, basically. So, I was at this dinner and it was the end of the dinner and I was talking to a very senior [Queen's Counsel]. I had been opposed to him in a case a few years before. And we had been on opposite sides, and the case, the case had run, and you know it was one of those ones that had been very hard fought. Anyway, he said to me at the dinner, he was very sort of friendly and jovial and said, as he put his hand on my rear, and gave me a squeeze, he said "I was very aggressive with you in that case." And I looked at him and I thought, you know, I could just go "whatever" and shrug it off, but I looked at him and I said, "Like you're being now" and he pulled his hand away, because I was two feet away from him staring at his face, and he pulled his hand away and I said, "I did not give you permission to touch me." And he laughed, anxiously, and he subsequently became a judge.

That was brave to confront him.

So it was like one of those things of, I didn't tell people, but there was another judge two feet away from me who was watching this and laughing at the fact, you know, that I slapped him down or put him down. So that was the end of it. Yeah, so that was the end of it. No, he never apologized. If he had apologized to me that would have been the end of it. Um, because [of a] misread of the situation, fair enough, I would have allowed that. But he didn't. And I always interpreted that as, not really sexual, but more aggressive, a power play. And what realized later on that what I was doing was putting some sort of favorable interpretation on it, to in a way diminish or excuse what he had done. Yeah, I didn't find, I found it sort of intrusive, but I didn't find it "traumatizing," if you like. It was just like "Ugh, creepy".

And then a couple of years ago, I was a country delegate to a new conference . . . You know, I walk around the world pretty confident in myself, and pretty clear about what I think my physical boundaries are with intimacy with other people . . . Sometimes I will give them a kiss hello or a hug if it's somebody I haven't seen for a long time and we are colleagues or shake hands. Anyway, I am at this international conference and I came downstairs, and some people were standing outside, there had been this big meeting that had been going on for hours. And I came outside and, a fellow who was one of the founders of the organization was standing in a group with the other founders. And they had all been revered and given lots of opportunities to talk throughout the conference, so we all knew this guy was the legend who dreamed up this international movement. And he said to me, I said hello, and he said, "You know you are in the presence of the founders," and I said "Oh, I am in the company of legends," and I sort of acknowledge them all and he said "Yes, so get down on your knees, baby." I looked at him, and I said, "No, you don't get to say that to me." And there was another pause, and everything that's going through my mind is [that] if I don't say this to him, who's going to? Who is going to push back, if I can't? So I said, "No, you don't get to say that to me, I have read your policies that you publish with the conference material, that talks about zero tolerance for exactly what you just said." And the four other founders, all standing two or three feet away, all just stared at me. And one of the founders, I don't know if he speaks English, started going off in another language, right? So, I walked away, and I thought well that was a bit greasy, of him again. What the hell? And I immediately found the group I was traveling with, and there were some others from some other countries, and I mentioned it. I said this just happened to me, and one of the guys there told a story about how he had denigrated a woman who was appointed to an international working group, [talking] about who she had to sleep with to get that role.

So, I report this to the group, and they tell me, oh, there's another example of that sort of bad behavior where he's denigrated somebody in public. And I thought, mmm, OK, and one of the Australians with us said, "Oh, do you want to do something about it?" And I said no, let me just think about it, because I feel like I put him back in his place and I feel like I took the power back myself, so I don't feel a compulsion to do anything about it, but let me think about it. And that night we were at dinner with some other internationals, and they said, "Oh, let me tell you what he did to us." And I thought, OK that's three strikes where he had used his position to demean a woman, using his sexuality, or her sexuality as the basis for the put-down. And I thought, that's it, OK, I have to be the one. Because if there's three of us then, and I don't really care what these people think of me (I mean I do, but you know).

So, I thought, OK, I am going to do something about this, and then I did notice I avoided him for the rest of the conference. Because I felt uncomfortable around him, and . . . he would approach from behind when we were in a conversation, . . . benign perhaps or perhaps not, and I would move away because I felt uncomfortable. And I thought OK, well there's a signal that . . . I am affected by this. So I wrote a letter, and in the end it was put to him by the board who were organizing the conference and they were mortified and they put it through a process, which they hadn't tested before, so it was a little clunky, but that's OK, they gave it a trial run. And in the end, it came back to me and it said I must have misinterpreted. That made me very angry. Because I thought I had four or five witnesses, whom I named. The response came back. And . . . they said that If I was offended that I must have misinterpreted, so it wasn't an apology.

It's unbelievable that this is still going on. It is so blatant.

Well, they were his mates, the founding fathers. So, the point for me was first that I'd become quite empowered that I had triggered the process and said firstly that I'd point my finger at him and said, "No, you don't get to do this to me," And secondly that I'd triggered the formal process at risk of being painted as the troublemaker from Australia, and said, . . . "This is happening from somebody who is senior in your organization. You need to know about it and do something about it."

[That] episode is sort of closed for me in terms of my own growing angst about it, but it does continually occur to me that if I was junior or had been previously traumatized, or if there was some other vulnerability there, that would have been a very upsetting episode potentially.

Absolutely. And the really horrifying thing about it is that in both instances, Fiona, you had people around you who could have helped.

[And] it also emphasizes how critical it is if you're a bystander to poor behavior, that you need to intervene. And sometimes all you need to do, [is if] a person's being aggressive, just ignore them and turn your attention to the other person to make sure they're OK. But if the person's not being aggressive you can take it up to them and say, "What're you doing?" You know, what is this? And my daughter said to me, when [women her age] get the sleazy comments. They always put their hands out, there is never a kiss in this sort of professional situation . . . they always put their hands out. And sometimes that surprises the senior people in their position, they are like, "Oh! A woman wants to shake my hand." Um, and then they say, they give it straight back [after a harassing comment] without edge. They say, "What did you say?" You know if you can do it without heat, then you're not hooked. Because often . . . what the person's looking for is a reaction.

It can be hard not to be reactive.

Especially if you feel like, how come I have been singled out? I want to be treated like an equal too, you know?

Of course, I understand.

So . . . my own experience suggests that if it's unwelcomed it generally is about the power play. When you know you've been diminished? And there are plenty of instances when you know they've been flirtatious, and you can just send the signal you aren't interested and that doesn't seem to worry me so much. I have heard numerous examples of young women who have been in much more frightening situations, and I believe there is a continuum of behavior, so that if you get away with this sort of comment and no one brings it up then [you think] it's OK to put your hands somewhere else, or to . . . put your hand on someone where they can't get away, like under a table with other people around. Or to push someone up against a wall or close the door on them, you know those sorts of things, I do think it's a continuum, when you don't get called out on the other stuff.

I agree. That's why I think what you're saying in your experience, . . . you had the strength to be able to confront these people who are in power situations.

And I think that's because I've been immersed in it, as a person who you can come and talk to about their situation. So, I do feel that responsibility to actually be the one who calls it out. Even though you know there's a risk you'll be ostracized, being the complainer.

You haven't been ostracized?

No, not for those two events. But of recent times, I have experienced . . . being run down by men who tell me directly, "That's not our way of doing things, we circle the wagons, we have the quiet word with the fellow, we tell him that the behavior is unacceptable, and if he does it again this will be the consequence. That's how we deal with things because we're . . . "gentlemen colleagues," whatever, who don't want to ruin these guys' lives. And they do see what I've done in being very proactive on behalf of women's equality and advancement as somehow disadvantaging men, and somehow . . .you know there's been personal attacks as well about [how] "you can't be any good because you've had to raise these things on behalf of other women." Oh yeah, well look that's the general conversation, because all the men find it very confronting and see that something that is naturally theirs is under attack or taken away when one group are the focus of advancement or promotion or whatever. You know, the idea that we've all been appointed on the basis of merit, historically somehow that's changing because women are now the subject of quotas or targets or some sort of campaigns to be promoted. So there's always a pushback . . .my girlfriends who've done it in other states and territories also have been on the end of a pushback, you know, "she can't be any good because she's [a] campaigning women." And you can't do that if you're no good. Young women who say they are afraid to do that because they don't want to be considered that way. They'd rather be seen as the superstar on their own merit. So we, you know, we're still grappling with this stuff, and heaven help if you have an intersectionality like you are a woman of color or you –. . . have a non-binary sexuality or something like that. It's very difficult.

The realization is that this is not just your little circle of people, that this is prevalent, and what drives me is I want where I work to be fair and just and reward enthusiasm and dedication, and it's not. It still has this imbalance in the power structures. And then, and then you look, and you go, "But I want the world to be like that" and women are not treated like that, so what do we do to fix it?

Right, it's kind of amazing as we sit here in 2020 and we're still grappling with issues and they're so very alive.

Did Kieran [Pender] tell you about the wet T-shirt competition? For the new associates?

[Although this occurred in 1983, this event demonstrates the historical nature of sexual harassment within the workplace. Due to protests from within the organization the event became a swimsuit contest which is not much better. The swimsuit contest went forward, and the winner was offered a position with the firm. One partner commented "she has a body we'd like to see more of." Other partners described the event as characteristic of the good fun that the company liked to have. This "good fun," is ultimately a blatant example of inappropriate and unacceptable behavior.] Where was this?

At a global law firm. So, this is one of the things in the international bio assessment report, one of the little stories or vignettes. A global law firm required the new applicants for the associate positions to have a wet T-shirt competition.

This is unbelievable, Fiona. How could they even think that this was remotely appropriate?

Because they knew the applicants have no power, and if they say no they just aren't on the list and they never expected it to come out.

Just unbelievable, it is actually startling.

Yes, I know!

[It's]almost unfathomable that people go forward and have these behaviors or try to get, you know, these younger women to participate in these kinds of events and think there isn't going to be any kind of . . . response. I'm glad you shared that.

**<u>Champion of Disclosure: "Lydia"</u>**

We have also been fortunate to have a student who was willing to write her story, which has been anonymized. "Lydia," whose name has been changed, is a law student in the United States. Her story is shared below:

Before law school, being sexually assaulted was compartmentalized into a box and placed in the back of my mind and only thought about on rare occasions. The assaults occurred throughout my childhood and during my first year of law school. Sexual assault and understanding what has happened to you is hard enough to process on its own, but law school confronts you with how society manages it, and how your peers view it daily.

In my second year of law school, I was studying for my final exam for professional responsibility. I sat down and made a chart of every example given in our book. My study group ran through each set of facts and arguments on each side. This was the easiest class in law school, but every time I felt exhausted and like I wanted to curl up in my bed and not get up for another week. As I flipped through my outline, I noticed that more than half of the cases we reviewed had gruesome facts of sexual assault: sexual assault by attorneys, sexual violence in the cases being argued, or inappropriate sexual behavior by judges. Being sexually assaulted multiple times, I understand the prevalence, and I understand the importance of discussing it, but these examples seemed unnecessarily cumulative.

The next term, I walked into evidence, and the person who raped me sat to my right. As soon as class ended, I bolted from the room feeling as if I were going to vomit. That feeling returned every night as I read other violent stories. I asked to take the class in a remote learning room. But even as I sat in that room alone, I wanted to cry. Sexual assault was brought up in every single class and nearly every reading. Every day I felt exhausted and like I just couldn't work anymore. Instead of doing my readings, I would skip dinner and lie in bed. It began to feel like I was reliving my past violence.

Sexual assault examples are used in every kind of class I have taken. Classmates are quick to raise their hands and state their opinions as facts, leaving those of us who have experienced the violence in real life feeling inadequate, vulnerable, and angry. The examples are simply not necessary. We can learn about confidentiality between a client and a lawyer without discussing a brutal rape case; we can learn about torts without discussing child molestation; we can learn about contracts without examples of degrading women; we can learn about relevance of evidence without discussing the entire background of a reoffender; we can even learn about sex discrimination without going into explicit details of teenagers being assaulted by their manager. But law school confronts you with them with such frequency it suggests that this is all your career will be.

The facts of these cases aren't something you can forget. You study the facts, take detailed notes, discuss them at length, and review them for exams. You don't get to close the book and walk away. Instead, they stay in your mind as you cook dinner, fall asleep, and go for a run. You think of all the ways the law failed these victims, and in turn how the laws have failed you. You are constantly reminded how women are devalued as you sit in a classroom with men who don't believe that, waiting in line to enter a career that is dominated by the class committing the violence.

The cases are no longer study material but become personal stories. The learning environment becomes an open court of judgment. And you go home, not feeling productive, but feeling like you have been in a fight all day and question if you can do it again. The box that was so neatly compartmentalized has been torn open and reminds you that you are just an untold case of facts for people to judge."

This is a sad and terrifying story. "Lydia" continues to attend law school and deal with all of its many pressures. Her story is hardly unique; she does not feel safe to disclose to the institution what has happened to her to get help. Not only is there the recurring issue of stigma, but what happens if no one believes her or no one does anything to help her?

### Section 2.12: What Can We Do About Sexual Harassment?

Some additional solutions:

- Provide continuing education on harassment globally.
- Provide real help for those who have been harassed in the form of counseling support, legal support, and institutional responses.
- Ensure that laws regarding sexual harassment are strengthened, expanded, and implemented in all countries.

### Section 2.13: What to do if you are being sexually harassed:

In his article "If You've Been Sexually Harassed, What's Next?" Robert Weiss recommends the following:

If you feel comfortable tell the person who is harassing you to stop. Follow the employee handbook or speak with someone from human resources on the anti-harassment policy, speak with a supervisor to help stop the behavior, decide if you want to file a complaint, know your rights about working in an environment that is safe and free of harassment as well as retaliation.[131]

The following is a list of agencies that help individuals who have experienced sexual harassment:

- United States: United States Equal Employment Opportunity Commission
- United Kingdom: Equality and Human Rights Commission, Citizens Advice Bureau
- Canada: Canadian Resource Centre for Victims
- Australia: Australian Human Rights Commission
- New Zealand: New Zealand Human Rights Commission

---

[131] Weiss, Robert. "If You've Been Sexually Harassed, What's Next?" *Psychology Today*, December 11, 2017. https://www.psychologytoday.com/us/blog/love-and-sex-in-the-digital-age/201712/if-you-ve-been-sexually-harassed-what-s-next.

I have created some easy additional tools in the form of mnemonics which can be displayed and acted on throughout the office environment to better help individuals who are being harassed. Please find the tools or mnemonics below.

# POWERFUL

**P**-protest out loud! Get the perpetrator's attention and everyone else in the room. (If you are reluctant to confront the perpetrator then seek the attention of someone whom you trust.)
**O**-orientate others to you- seek their support and help.
**W**-words are powerful use them. "Sexual harassment is not tolerable- stop."
**E**-expect a reaction- be prepared for denial, minimizing and/or out-right anger.
**R**-respect yourself and reinforce your own personal courage and integrity.
**F**-feel your feelings and share them with colleagues, your health group, and identified authorities who handle these issues within your institution or firm.
**U**-understand it is not about you, it is about power.
**L**-listen to those who are supportive and love yourself.

## Section 2.14: What bystanders can do

If you witness sexual harassment, do not look away or walk away or pretend that you do not see it. Go to the aid of the person being harassed. Stand next to the person so that they know that they are not alone and the person who is doing the harassing knows that he or she is being observed.

Work and school environments should be safe places and free of harassment of any sort. However, as we have seen by the studies and the shared stories, sexual harassment occurs frequently.

Another tool/ mnemonic which can be used by bystanders is REACH. This tool like the tool, POWERFUL can also be displayed around the office for ease of memory and use.

# REACH

**R**-react, be there in person, on the scene.
**E**-estimate the need for help using the IMPACT and CARE Tools.
**A**-act on your findings.
**C**-communicate immediately what you have witnessed to identified authorities and consider taking it outside of the institution or firm.
**H**-honor your efforts-you are part of movement against harassment and violence!

## Section 2.15: What Groups Can Do

Create a health group. On a regular basis provide continuing education and a forum for discussion on these issues. Bring in speakers to talk about sexual harassment. Check the group's willingness to share by creating a yes or no questionnaire that asks critical questions such as "have you experienced or witnessed sexual harassment and how did you react?" Discuss the findings as a group.

Implement REACH – display the mnemonic in places around the office and repeat the survey again, over time.

Make sure that your firm or institution has identified and made it easy to find advocates and/or human resource people who specialize in these issues. Place this information with the REACH information so that it is easily accessible when needed.

Everyone is affected by sexual harassment. In environments where sexual harassment occurs, no one feels safe. Sexual harassment is an overwhelmingly female issue. It is pervasive and cross cultural. The effects of sexual harassment can be long lasting, and often includes psychological and physical distress. We must take action at all levels. And indeed, people are taking action or want to take action all over the world. It is up to us as individuals and collective groups of people, representing the law in particular, to set an example. If you see it, hear it, experience it, do something about it. Do not let this menace continue for another generation.

## Discussion Questions:

- What is bullying, harassment, and incivility?
- How widespread are the issues of bullying, harassment, and incivility within the legal profession?
- What actions can you take if you are bullied or if you see someone being bullied?
- What do you think about the legacy question that Fiona McLeay poses?
- What is sexual harassment? What are some of the behaviors that are examples of sexual harassment? What are the possible effects of sexual harassment?
- What is the difference between sexual harassment and sexual violence?
- What is institutional betrayal? Provide an example of institutional betrayal. What is one possible remedy for institutional betrayal?
- What do the statistics from the United Nations reveal about the state of sexual violence against women?
- What does the data gathered by the International Bar Association tell you about sexual harassment within the legal profession?
- What can you do if you are sexually harassed? What government agency can you go to for assistance?
- What are some of the reasons individuals do not report sexual harassment or sexual violence?
- Why is the gender wage gap an important issue?
- What are the three dimensions of sexual harassment?
- What are the initial findings of the large survey that Attorney Fiona McLeay shared with us?
- What does Professor Catharine MacKinnon say about the demographics of sexual harassment?
- What are some recommendations to help end sexual harassment?
- Where were the highest rates of sexual harassment per location according to the World Health Organization?
- What are Professor Charlotte Proudman's main points?
- What did you learn from Champion of Disclosure Fiona McLeod?
- What is your response to Lydia's Story?

# References

Australian Institute of Health and Welfare 2018. Family, domestic and sexual violence in Australia 2018. Cat. no. FDV 2. Canberra: AIHW © Australian Institute of Health and Welfare 2018 under Creative Commons BY 3.0 (CC BY 3.0) license.

Baron, Paula, and Lillian Corbin. 2015. "Robust communications or incivility – where do we draw the line?" *Legal Ethics* 18 (1): 123).

Bowcott, Owen. 2019. "Bullying and Sexual Harassment Rife among Lawyers, Global Survey Finds." *The Guardian*, May 14, 2019. https://www.theguardian.com/law/2019/may/15/bullying-and-sexual-harassment-rife-among-lawyers-global-survey-finds.

Burn, Shawn M. 2017. "What Do Psychologists Say About Sexual Harassment?" *Psychology Today*, Apr 29, 2017. https://www.psychologytoday.com/us/blog/presence-mind/201704/what-do-psychologists-say-about-sexual-harassment.

Catalyst. 2018. "Women in Law: Quick Take." Catalyst, October 2, 2018. https://www.catalyst.org/research/women-in-law/.

Cotter, Adam and Laura Savage. "Gender-based violence and unwanted sexual behaviour in Canada, 2018: Initial findings from the Survey of Safety in Public and Private Spaces." Government of Canada, Statistics Canada, December 5, 2019. © Her Majesty the Queen in Right of Canada as represented by the Minister of Industry, 2018

Daicoff, Susan Swaim. 2014. Lawyer Know Thyself: A Psychological Analysis of Personality Strengths and Weaknesses. American Psychological Association.

Dinovitzer, Ronit. 2015. *Law and Beyond: A National Study of Canadian Law Graduates*. May 27, 2015. http://dx.doi.org/10.2139/ssrn.2615062.

Freyd, J.J. (2020). Institutional Betrayal & Institutional Courage Retrieved [2/21/2020] from https://dynamic.uoregon.edu/jjf/institutionalbetrayal/

Gautier, Chantal. 2018. "Are You a Bully? Here's How to Tell." *The Conversation*, November 1, 2018. This article is republished from https://theconversation.com The Conversation under a Creative Commons license

Gordon, Sherri. "How Workplace Bullying Negatively Affects the Victim and Profits." Verywell Mind. Verywell Mind, March 10, 2020. https://www.verywellmind.com/what-are-the-effects-of-workplace-bullying-460628.

Hango, Darcy, and Melissa Moyser. "Harassment in Canadian Workplaces." Government of Canada, Statistics Canada, December 17, 2018. https://www150.statcan.gc.ca/n1/pub/75-006-x/2018001/article/54982-eng.htm. © Her Majesty the Queen in Right of Canada as represented by the Minister of Industry, 2018

Kelk, NJ, Luscombe, GM, Medlow, S, Hickie, IB (2009) Courting the blues: Attitudes towards depression in Australian law students and lawyers, BMRI Monograph 2009-1, Sydney: Brain & Mind Research Institute

Krug, Etienne G., Linda L. Dahlberg, James A. Mercy, Anthony B. Zwi, and Rafael Lozano, ed. 2002. *World report on violence and health*. Geneva, World Health Organization.

Larkins, Christopher M. 'Judicial Independence and Democratization: A Theoretical and Conceptual Analysis" (1996) 44 *American Journal of Comparative Law* 605 at 609).

McLeod, Fiona. 2019. "#Metoo—All Sound and Fury or Signifying Something?" Griffith University: Michael Whincop Memorial Lecture. August 2019. https://www.youtube.com/watch?v=4VMQ5c2RH8w&feature=emb_title.

Monahan, Alison. 2019. "Understanding the Gender Wage Gap in the Legal Profession." The Balance Careers, updated May 5, 2019. https://www.thebalancecareers.com/understanding-the-gender-wage-gap-in-the-legal-profession-4000621.

New Zealand Ministry of Justice. n.d. "Sexual Violence." Accessed December 18 2019. https://www.justice.govt.nz/justice-sector-policy/research-data/nzcass/survey-results/results-by-subject/sexual-violence/. Published by the Ministry of Justice © Crown Copyright Licensed from the Ministry of Justice for use under the creative commons attribution licence (BY) 4.0.

Office for National Statistics. 2017. "Crime in England and Wales: year ending March 2017." https://www.ons.gov.uk/releases/crimeinenglandandwalesyearendingmarch2017 Contains public sector information licensed under the Open Government Licence v3.0.

Office for National Statistics. 2019. "Crime in England and Wales: year ending December 2018." Office for National Statistics, April 25, 2019. https://www.ons.gov.uk/peoplepopulationandcommunity/crimeandjustice/bulletins/crimeinenglandandwales/yearendingdecember2018 Contains public sector information licensed under the Open Government Licence v3.0.

Omari, Maryam, and Megan Paull. 2013. "'Shut up and bill': Workplace bullying challenges for the legal profession." *International Journal of the Legal Profession* 20, issue 2 (2):141–160. https://doi.org/10.1080/09695958.2013.874350.

Pender, Kieran. 2019. Us Too? Bullying and Sexual Harassment in the Legal Profession. International Bar Association.

Rape Crisis England & Wales. n.d. "About sexual violence." Rape Crisis England & Wales. Accessed December 18, 2019. https://rapecrisis.org.uk/get-informed/about-sexual-violence/statistics-sexual-violence/.

RAINN. n.d. "Sexual Harassment." Accessed December 17, 2019. https://www.rainn.org/articles/sexual-harassment.

Ryan, Holly. "Law Profession Has Widest Gender Pay Gap: YUDU Survey." NZ Herald. NZ Herald, July 2, 2018. https://www.nzherald.co.nz/business/news/article.cfm?c_id=3&objectid=12081261.

Sexual Abuse Prevention Network n.d. "Statistics." Accessed December 17, 2019. http://sexualabuseprevention.org.nz/who-we-are/statistics/.

Sharpe, Michelle. "The Importance of Civility" *Law Institute Journal* Vol 93 No. 6, June 2019, pages 29-33

Siegel, Reva. 2003. *Introduction: A Short History of Sexual Harassment*. Directions in Sexual Harassment Law. New Haven: Yale: 1-39. 10.12987/yale/9780300098006.003.0001.

United Nations Population Fund. 2019. "Protection from Sexual Exploitation, Sexual Abuse and Sexual Harassment." December 20, 2019. https://www.unfpa.org/protection-sexual-exploitation-sexual-abuse-and-sexual-harassment.

Vartia, M. 1996. "The sources of bullying – psychological work environment and organizational climate." *European Journal of Work and Organizational Psychology* 5(2): 203.

Weiss, Robert. "If You've Been Sexually Harassed, What's Next?" *Psychology Today*, December 11, 2017. https://www.psychologytoday.com/us/blog/love-and-sex-in-the-digital-age/201712/if-you-ve-been-sexually-harassed-what-s-next.

"Why Does the Gender Wage Gap Persist in Law?" Legal Mosaic, March 27, 2019. https://www.legalmosaic.com/why-does-the-gender-wage-gap-persist-in-law/.

Willer, James. "The UK Gender Pay Gap 2018: What Do The Numbers Actually Tell Us?" Law.com, May 1, 2019. https://www.law.com/2019/05/01/the-uk-gender-pay-gap-2018-what-do-the-numbers-actually-tell-us/?slreturn=20191117132609.

World Health Organization and Pan American Health Organization. 2012."Understanding and addressing violence against women: intimate partner violence." World Health Organization. https://apps.who.int/iris/bitstream/handle/10665/77434/WHO_RHR_12.37_eng.pdf?sequence=1

# Chapter 4 Abstract: **The Commonality of Stigma**

In this chapter we will be exploring the nature and consequences of stigma. We will learn how stigma is pervasive in cultural attitudes towards mental health. We will learn about the commonality of stigma and how stigma impedes the ability to get help. We will explore four types of stigma; social stigma, self-stigma, structural stigma, and stigma created by mass media. We will be exposed to various studies on stigma and mental health. We will learn the role of stereotyping and its impact. We learn of extraordinary historical and present-day individuals who have coped with mental health issues and alcohol and other drug issues and live or have lived brilliant, productive lives. We will learn about recommendations and strategies for eradicating stigma. Finally, we will meet our Champions of Disclosure, who share their own stories of overcoming stigma.

# Chapter 4: The Commonality of Stigma

"This stigma is the most significant hindrance to thinking about and actually addressing the problem of mental health and wellbeing in the profession."[132]

—Angus Lyon

## Section 1: What is Stigma?

"Stigma and discrimination against patients and families prevent people from seeking mental health care. Misunderstanding and stigma surrounding mental ill health are widespread. Despite the existence of effective treatments for mental disorders, there is a belief that they are untreatable or that people with mental disorders are difficult, not intelligent, or incapable of making decisions. This stigma can lead to abuse, rejection and isolation and exclude people from health care or support. Within the health system, people are too often treated in institutions which resemble human warehouses rather than places of healing."[133]

Stigma is a discrediting and shaming behavior that causes great pain for those individuals and groups who suffer from it. It is a belief or story that is not founded in reality or fact and has negative consequences for the individuals or groups for which it is promulgated.

"Stigma can be defined as a mark of shame, disgrace or disapproval which results in an individual being rejected, discriminated against, and excluded from participating in a number of different areas of society."[134]

Groups and individuals have been fighting against mental health stigma for decades. In 2013, The World Health Organization European Mental Health Action Plan recognized the challenges that stigma and discrimination pose to people with mental health problems. "Many people with mental health problems choose not to engage or maintain contact with mental health services, due to stigma and discrimination."[135]

---

[132] Lyon, Angus. 2015. *A Lawyer's Guide to Wellbeing and Managing Stress.* London: Ark Group.

[133] World Health Organization. n.d. "10 Facts on Mental Health." World Health Organization.

Accessed March 5, 2020. https://www.who.int/features/factfiles/mental_health/mental_health_facts/en/index5.html

[134] World Health Organization. 2007. "Chapter 1: A Public Health Approach to Mental Health." World Health Organization. World Health Organization, June 13, 2007. https://www.who.int/whr/2001/chapter1/en/index3.html.

[135] World Health Organization. n.d. "Stigma and Discrimination." World Health Organization. Accessed March 5, 2020. http://www.euro.who.int/en/health-topics/noncommunicable-diseases/mental-health/priority-areas/stigma-and-discrimination.

More individuals and groups continue to actively open up the conversation about stigma among legal professionals and students. Professor Richard Collier of the United Kingdom also addresses the issue of stigma as an issue of concern. Professor Richard Collier speaks to one of the critical issues facing legal professionals as the "pervasive cultural stigma around disclosing mental health problems as a key issue and the widespread concerns about poor work-life balance in law."[136]

From the student realm, research from the report *Under the Radar, the Mental Health of Australian University Students* examined mental health among the roughly 1.4 million students in Australia in 2015. Roughly one in four students experienced some sort of mental illness in a year. The research suggested that the reason students do not disclose or seek support for mental health issues was due to stigma and the lack of understanding among academic or administrative staff about these conditions.[137]

## Section 2: Types of Stigma

### Social stigma

Social stigma is what most people think of when they think of stigma. "Social stigma is the disapproval of, or discrimination against, a person based on perceivable social characteristics that serve to distinguish them from other members of a society. Social stigmas are commonly related to culture, gender, race, intelligence and health."[138] One example is someone disclosing he has a mental illness. In response, others question his ability to do his job or parent effectively due strictly to the issue of the mental illness without any viable examples of failure in the workforce or failure in parenting.

"Stigma is a major cause of discrimination and exclusion: it affects people's self-esteem, helps disrupt their family relationships and limits their ability to socialize and obtain housing and jobs. It hampers the prevention of mental health disorders, the promotion of mental well-being and the provision of effective treatment and care. It also contributes to the abuse of human rights."[139]

In a conversation with Professor G. Andrew H. Benjamin, he noted that "more than 40 [U.S.] states continue to discriminate against [law] students who obtain mental health or alcohol/drug treatment services by forcing applicants to the bar exams to disclose their treatment. This has a chilling impact on

---

[136] Collier, Richard. 2019. "Anxiety and Wellbeing Amongst Junior Lawyers: A Research Study" Anxiety UK, March 2019. https://www.anxietyuk.org.uk/wp-content/uploads/2019/05/Collier-Anxiety-UK-Final-Report-March-2019.pdf

[137] Orygen. 2017. *Under the radar: The mental health of Australian university students.* Melbourne: Orygen, The National Centre of Excellence in Youth Mental Health.

[138] Haddad, Peter, and Isabelle Haddad. 2015. "Mental Health Stigma." *British Association for Psychopharmacology*, March 3, 2015. https://www.bap.org.uk/articles/mental-health-stigma/.

[139] World Health Organization. n.d. "Stigma and Discrimination." World Health Organization. Accessed March 5, 2020. http://www.euro.who.int/en/health-topics/noncommunicable-diseases/mental-health/priority-areas/stigma-and-discrimination.

---

students obtaining services when symptoms first emerge in law schools. We changed the law and bar application questions in Washington State."

## Self-Stigma

Self-stigmatization has been defined as "the process in which a person with a mental health diagnosis becomes aware of public stigma, agrees with those stereotypes, and internalizes them by applying them to the self."[140]

For some people, once they have a condition or a diagnosis such as depression or anxiety, regardless of the prevalence cross-culturally, they may self-label and limit themselves. Instead of being a whole person who has a condition, they *become* the condition and believe cultural stereotypes about the condition and thus about themselves.

With self-stigma, the use of language has a profound effect on how we perceive ourselves. For example, a man with mental issues might readily hear the phrase, "He is bipolar," Thus, he becomes bipolar instead of a son, father, friend, colleague, attorney, student, community member, musician, etc. The diagnosis seems to define the person. We must be careful with painting ourselves and others with broad brushstrokes. Yes, you or someone you know may have a condition or a diagnosis, but it certainly does not define you or them or begin to describe you or them as human beings.

In a wonderfully written article by Patrick W. Corrigan and Amy C. Watson, "The Paradox of Self-Stigma and Mental Illness, the authors argue that that public stigma fuels discrimination and misunderstanding about mental illness and ultimately impacts the individuals with mental illness in all areas of their lives including employment, housing, and other opportunities. When stigma is inherent within a culture, individuals tend to accept the stigma without challenging it."[141]

As a result, they argue that these persons lose their self-esteem and self-efficacy. Corrigan quotes Kathleen Gallo on this kind of self-stigma:

"I perceived myself, quite accurately unfortunately, as having a serious mental illness and therefore as having been relegated to what I called 'the social garbage heap.' I tortured myself with the persistent and repetitive thought that people I would encounter, even total strangers, did not like me and wished that mentally ill people like me did not exist. Thus, I would do things such as standing away from others at bus stops and hiding and cringing in the far corners of subway cars. Thinking of myself as garbage, I would even leave the sidewalk in what I thought of as exhibiting the proper deference to those above me in social class. The latter group, of course, included all other human beings."[142]

---

[140] Corrigan, Patrick, Jonathon Larson, and Kuwabara. 2010. *Social psychology of stigma for mental illness: Public stigma and self-stigma.*

[141] Corrigan, Patrick W., and Amy C. Watson. 2006. "The Paradox of Self-Stigma and Mental Illness." *Clinical Psychology: Science and Practice*9:35–53. 10.1093/clipsy.9.1.35.

[142] Corrigan, Patrick, Jonathon Larson, and Kuwabara. 2010. *Social psychology of stigma for mental illness: Public stigma and self-stigma.*

In *Social Psychology of Stigma for Mental Illness*, Corrigan et al. created a stage model of self-stigma: "A person with an undesired condition is aware of public stigma about their condition (Awareness). This person may then agree that these negative public stereotypes are true about the group (Agreement). Subsequently, the person concurs that these stereotypes apply to him/herself (Application). This may lead to harm, to significant decreases in self-esteem and self-efficacy."[143]

## Structural Stigma

Structural stigma comprises the "societal-level conditions, cultural norms, and institutional practices that constrain the opportunities, resources, and wellbeing for stigmatized populations."[144]

Individuals operating within these systems may not be aware of the structural stigma. "Structural stigma can be intentional or unintentional. Intentional structural stigma requires conscious and purposeful effort to restrict the rights and opportunities of people with mental illnesses. This can be overt, such as policies that disqualify people from health insurance coverage because of having a mental illness. Alternatively, it can be covert, in which case institutions deliberately use a criterion that is strongly correlated with mental illness (i.e., a proxy) to deny equal opportunities to people with mental illnesses. An example of this would be organizations who deny jobs or volunteer opportunities to individuals who have a police record, knowing that the practice causes unequal harm for people with mental illnesses who routinely use the police to access emergency mental health services. Covert structural stigma might also take the form of institutional leaders who fail to mitigate known inequities and injustices. An example would be police officials who continue to support the disclosure of mental health-related information (e.g., mental health apprehensions, suicide attempts) on routine police or criminal record checks after becoming aware that such a practice arbitrarily limits the life opportunities of people with mental illnesses, such as obstructing volunteer and employment opportunities. Unintentional structural stigma produces inequities for people with mental illnesses through inadvertent means. Usually, this occurs because of people with mental illnesses being disproportionately represented in certain groups find themselves the subject of a given social policy. For instance, 'tough on crime reforms' that impose harsher sentences for less serious offences (e.g., drug offences) will have disproportionate effects on people with mental illnesses because of the prevalence of concurrent mental health and substance use problems."[145]

## Stigma Created by the Mass Media

According to the World Health Organization, it is apparent there exists strong negative views about people with mental health problems and an overriding gross representation that these individuals represent a danger to the community. This view is strongly reinforced by the media.

---

[143] Corrigan, Patrick, Jonathon Larson, and Kuwabara. 2010. *Social psychology of stigma for mental illness: Public stigma and self-stigma.*
[144] National Academies of Sciences, Engineering, and Medicine. 2016. Ending Discrimination Against People with Mental and Substance Use Disorders: The Evidence for Stigma Change. Washington, D.C: The National Academies Press. https://doi.org/10.17226/23442.

[145] Livingston, J. D. 2013. *Mental illness-related structural stigma: The downward spiral of systemic exclusion.* Calgary, Alberta: Mental Health Commission of Canada. https://www.mentalhealthcommission.ca/sites/default/files/MHCC_OpeningMinds_MentalIllness-RelatedSructuralStigmaReport_ENG_0_0.pdf.

According to Harnois, violence due to mental illness does exist however, it is very low when compared to other forms of violence. The media frequently portray individuals with mental illness in a negative light. Almost half of health journalists have serious misconceptions concerning mental illness. As a result, it is recommended that a code of ethics should strictly be adhered to to prevent the frequent "sensationalism" of "alleged" mental health issues among individuals.[146]

According to Overton and Medina, the stereotypes associated with mental illness may be more harmful than the mental illness. Overton and Medina point out that during the Middle Ages, people were jailed or put to death for mental illness. Individuals with mental illness were considered to be the "living examples of the weakness of humankind."[147] I wonder sometimes how far we have really moved from these notions.

## Section 3: Addiction Stigma

People with addictions are generally stigmatized in an even more negative light than people with mental health issues. According to the Hazelden Betty Ford Foundation (n.d), "Drug and alcohol addiction is too often seen as a moral issue or a criminal matter rather than a health problem. Many public policies and practices related to housing, education, jobs, voting rights and insurance discriminate against individuals who have addiction, even after they've established long-term recovery. And despite advances in understanding addiction as a disease, substance use disorder remains largely marginalized by the mainstream medical field, starting with a lack of robust education on the topic in medical school."[148] As we all know, stereotyping about addiction is an ongoing issue. If legal professionals or students reveal they are struggling, there is a fear, they will not be accepted or respected within the profession.

There are many reasons for the lack of treatment, and stigma continues to be one of the pervasive issues. As we have seen, stigma can affect everyone: individuals, children, and families.

It is sad that not only do we stigmatize in general, we also have degrees of stigmatization. For example, a study by Johns Hopkins Bloomberg School of Public Health, demonstrated the general public was more likely to have negative attitudes toward those dealing with drug addiction than those who were dealing with mental illness. Additionally, researchers found that people don't generally support insurance, housing, and employment policies that benefited people who were dependent on drugs.[149]

---

[146] Harnois, Gaston, Gabriel, Phyllis, World Health Organization & International Labour Organisation. (2000). Mental health and work. impact, issues and good practices. World Health Organization. https://apps.who.int/iris/handle/10665/42346.

[147] Overton, Stacy L., and Sondra L. Medina. "The Stigma of Mental Illness." *Journal of Counseling & Development* 86, no. 2 (2008): 143–51. https://doi.org/10.1002/j.1556-6678.2008.tb00491.x.

[148] Hazelden Betty Ford Foundation. n.d. "Smashing the Stigma of Addiction." Accessed December 18, 2019. https://www.hazeldenbettyford.org/recovery-advocacy/stigma-of-addiction.

[149] Desmon, Stephanie, and Susan Morrow. 2014. "Drug Addiction Viewed More Negatively than Mental Illness, Johns Hopkins Study Shows." The Hub, October 1, 2014. https://hub.jhu.edu/2014/10/01/drug-addiction-stigma/.

Due to the stereotypes surrounding drug and alcohol addiction specifically, individuals may find it difficult if not impossible to identify alcohol or other drug issues. Many of these alcohol and other drug issues may stem from an underlying mental health condition such as depression or anxiety. Some stereotypes regarding addictions include the idea that individuals with these issues lack credibility and cannot accurately assess situations. Worldwide, due to all of these stereotypes and stigma, only 2 in 5 people who experience a mood, anxiety, or substance abuse disorder seek assistance within the first year of the disorder.[150]

Of course, the legal profession has its own stereotypes and stigmas. For instance, one is that legal professionals are superhuman and therefore either don't experience or "can handle" mental health and alcohol and other drug issues. Let us take a look throughout history. Many of the individuals who were leaders in their professions and areas of expertise have experienced many kinds of mental health issues and alcohol and other drug issues. For example, we can think of Vincent Van Gogh, who cut his own ear off. But people have dismissed this saying that "he is an artist and artists do all kinds of odd things." This is another stereotype. Other historical figures who have struggled with mental illnesses, specifically depression include Abraham Lincoln, Edgar Allen Poe, William James, Sigmund Freud, Georgia O'Keefe, Charles Dickens, Winston Churchill, Virginia Woolf, Ernest Hemmingway, Martin Luther King Jr., and many more.

There are multiple groups that are trying to reduce or end stigma around the world. For instance, Australia's Globe University has created a program highlighting the discrimination specific to alcohol and drug use, "Reducing stigma and discrimination for people experiencing problematic alcohol and other drug use." The monograph contains 34 recommendations, which could be a powerful springboard for moving this issue forward in other regions including training everyone on anti-stigma awareness and methods and overall investing in alcohol and other drug abuse services.[151]

## Section 3.1: Prevalence of Addiction Stigma by Country

### United States

We live in a society where millions are dependent on drugs and/or alcohol; yet only a small percentage receive treatment at a facility. A 2014 national survey on drug use and health found that 21.5 million Americans age 12 and older had a substance use disorder in the previous year; however, only 2.5 million received the specialized treatment they needed.[152]

---

[150] World Health Organization. 2013. "Gender and Women's Mental Health." World Health Organization, June 24, 2013. https://www.who.int/mental_health/prevention/genderwomen/en/.

[151] Lancaster, Kari, Kate Seear, and Alison Ritter. 2018. Monograph No. 26: "Reducing stigma and discrimination for people experiencing problematic alcohol and other drug use." DPMP Monograph Series. Sydney: National Drug and Alcohol Research Centre. http://doi.org/10.26190/5b8746fe72507.

[152] Center for Behavioral Health Statistics and Quality. 2015. Behavioral health trends in the United States: Results from the 2014 National Survey on Drug Use and Health (HHS Publication No. SMA 15-4927, NSDUH Series H-50). Retrieved from http://www.samhsa.gov/data/.

## United Kingdom

In the United Kingdom, of the estimated 595,131 people suffering from alcoholism and less than one-fifth receive help.[153]

## Australia

The statistics that follow will demonstrate the wide gulf between those that need treatment and those who actually obtain treatment. According to a study by the Australian Institute of Health and Welfare, 952 publicly funded alcohol and other drug treatment services in the country treated an estimated 130,000 clients in 2017–18.[154]

## Canada

It is estimated that approximately one in five Canadians aged 15 years and older experiences a substance use disorder. Studies show that only 15% of Canadian respondents with a substance use disorder reported that all of their perceived health care needs were met.[155]

## New Zealand

According to New Zealand Drug Foundation, one in three New Zealanders experience a family member who is struggling with the effects of alcohol or drug use, yet a survey demonstrated that 15% of New Zealanders don't know where to go for help when faced with a family member who has an alcohol or drug problem.[156]

# Section 4: Champions of Disclosure

### *John Broderick Jr.*

The Honorable Judge John Broderick Jr. served as Associate Justice of the Court of New Hampshire from 1995 to 2004 and as its Chief Justice from 2004 to 2010. He served as Dean and President of the University of New Hampshire School of Law until May 2015. Since 2015, Judge Broderick Jr., has been working to end the stigma surrounding mental health in New Hampshire,

---

[153] Smith, Cooper. 2019."Addiction in the UK." Addiction Center, last edited December 5, 2019. https://www.addictioncenter.com/addiction/addiction-in-the-uk/.

[154] Australian Institute of Health and Welfare. 2019. "Alcohol and other drug treatment services in Australia 2017–18." Australian Institute of Health and Welfare, July 25, 2019. https://www.aihw.gov.au/reports-data/health-welfare-services/alcohol-other-drug-treatment-services/reports

[155] Government of Canada. 2018. "Strengthening Canada's Approach to Substance Use Issues." Government of Canada, September 10, 2018. https://www.canada.ca/en/health-canada/services/substance-use/canadian-drugs-substances-strategy/strengthening-canada-approach-substance-use-issue.html.

[156] New Zealand Drug Foundation. 2014. "1/3 Of NZ Families Affected by Alcohol and Drug Problems." February 20, 2014. https://www.drugfoundation.org.nz/news-media-and-events/nz-families-affected-by-alcohol-and-drug-problems/.

Vermont, and elsewhere. He's given more than 160 talks and spoken to more than 20,000 people. Judge Broderick Jr. is asking kids to REACT. (The acronym stands for "Recognize" the signs of emotional suffering, "Express" concern and offer support, "Act now" and tell someone you trust, "Care enough" to follow up, and "Text" or call a number for extra support.) REACT was developed by Dartmouth-Hitchcock Hospital, where Broderick is the Director of Public Affairs, and New Hampshire's Department of Education. It's intended to provide tools that students and non-professionals can use once they recognize someone, they care about may be having a mental illness issue or event.

What I am seeing, Judge Broderick, is stress and secondary trauma occurring and a lot of unhealthy ways of coping. The theme that I am seeing throughout these five countries that I would like to address with you is the role of stigma. Because of the role of stigma, people are reluctant to get help, and some people do not get help because they don't recognize basic signs and symptoms of mental health issues.

I think you are 100% correct on that.

Can you tell me about your background and a bit about your story with the REACT Program?

I was a trial lawyer for 22 years so, I know what stress feels like it. Not that I didn't love it, I loved being a lawyer. When I was chief justice, I started the lawyer assistance program, which was not just volunteer. We had a full-time director, and it was one of the most consequential things I think that I did.

Because I grew up in a world where everyone had perfect mental health and every marriage was happy. I mean I come from that bubble. Everyone was perfect, and when our own family got into trouble, I did not have the wherewithal or knowledge to understand it, and I was probably too proud to reach out, and it took my family to bad places. Thank God we have all come out whole. We really have . . . about three and a half years ago I found Barbara Van Dahlan, of Change Direction; ChangeDirection.Org. She was the genius behind the "five most common signs of mental illness." She launched it in New Hampshire. I knew I was not alone in the valley of mental illness when we launched this nonpartisan non-political change direction campaign, The Five Signs. we launched it in an empty house chamber in our statehouse on a Monday morning, May 23, 2016, and I said, this could fail miserably. It is a Monday; a workday and it is mental health. No one talks about it. We did what we could.

We put it on social media to let people know we were launching it, and 425 people showed up; the Catholic bishop, the Episcopal Church, the Jewish community, three members of the Supreme Court, the chief justice of the Superior Court, the attorney general, hospital CEOs, law enforcement, it was unbelievable. Barbara said to the room, "Is there anyone here this morning who has been untouched by mental health problems, themselves or their family or extended family, friends, or coworkers? If you have been untouched, I would like to raise your hand," and not one hand went up. Everyone had been touched. I said to Barbara, how is that possible. She said, John, it's mental illness, people don't talk about it. They are ashamed of it. What I also learned that day, and now I see it every time I go out: half of mental illness arises by age 14, there have been more suicides than car accident victims last year, we lose a veteran every 90 minutes to suicide, we lost more police officers last year to suicide then homicide. After we launched it our entire congressional [members] and governor came. It was stunning. We didn't know what to do next.

I have spoken over 500 times to over 100,000 people since May, 2016. In my travels I have spoken at over 200 schools to over 80,000 students, grades 7-12. Anxiety and depression are epidemic among young people. I have hugged hundreds and hundreds of kids in high school gyms and they thank me for coming and talking about this. In the last month I have hugged five kids who have tried to kill themselves. Do you know, you are not your mental illness? If you break your ankle you do not become a broken ankle. It is not who you are, it is what you are dealing with. One girl came up to me in the 4th, 5th grade and said, you said it is OK to have a mental health problem. It is not your fault it is not your choice. You are not your mental illness. It is OK to have a mental health problem. It is not your fault. Treatment is possible. The little girl said, I never hear that. I just hear how bad it is.

I know in the world of law; I know the stats are alarming for the legal profession; the striving to always be perfect, to always win. Some of it is the A-type personality. And the competition in the legal profession: some of it is because of technology and the speed of practice because of the internet has sped up dramatically, competition has increased.

I practiced law until 1995 when I went on the Supreme Court and people say, John, you would not recognize the practice today. It has sped up. You had time to reflect. Reflection time is being lost, and when you are a professional that is the realm; thought, thinking, and time, and you're working in a space where thought and thinking [is important] and there really isn't time for that. You are supposed to be a computer. What is the answer? And if you're not doing it, the law firm down the street would get the business. It's a lot more expensive to practice law now, with all of the technology. Even though you are a small firm, you have to have big technology if you want to compete. So, the pressure is on these people. I understand it. I didn't live it, that world. I had pressure when I practiced, but it was mostly self-imposed.

Yes, I see it with my colleagues, and it is concerning because I feel it is becoming a conversation and I am so thrilled to hear what you have to say.

I spoke in the City of Keene at the Keene Chamber of Commerce's Annual Dinner . . [so] I am up there talking about mental illness. When I finished speaking the room stood up and applauded for almost a minute. It was stunning to me. Other people cared too. One woman told me, I have been depressed for years and I never had the courage to tell anyone, and I am thinking oh my God, what are we doing to ourselves? And now all of these months later, it doesn't matter. You could go into a gas station and get everyone's attention or a bowling alley or a university, it doesn't matter. They are either dealing with it or someone they love is dealing with it. I went to a prep school and spoke to 525 kids; I asked if there is anyone in the auditorium who has a mental health problem or someone you love has a mental health problem—500 stood up. Now I think the other maybe, the other twenty-five were too embarrassed. Lawyers are high-achieving people, and they are under a time crunch and achievement expectation that is not reachable for most of them, and then they self-medicate. And because of their profession, because they are supposed to be perfect or above reproach, they are not going to share that.

So that is the issue. How do we get to that, Judge Broderick?

I am going to a law firm for a second time to speak to the lawyers. I thought, well, lawyers are kind of proud and they wouldn't be too interested. I could hear a pin drop! [And] they asked me to come back to speak with the staff.

The way it will change is when we start talking about it in a nonjudgmental, non-stigmatizing way. It will not change until then. Until the risk of disclosing is minimal, people will keep it a secret. They will! And so, a lot of it is, we have told these people it is a weakness, it is a flaw, it is an imperfection, and we put them on the spot. And so, you are trying to be a high achiever, a lawyer, and you reveal you have that problem—oh my God, you are a weak person! That's the problem.

And the perception that weak people are targeted more often.

They are! I had a call from the dean at Northeastern University Law School in Boston. I was dean of the law school at UNH, we did not speak much about [mental illness] then, it was before this campaign, but now I would be talking about it. Today if I was the dean, I would talk to law students openly, candidly about it.

I am trying to create small groups in schools and firms and actively have tools available. I am hoping to encourage better coping and healthier lawyers.

It has to be part of the culture. You can change the culture. I grew up in a world where ashtrays were everywhere. Try to find one today. And you can't find one today. I grew up in a world where if you were black your odds of being president of the United States was zero. And now we have elected an African American president. So, I say to them, things happen, something changed and mental health is the last frontier of medicine. We accept AIDS, we accept everything, and we should. We treat every physical illness with empathy, respect, and understanding. When it comes to mental health, we treat it like witchcraft. Like maybe you're possessed. If you were a better person, a stronger person—well, snap out of it. We say to people and we would say, I met someone today with heart disease. If we met someone with mental health issues, we would likely say, I met someone today who is mentally ill, not who has mental health issues.

Yes, you are right, most people would.

I would never say, I met someone who is cancer. Why do we do it [with mental illness]? We do it because it scares us and we do not know much about it. When I was a kid, [my mother] would whisper about her cancer. She would whisper! I would think, will I catch it? And now I know, there were women in my town who died of breast cancer in their forties. When I was a child, no adult ever said the word, breast. And they whispered the word cancer and now we say, breast cancer and we have a color. The answer to the problem is multifaceted, but my view of the problem is we are not going to fix it overnight. We need to imbue our schools with social and emotional learning so kids can know how to deal with feelings, express feelings and deal with other people's feelings before they even know the language of mental health. We can't pretend, we can't do anything. I would go after law schools and have it be part of every law school curriculum and I would make it part of the known fabric. We need people with authority to say it is not an issue here. The only issue we have is, if you are suffering and you don't get help. That is on you. There is no reason to do that.

Yes, I understand.

That is how it will change. Until it is OK to say, "I think I am depressed," and people won't start walking backwards. That is, if you live in a world where it is stigmatized you sure as hell aren't going to raise your hand and say that is my problem. In a world of professional growth where that is not a plus, so you hide it and often you drink to hide it or take drugs. It is not a mystery to me anymore, I see it now.

I see it cross-culturally. It is common. It is a thread, and the people responding to the survey, it's anonymous, taking sleeping pills and talking about panic attacks and stress and what they are exposed to not only in family law or criminal law but business law, really all of law.

We live in a culture . . . it works both ways. If you are a woman and you express your emotions, it means you are just not really all together. If you are a man and you express, it is a weakness. It is true.

It is still stigmatized.

. . . If you look at New Hampshire youth risk surveys, [from the] New Hampshire Department of Education, the future lawyers and doctors of America, [with a] 86% response rate . . . 20.7% of 7th and 8th grade girls said in this survey that they have suicidal thoughts. So, let's not talk about that. Let them suffer and then they will tell their parents. One girl said to me, I think I have depression, and that is good. You know that I didn't see it in my own son and the important thing is, you get help. I said why don't you start by talking to your parents. She said, I talked to my dad and he just laughs at me. That is the problem, you can have a broken leg, you can have AIDS, but you can't have depression. It is just you that is the problem. We need to start talking about it, not in the language of mental illness but we need to talk about social emotional learning, adversity resiliency, dealing with adversity, feelings. Men have to grow up knowing they can cry. When you bury stuff, you bury a lot, and it comes out. ACEs, Adverse Childhood Experiences, trauma plays a big role in it. You can read literature about it through ABA. Talking about it and doing something are two different things. Every law firm in American is dealing with it, there must be law firms dealing with it in a little bit of a shroud. If we have to do it, we will, but we are not proud that we are doing this. When that changes it will be better.

I agree. I hope the ideas and tools in the book can be used in the very beginning in the law schools and law firms.

Well, that is how it needs to move, from the law schools into the law firms. Last year the attorney general in Vermont asked me, the governor, [now-]Senator Hassen to come to the schools. It is not about politics. It is about mental health. It is neutral ground, and in America these days it is impossible to find! This is about awareness. They asked me to come to the office retreat in Vermont, so

I could give my talk on mental illness, and a senior lawyer stopped me and said, "I have had mental illness for years, I get help, but I don't talk about it much. But I am doing so much better now." And he was talking about it like if this gets out anywhere, my life is over, and he was obviously very successful. When I meet people like that, I think you must be incredible! It is hard [enough] to be successful when you feel great. It is like being a marathoner with a bad foot. But they will do it! Every law school has orientation and every law school dean in America . . . should say, we care about you. We care about your physical health and we care about your mental health too. And this is a no-shame school you just entered. No shame here. We are going to change it; we are going to change it, here. Don't worry about it. If you are not feeling well. You can see someone here.

That is so powerful.

That is how it will change. We need a new conversation in all levels of society and in the profession of law, especially.

Yes, there are just too many people suffering, and they are suffering silently.

I will tell you who is suffering too, the people who love them are suffering too. Every time you help someone with a mental health problem it multiplies to helping all the people who love them. And if someone you love is not doing well, you are not doing well. So, multiply those lawyers by their families or spouse or boyfriends, girlfriends are all impacted. It affects a lot of people who themselves are not affected, but they are impacted.

One of the things that I saw was the impact. They were recognizing [the role of] photographs, evidence, or narratives from clients causing what looked like secondary trauma. Do you see that also as a factor in the whole mental health issue?

Absolutely, just in the world of first responders, people don't see what they want to see, they don't have to walk over and look in. Just in the world of first responders, I spoke with a police officer recently and he said that in car crashes the average person slows down, but they don't see what we see: walking over bodies, or the screaming and pain. You don't just go home at night and turn on the news and relax. We are not capable of doing that. It becomes part of you. Lawyers are people too. They have adverse experiences.

I think the law, though, is special. Because people like me, [psychotherapists], when we were in training, we learned a lot about this ourselves, how to be protective and healthy ourselves. [For] police officers, it might be a little more common to talk about that. But there is a perception or notion that judges, and lawyers are not touched by this; almost as though people are machines and are not impacted by the experience.

It is true. It is very true. One of the problems lawyers have and doctors too, but many professions, you are held in high esteem, you are deemed to be well educated and thoughtful and therefore some people mistake that with the ideal of being perfect or being "hollow," so you don't have the same feelings. You can deal with anything. So that is the expectation, that you are always going to have the best answer in the room, you will always be able to cross-examine the witness effectively, you will have the best memo, the best argument, you're going to bill the most of anyone in your law firm. So, there are all of these pressures, and people know to their bone that they can't do all of those things well, but they won't tell you that. Because there is always someone in the next office, you think, who is smarter or faster or bills more. And because of all of the technology there is no space anymore. There is no space [between] your office on the 35th floor and your living room. They are the same thing. In my own life, I had the benefit of the dining room table, with my parents and we had breakfast and we had dinner. And I learned a lot of civics from my parents, and they said how is your day going, what are you doing. A lot of the kids I am meeting don't have that. It went away.

No, they don't. They don't have the opportunity for support or nurturing. I think it is basic nurturing, really.

It is basic nurturing. If you said to a lot of young people, how many friends do you have. They would say 72 or 128, and if you asked me, I would say maybe three. And so that the world allows them; you could today move to your basement, order your food, pay your bills, get your cables, faxes; you don't need to interact nearly as much and therefore people who have any issues can still survive. The kids that I am seeing; if we don't finally say, hey folks, we can fix this, it is not hopeless, but it *will* get worse until we address it and talk about it.

Talking about it is what normalizes it.

I agree. When a suicide happens, people come out and they think what happened? This is terrible. What can we do? But by Tuesday they are back, paying bills? It's hard to stay focused. At some point, we have to say we are tired of going to funerals.

It has to become more of the fabric of the basic conversation.

I agree. I couldn't agree more. The kids that come up to me and say their parents are ashamed and they are ashamed.

I see so many adolescents in my practice whose parents have told them this is a secret, we are not sharing it with others, and they view the child as the problem, [as opposed to] having a problem. You know, they are a sister, a brother, a daughter, a son, and they may have a mental health issue, but they are not the issue or the problem.

No, they are not. It is shameful. The attorney general of Vermont came to me and asked me to go to more schools. He said [that] to these kids, no one talked about it. I had four brothers and sisters, and my older sister had serious mental health problems and I was so ashamed of her. I realize now I should have been ashamed of myself for feeling that way. That was where we were. That is where we need to go. Changedirection.org I looked her up (Barbara), and she was on Time Magazine 100 list in. I instantly liked her. She created something called give an hour. Give an hour campaign has thousands of mental health workers that volunteer one hour a week to veterans at no cost.

This is indeed a wonderful project. Which brings us to working on mental health issues and that is what happened with your son. Can we talk about that?

My son is a great person, one of the smartest people I know. He is a self-taught musician, but I did not see it because it came out at age 13 and I did not know anything about it at the time. He would spend a lot of time in his room drawing . . . today I would call it withdrawing. He had friends, but not as many. He started smoking in high school. I did not know that. He was more of a loner and home more than he was not. Then he went away to college and started drinking and it was alarming, and it got so bad. He got his master's degree, and I don't know how he did it. And finally, he assaulted me and we had to put him on the street because that was the only hope and he told me, Dad, if I did not have these feelings, I would not be drinking. I mentioned that to the alcohol people, and they said that he was an alcoholic and that is what you do. He had mental health problems, and when we put him out, his underlying mental health problems exploded. He went to prison and we were at the prison, it was all over the news and it was on the *Today* show and it was not a good time after prison. The psychologist said, your son is great, I love your son. He is really smart. He said, your son has really serious depression. He has panic attacks and anxiety that are almost out off the charts. If you didn't know it was a mental health [issue], you would be drinking too. He was self-medicating. [Now,] he has not had a drink in 12 years. His wife is amazing, and she won an Emmy in New Hampshire. I have a granddaughter now too. Every time I go out and speak, my son will write me or call me, and I apologize to him because I did not know anything. Ignorance is never your friend, and silence never solve any problems. I see it now. So, I do what I can do.

You are doing an amazing job. What you are doing is bringing relief and a discussion to many people. Many alcohol and other drug counselors can't do duel diagnosis, so opportunities to discuss mental health like anxiety or depression can't be diagnosed.

We treat these problems like they are in their own silos.

So many of the people have an emotional issue that brings them to coping with alcohol or other drugs.

In the world we occupy you're a drug addict, you're a domestic abuser. But probably there is something else going on. We never roll the film back and say, oh, now I see it, because we are not looking for it and we don't even know what to look for and we are frightened to find it. Once we are no longer frightened, we will solve this problem and we will find the resources, because families will say, I am not ashamed anymore, [but] I can't get in to see someone: we need resources. That is the only answer, if we say we need more money they will say sure, we all do. I understand the scope and the depth of this problem. I understand the onset. I see the suffering. It is not morally right; it is not medically right. It is so obvious to me now, and it was hiding most of my life. Now it is not hiding. It is horrible that we allow it.

The suffering is immense.

It is horrible that we allow it. I believe that people armed with good information most often do the right [thing], for the right reasons but if they don't act it often means they don't know. A lot of people are hiding. For example, you have a daughter, and your daughter has mental health problems and she was in college and now at home and someone walked up to you in a grocery store and said, "Hey, how is your daughter doing?" that is like saying "Is Anne Frank hiding in your house?" Now if your daughter were home and she broke her leg in a soccer game, she had a horrible injury to her knee etc., but if it is mental health, oh no, I can't tell them—why?

I don't get it.

I don't get it either. It hasn't made sense for generations. That is what we are up against.

If you smoke outside today on the Boston Commons, it is a violation of the city ordinances. Not so long ago you could smoke on airplanes. Smoking, no burning talk about it, every car had an ashtray so something changed that was a lot more arduous then saying could we just stop being ashamed. It is going to take leaders to speak up. I grew up in a world where everyone had perfect mental health. Everyone was perfect.

Thank you so much, Judge Broderick, Jr. I wish you the best in your continued endeavors to help eradicate stigma and educate on mental health.

Judge Broderick, Jr.'s interview represents the issue of stigma on multiple levels. His ability to articulate the changes that culture has undergone regarding other stigmatized issues, such as breast cancer or cigarette smoking is truly hopeful.

## Champion of Disclosure

### *The Honorable Michael Kirby*

The Honorable Michael Kirby is an Australian jurist and academic. From 1996 to 2009 he served as a Justice of the High Court of Australia. In May 2013, he was appointed by the United Nations Human Rights Council to lead an inquiry into human rights abuses in North Korea.

Thank you for taking the time to talk with me today about these important issues.

Yes, I went to a judge's conference in Canada in 1996 or 1995 and I saw the judges there talking candidly about issues of judicial stress, isolation, and bullying. So when I came back to Australia I gave a lecture on the subject, and I found a lot of hostility and objection to even mentioning it, but now it has become a very common issue in all or most legal and judicial conferences.

Oh, very good. Is it being talked about or taught in law school at all?

I ask that when I go to law schools, which I go to all the time, and the answer that I get is, it is talked about in orientation when the new students arrive but there is very little follow-up. It varies from law school to law school. It has cracked into the discussion but not very effectively so far.

The survey I mentioned, shows us that the conversation about secondary trauma is becoming more open but is still quite stigmatized.

Well, I think that is a correct discovery. I do find less pushback now [than when] I spoke about it originally in 1996. There was hostility and discomfort and a mocking attitude towards it, but there certainly isn't that now. I think the fact that there has become now an increasing number of women appointed to the judiciary in Australia in the last 20 years that has helped somewhat. because women are much more likely to talk about a subject like this then men. There may be some sort of gender element in pushback.

Well, that is a great question. So, it sounds as though in Australia that the conversation is becoming a little more normalized?

Well, I think that's only really the first step, to normalize the conversation. [Then] one has to organize the reaction and the response and the institutional responses to these issues, and I am not sure that has happened on a widespread basis in Australia just yet. Australia can be sometimes be a sort of macho kind of society, not all that different from the United States. And I think the poor little boys when they are tiny are told you can't, or you are not allowed to cry and you have to keep a stiff back and get on with life. I think it is a matter of gender training rather than anything in the DNA.

Interesting, I just spoke with a former Supreme Court Jjudge from the State of New Hampshire, John Broderick Jr., and he was telling me pretty much the same thing. It is a matter of how these boys are being trained and the idea that men cannot cry. They are not having a conversation about emotionality at all. He is doing work on developing a program that school children can have the ability to talk about mental health issues and begin to be open about it. He is looking at social and emotional learning and I think that is a big piece of what is missing in this puzzle.

Yes, there is quite a lot of resistance to this in certain political circles and people are getting quite upset with people thinking boys are being turned into wet socks and this is not good for masculinity and society, and this arises often in the issue of transgender children at schools and how to respond to them. And we have many of the same kinds of debates that I see that you have in the United States. Because of my own sexual orientation, as a gay man I was much more ready to talk about these things, and because that really was the only way we began to make progress on the LGBTQ+ issues by speaking about them and by being confronted with members of the different sexual minorities and by learning about their lives and beginning to appreciate the overwhelming commonality of lives. The more you get to know about it and the more you get to know people affected by it, the more understanding you have, and the less ignorance and counterproductive attitudes policies and laws are likely to get in the way.

LGBTQ+ issues may be an area that is more difficult to talk about.

Yes, well the deal that was struck between society and gay people twenty years ago, thirty years ago was, we will leave you alone if you keep very quiet about your identity and if you don't make us think about you and the non-binary nature of society. Now, I knew all about that and I played along with that rule for a very long time. This was the rule of "don't ask, don't tell," but eventually the irrationality of that rule dawned on me, and also the fact that it is a rule that leads to silence about the reality of minorities and therefore, to oppression of those minorities. So, they are in effect being cajoled into conspiring in their own denigration. My partner, Yohan, who is from the Netherlands is ultimately the person who insisted that we stand up and confront this, because the culture in the Netherlands is much more direct and honest and blunt, and that ultimately persuaded me and I think it was a good thing.

Do you feel as though what I was talking about earlier with regards to the LGBTQ+ community and a level of silence and difficulty is still applicable?

Yes, well it is still difficult for some particularly, for people that live in families with strong religious or cultural norms, but even they, if they live in a country like the United States or Australia are being constantly exposed. Change does happen, but it only happens if people stand up and if they confront the wrong attitudes and if people talk about it. Quietly, respectfully, and intelligently and backed up by scientific data that has a big impact. Another big impact in particular [are] instances of suicide or self-harm in Australia. We have had quite a few cases in law school of young, generally male [suicides]. Every case I know of a young male law student [is] in a highly pressurized circumstances of law schools who take their lives and this comes as a terrible shock to people. And then questions come out: What did we do wrong, is there anything we can do, what should we be doing? And the answer: you did do things wrong, and what you should do is engage people and talk about it and find ways to help people. If they are feeling stressed and pressured, you have got to talk. You have to find friends and buddies who will lend support. By no means are all people who suffer from stress of this kind gay, but a number are, and it really behooves people who are gay in important positions to stand up and say enough is enough . . . and we just have to confront this demon and it is in everybody's interest to do it and not when it is too late.

In my research, I have not seen a framework that allows for this discussion to start to occur. Can you tell me what you see in your experience, as the most pressing health concern for legal students and professionals?

Most pressing health concern is health generally; aging, exercising, and having a good and loving relationships having an agreeable sexual life and being willing to talk about these issues with colleagues and to confront the demons that inhabit the minds of those who don't feel able to talk. I think this is why my talk, even though I had just been appointed to Supreme Court, my talk really was very confronting to a lot of judges because it hadn't been done before. But I knew from the conference of Canadian judges that I had just come from, that was happening in Canada. Canadian people are kind to each other. The Canadian judges were talking about this, so I knew I was on to a good topic and I resisted when they pushed back, I pushed back further against them. Because I had a long-term relationship which is now coming around to fifty years, I never really felt suicidal or pressured. I mean there is always pressure in the law, but I never felt that I was unworthy, and I didn't allow people to bully me because I am a pretty tough cookie. I knew from what I read, this is a very common thing especially in law schools, that the rates of stress and pressure in law schools is much higher than other faculties, even higher than dentistry. Therefore, you must ask, why is this so? These are all by definition, if you have got into a law school, they are clever young people and why are there these problems? There are a whole lot of explanations, but then what can we do about it?

I think one lecture in orientation at the beginning of a law course is not really enough. It is not the right way to think you have solved the problem by just having an initial lecture, it requires sustained efforts and organizing young people so they have at least one person they can talk to if they get into a corner and feel everything is going wrong. I think what needs to be coming is the grafting onto of regular discussions at every year in a law course that deals with these issues that deals with what has been discovered and brings people forward to talk about it. In Australia there are one or two judges and a number of barristers, the advocates who talk about their own depression, the so-called black dog symptom and how they have coped with it and what they do about it. I think in the law schools and professional courses given by bar associations this is something that can be a whole of life experience, just as I talk regularly at law schools and in the community about LGBTQ+ issues. It is a good thing, if people who have been into the valley of despair could come out of the other side and talk about it. There is a very good professor in England Louis Wolpert who has suffered from serious clinical depression. He speaks about it at conferences, and he is extremely powerful. He is a top scientist. His area is biology. If you can get people who others identify with and respect that's very useful. I think the fact, that I as a Supreme Court judge was talking about these things was quite a good thing in Australia on LGBTQ+ and also on depression, stress, and suicide.

You have allowed the conversation to start and be a little more normalized.

Lawyers are very combative, ambitious and aggressive. If they are confronted and told this is a serious thing, they might just start to take it a bit seriously. In Australia, unfortunately, after my initial efforts, I didn't keep in the forefront, but there were lots of people to take my place and they were organizations established to conduct research and to conduct conferences and provide speakers at law conferences. You just have to build a momentum out of the initial rejection. It has grown first of all a vague feeling [that] maybe there is something in this, hopefully, that can grow into a programmatic response that looks at what we can do about it. The bar associations have been quite good, better than the judiciary. The judiciary is still worried that if they reveal that there are judges who suffer from depression, then people will say that we just don't want them in the judiciary. They have to be thrown out; which is difficult in a country like Australia or the United States, because judges generally have tenure. But the judiciary is a bit circumspect about these issues, but there are some judges that give it support and it is good to get them because law is a very hierarchal profession. Target and get people to talk about the difficulties of coping, work-life balance, and the value of exercise, the value of discussion with colleagues, the value of setting aside time for social events, all of these things can help, and I think it is common sense really to work toward providing it. The firms will provide occasions and use their offices and encourage their young members to organize themselves to have chapters to talk about these issues and LGBTQ+ and gender issues and #MeToo issues and bullying by judges and all of the other issues that are interconnected.

Michael Kirby shared with us multiple issues, including some of his outspoken work on secondary trauma in 1996 as well as the issue of stigma and the need to continue to address stigma on multiple fronts.

## Champion of Disclosure

### *Brian Cuban*

Brain Cuban is an American attorney, author, and speaker. He is a regular writer for Above the Law and the author of *The Addicted Lawyer* and *Shattered Image: My Triumph Over Body Dysmorphic Disorder*. He is an authority on male eating disorders and drug addiction, drug rehabilitation, and alcoholism.

We all come into our professions and our adult lives with stories and experiences of how we came to where we are. For many, these stories include trauma. These traumas may be primary traumas or secondary or generational. They can also be life-defining events. For many, these events never receive proper care or treatment due to stigma.

During our interview, Brian told me, "There is a tendency of the profession to avoid dealing with trauma. How we deal with our story affects how we deal with stress. If we do not handle the trauma, we can't handle the stress in our everyday lives." Traumas such as "adverse childhood experiences (ACEs) not dealt with lower the trigger threshold for self-medicating [if they] deal with it the threshold becomes a lot higher." And "compassion fatigue and secondary trauma triggers become a lot lower as well." Lawyers may not reveal these issues, according to Brian, because of stigma, and they "associate these issues with vulnerability, and lawyers are trained to take advantage of vulnerability."

*Brian created the following funnel description of stigma:*

Level 1: the lowest level of the funnel, is social stigma: the societal stigma every person is socialized to while growing up and living life.

Level 2: the middle layer, is family stigma, - what your family teaches you.

Level 3: the top layer of the funnel, is professional stigma, which is what the profession teaches you.

*Using the example of depression:*

Level 1: when Brian and I were growing up, society taught that depression was not something you talked about.

Level 2: families didn't really consider depression or anxiety or mental health in general, and it was not talked about or acknowledged at home.

Level 3: lawyers are taught not to talk about it, while therapists learn something a little different. (Therapists can talk about it, but there is still shame and stigma at the professional level.)

As Brian put it, "lawyers are lawyers—not everyone is an advocate or rewarded for being vulnerable." However, he also pointed out that he gained healing through his story and gained praise for his vulnerability.

Finally, Brian and I discussed there have been very few studies on law students and unresolved personal trauma; it's an area that continues to need further study.

## Section 5: The Power of Shame

We must assess the role that shame, guilt, and embarrassment play in our lack of willingness to communicate with each other. We sometimes forget that these very basic emotions play a role in our lives from time to time. They all affect our self-image, which we carefully create, maintain, and monitor. When embarrassment, guilt, or shame emerge, our self-image has been damaged.[157]

For so many, shame and stigma go hand in hand with issues of trauma. Professor Brené Brown studied shame and how and why we use shame to change people. She found that if we focus on a weakness or exposed vulnerability, (as lawyers are trained to do), a very swift behavioral change occurs, but the change does not last and it has the potential to harm the person being shamed. Professor Brown also notes, shame is the number one issue that brings people into mental health treatment. Yet no one really talks about shame in mental health, school, or business settings. Professor Brown found descriptions of shame such as "devastating, noxious, consuming, excruciating, filleted, small, stained, incredibly lonely, rejected and the worst feeling ever."[158]

Brown's work identifies such terms as embarrassment, guilt, and humiliation as being closely linked and often used interchangeably with shame. She defines shame as "the intensely painful feeling or experience of believing we are flawed and therefore unworthy of connection and belonging." She notes, embarrassment is defined as "something fleeting and often eventually funny and very normal. Guilt is most confused with shame. Guilt can be a positive motivator; it is holding an action or behavior up against our ethics, values and beliefs, shame is about the fear of disconnection."[159]

There also exists for many people a sense of shame paired with a sense of powerlessness. An example of this comes from Brian Cuban's book *The Addicted Lawyer*:

---

[157] Henricks, Thomas. 2017. "Embarrassment, Guilt, and Shame." *Psychology Today*, September 4, 2017. https://www.psychologytoday.com/us/blog/the-pathways-experience/201709/embarrassment-guilt-and-shame.
[158] Brown, Brené. 2008. *I Thought It Was Just Me (but It Isn't): Telling the Truth about Perfectionism, Inadequacy, and Power.* New York: Gotham Books.

[159] Brown, Brené. 2008. *I Thought It Was Just Me (but It Isn't): Telling the Truth about Perfectionism, Inadequacy, and Power.* New York: Gotham Books.

"I was in therapy but lying to my psychiatrist or leaving out critical facts about events that injured me to the core of my identity. Shame knows no hourly rate. More comfortable to leave things off the couch than face the past. Easier to gauge my trauma by those in our profession who appear 'strong.' Maybe those who post in social media to 'get over it" or "stop whining.' Good for them. They are not you. My guess is that they are less than honest with themselves about the impact of trauma on their lives.

Here is something I did that may help you. I made a list of every single event in my life I could remember that I considered traumatic. Nothing was too small or too big. I read it to my therapist. It was the first step. Acknowledging the trauma. It starts there. Give it a try. There is no doubt in my mind that allowing ourselves vulnerability in looking at our past or ongoing trauma is a gatekeeper to wellness and something that has helped me stay sober and deal with depression."[160]

As we have discussed, law students, lawyers, and judges are not always able to cope with the shocking information they work with on a daily basis. This idea, similar to ideas about those in the medical profession, paints those in law as strong, smart, and invincible. The general population may think that lawyers are able to handle such upsetting information, but in some cases they are not. When legal professionals and law students have a negative response to egregiously upsetting information, many of them are ashamed by their perceived weakness. They feel that they should not be having these feelings and should be able to deal with it like "everyone else does," when in fact everyone else may be dealing with it less-than-healthy or productive ways.

Guilt emerges after doing something wrong, intentionally or accidentally, or from not doing something you should have. A person's sense of guilt usually relates to their moral code.[161] Individuals can be so guilt-ridden that they cannot move, they get stuck or paralyzed or begin to feel as though they cannot do their work or help people adequately. Ultimately, with guilt, people may feel a sense of inferiority, feeling that because they are "less than" they could not have made outcomes better or different.

Sometimes feelings of guilt, may actually be disguised sadness that you could not do more to help, or disappointment that you did not achieve your desired goal. Guilt can also be confused with anger for not doing as well in a given situation as you could have. Check yourself and your feelings of guilt and shame periodically.

Embarrassment is an uncomfortable but important emotional state that many researchers believe enables "people [to] feel badly about their social or personal mistakes as a form of internal (or societal) feedback, so that they learn not to repeat the error."[162]

---

[160] Brian Cuban, *The Addicted Lawyer: Tales of the Bar, Booze, Blow, and Redemption* (Brentwood, TN: Post Hill Press, 2017).

[161] GoodTherapy. 2019. "Types of Guilt." GoodTherapy, November 21, 2019. https://www.goodtherapy.org/learn-about-therapy/issues/guilt.

[162] *Psychology Today*. n.d. "Embarrassment." *Psychology Today*. https://www.psychologytoday.com/us/basics/embarrassment.

---

This can include the perception of not doing as well as one expected in mock trial or court, or other public venue. Like shame and guilt, embarrassment can cause people to avoid social situations and avoid trying again. Sometimes these strong emotions can lead to people temporarily shutting down or isolating themselves.

## Section 6: Moving Beyond These Feelings

The three emotions we have been discussing are important. How has this kind of culture, which elicits these feelings for many, been created and how does it continue? Think about these emotional states. Do you want to be a contributor to, or a sustainer of these states? Or would you rather be a contributor and sustainer of compassion and respect? No one should feel shame, embarrassment, or guilt regarding stress or other mental health issues, but we are yet not there in terms of acceptance culturally.

Of course, legal professions are not the only professions where difficult information is received. Doctors, nurses, police officers, and psychotherapists often receive and work with traumatic information on a daily basis. However, the legal profession is different for two important reasons. First, the legal profession in general does not have the specific training and education on these issues. Second, because the legal profession is so competitive, and its members strive for personal and professional perfection, there exists profound feelings of shame, embarrassment, and guilt when they fail.

Over the course of writing this book, I have heard repeatedly that in the legal profession anyone or thing that looks weak, is a target both at school as well as within work environments. There is a perceived notion, not only in our culture but particularly in law, that sharing anything, but perfection could harm one's professional goals and outcomes. No wonder individuals are experiencing feelings of shame, embarrassment, and guilt.

According to Brown, there is no way to permanently avoid shame, but we can become more resilient to it. Empathy from others also helps us recover from shame. Sharing with an empathic person helps to lessen and eventually stop the feelings of shame.

Shame resilience is the ability to recognize and accept vulnerability, awareness of social and cultural expectations, and the ability to form empathic relationships where the individuals are able to talk about shame.[163] Shame is a universal emotion but can have serious consequences on resilience and mental health in general. Shame Resilience Theory (SRT) looks at how people respond to shame as well as their ability to move beyond it to empathy and freedom, which the theory posits are the opposite of shame. According to the social work researcher Brené Brown, shame causes people to feel "trapped, powerless, and isolated."[164]

---

[163] Brown, Brené. 2006. "Shame Resilience Theory: A Grounded Theory Study on Women and Shame." *Families in Society* 87, no. 1 (January 2006): 43–52. https:// https://doi.org/10.1606/1044-3894.3483.

[164] Brown, Brené. 2006. "Shame Resilience Theory: A Grounded Theory Study on Women and Shame." *Families in Society* 87, no. 1 (January 2006): 43–52. https:// https://doi.org/10.1606/1044-3894.3483.

---

To move forward, Shame Resilience Theory proposes that "shame resilience is essentially made up of four steps:

1. Recognizing the personal vulnerability that led to the feelings of shame
2. Recognizing the external factors that led to the feelings of shame
3. Connecting with others to receive and offer empathy
4. Discussing and deconstructing the feelings of shame themselves" (Selva 2019).

In other words, shame needs to be acknowledged and understood before it can be overcome. Shame may be most harmful when it goes unacknowledged and is not spoken of.[165] Communication and sharing, whatever the source of the shame is, can help. According to Brown, when the four elements are practiced together, they can move people toward resilience.

---

[165] Selva, Joaquin. 2019. "Shame Resilience Theory: How to Respond to Feelings of Shame." PositivePsychology.com, July 29, 2019. https://positivepsychology.com/shame-resilience-theory/.

## Discussion Questions

- What is stigma?
- Outline and define the different types of stigma.
- What makes stigma about alcohol and drugs unique?
- Name several recommendations created in Australia to help with the issue of stigma and alcohol and drug use.
- What are some examples of mental health stigma?
- How is mental health stigma portrayed in media?
- Are there some issues that are more stigmatized than others?
- What kinds of cultural changes have taken place regarding stigma that Judge Broderick, Jr. discussed?
- According to the World Health Organization, what percentage of people who experience a mood or substance abuse disorder actually obtain help within the first year?
- What does the Honorable Michael Kirby tell us about changes in the discussion of secondary trauma from the mid-1990's to present?
- What are the three levels of stigma that Brian Cuban defined?
- What role does shame play with stigma?

# References

Ando S, Clement S, Barley EA, Thornicroft G. The simulation of hallucinations to reduce the stigma of schizophrenia: A systematic review. Schizophrenia Research 133 (2011) 8–16

Australian Institute of Health and Welfare. 2019. "Alcohol and other drug treatment services in Australia 2017–18." Australian Institute of Health and Welfare, July 25, 2019. https://www.aihw.gov.au/reports-data/health-welfare-services/alcohol-other-drug-treatment-services/reports

Brown, Brené. 2006. "Shame Resilience Theory: A Grounded Theory Study on Women and Shame." *Families in Society* 87, no. 1 (January 2006): 43–52. https:// https://doi.org/10.1606/1044-3894.3483.

Brown, Brené. 2008. I Thought It Was Just Me (but It Isn't): Telling the Truth about Perfectionism, Inadequacy, and Power. New York: Gotham Books.

Center for Behavioral Health Statistics and Quality. 2015. Behavioral health trends in the United States: Results from the 2014 National Survey on Drug Use and Health (HHS Publication No. SMA 15-4927, NSDUH Series H-50). Retrieved from http://www.samhsa.gov/data/.

Collier, Richard. 2019. "Anxiety and Wellbeing Amongst Junior Lawyers: A Research Study" Anxiety UK, March 2019. https://www.anxietyuk.org.uk/wp-content/uploads/2019/05/Collier-Anxiety-UK-Final-Report-March-2019.pdf

Corrigan, Patrick W., and Amy C. Watson. 2006. "The Paradox of Self-Stigma and Mental Illness." *Clinical Psychology: Science and Practice*9:35–53. 10.1093/clipsy.9.1.35.

Corrigan, Patrick, Jonathon Larson, and Kuwabara. 2010. *Social psychology of stigma for mental illness: Public stigma and self-stigma.*

Desmon, Stephanie, and Susan Morrow. 2014. "Drug Addiction Viewed More Negatively than Mental Illness, Johns Hopkins Study Shows." The Hub, October 1, 2014. https://hub.jhu.edu/2014/10/01/drug-addiction-stigma/.

GoodTherapy. 2019. "Types of Guilt." GoodTherapy, November 21, 2019. https://www.goodtherapy.org/learn-about-therapy/issues/guilt.

Haddad, Peter, and Isabelle Haddad. 2015. "Mental Health Stigma." *British Association for Psychopharmacology*, March 3, 2015. https://www.bap.org.uk/articles/mental-health-stigma/.

Harnois, Gaston, Gabriel, Phyllis, World Health Organization & International Labour Organisation. (2000). Mental health and work: impact, issues and good practices. World Health Organization. https://apps.who.int/iris/handle/10665/42346

Hazelden Betty Ford Foundation. n.d. "Smashing the Stigma of Addiction." Accessed December 18, 2019. https://www.hazeldenbettyford.org/recovery-advocacy/stigma-of-addiction.

Hatzenbuehler, M. L., and B. G. Link. "Introduction to the special issue on structural stigma and health." *Social Science & Medicine* 103:1–6. https://doi.org/10.1016/j.socscimed.2013.12.017.

Government of Canada. 2018. "Strengthening Canada's Approach to Substance Use Issues." Government of Canada, September 10, 2018. https://www.canada.ca/en/health-canada/services/substance-use/canadian-drugs-substances-strategy/strengthening-canada-approach-substance-use-issue.html.

Lancaster, Kari, Kate Seear, and Alison Ritter. 2018. Monograph No. 26: "Reducing stigma and discrimination for people experiencing problematic alcohol and other drug use." DPMP Monograph Series. Sydney: National Drug and Alcohol Research Centre. http://doi.org/10.26190/5b8746fe72507.

Livingston, J. D. 2013. Mental illness-related structural stigma: The downward spiral of *systemic exclusion*. Calgary, Alberta: Mental Health Commission of Canada. https://www.mentalhealthcommission.ca/sites/default/files/MHCC_OpeningMinds_MentalIllness-RelatedSructuralStigmaReport_ENG_0_0.pdf.

Lyon, Angus. 2015. A Lawyer's Guide to Wellbeing and Managing Stress. London: Ark Group. National Academies of Sciences, Engineering, and Medicine. 2016. Ending Discrimination Against People with Mental and Substance Use Disorders: The Evidence for Stigma Change. Washington, D.C: The National Academies Press. https://doi.org/10.17226/23442.

New Zealand Drug Foundation. 2014. "1/3 Of NZ Families Affected by Alcohol and Drug Problems." February 20, 2014. https://www.drugfoundation.org.nz/news-media-and-events/nz-families-affected-by-alcohol-and-drug-problems/.

Overton, Stacy L., and Sondra L. Medina. "The Stigma of Mental Illness." *Journal of Counseling & Development* 86, no. 2 (2008): 143–51. https://doi.org/10.1002/j.1556-6678.2008.tb00491.x.

Orygen. 2017. Under the radar: The mental health of Australian university students. Melbourne: Orygen, The National Centre of Excellence in Youth Mental Health.

*Psychology Today*. n.d. "Embarrassment." *Psychology Today*. https://www.psychologytoday.com/us/basics/embarrassment.

Selva, Joaquin. 2019. "Shame Resilience Theory: How to Respond to Feelings of Shame." PositivePsychology.com, July 29, 2019. https://positivepsychology.com/shame-resilience-theory/.

Smith, Cooper. 2019."Addiction in the UK." Addiction Center, last edited December 5, 2019. https://www.addictioncenter.com/addiction/addiction-in-the-uk/.

World Health Organization. 2007. "Chapter 1: A Public Health Approach to Mental Health." World Health Organization. World Health Organization, June 13, 2007. https://www.who.int/whr/2001/chapter1/en/index3.html.

World Health Organization. 2013. "Gender and Women's Mental Health." World Health Organization, June 24, 2013. https://www.who.int/mental_health/prevention/genderwomen/en/.

World Health Organization. n.d. "Stigma and Discrimination." World Health Organization. Accessed March 5, 2020. http://www.euro.who.int/en/health-topics/noncommunicable-diseases/mental-health/priority-areas/stigma-and-discrimination.

World Health Organization. n.d. "10 Facts on Mental Health." World Health Organization. Accessed March 5, 2020. https://www.who.int/features/factfiles/mental_health/mental_health_facts/en/index5.html

# Chapter 5 Abstract: Core Values and Self-Care

What are core values? What is self-care? How do we achieve these things? These are the topics which we will be exploring in this chapter.

Values and ethics are frequently used interchangeably. They are different. Our core values are deeply personal and vary from individual to individual. Core values are the principals that help us to determine our priorities and our behaviors. We suffer emotionally from conflict or confusion when we lose our core values or when we are distanced from our core values as we will see in Self-Determination Theory. Ethics are organizational, professional and societal and provide guidelines for behavior that help to determine morality. Self-care is about how we live our lives and take care of ourselves on a daily basis in accordance with our values, whether at home, at school, or at work. As we will see, core-values play a crucial role in health and well-being.

Your judgment and ability to do good work depend on your lifestyle, how you react to stressors and exposure to trauma, how you acknowledge and handle mental health concerns, and how you build social support within your life. In a nutshell, it is your physical and emotional self that you are valuing and taking care of.

There is growing momentum to help rediscover, retain, and articulate core-values and working to achieve better self-care. We will see the history, progress, setbacks, and the resurgence of this movement.

# Chapter 5: Core Values and Self-Care

The best care is living one's life according to one's values in a balanced and healthy way.

## Section 1: Core Values

Core values are important deep values that are central to who we are. They express what we believe about life and the world. Personal values are not central to who we are and do not affect what we believe about the world. For example, I may value the cost of my clothing over the cost of my shoes. This value does not impact my view of life. Finally, values are not necessarily moral in nature. There are many different core values for individuals and organizations. Here is a list of some of the values that you might think about. They are from Rushworth M. Kidder's *Moral Courage:*

- Honesty
- Spirituality
- Dependability
- Sense of Justice
- Flexibility
- Reliability
- Loyalty
- Commitment
- Open-mindedness
- Consistency
- Efficiency
- Innovation
- Creativity
- Good humor

- Compassion
- Spirit of adventure
- Motivation
- Positivity
- Optimism
- Passion
- Respect
- Fitness
- Courage
- Education
- Perseverance
- Patriotism
- Service to others
- Environmentalism[166]

---

[166] Kidder, Rushworth M. 2006. *Moral Courage.* New York: Harper.

Much of the discussion from Australian professor Adrian Evans, who we will hear from later in this chapter, addresses values. In his book *The Good Lawyer*, he identified three of Segilman's values as particularly relevant to lawyers:

- Wisdom and knowledge: cognitive strengths that entail the acquisition and use of knowledge.
- Creativity
- Curiosity
- Open-mindedness
- Love of learning: mastering new skills, topics, and bodies of knowledge whether on one's own or formally
- Perspective
- Courage: emotional strength that involve the exercise of will to accomplish goals in the face of opposition, external or internal.
- Bravery
- Persistence
- Integrity
- Justice: civic strength that underlines healthy community life.
- Citizenship
- Fairness: treating all people the same according to notions of fairness and justice; not letting personal feelings bias decision about others; giving everyone a fair chance
- Leadership: encouraging a group of which one is a member to get things done, at the same time maintaining good relations within the group; honoring group activities and seeing that they happen.[167]

Core values are important to our health, well-being, and general life satisfaction. Professor Lawrence Krieger argues, "satisfaction and professional behavior are inseparable manifestations of a well-integrated and well-motivated person; and that depression and unprofessional behavior among law students and lawyers typically proceed from a loss of integrity—a disconnection from intrinsic values and motivations, personal and cultural beliefs, conscience, or other defining parts of their personality and humanity." Satisfaction and professional behavior are integral to a well-integrated and motivated person. Professor Krieger also noted that a disconnection from intrinsic values and motivations may precede depression and unprofessional behavior among lawyers and law students. [168]

What are your core values? Do you remember them? Are you living your life on a day-to-day basis congruent to those values? Or do you ever find yourself in a situation where you are in conflict with your core values? Think about how you have behaved and coped just yesterday and today. How did you interact with those around you, family, friends, colleagues? What healthy behaviors did you participate in? Did you eat breakfast and exercise, or did you drink too much coffee or alcohol and sleep

---

[167] Evans, Adrian. 2014. *The Good Lawyer*. Cambridge: Cambridge University Press.

[168] Krieger, Lawrence S.. 2005. "The Inseparability of Professionalism and Personal Satisfaction: Perspectives on Values, Integrity and Happiness." *Clinical Law Review,* Spring 2005: 425–45. http://ir.law.fsu.edu/articles/97.

until the last moment; perhaps because you pulled an all-nighter? Are these behaviors congruent with your values? Self-care maybe a core value. We will discuss more about self-care later. With the loss of core values, we may find much internal conflict and distress. It is important to regain core values, as they are a kind of a compass, directing and moving us toward our life goals.

## Section 1.1: Finding Your Values

G. Andrew H. Benjamin, an American clinical psychologist and law professor at the University of Washington–Seattle, has been asking values questions of law school students and professionals. During one of our conversations, Dr. Benjamin noted that "lawyers chronically violate physical, emotional, and spiritual values because of the perceptions about 'time famine' and their overall workload."[169] A time famine is the perception that there is not enough time to get done all of the things that are important to us. As we make choices, some of our core values may be left behind. Over time, we may find a change or permanent shift in core values. In fact, we may lose core values completely as we try to operate within systems where with the values around us are in conflict with our core values.

In his work with students and professionals, Dr. Benjamin created a True Self Values Worksheet. This worksheet helps to rediscover core values. A version with modified directions on how to use it is below. After you work on the worksheet, consider if you need to regain or reaffirm any of your core values.

Consider the best decisions and the best interactions you have had with people during the course of your life. During these positive interactions, were your behaviors congruent with your deeply felt values?

The assignment is to identify those values, and to make them quite concrete for each of the 16 competencies in the worksheet. Note, that an example is included under each competency (values should always be listed in an affirmative manner). But they are just examples— you have your own values. The examples demonstrate the expected form and specificity required. Remember to delete the sample value and provide three of your own values for each competency.

Please reflect and write (no more than 50 words on any occasion) about any feeling state you might be stuck in, what that feeling state means in the way of an unmet need, and what values you could activate to meet that unmet emotional need.

---

[169] Benjamin, G. Andrew H., and Cynthia Alexander. 2011. "Civility is Good for Your Health." *Washington State Bar News*, April 1, 2011. https://ssrn.com/abstract=1803904 Reprinted with permission of the Washington State Bar Association from the April 2011 issue of the *Washington State Bar News*.

# True Self Values Worksheet

## <u>NURTURING</u>

Example: I express appreciation when an individual enters my presence.
1.
2.
3.

## <u>COMMUNICATION:</u>

### *SENDING*
Example: I am clear and specific in my verbal communication.
1.
2.
3.

### *RECEIVING*
Example: I detect underlying themes and patterns in others' communication.
1.
2.
3.

## <u>ATTITUDES</u>

Example: I focus on the likely positive outcomes in given situations.
1.
2.
3.

## <u>PHYSICAL HEALTH</u>

Example: I get sufficient exercise to promote physical fitness.
1.
2.
3.

## <u>ETHICS</u>

Example: I act with integrity.
1.
2.
3.

## EMOTIONAL HEALTH

Example: I diligently clarify the actions of others that generate strong feelings.
1.
2.
3.

## MANNERS

Example: I am silent about others' shortcomings unless there is a good reason to bring them up.
1.
2.
3.

## WORK HEALTH

Example: I diligently use a time management system in my daily life.
1.
2.
3.

## SPIRITUALITY

Example: I evaluate pursuit of my values in the context of my faith.
1.
2.
3.

## RECREATION

Example: In my recreational activities, I pursue intellectual stimulation.
1.
2.
3.

## ROMANCE/MARRIAGE

Example: I engage in full partnership by being assertive about my needs.
1.
2.
3.

## **MONEY**

Example: I plan how to save and spend money with my partner.
1.
2.
3.

## **SEX**

Example: Whenever I feel uncomfortable, I redirect my partner to touch me in another way.
1.
2.
3.

## **CHILDREN**

Example: I am available to my children.
1.
2.
3.

## **FRIENDSHIP**

Example: I am dependable and faithful to my friends.
1.
2.
3.

## Section 1.2: Giving Voice to Values

Once you have regained perspective on your values, what is the next step? How do you enact those values? To find out more about how to do this, I spoke with a pioneer in the field of how to articulate one's values, Professor Mary Gentile. Professor Gentile is the Darden Professor at the University of Virginia and creator of Giving Voice to Values or GVV. GVV helps individuals to create scripts and practice utilizing communication skills to effectively act on values. It helps individuals ask these questions: What if I were going to act on my values? What would I say and do? How could I be most effective? Since its inception, GVV has helped to implement programs in over 1000 schools and businesses.

In an interview, Professor Gentile noted, "people know what to do, they just didn't think they could do it. They did not have an action orientated way of moving forward." In her book *Giving Voice to Values*, Professor Gentile talks about having an "ethical muscle" and using scripts, plans, and practice to get in the habit of voicing values. "If we are not voicing our values, we are not bringing our whole selves to work or to school for that matter."[170]

## Section 1.3: Case Studies

### *Adrian Evans*

Adrian Evans has practiced, consulted and taught law for thirty-five years at LaTrobe and Monash Universities. He was coordinator of the Springvale Legal Service Inc. from 1988-2000, the largest Australian Clinical Site. Professor Evans has conducted research and published on values in relation to law students' and lawyers' values, and best practice' ethics for lawyers and law firms, among other areas of interest.

Professionals and students suffer from emotional conflict and confusion due to the loss of core values. They are suffering emotionally from conflict or confusion due to this loss. So, it seems like in Australia you have found something different? Can you please tell me why you think there may be differences?

It's more a case that in Oz that research is coming up to twenty years old, and in that early period, there was little if any effort to inculcate or strengthen formative values in law students. Ethics education was (and often still is) rules-based rather than values-based. My view is that in this country, core values, whatever they were and regardless of law school, were pretty much left unaltered by legal education.

How do we overcome stigmas associated with issues of stress and secondary trauma as well as mental illness?

---

[170] Gentile, Mary. 2010. *Giving Voice to Values: How to Speak Your Mind When You Know What's Right*. New Haven: Yale University Press.

Many strategies help: thorough whole-of-person values identification programs for first years; good intra-law school availability of counsellors and mentors (which will include counselling to leave the law); and frequent public statements by deans and teachers about availability of support, etc. But I am sure all this and more is already well on your radar.

*We will now look at the work of Professors Sheldon and Krieger,*
*whose studies are referenced many times in the literature.*

Together, Sheldon and Krieger studied the issues of values, subjective well-being, and motivation among law students in Florida and Arizona. Their studies revealed that law students, compared with undergraduates, began their studies with higher levels of subjective well-being. However, by the end of the first-year subjective well-being had dramatically decreased. The changes they discovered correlated with decreases in intrinsic motivation, (individually defined essential actions and goals) over the first year and increases in more extrinsic characteristics such as appearance values and decreases in community service values.[171]

They also found those with the most intrinsic motivations obtained the highest grades, which supports Self-Determination Theory. The high grades were predictive of shifts in career preferences toward more lucrative careers, as opposed to more service-oriented ones.

### *Kennon M. Sheldon*

Kennon M. Sheldon, Ph.D. is a Psychology Professor at the University of Missouri and the coauthor (with Professor Krieger) of "What Makes Lawyers Happy? He studies motivation, goals, and well-being from both Self-Determination Theory and a positive psychology perspective.[172]

Highlights of my discussion with Professor Sheldon about Self-Determination Theory are below.

Your 2014 article talked about happiness and noted the change in values that people experience as they study law. It noted that prestige and income were nor factors that helped individuals to gain more happiness, even though prestige and income became goals for them.

[Self-Determination Theory] says that people have a need for autonomy and that it is often thwarted because of the power dynamic that people encounter in the world, where authorities don't support their autonomy, so they are treated in controlling ways. They end up kind of in a deficit position, where their needs are not being met, they feel controlled, they are not happy, they do not know what to do. Their ability to make fully informed decisions based on their own internal processes is compromised, so they start to make choices to get some type of satisfaction and so they make choices in ways that are compensatory and probably are not going to work very well. So, from this point of view,

---

[171] Sheldon, Kennon M., and Lawrence S. Krieger. (2004). "Does Legal Education have Undermining Effects on Law Students? Evaluating Changes in Motivation, Values, and Well-Being." *Behavioral Sciences & the Law* 22, issue 2:261–86. https://doi.org/10.1002/bsl.582.

[172] Krieger, Lawrence, and Kennon Sheldon. 2014. "What Makes Lawyers Happy? Transcending the Anecdotes with Data from 6200 Lawyers." SSRN Electronic Journal. 10.2139/ssrn.2398989.

materialism and narcissism, [and] drug use . . .There is sort of a common thread underneath the syndromes for compensating, for thwarting, the real needs not being met. [They] end up in a little bit of a downward spiral.

So, the application of that to law school, where it fits with Larry's stuff, [is] that legal education is basically quite controlling. [We] found that yes, students in Florida State, our first article, they did tend to lose or become more extrinsic or material in their values over time. They do tend to feel controlled by the situation, the context. There is reduction in needs satisfaction that create reduced happiness and reduced high-level functioning in general. That is kind of the big overview.

After moving to extrinsic values like materialism, do you think people can regain their core values?

I do think people can regain their former state or wake up, but it can be difficult . . . People get stuck in this limited view of themselves, which cuts them off from deeper sources, and it's like trying to use a broken tool to do a job. [It] is really not going to work, but there is still some part of them that can inform them, but they still have to ask for that and be open to it and then be courageous enough to implement [them] once they get those insights.

[The] growth process from that point of view is being discontent and starting to ask questions like, is this all there is? What's wrong with me? Which then primes nonconscious cognition to start working on the problem. It's like creativity, you solve a problem and then you're stuck and there is an incubation period and then an aha moment and then you have to take that insight and run with it. So, we are thinking about personal growth in that way. It involves being unhappy and stuck in a place and you start to ask questions, to where you open yourself up for your deeper self to start telling you how to make changes.

What role do you think stigma plays as people move away from core values and start to struggle with mental health issues or alcohol or other drug issues?

Well, I think that is an issue for anyone who is struggling. I don't know if it is for lawyers in particular. Do you think it is?

I do think it is. There is this particular self-narrative for lawyers that they should be role models, they have to be perfect, they have to keep pushing through even though they are tired or sick. They can't really show any signs of being "less-than" because even their colleagues might be attacking. Or they might be viewed as incompetent to take a certain case or incompetent to take the bar.

I mean I think that definitely happens. I think it doesn't happen only in the law. I think Larry might say the law encourages people to ignore or minimize their feelings, because . . . they have a case to handle. So maybe that is sort of a vocational norm that creates a special problem. I am not sure of that. It seems reasonable.

## *Lawrence Krieger*

Professor Lawrence Krieger's work focuses on well-being, satisfaction, values, relatedness and the motivations of law students and lawyers. His publications on law students and career planning have been used internationally. He codirects the externship program and supervises criminal justice externships at the College of Law at Florida State University. He was one of twenty-six law professors featured in the 2013 book *What the Best Law Teachers Do,* He is also the co-author of the study, "What Makes Lawyers Happy? Transcending the Anecdotes With Data From 6200 Lawyers."[173]

According to Krieger, his "focus is mainly on the 'primary trauma' . . . of students and lawyers losing their connection to their values, morality, [and] caring side, as practically a rite of passage into the profession (for many, certainly not all, but it is pervasive). Once that happens it is very hard to reverse, and it also makes law students and lawyers even more vulnerable than the rest of the population to the insanity about success, high pay, partnerships, etc. that also mainly distracts people from well-being. Then the law practice, adversarial system, and vicarious trauma piled on top of that, [which is] not a likely scenario for thriving at all." He looks at "internal values/motivations, one's sense of true self, and true values," which law professionals also need in order "to have the core personality integration" required to handle the stress of their job.

Here are more results from our discussions:

Self-Determination Theory tells us that we have be autonomous to be happy and yet law school and the Socratic Method is very controlling. Can you comment on this?

You can read Professor Elizabeth Mertz's *The Language of Law School*[174] to see just how unsettling the law school classroom can be. ["What Makes Lawyers Happy?"] was sponsored by the American Bar Foundation, in fact. And it shows, along with our research on law students, that the more profound negative effect is that law training actually directly pressures students to distance from their conscience, their values, and caring for people, to learn legal analysis. Those inner factors are the source of ethical and moral decision-making and the core of the "autonomy" need as we measure it.

What role do you think stigma plays as people move away from core values and start to struggle with mental health issues or alcohol or other drug issues as a way of compensating or coping?

Right, not just stigma, but greed, the need for money or power, high opinion from other people . . . all these external inputs that can temporarily make us feel better can come to the fore in the absence of the deep sense of well-being that autonomy, relatedness to others, and purpose in work provide to well-adjusted people. Those things specifically are known to fade during law school, making people ripe for a more external, and therefore unmanageable source of well-being. People become more vulnerable to outside influences when their internal groundedness is lost.

---

[173] Krieger, Lawrence, and Kennon Sheldon. 2014. "What Makes Lawyers Happy? Transcending the Anecdotes with Data from 6200 Lawyers." SSRN Electronic Journal. 10.2139/ssrn.2398989.

[174] Mertz, Elizabeth. 2007. *The Language of Law School: Learning to "Think Like A Lawyer"* Oxford: Oxford University Press.

Do you think you have seen any changes in the field since "What Makes Lawyers Happy?" came out?

Yes, probably not as a result of the study, but it is part of a national trend to focus more on lawyer and law student wellness and be less accepting of, or resigned to, the inevitably of a difficult and stressful life as a lawyer. It will take a lot longer for this emphasis, if it continues, to filter down to the core law firm, [to the] agency lawyer, but there is so much more attention, task forces, working groups, and such nationally now, so it is encouraging.

There is a widespread loss of character service commitment. What does this mean for the individual and for the profession? Is this a primary conflict?

I think "character" relates to the loss of autonomy, loss of connection to conscience, values, morality, caring for others . . . For the service values, yes, they are lost, there is a lot of research on that. You can see why from the previous response, loss of caring as students become less connected to internal sources of well-being and start to seek outside to fill the hole—via grades, competitions, money jobs, and for many, alcohol, drugs, etc.

It is all a displacement from internal to externally based satisfaction, and our research shows that none of the externals work. Common sense shows the same thing. Service values are one of the "internal" sources of well-being, and when one follows those values their choices also bring more experiences of connecting to others, feeling meaning and purpose in life (internal motivation), and autonomy (following one's values, conscience, and caring side). It is a big loss that is integrated with the rest of the findings very tightly.

Looking at Self-Determination Theory and the issues of autonomy, competence, and relatedness, how is relatedness reflected in terms of secondary trauma?

Secondary trauma needs its own training and awareness for lawyers and students, because it is a definite stressor that can generate burnout and depression without awareness and technique. Beyond that, when people (as stated several times now) lose their internal groundedness they search harder for fulfillment outside. It is a lot harder to find outside, because most of the external factors are out of one's personal control. But greater focus on outcomes, wins, and potentially "fixing" other people's problems is one result, and it generates burnout because one cannot reliably do these things. I do teach this to my students, how to keep their focus on what they can reliably do to help others (and themselves), and to stay satisfied there where they have control over their actions.

There appears to be no platform for the discussion of relatedness in a practical, methodical way. It is my opinion that we are not talking about relatedness due to stigma. If we are supposed to include all components, why are we not talking about this one and what is your suggestion?

As above, yes, relatedness to others is critical to well-being. When we get into legal-analytical mode (first week of law school) and competition against capable others as the be-all of success in our profession, relatedness falls to the side. Talking about it is useful but that doesn't fix anything, agreed. Talk stays up in our heads, that is where the problems are, frankly. [There should be] more focus for students and lawyers on reconnecting first to the body—the place where our life, all our feelings, and our energy to achieve all reside. Once we start to reconnect there, reconnecting with the natural desire to be close to and get along with others increasingly takes place. Lots of things people emphasize now help with this reconnection, including exercise, mindfulness, journaling, breathing and stress resilience practices. They all overlap tremendously, all for the good. In other words, it is not another intellectual discussion, it is back to common-sense basics of human life, especially now that the research shows what those are.

Do you think with the acceptance and usage of the right tools, [law professionals] can get their values back after losing them?

Yes, but it is very hard to get people's attention once they are distracted onto external "salvation" if you will, those values are so strongly established by traditional law school and practice institutional values. Anyone can change anything, [but] it takes real persistence, which takes deep understanding of the what and why of it all—connection or disconnection.

Tools have been in existence for some time, including tools created by lawyers and mental health professionals dating back to 1995. Why do you think they are not being utilized? Do you think this is because of the stigma surrounding mental health issues and coping?

I think stigma is less important, but a factor, whereas just feeling lost and grabbing onto dysfunctional sources for the lost well-being are the key.

The loss of values, morality and one's caring side are bold, brave statements. How do students or early professionals reconcile this?

Those are empirical facts and realities. They are bold and brave only because our training and profession take people in another direction without really intending to. It is the nature of legal analysis and argument, but it is counterproductive for well-being.

What roles do civility and values play when we are being taught to be competitive and adversarial?

A bit more on civility, it is like integrity I would say. Lecturing on it is true but not effective. And people can feign civility from the outside; it is surface and obviously [only on the surface], or it naturally proceeds from the inside. A person who is connected to her conscience, morality, decency, simply cannot be nasty, manipulative, dismissive, abusive toward any other being without feeling that pang of conscience. Hence in literally every paper I write I have a section on professionalism and ethics pointing out that in a healthy person there is no choice but to be ethical and respectful, it comes with the same territory as well-being, the very same foundations of authenticity (integrity!), relatedness to others, purpose in work. for the others, it is a surface add-on that will lapse under stress or simply never be there at all without effort for it.

## **Section 1.4: The Importance of Civility and Ethics**

We can see that living and articulating our core values is essential to our health. What do we do with peers and colleagues that are demeaning or even cruel when we behave in ways consistent with our values? What do we do when we are publicly criticized for articulating our values? One solution is to create an environment where civility is the norm and incivility is not tolerated. Professor G. Andy Benjamin works on the issue of civility and how the value of civility benefits individuals as well as the community. In the article "Civility is Good for Your Health," Benjamin and Cynthia Alexander found that social support is linked to happiness, and that the happiest people have the strongest social connections.[175]

"If your character is known to be good—that is, if you are known to keep your promises, if you're industrious, if you treat opponents fairly and do not deceive them- then your reputation will not only add to your success in material terms, but it will sustain your self-respect."[176]

Another way to potentially improve your surroundings would be working in a law practice that uses the concept of Collaborative Law. The Collaborative Law Institute of Minnesota (n.d.) encourages lawyers to use what could be called pro-social values: peace, dignity and "respect through a commitment to being non-adversarial and engage in active listening, transparency and "common understanding while discouraging argument, accusation and deception."[177] Would this not be an interesting approach to work and school in general?

## **Section 1.5: Champions of Disclosure**

### *Stu Webb*

Stu Webb shares with us his journey to mental health, consciousness, and the creation of Collaborative Law. In 1990, Stu Webb was a senior divorce attorney. After working in the field for numerous years he was tired of the adversarial work. He wanted to really help people but not in the way he had been. It was burning him out. It was through this process that Stu created Collaborative Law.

Stu it is so nice to talk with you. As I had been writing, I had already made the suggestion that people look into collaborative law rather than continue to work in this more adversarial and difficult way that they have been practicing. After talking with various people, they referred me to you.

How did you formulate this new way of doing divorce law practice? What is the story behind it?

I am totally transparent. I have no reason not to disclose anything. When I was going through my different things my manic-depressive stuff and hospitalization there was an article in the paper where I

---

[175] Benjamin, G. Andrew H., and Cynthia Alexander. 2011. "Civility is Good for Your Health." *Washington State Bar News*, April 1, 2011. https://ssrn.com/abstract=1803904 Reprinted with permission of the Washington State Bar Association from the April 2011 issue of the *Washington State Bar News*
[176] Evans, Adrian. 2014. *The Good Lawyer*. Cambridge: Cambridge University Press.
[177] Collaborative Law Institute. n.d. "Mission, Vision and Values." Collaborative Law Institute. Accessed January 1, 2020. https://www.collaborativelaw.org/mission-vision-and-values/.

was interviewed. I learned the hard way that you can't hide things. There is a stigma, and you think there is a stigma. When you share, people have open arms. It is a savior to share. It is dangerous to hide. In the first 40 years of my life, I was hiding. Up to the time of going to law school, my job was to make everyone like me. So, up until that time I hid so everyone liked me. And that worked perfectly through adolescence, college, navy, law school. When I came to be a lawyer, no one likes you. Your client doesn't like you; the judge doesn't like you; the other attorney doesn't like you. So, my world was turned. So, I went to this workshop and the leader said what is the one thing in life that if you lost it you would die or be destroyed. If I screwed up in life and everyone in the world new it and at the same time, they all turned around and pointed their finger at me I would disappear. The insight was what a lot of power to be giving to other people. THE AWARENESS from that sharing: I thought holy mackerel, EVERYONE HAS the power to kill me. The lesson was to open up myself. The lesson was not to have a defense. Open up.

Which is the exact opposite of what you learned in law school?

It was the exact opposite of what I learned in life- in the first 40 years of my life. I hid everything that would be negative. It was part of the release what happened was that I had a two-week period following the insight I just described, of total consciousness. I was totally conscious for 2 weeks and like spirituality leader, Ram Das said if you think you are enlightened, spend a week with your family. That is exactly what happened. It was at Christmas time family was around and I lost it. It started a search. Search, search, search- total search. The search was reaching to feel good and that was the manic and I would usually get caught by the police or other metal health professionals and be locked up on 72 hour holds and often abused beat up and stripped of all that stuff. So, coming out of manic with 2 weeks of total power and that is followed by 6 months of depression. Tremendous depression barely get out to work and then gradually comes the manic again and it was a big cycle and breaking that cycle was what saved my life. My vocation is higher consciousness and learning how to do it. So, I finally learned how to do it. I have no depression or worry for the last 5 years. It is normal living. We are habitually caught up in love fear and we have no control over it. We try to be loving and we watch the news and bing. Back in the 80s I wrote the book, The Serenity Space. It is learning how to shift from dualistic point of view to a non-dual point of view. That is what is going on in the world, the consciousness is raising. The question is, will enough consciousness be raised so there is a tipping point where enough people are in a non-duality where we can then shift the world. As consciousness is raised a lot of trauma gets erased. For me, as I learned from you, the term secondary trauma, I think secondary trauma is erased by higher consciousness. You have an idea, and you bring it out but someone in the group will say yes what about liability and you feel the energy – and it silently dies and that is what duality does. I was burned out after 20 years and you never know what is going to happen and you have your day all planned and your day blows up and I said I am not going to do this anymore. So, I started to take some classes over at the U to become a psychologist so I was still practicing but I thought if I am willing to quite the practice maybe I could do it differently Do the things I like to. And I started to experiment. So, I shared office with another lawyer and we each picked a client and it worked for half dozen cases and we settled things. The secret is if you are a settlement lawyer you get out of the case if it doesn't settle. That is collaborative law. On Jan 1st of 1990 There weren't any other ones. So, I had to send out a letter to 12 other lawyers who may be interested and that was the start of collaborative law. There is now 30,000 practitioners in 20 countries. Because of the lawyers the words spread slowly and lawyers doing all of this fighting and it was taking its toll on them and they were saying my God I can do this and be there to help people. We shifted, it is a paradigm shift, what I call a change a shift to higher consciousness in a legal setting. You shift from being in litigation down to the energy of the client and you move up to where you are looking at it from a higher place. The discovery is that you can't really hold the loving space in the duality system. I couldn't figure out why my Serenity Space brochure wasn't working. You can't get there from duality, you can get there other ways.

Do you teach it to your students?

Yes, that was messages to the collaborative family, and I did a webinar for the overall collaborative family. 90 people responded and we formed a global group called Coming Home. Since then, it keeps growing and growing and getting easier and easier. It is the most hopeful thing there is. The work you do is wonderful because I see the examples of trauma.

It gives some hope.

It is beyond hope. It is knowing.

Stu's story moves through tumultuous times in his life surrounding his issues of mental health to his creation of a new way of practicing law, Collaborative Law and finally, to the raising of his consciousness and that of others through what he calls enlightenment.

As the guidebook *Being Well in the Law* puts it, it's not easy to match your values with that of those around you, but it's worth it. "This convergence might be constrained by commercial realities and pragmatic limitations but working hard to find an ethical fit was important."[178]

*As we have seen, values and ethics play a crucial role in well-being,*
*as the attorney and academic Anneka Ferguson explains below.*

Anneka Ferguson is an Honorary Senior Lecturer at the Australian National University and Senior Lecturer at the University of New South Wales Australia. She has degrees in both law and psychology. Her areas of focus include legal ethics and promoting the development of well, professional, competent and ethical law graduates. Attorney Ferguson initiated a study of over 2,000 individuals looking at the issues of value and ethical conflicts. She shares her insights about ethics and common myths about lawyers and mental illness with us below.

---

[178] Rowe, Margie, Stephen Tang, Tony Foley, Vivien Holmes, Colin James, and Ian Hickie. 2016. *Being Well in the Law: A Guide for Lawyers.* The Law Society of New South Wales, November 3, 2016. https://ssrn.com/abstract=2861586 This publication is licensed under the Creative Commons Attribution-NonCommercial-NoDerivatives 4.0 International License

Anneka Ferguson: What Does Well-Being Have to Do with the Interaction Between Ethics and Values?

My research and writing on legal ethics and values started first with a question regarding the impact of legal education on the well-being of law students, rather than their ethical outlook. It started out of a desire as a fellow human to work out whether the new integrated, simulated and collaborative curriculum we had devised (see Ferguson 2015)[179] for the Graduate Diploma in Legal Practice was making or breaking our students. (The GDLP is the mandated course that law graduates in Australia need to complete to be admitted to the courts, in place of articles or bar examinations.

My initial logic, somewhat colored by my own experiences of tertiary legal education not preparing me for legal practice—was that grades were a poor indication of a student's ability to succeed and have a healthy and professional relationship with legal practice.

To examine this and extend on the already valuable information in this area, my colleague Stephen Tang and I developed a research project that surveyed almost 2000 students at the beginning and end of our core course. Done with approval from the ANU Ethics Committee. the survey was designed to examine the following issues:

- expectations/experiences of the course,
- indicia of professionalism,
- management of value and ethical conflicts; and,
- psychological wellbeing/distress

Analysis of this data suggested that we weren't doing the harm that many other studies of the law student experience in Australia and the U.S.

In short, we found evidence that the insulating factors for undesirable psychological outcomes of depression, anxiety, and stress were to be found in the creation of an legal educational environment that helped students feel that they are making progress towards their values and where their self-determination theory factors of autonomy, competence and relatedness were supported[180] (Tang and Ferguson 2014,[181] Ferguson 2015,[182] Ferguson and Tang 2019[183]). More important, we were able to provide some evidence that it was possible to create an educational environment for law students that supported their progress towards their values through autonomy and relatedness (Ferguson and Tang

---

[179] Ferguson, Anneka. 2015. "Creating Practice Ready, Professional and Well Law Graduates." *Journal of Learning Design* 8 (2):22 This work is licensed under a Creative Commons Attribution 4.0 License.

[180] Ferguson, Anneka. 2015. "Creating Practice Ready, Professional and Well Law Graduates." *Journal of Learning Design* 8 (2):22 This work is licensed under a Creative Commons Attribution 4.0 License

[181] Tang, Stephen, and Anneka Ferguson. 2014. "The Possibility of Wellbeing: Preliminary results from surveys of Australian Professional Legal Education Students." QUT Law Review 14 (1):27. https://ssrn.com/abstract=2413269

[182] Ferguson, Anneka. 2015. "Creating Practice Ready, Professional and Well Law Graduates." *Journal of Learning Design* 8 (2):22 This work is licensed under a Creative Commons Attribution 4.0 License

[183] Ferguson, Anneka, and Stephen Tang. 2019. "Chapter 5: The Value of Determination." In *Educating for Well-being in Law*, edited by Caroline Strevens and Rachael Field. New York: Routledge, 2019.

2019), as well as improve their sensitivity to enacting their values and ethical obligations. With this new evidence it became important to focus further on how values and ethics interacted in the legal education environment to create practice ready and psychologically well legal professionals.[184]

In many discussions on legal ethics in the classroom (perhaps determined by the way in which competencies are written for this work), the interaction between personal values and legal ethics as defined by the rules, as well as the values being promoted within the legal curriculum/classroom is ignored. However, as the research on well-being in legal education suggests, ignoring this interaction could potentially undermine the well-being and the ethical behavior of students. Personal values are incredibly powerful motivators, and the legal practice environment is also incredibly influential on the promotion of ethical or unethical behavior.

Thus, by discussing ethics as a set of rules, that is, a minimum standard to be followed, we are not arming graduates with the ability put these rules into action in environments where there are clashes between ethical principles and rules, or between ethical rules and their own values. Furthermore, this inability to bring their whole selves to work and to resolve ethical conflicts in a manner that also recognizes their personal values could lead to the poor well-being outcomes and symptoms we see in the many studies of law students and the legal profession. Viewing the interactions between values, ethics and well-being in this interrelated manner, where the chicken-and-egg paradox of what comes first is not clear, suggests that efforts to improve well-being must necessarily examine how to support individual values and professional ethics; and efforts to improve ethical behavior and values based action cannot be divorced from well-being.

What does an acknowledgement of this interaction look like in a practical sense?

In terms of framing how you turn this research into practical tips for improving both the ethical behavior and the well-being of the legal profession, my suggestion is that it is useful to examine a few myths that often get raised when questions on this are raised:

- Myth #1: Diagnosed mental illness equates to bad ethical behavior
- Myth # 2: Well-being and ethics are just about individual responsibility and sexy well-being add-ons
- Myth #3: All you need to do to "be ethical" is follow the rules. Ethics is common sense, and only bad people do unethical things.
- Myth #4: Lawyers are values-neutral and emotionless robots

*Myth #1 –Diagnosed mental illness equates to bad ethical behavior*

One of the side effects of the studies that now show the often poor mental health of legal practitioners is that the regulators of the profession (at least in Australia) have attempted to address this through mandatory reporting of psychological episodes and psychological diagnoses at the time that a

---

[184] Ferguson, Anneka, and Stephen Tang. 2019. "Chapter 5: The Value of Determination." In *Educating for Well-being in Law*, edited by Caroline Strevens and Rachael Field. New York: Routledge, 2019.

law graduate makes an application for admission to practice. The good intentions behind this practice are that examining these issues on admission will assist in protecting the public from unprofessional and unethical practices by practitioners with psychological illness. The side effect of these good intentions is that the assumption is being made that mental illness equates to bad ethical behavior. However, this assumption does not recognize several issues:

- The range of mental illness (just as there is a vast range of physical illness)
- The often-transient nature of such illnesses
- The fact that mental ill health does not immediately translate to ethical dysfunction in the legal practice environment.

To take an example close to my experience, even a cursory examination of the disciplinary cases before the Civil and Administrative Tribunal (Occupational Division) for the Australian state of New South Wales (NSW) for the January–November 2018 period suggests this focus on mental illness at the time of admission may be ill conceived in terms of protecting the public from unethical behavior. For example, of the thirty-nine cases examined only four made (just over 10% of the recorded cases) made mention of mental illness as part a possible mitigation of the alleged unethical behavior. Three of the four were diagnosable illnesses: major depressive disorder, post-traumatic stress disorder and acute stress disorder. Two of these diagnoses were to do with factors outside of legal practice, including domestic violence at home and being the victim of kidnapping.

This examination of the cases suggests that there was no indication that the conditions existed at the time of admission to practice and, in any event, the reference to the illnesses was not accepted as mitigation for the unethical behavior (generally the mishandling of legal practice trust account funds). Of the remaining cases where there was no mention of mental illness and the mitigating factors raised to explain the poor ethical behavior were focused on:

- Poor physical health,
- Being a "busy" partner,
- Personal external stressors (such as moving to a new house, surgery, family health and marital issues),
- Financial difficulties and bankruptcy; and,
- A lack of knowledge of ethical obligations.
- Finally, all cases involved sole or small firm practitioners and primarily involved practitioners with over ten years' experience.

Based on even this cursory examination of the factors that contribute to unethical behavior, it appears that the emphasis on mental illness as a primary driver is ill-conceived. In the vast majority of cases that don't involve out-and-out fraud (although even then) there was a general trend towards a lack of general well-being: stresses at home, being overworked or under supported, bad physical health, financial pressures, needing a break. This suggests to me that any regulation of the profession that aims to reduce unethical complaints or behaviors may need to support legal practice structures that encourage general well-being. This could include increased focus on the reasons that lead good people to do bad things. Examples of this could be behavioral ethics supports and professional development training that recognizes the behavioral ethics pitfalls that are possible for all practitioners rather than "if you have a mental health issue, you will be unethical" (which is simply not borne out by an examination of the cases).

*Myth #2: Well-being and ethics is about individual responsibility and add-ons*

While individual lawyers should not eschew individual responsibility for their ethical behavior and well-being, the constant focus on the individual lawyer in both the regulation of ethical behavior and the support for well-being ignores structural issues that lead to poor behavior and poor well-being outcomes and that require reaching a very high level of distress (a crisis point) before any support can be given. Although a disciplinary judgement may make mention of the structural problems of the law firm, such as time billing, a culture of long hours and undervaluing staff or prioritizing client requirements over ethics, it is ultimately the individual lawyer that bears the brunt of the consequences of the behavior, whilst the law firm continues to benefit from the same practices that lead to the behavior. Unless something happens to adjust this framework to the level of the law firm, the individual mindfulness of the individual lawyer, or whether the law firm offers gym passes or nutritious dinners in the office are nothing more than a Band-Aid covering up a ubiquitous sore of profits over people.

*Myth #3: Just follow the rules to be ethical. Ethics is just common sense;*
*only bad people do unethical things*

There are many potential (and arguably very obvious) pitfalls in just teaching the legal ethical rules or suggesting that the rules are just common sense. The rules are a minimum standard. They simply will not cover every situation lawyers find themselves in. Invariably there will be clashes between obligations and grey areas for interpretation. Furthermore, what is "common sense" to one person will be dictated by values, environment, experience, education, and upbringing. Accordingly, there is the very real possibility that legal practitioners with all the best of intentions may behave unethically if they fall into one of the behavioral ethical traps of their environment, or simply take their sight off the ethics of a situation in favor of some other aspect of their situation. As the brief analysis (above) of the disciplinary matters in the state of NSW indicated, behaving unethically could simply be the result of overwork, physical illness or social stressors of family or finances.

The suggestion that only bad people do unethical things unhelpfully removes questions of how to support lawyer well-being for better professionalism from the equation. It also stymies broader useful discussions on the interactions between different legal ethical rules, legal ethics and morality, and legal ethics and personal values.

*Myth #4: Lawyers are values-neutral and emotionless robots*

It is always interesting discussing the role of values and emotions in legal practice with students and legal practitioners. Frequently, the suggestion will be made that the role of the lawyer is not to exercise their values, as they are the mouthpieces of their clients. Similarly, it is often intimated that all emotional responses are to be suppressed to serve your client.

Given the research on the importance of being able to progress your values to well-being (indicated above) and that, as humans, we make our emotional judgments quickly and prior to intellectually rationalizing them, it is an absurd myth to pursue, both for the lawyers and the clients. Which is not to say we all need to be hugging each other and singing "Kumbaya."

Instead, I suggest a more pragmatic approach of encouraging lawyers and law students to identity their values and providing a framework for voicing them effectively and constructively– for example, the Giving Voice to Values curriculum (Gentile 2010). Similarly, instead of discouraging the recognition of emotional responses that individual lawyers may have to particular situations, it is healthier and more effective in serving the clients' interests if lawyers and law students are encouraged to actively reflect on their emotional responses to situations.[185] By slowing down their thinking in this manner, it provides space for legal practitioners to test their initial emotional response and consider making a more considered decision for their client. This process of making the implicit explicit can also potentially improve the ethical behavior in situ, as well as ameliorate the power of implicit biases on lawyer actions. Thus, it will serve both the clients and the community better than if these emotional responses and implicit biases go unchecked.

The interaction between legal ethics, values, and well-being is complex. It is interdependent rather than linear, and very reliant on the context in which situations occur. This complexity requires us to lean into the challenge of providing dynamic and contextually aware discussions and skills in the education of law students and lawyers rather than trying to simplify the process through a rules-based legal ethics approach or a reliance on sexy well-being add-ons such as mindfulness to resolve the very often structural stressors of being a legal professional.

As Anneka Ferguson demonstrates, it is important that we continue to support individual values and professional ethics. Values and ethics are essential components for well-being, and it is equally as important for law firms to support lawyers with ethical issues.

---

[185] Gentile, Mary. 2010. *Giving Voice to Values: How to Speak Your Mind When You Know What's Right*. New Haven: Yale University Press.

## Section 2: Spirituality

Spirituality is important for many reasons, including general well-being, coping, and finding meaning and balance in life. Lawyers and law students encounter suffering as part of their work. Spirituality can be used to help understand and cope with that suffering.

As the Substance Abuse and Mental Health Services Administration (n.d.) states, "Spirituality is a broad concept with room for many perspectives. In general, it includes a sense of connection to something bigger than us, and it typically involves a search for meaning in life. As such, it is a universal human experience—something that touches us all."[186] For many, spirituality is a component of a balanced life.

Numerous studies demonstrate that spirituality improves physical as well as mental health. In one study, individuals with higher spirituality and religiosity levels had an 18% reduction in mortality rates.[187]

"Here are just a few more of the many positive findings related to spirituality and its influence on physical and mental health:

Canadian college students who are involved with campus ministries visited the doctor less. They also scored higher on tests of psychological well-being and coped with stress more effectively.

Older women are more grateful to God than older men, and they receive greater stress-buffering health effects due to this gratitude.

Those with an intrinsic religious orientation, regardless of gender, exhibited less physiological reactivity toward stress than those with an extrinsic religious orientation. They were also less afraid of death and had greater feelings of well-being. (Those who were intrinsically oriented dedicated their lives to God or a 'higher power,' while the extrinsically oriented ones used religion for external ends like making friends or increasing community social standing.)"[188] (Scott 2010).

---

[186] Substance Abuse and Mental Health Services Administration (SAMHSA). n.d. "Talking About Spiritual and Religious Factors in Wellness." https://www.samhsa.gov/sites/default/files/programs_campaigns/wellness_initiative/spirituality-fact-sheet.pdf

[187] Lucchetti, Giancarlo, Alessandra L. G. Lucchetti, and Harold G. Koenig. 2011. "Impact of spirituality/religiosity on mortality: Comparison with other health interventions." *EXPLORE: The Journal of Science and Healing* 7(4): 234–238. https://doi.org/10.1016/j.explore.2011.04.005

[188] Scott, Elizabeth. "Spirituality Can Improve Many Aspects of Your Life and Health." Verywell Mind. Verywell Mind, March 13, 2020. https://www.verywellmind.com/how-spirituality-can-benefit-mental-and-physical-health-3144807.

## Section 2.1: Thoughts on Spirituality

Peter Gabel is a professor of law, the author of numerous books, a former college president, and a community activist. In our discussion, Peter shared that, "a lawyer should be a healer of human conflict, not someone who makes it worse." He proposes a "social-spiritual way of seeing the world," and has written that law "is not a body of rules but rather a culture of justice in which the moral and spiritual dimension of human relations is given expression."[189]

In his book, *The Desire for Mutual Recognition*, Peter recommends utilizing social-spiritual activism in concrete ways. He proposes that we start with ourselves right now, right where we are. He creates three concentric circles. In the innermost circle, is the person, you or I or "we." In this circle we can use "spiritual practices that strengthen the presence of the person," such as meditation, yoga, chi gong, tai chi, walking in nature, and prayer. As he states in our discussion, "the purpose of the innermost circle practices is to remain in touch with our soul, you might say, instead of being drawn out of ourselves repeatedly and back into the learned performances of the self (along with 'the news, the demands of work, the learned roles of the family, etc.)."

The second circle is the surrounding social field. "The Second Circle: Social-Spiritual Practices that Strengthen the Internal Confidence of the Group in the Present Moment through Intentional Creation of a Parallel Universe." That is a "confirmatory environment" that provides mutual recognition. Peter uses as an example, spiritual practice associated with religion. As Peter told me, "the aim is to create a 'parallel' social world in which our deepest selves can be elicited and confirmed by others. Sometimes religious practice can help accomplish this, but also labor unions can, and emergent social movement practice can." Family is also part of this second circle.

The third circle, the future, is where we "aspire to spiritualize social policy and other incarnations of the world we are trying to bring into being." Peter noted in our email correspondence, "the third circle means that proposals for social policy are actually evocations of the future possible world and thus must be articulated in a framework of meaning that would realize the social bond we all long for!" [190]

## Champion of Disclosure

### *Mary J. Novak*

Below, our Champion of Disclosure Mary J. Novak discusses how spirituality impacts her and those she works with at the Georgetown University Climate Center.

Mary Novak serves Georgetown Law Center and the School of Continuing Studies as a mission integrator, chaplain, spiritual director, and adjunct professor of law. She also currently serves as Chair of the Board of the Catholic Mobilizing Network to End the Use of the Death Penalty and Promote

---

[189] Gabel, Peter. 2013. *Another Way of Seeing: Essays on Transforming Law, Politics and Culture.* New Orleans: Quid Pro Books.

[190] Gabel, Peter. 2018. *The Desire for Mutual Recognition: Social Movements and the Dissolution of the False Self.* New York: Routledge.

---

Restorative Justice. What follows expands on a presentation from the Fall of 2019 Symposium of the University of St. Thomas Law Journal, Restorative Justice, Law, and Healing (October 25, 2019), and a similar narrative appears in her article in 17 U. St. Thomas Law Journal.

## Lawyers Making Meaning of Our Secondary Trauma Response

Man's search for meaning is the primary motivation in his life and not a "secondary rationalization" of instinctual drives. This meaning is unique and specific in that it must and can be fulfilled by him alone; only then does it achieve a significance which will satisfy his own will to meaning.[191]

—*Man's Search for* Meaning, Viktor Frankl

Coming to realize we are prone to secondary or vicarious trauma in the study and practice of law is such an important step. Until recently, nothing in our legal education prepared us for dealing with traumatized clients. As described in Chapter 1 of this book, coming to terms with the actual fact that we are exhibiting signs of a response to trauma exposure is a courageous step indeed. As we become conscious of our own suffering, we are well on the way. Making a choice about what to do with that suffering is our ultimate goal, and in so doing, we must grapple with how we make meaning of our suffering and the suffering of others.

Trauma interferes with how we have made meaning in the past. We must learn how to remake meaning after trauma to continue to build resilience. This is the gift Viktor Frankl gave us after he survived the death camps of Dachau and Auschwitz, the understanding that trauma and meaning are inextricably linked. What Frankl observed in the camps is that people making meaning (relying on old ones or creating new ones) meant the difference between life and death[192] (McAdams and Jones 2017, 3).

Below, we explore how trauma intersects with our categories of meaning making, offer a case example of a group of lawyers, scientists, and communicators as they grapple with their secondary trauma, and make suggestions for your own meaning making in the study and practice of law.

## How Trauma Impacts Our Meaning Making

C. L. Park offers an important model of meaning making for our purposes. She suggests that people navigate their lives through their global meaning systems. These meaning systems comprise people's fundamental beliefs—about themselves, the world, their place in the world, and their sense of meaning and purpose—as well as their unique hierarchies of goals and values. Global meaning systems inform people's understanding of themselves and their lives and direct their personal aims and projects

---

[191]Viktor Frankl, *Man's Search for Meaning* (New York: Pocket Books, 1984), 121. Pardon the use of gendered language in this quote; I am loathe to change the text of a giant like Frankl and trust readers to understand he was using the language of his time.
[192] McAdams, D. P., and B. K. Jones. 2017. "Making Meaning in the Wake of Trauma: Resilience and Redemption." *Reconstructing Meaning After Trauma: Theory, Research, and Practice*, edited by Elizabeth M. Altmaier. London: Academic Press.

and, through them, their general sense of well-being and life satisfaction.[193] (Park and Kennedy 2017, 18)

These global meaning systems include beliefs about the self and world such as predictability, controllability and the benevolence of humanity. They include our goals for companionship, self-acceptance, financial security and achievement as well as a general sense of meaning or purpose.[194] (Wade et al 2017, 71–72). When we are faced with a trauma, whether consciously or not, we make appraisals related to the situational meaning of the event (e.g., why did it happen, the degree of threat and controllability). And we experience distress when we experience a discrepancy between our global meaning and situational appraisals; this distress then initiates a process of meaning making."[195] (Wade et al 2017, 71–72).

Oftentimes, students first experience this distress as they become exposed to the legal system, especially the part of the system that addresses criminal law, generally a requirement for all first-year law students. Legal practitioners in that part of the system as well as those in the area of immigration and family law are confronted with this discrepancy relentlessly. Increasingly, we are seeing this discrepancy in those who practice environmental law, as we will discuss below. This discrepancy does not usually happen in a moment, but rather over the course of time and thus, it can sneak up on us. How we navigate this meaning making in the face of the discrepancy between our global meaning and situational appraisal can often determine our ability to grow from our secondary trauma. But first, we have to prepare ourselves to do this meaning making.

## Preparing the Way for Meaning Making

Like those who are directly exposed to trauma, those of us in the legal profession who are exposed secondarily or vicariously can have physiological and acute emotional impacts that need to be addressed prior to the difficult work of meaning making. For example, as Champion of Disclosure Attorney Dan Lukasik, discussed in the chapter on depression, he did not recognize self-care as a priority. Once he realized the need to prioritize his self-care, he had better work-life balance and ultimately created his support group and online community.

Once this baseline healing is underway and our strength is returning, we can start the multifaceted process of making sense of our trauma exposure and the meaning making of our secondary trauma response.

---

[193] Park, C. L., and M. C. Kennedy. 2017. "Meaning Violation and Restoration Following Trauma." In *Reconstructing Meaning After Trauma: Theory, Research, and Practice*, edited by Elizabeth M. Altmaier. London: Academic Press, 2017.

[194] Wade, N., J. M. Schultz, and M. Schenkenfelder. 2017. "Forgiveness Therapy in the Reconstruction of Meaning Following Interpersonal Trauma." In *Reconstructing Meaning After Trauma: Theory, Research, and Practice*, edited by Elizabeth M. Altmaier. London: Academic Press.

[195] Wade, N., J. M. Schultz, and M. Schenkenfelder. 2017. "Forgiveness Therapy in the Reconstruction of Meaning Following Interpersonal Trauma." In *Reconstructing Meaning After Trauma: Theory, Research, and Practice*, edited by Elizabeth M. Altmaier. London: Academic Press.

## Making Sense of Our Trauma Exposure

Let us be clear about what we mean by making meaning out of our secondary trauma. A good place to begin is with trying to make sense of the trauma exposure we have experienced by thinking about what caused this situation to happen, how and why it came to be. Making sense of our experience is an invitation to understand more fully the general systemic dynamics at play. We might be drawn, for example, to understand better the oppression institutionalized in our society's structures and how our clients experience the embedded violence that systematically implements ethnocentrism, racism, sexism and all other isms.[196] Or we might be drawn to a better understanding of the newest research of the causes for the growth in child pornography worldwide or the rise in domestic violence in areas where women's empowerment programs are flourishing.[197]

Making sense of the how and why can also be an invitation to understand the pain and suffering in the people we accompany and represent as attorneys and law students. In other words, what is happening in the specific situation of our clients. For example, if we are representing juveniles in the local juvenile legal system, it can mean understanding how adverse childhood experiences impact the growing brain of youth who end up in that system.[198] It can mean understanding how the national "war on drugs" has impacted the segments of the local community from which those juveniles are hailing.[199]

Davis labels this kind of activity "sense making." By way of this process, we gain constructs for our understanding of our client's pain and suffering, the pain and suffering caused by those we are adjudicating or whatever is the nature of the pain and suffering to which we have been exposed in our work as lawyers. With these understandings, our own secondary trauma can begin to be ameliorated,[200] because we have begun to make meaning of it.

As we progress in the practice of any specific area of the law, our sense making must be updated over time as the knowledge in our area of the law grows, especially when leaps of knowledge occur. What this requires is updating our knowledge of the law as well as the underlying conditions in which it operates, for example sociology, psychology, criminology, and foreign affairs. If we are not continually updating our knowledge of the portion of society in which we are operating, we will be engaging the law with antiquated constructs that neither serve us nor the people we serve. Such antiquated constructs can over time limit our ability to make sense of what we are experiencing and thus limit our ability to understand the trauma to which we are exposed.

---

[196] For example, in the criminal system, Michelle Alexander, *The New Jim Crow: Mass Incarceration in the Age of Colorblindness* (New York: The New Press: 2012); Paul Butler, *Chokehold: Policing Black Men* (New York, The New Press: 2018); and Angela Davis, ed., *Policing the Black Man: Arrest, Prosecution, and Imprisonment* (New York: Vintage Books: 2017).

[197] Mara Bolis and Christine Hughes, Women's Economic Empowerment and Domestic Violence (Oxfam: 2015); The Scourge of Child Pornography: Working to Stop the Sexual Exploitation of Women, Washington: FBI: April 25, 2017. Accessed November 2, 2019. https://www.fbi.gov/news/stories/the-scourge-of-child-pornography.

[198] Eduardo Ferrer, "Transformation Through Accommodation: Reforming Juvenile Justice by Recognizing and Responding to Trauma." *American Criminal Law Review* (2016).

[199] James Forman, *Locking Up Our Own: Crime and Punishment in Black America* (New York: Farrar, Straus and Giroux: 2017).

[200] C. G. Davis, "The tormented and the transformed: understanding responses to loss and trauma," in R. A. Neimer, ed., *Meaning reconstruction and the experience of loss*, 135–155 (Washington, DC: APA Books, 2001).

*Making Meaning of Our Secondary Trauma*

In whatever way we make sense out of our trauma exposure, we need to also do the hard work of examining and potentially changing our own global meaning systems if we are to healthily stay engaged as legal practitioners. The personal meaning making we do of our secondary trauma response requires us to understand how the part of the legal system we engage affects us, our worldview and our ongoing life narrative.

*How does Secondary Trauma Exposure Affect Us?*

When reflecting on our own secondary trauma response as law students or lawyers, the work of emergency medical dispatchers (EMDs) is very instructive:

EMDs say that they all have their own personal triggers, as seen with the description of one dispatcher, Julia: "those teenage suicides, they throw me off my game. They're not the kids with SIDS [sudden infant death syndrome], not the big cases, but the unnecessary ones." Personal connections to a caller's story also reverberated as a traumatic moment. Julia recalled a case that was particularly difficult because she felt an emotional and personal connection to the caller: "There was a call when I first came to [location] who sounded just like my mum and I think that call was a trigger. Like my heart rate went up and when I was off the phone, I said I have to get out of here and I think that was what triggered it all." Here Julia is referring to the symptoms of traumatic stress she began to experience. Personal connections can allow for a permeation of their thin but clear professional emotional boundary with the caller. And the caller's trauma can then seep into their one psyche[201] (Shakespeare-Finch and Adams 2017, 121).

Like EMDs, how we legal practitioners are aware of our personal connections to the trauma to which we are exposed demands consistent attention to what is happening within us. Just as Julia does in this example, we need to notice when our bodies respond and when we feel like fleeing or any of the other base responses to trauma (freezing, fainting, or fighting). With the knowledge of our personal triggers, we can then find strategies that maintain our mental health in a context where the threat of trauma exposure is constant. With this knowledge also comes the invitation to explore our prior connections to trauma—the ones that were triggered. Of course, the bodily responses must first be addressed, as has been discussed in Chapter 2.[202]

---

[201] Shakespeare-Finch, J., and K. Adams. 2017. "Growth and Meaning From Negotiating the Complex Journey of Being an Emergency Medical Dispatcher." In *Reconstructing Meaning After Trauma: Theory, Research, and Practice*, edited by Elizabeth M. Altmaier. London: Academic Press.

[202] The bodily responses are also personal, and often culturally as well as racially based; for instance see Resmaa Menakem, *My Grandmother's Hands, Racialized Trauma and the Pathway to Mending Our Hearts and Bodies* (Las Vegas, NV: Central Recovery Press, 2017).

*How does the Secondary Trauma Exposure Affect Our Worldview?*

Once we are ready, however, it's time to revisit how what we experienced in the prior trauma disagreed with our global sense of meaning. In other words, to look at how our prior trauma was inconsistent with our belief about ourselves in the world, how predictable and controllable it is, and whether humanity is good or not.

When we allow ourselves to engage these more ultimate beliefs in the face of trauma, we open the door to subjects many of us have not examined since childhood or maybe never examined directly but simply received indirectly from our families and society. Our spirituality, whether located in a religious tradition or not, whether conscious of it or not, often informs the global beliefs that are so important to our making meaning out of our secondary trauma responses.

For many of us, spirituality, including our beliefs about God or the Divine as loving and benevolent, wrathful, or distant, informs our core beliefs about the nature of people (e.g., inherent goodness, made in God's image, sinful human nature) and this world (e.g., the coming apocalypse, the illusory nature of reality), as well as, often, the next, including heaven and reincarnation[203] (Park and Kennedy 2017, 20).

Uncovering how our core beliefs are informed by our spirituality can be revelatory in making meaning of our secondary trauma response. Our spirituality can be a positive influence on our global beliefs,[204] leading to profound healing when we do the deep work of exploring and integrating our secondary trauma response.[205] When our spirituality promotes the following traits, not only is it the basis for a good integration of our secondary trauma response, it might even serve as a protective strategy against the deleterious effects of trauma exposure[206] (Murdoch 2004, 494): honest self-esteem which includes an accurate assessment of our limitations; wonder in the face of inexplicable grace; friendship through betrayal and pain; courage to forge such friendships; a willingness to learn; tolerance of pain, suffering and difference; finding joy despite adversity; interdependence on the journey; perseverance; freedom to choose; love; generativity; balance; various prayer forms including external and internal; careful and well-boundaried forgiveness;[207] gratitude for simple gifts; situationally appropriate playfulness and lightness; commitment and fidelity; theological hope; and non-anxious restlessness.[208]

---

[203] Park, C. L., and M. C. Kennedy. 2017. "Meaning Violation and Restoration Following Trauma." In *Reconstructing Meaning After Trauma: Theory, Research, and Practice,* edited by Elizabeth M. Altmaier. London: Academic Press, 2017.

[204] "Some spiritual beliefs can have negative content or exert negative influences on the believer as well. For example, some religious beliefs, such as those in an angry, uncaring, or punitive God, can have powerfully destructive implications for personal and social functioning in the context of stress or trauma" (Park and Kennedy 2017, 20).

[205] Teresa Rhode McGee, *Transforming Trauma* (Orbis, 2005)

[206] Murdoch, Lynda L. 2000. "Psychological Consequences of Adopting a Therapeutic Lawyering Approach: Pitfalls and Protective Strategies." *Seattle University Law Review* 24: 494.

[207] Dennis Linn, Sheila Fabricant Linn and Matthew Linn, *Don't Forgive Too Soon: Extending the Two Hands That Heal* (Mahwah, N.J.: Paulist Press, 1996).

[208] Melannie Scoboda, *Traits of a Healthy Spirituality* (Twenty-Third Publications, 1996).

For many, this reflection may also be aided by examining and interrogating our understanding of suffering and evil. Often, this is an area of our global sense of meaning we indirectly inherited from our families and communities and have never examined directly as adults. Possessing an undeveloped theodicy can seriously limit our ability to process and integrate our trauma exposure response.[209]

### *How Secondary Trauma Affects Our Ongoing Life Narrative*

Similarly, how we understand ourselves in our roles in the legal system we inhabit must integrate our trauma exposure experiences and how we make meaning of them. The good news is the process of professional identity formation has been well-developed in the last decade for law students,[210] such that this kind of reflection began for many lawyers before they graduated from law school. To stay healthily engaged as legal practitioners, reflecting on our life narrative needs to continue on an ongoing basis to incorporate and integrate our experiences, especially to integrate how we make meaning of our secondary trauma experiences. In other words, once formed, we must actively reform our identities at critical junctures in our lives as lawyers because this is not a one-and-done process.

As part of some of the clinics here at Georgetown University Law School, when the clinical psychologist and I are introducing trauma exposure responses, I invite law students to reflect on who they are to their clients and who their clients are to them. Then I give them two poles as examples, explaining they are probably somewhere between them.

The first pole is where the students understand themselves in relationship with their clients at arm's length. It can mean the client relationship is one for the student to get a chance to "give back," or where they are "saving their clients from themselves," or "making a difference," or "empowering them" or "being a voice for the voiceless."

The other pole draws from the aboriginal saying: "If you are coming to help me you are wasting your time. But if you have come because your liberation is bound up with mine, then let us work together." In other words that you were sent to the margins NOT to make a difference but rather, so that the folks on the margins, the clients, will make you different; that you are called to surrender to their leadership and listen to them. Or that your clients return you to yourself, to your own brokenness and your deeper desire to show mercy. Or what the Koran teaches, that God created diverse tribes so that we might come to know each other, simply know each other. Or in a hope that was not about some assurance that everything will work out but rather about a confidence that purpose and luminous meaning can be found in this work together, no matter how things unfold[211] (Murdoch 2004, 494).

---

[209] One of the most popular and helpful explorations of theodicy across the faith traditions is Harold Kushner's *When Bad Things Happen to Good People* (New York: Random House Inc., 1981).

[210] See, for instance, Neil W. Hamilton, "Professional Formation with Emerging Adult Law Students in the 21-29 Age Group: Engaging Students to Take Ownership of Their Own Professional Development Toward Both Excellence and Meaningful Employment," *Journal of the Profession Lawyer* (2015).

[211] This framing comes generally from Gregory Boyle, *Barking to the Choir: The Power of Radical Kinship* (New York: Simon & Schuster, 2017); Bryan Stevenson, *Just Mercy: A Story of Justice and Redemption* (New York: Spiegel & Grau, 2014); and Jon Sobrino, *No Salvation Outside the Poor: Prophetic-Utopian Essays* (New York: Orbis, 2008).

It might come as a surprise that the students and lawyers who are grounded closer to the first pole will likely experience less impacts of secondary trauma exposure initially than those who fall closer to the second pole. It is because their meaning making constructs distance them from their clients. Those closer to the second pole initially experience more secondary trauma impact because, by way of their empathy, they open themselves up to the client in ways that those closer to the first pole do not[212] (Murdoch 2004, 494).

As we move toward the second pole in our practices of law by way of various movements in legal education,[213] we therefore need to train ourselves to do the important work with our own trauma exposure as do those in other helping professions. This important work includes forming and reforming our philosophies and narratives of life and work consistent with our chosen roles in the legal profession while we employ practices of care for our bodies, emotions and spirit. This is the kind of grappling the Georgetown Climate Center (GCC) has been doing, the next Champion of Disclosure in this book.

*The Georgetown Climate Center*

When I first started at Georgetown Law Center, I very quickly became familiar with the Georgetown Climate Center (GCC) and its internationally recognized analytic, policy and advocacy work. As a former environmental lawyer, I was drawn to and in great admiration of its multidisciplinary approach to climate change. As I got to know them, however, I started to note very familiar signs of the deleterious impacts of this work when individuals and groups engage it for the long-term. I myself had experienced what I later came to understand as significant secondary trauma response (e.g., feeling helpless and hopeless, a sense that I could never do enough, hypervigilance, chronic exhaustion and physical ailments, numbing, minimizing, diminished creativity) when I practiced California environmental law over 20 years ago. Except no one was making the connection back then between my symptoms and my vocation.[214]

While today we know so much more about the impacts of climate change on mental health and well-being, especially for those who work in it day-in-and-day-out,[215] when I started to experience the symptoms of trauma response over two decades ago, I began to question my vocational choice to be an environmental lawyer. This led me to engage the more ultimate questions of meaning and purpose, but I had no faith community with which to discuss them. I was therefore left to simply engaging health-care practitioners to alleviate my mounting physical and emotional symptoms (debilitating body aches, gastrointestinal distress, exhaustion, difficulty sleeping, emotional numbing, feelings of alienation). I also began reading apocalyptic literature, both ancient and new, without the theological training to put it

---

[212] Murdoch, Lynda L. 2000. "Psychological Consequences of Adopting a Therapeutic Lawyering Approach: Pitfalls and Protective Strategies." *Seattle University Law Review* 24: 494.

[213] Trauma-informed legal education, therapeutic lawyering, practicing law as a healing profession, religious lawyering, law student well-being, ethical profession identity formation, to name a few.

[214] Frederick Buechner defines vocation broadly, saying that the place "God calls you to is the place where your deep gladness and world's deep hunger meet." Accessed November 3, 2019. http://www.calledthejourney.com/blog/2014/12/17/frederick-buechner-on-calling.

[215] See, e.g., Lipsky, *Trauma Stewardship,* 52-58; Susan Clayton, Christie Manning, Kirra Krygsman and Meighen Speiser, *Mental Health and Our Changing Climate: Impacts, Implications, and Guidance* (American Psychological Association, Climate for Health and ecoAmerica: 2017). Accessed November 3, 2019. https://www.apa.org/news/press/releases/2017/03/mental-health-climate.pdf.

in context. By sheer grace, a friend invited me to his faith community, which engaged faith and reason, religion and science, contemplative practices as well as the work for the common good. In this community, I both found a home and a place to engage my ultimate questions, including my deep concerns about what we humans were doing to the planet, the role of religious traditions in our collective disconnection from Mother Earth and my finitude in the midst of it all.

These reflections and ponderings led me to teach law and study theology at night to continue the process of integrating my secondary trauma responses and the meaning I was making out of them. It is now my privilege to serve as a trauma-informed chaplain and spiritual director to law students and lawyers and it is from this space of gratitude that I received the invitation to journey with the GCC last year.

Preparing to celebrate the GCC's tenth anniversary in 2018, its director invited her staff to retreat from the office to do some strategic planning. She invited me into the process of planning the retreat, as I had been sharing with her the literature on the impacts of climate change on mental health and well-being. In the middle of fall, when autumn's beauty was still so apparent, GCC's staff and I gathered at Georgetown's Calcagnini Contemplative Center near the Appalachian Trail in Virginia. We chose to be outside of Washington, D.C. because GCC's offices are on and near Georgetown's Law Center campus on Capitol Hill, an intense place under the best of circumstances.

At the beginning of the retreat, we invited the GCC staff of attorneys, climate scientists, policy and communications experts, and administrators to share with each other what moved them to devote their lives to climate change work. The stories were rich, moving, and sometimes quite humorous. We then suggested the GCC staff take a thirty-minute silent walk-in nature, inviting them to choose either a secular or theistic version of a mindfulness exercise, whichever was most comfortable to them and whichever fit best within their own meaning making constructs. Later in the afternoon, after exploring where GCC had been and where it is going in light of the state of the national, state, and global situation, we took a break to hike, read, rest or play. Each GCC member was then invited to read the introduction to *Trauma Stewardship* which included the following paragraph:

We cannot ignore emerging information about the profound levels of trauma exposure among people in the front lines of the environmental movement—those fighting to stop the juggernaut of global warming and those who strive desperately, in the face of mounting losses, to ward off the extinction of countless species of plants and animals.[216] (Lipsky 2009, 5–6)

After grounding ourselves in our vocation stories, directly experiencing the creation to which we are devoting our lives, reflecting on our work, attending to our bodies and being invited to consider trauma exposure as a framework, we reconvened to explore and reflect upon the our own trauma responses in the face of climate change. To a person, the GCC staff acknowledged how they did not feel entitled to these feelings—or to labelling them as trauma—- as a result of climate change. They explained their resistance was because their own exposure paled in comparison to what the people they

---

[216] Lipsky, Laura van Dernoot, with Connie Burk. 2009. *Trauma Stewardship: An Everyday Guide to Caring for Self While Caring for Others.* San Francisco: Berrett-Koehler.

served were facing, for example, forced relocation due to climate change, often while simultaneously navigating the adverse effects of chronic poverty.

Acknowledging and honoring this disparity of experience, I invited them to consider how they could be suffering even if those they serve were suffering more. I noted how I had no investment in whether they were experiencing a trauma response but invited them to be open to the possibility. We then reviewed much of what is covered elsewhere in this book, the definition of trauma and secondary trauma, and how recognizing it in ourselves is not easy. After inviting them to take a deep breath, remain curious and inquisitive, be nonjudgmental and maintain a sense of humor, I suggested they write down any trauma exposure warning signs that resonated for them[217] (Lipsky 2009, 47–113). The room got quieter and heavier as I made my way through the warning signs explained more fully in Chapter 1.

Explaining how "if we are to alleviate the suffering of others and the planet in the long term, we must respond to even the most urgent human conditions in a sustainable and intentional way"[218] (Lipsky 2009, 11), I channelled the clinical psychologist colleague with whom I often teach on this subject. At this point in the process, he aptly notes how bearing witness to trauma forces us to juxtapose our life with the life of others. Often, we are called to acknowledge that we have experienced a great deal more privilege than the people we serve, and secondary trauma often forces us to engage in the resulting philosophical questions about life. This internal dialogue happens with or without our consent, consciously or unconsciously, and if we are not mindful of it, our core values can shift without our even knowing. He goes on to explain how often people find out that they have had a trauma response when they become shocked by their own behavior. People catch themselves behaving in ways they never would have thought they could, and this often happens because they were not aware of the small and large ways in which, what they were exposed to, began to change them. Trauma stewardship is about developing an awareness of those things and being able to reconcile personal joy and privilege with the undeniable suffering we have witnessed in others.[219]

My clinical psychologist colleague also explains how many of us might believe secretly or not so secretly that our commitment to our work may be measured by our willingness to martyr ourselves, to suffer alongside our client. While others may believe the only way they can show up to work every day is by compartmentalizing or walling off the degree of trauma and injustice they witness, neither are optimal ways of living. We must find a balance, and that begins with paying attention on purpose to what is going on within us as we engage in our world. We can be preventative by cultivating an awareness which allows us to gauge our trauma response level and assess what we need to do about it, and the earlier, the better.[220]

---

[217] Lipsky, Laura van Dernoot, with Connie Burk. 2009. *Trauma Stewardship: An Everyday Guide to Caring for Self While Caring for Others*. San Francisco: Berrett-Koehler.

[218] Lipsky, Laura van Dernoot, with Connie Burk. 2009. *Trauma Stewardship: An Everyday Guide to Caring for Self While Caring for Others*. San Francisco: Berrett-Koehler.

[219] Justin S. Hopkins, Psy.D., *Secondary Trauma and Self-Care,* Georgetown Law Juvenile Justice Clinic PowerPoint, February 26, 2019.
[220] Ibid.

With that foundation, I announced to the group how strategies existed for coping with our trauma responses once we become aware of them and realize the need to employ these ways forward. Starting with the practices we had been employing together on retreat, I named the self-care strategies of sleep, eating healthy, exercising, being outside and appreciating our environment, breathing, and practicing mindfulness. From there, we spoke about spiritual practices such as meditation, prayer and rituals in communities of faith as well as doing things just for fun. When seeking social support from folks, we spoke about being with those who "get it" so we can be seen and truly heard, and we spoke about how important it is to also be around folks who are completely outside our realm. Raising up the importance of a disciplined debriefing with peers as well as getting consultation and supervision in our trauma response, I also mentioned how counseling, psychotherapy and working with an elder in one's spiritual tradition can be especially helpful when we have not attended to our trauma responses in a while. To that, the GCC staff suggested pets as a critical strategy, and this led to a lively discussion of what else to add to the list. After a scrumptious dinner, we finished the evening playing instruments and singing together, celebrating our common journey in this important work.

It has been about a year since we gathered, and in preparation to write this chapter, I asked GCC staff members how they have navigated this period since becoming conscious of the impact of trauma exposure on their lives. One of the lawyers noted she has more readily been able to name her trauma exposure response and has given herself permission to take breaks, to work out, to leave work at work when it is not completely necessary for deadlines, and to do fun things such as vacations, even if short and brief. She noted how she is growing in the "understanding that we are fortunate and in a privileged position to do this work—rather than dealing with the impacts directly—but this does not exempt us from trauma; and to be able to do this work properly and create a positive impact for those affected, we must take care of ourselves." In her list of strategies, this attorney explained how she is now "building a stronger relationship with God and has joined a church officially" to which she is "tithing (sharing my blessings from this work for the greater good)."

Another GCC staff member was also more readily able to name her trauma response and acknowledged that doing this work for decades and not seeing much progress sometimes feels overwhelming: "No matter how hard or how much I work, I will not be able to solve the climate crisis alone and [therefore] strive to find some balance and take breaks from thinking about and working on it." She now tries "to take walks in nature, to reconnect with friends and say yes to opportunities to get a break from work—sometimes very short (coffee or lunch break with an old friend) or more extended (trip to the Grand Canyon, off the grid for a week and feeling the long arc of geologic time and our relatively small place in the universe)." She further noted how she seeks to be more spiritually grounded when feeling frazzled or depressed by using the Ignatian Examen[221] and spiritual reading as well as being outdoors. She also explained how she learned that different people react differently in the face of information that is difficult to absorb. "In addition to being more attuned to the toll it is taking on me, I am trying to be more aware of how recent developments on climate change (increasing scientific certainty about adverse impacts, devastating fires, etc., as well as policy setbacks) affect my staff, students and the audiences to whom I speak. I try to balance raising awareness of the threat with a

---

[221] Jesuitresrource.org: "St. Ignatius Loyola's Examen is an opportunity for peaceful daily reflective prayer. It invites us to find the movement of God in all the people and events of our day. The Examen is simply a set of introspective prompts for you to follow or adapt to your own character and spirit."

message of hope that we can meet the challenge if we all pull together. I also emphasize self-care and the need to enjoy life in conversation with others."

The writer Andrew Solomon challenges us to "forge meaning" and "build identity" in the face of adversity to find hope and build resilience[222] (2014). At first, the adversity I experienced as a result of prolonged environmental work led me away to forge new meaning making constructs and build a new (and hopefully improved) identity. During this exploration, I spent time with my tradition's understanding of the role of martyrs,[223] those who suffer persecution and often death for advocating a religious belief or cause. As the earth continues to create (advocate for) life all the while slowly dying because of humanity's destruction and greed, her struggle could be a source of desolation and despair in me. Like the martyrs in my tradition, however, the earth's process is one of great inspiration to me, as is being among colleagues who have devoted their lives to her salvation. Being with those who are grappling with what this all means on all levels for us individually and communally has changed everything for me. Instead of running from this important work, I am leaning into it with far more sanity and maybe a bit more wisdom. We cannot do this kind of meaning making alone, and I am grateful for this community of trauma-informed legal practitioners who remind me often why we do what we do. Because of them and people like Andrew Solomon, I am called to go deeper into myself and into the world when challenged by an exposure to trauma in any form.

Here are some suggestions for dealing with secondary trauma in your own life:

- Ask yourself when the last time was you set aside time to make meaning of your life, to reflect. How often do practice reflection? (We often do not take time to reflect, because it is hard work, and without practice, we are not that good at it.)
- After processing your feelings, thoughts, and motivations around a trauma response you have experienced, ask yourself how you make sense of the pain and suffering of the source of your trauma.
- Are there areas of research you need to review to better equip yourself to make sense of the legal and societal environment in which you operate?
- How does your worldview and spirituality differ from your understanding of the world in light of the trauma to which you have been exposed?
- Are there unhelpful aspects to your worldview and spirituality relating to the trauma to which you were exposed that might need deeper exploration with an elder in your spiritual community?
- After processing your feelings, thoughts, and motivations, draft an updated personal life narrative that affirms a positive understanding of yourself in the face the pain and suffering of the world you witness in your day-to-day work as a legal practitioner.
- What self-care goals do you have for the coming year? How can you be accountable for those goals?

---

[222] Solomon, Andrew. 2014. "How the worst moments in our lives make us who we are." TED2014. https://www.ted.com/talks/andrew_solomon_how_the_worst_moments_in_our_lives_make_us_who_we_are?language=en.

[223] Also helpful is Niels Gregersen's concept of "deep incarnation" as a "radical divine reach." Elizabeth A. Johnson, *Creation and the Cross: The Mercy of God for a Planet in Peril*, (Maryknoll, NY: Orbis, 2018), 184-85.

# Section 3: Self-Care

Self-care is critical for our well-being and happiness, and it involves every part of us, from how we take care of ourselves physically and emotionally, to how we engage with our work and the world. For example, research has shown "that lawyers who are more engaged by interest and meaning in their work are much more likely to be happy than others; such engagement also makes high productivity more likely."[224]

Self-care and the implementation of self-care remain difficult to sustain. Throughout writing this book, however, I have met many people, all caring individuals who are invested in changing the culture to promote health and well-being and destigmatize mental illness.

The World Health Organization, which monitors health situations and health trends across the globe, defines self-care in this way:

"Self-Care is what people do for themselves to establish and maintain health, and to prevent and deal with illness. It is a broad concept encompassing hygiene (general and personal), nutrition (type and quality of food eaten), lifestyle (sporting activities, leisure, etc.), environmental factors, (living conditions, social habits, etc.) socio-economic factors, (income level, cultural beliefs, etc.) and self-medication."[225]

In its *Self-Care for Health: A Handbook for Community Health Workers and Volunteers*, the World Health Organization recommends that work be handled in a way in which it does not become a chronic stress and that self-care be used to preserve and promote health as well as to prevent disease. These notions most certainly could be applied to the legal profession and law students.[226]

Keep in mind that it really wasn't until relatively recently, the 1970s, that the legal profession considered the emotional impact of criminal victimization on individuals. Therefore, it may not be that much of a stretch to understand why legal professionals and law students did not recognize until recently they can be affected too. Of course, there was a scattering of individuals writing about these issues within the profession and concentrating on students in particular. In the 1970s, concepts like the "faculty friend" arose. Such concepts over time faded away. In 1990, similar issues were brought up by the Australian Supreme Court Justice Michael Kirby, who voiced concern over the issue of bullying. The

---

[224] Krieger, Lawrence, and Kennon Sheldon. 2014. "What Makes Lawyers Happy? Transcending the Anecdotes with Data from 6200 Lawyers." SSRN Electronic Journal. 10.2139/ssrn.2398989.

[225] World Health Organization. 2014. *Self-Care for Health: A Handbook for Community Health Workers and Volunteers*. WHO Regional Office for South-East Asia. https://apps.who.int/iris/handle/10665/205887.

[226] World Health Organization. 2014. *Self-Care for Health: A Handbook for Community Health Workers and Volunteers*. WHO Regional Office for South-East Asia. https://apps.who.int/iris/handle/10665/205887.

ensuing debate led to much controversy and derision, but also faded away. These were pioneer thinkers, but the community was not ready to move forward.

We now recognize that better self-care is not only about taking care of ourselves at school and at work; it is about how we live every aspect of our lives. If we take good care of ourselves, we will live happier, more peaceful, and ultimately more productive lives. We will be healthier, stronger, and more resilient. After all, not taking care can result in impaired decision making, which can ultimately result in problems in performance at work and school. Such dangers were exemplified in the study, "Disciplinary Tribunal Cases Involving New Zealand Lawyers with Physical or Mental Impairment, 2009-2013." The study found that the impairments, which included depression, anxiety, substance misuse and stress, among others, either contributed to or were responsible for various lawyers' misconduct.[227]

Better self-care allows us to have a balanced, productive life, one that's fulfilling and enjoyable. Yes, we may be in law school or in a big trial, but we still have to eat (and not just junk food). We eat well so that we can have better focus and be fortified for school, for work, for our lives in general. The love and companionship of family, friends, and companion animals reenergizes us; gives us a minibreak and ultimately should remind us why we are working so hard. Do you remember why you are working so hard? Hopefully, you are working so hard to create a better life for yourself and your family and perhaps, you are hoping to improve the world too.

A simple behavior we can initiate to bring balance to our lives and to lessen the stressors of our lives is to do things we enjoy during our downtime or off work time. However, first and foremost, we must make the time to have downtime and off-work time. Maybe you are working so hard that you have lost the ability to sleep. Or perhaps, you do not have time with your family or friends? I can imagine that your motivation is certainly not to work so hard that you get sick or that you are not as available to the ones you love. Think about what you are doing, how you are doing it, and why. Remember that others will be watching and looking to you as a role model; model for them what is healthy and sustainable.

A global answer for learning more about better self-care enables individuals, schools, governing bodies and corporations to develop additional tools which are needed for mental, emotional, social and physical well-being now and in the future. These tools will help individuals and groups to create processes and make informed decisions to improve lives globally. Through better self-care, individuals and groups will learn to experience challenge in different ways and to experience enjoyment within the challenge. They will also learn how to experience healthy living in all sectors of their lives. These healthy experiences reinforce positive behaviors and become sustainable throughout one's life, thus creating a healthy lifestyle.

Every country we have examined in this book has some type of self-care or well-being initiative, and the law bodies within the countries also promote self-care and well-being. So better self-care is important—in fact, it may be the most important contribution we make to our lives and those around us.

---

[227] Moore, Jennifer, Donna Buckingham, and Kate Diesfeld. 2015. "Disciplinary Tribunal Cases Involving New Zealand Lawyers with Physical or Mental Impairment, 2009–2013." *Psychiatry, Psychology and Law* 22:5" 649–672. http://dx.doi.org/10.1080/13218719.2015.1055624.

## **Section 3.1: Mimicry, Empathy, Sympathy, and Compassion**

An example of mimicry could be walking into a room in which people are yawning and tired. You may have had moderate energy when you walked in, but by the time you walk out you may be yawning and tired. This is because we unconsciously take on the behaviors, manners, and postures of others.

What role does mimicry play when we are exposed to clients? What do you find yourself doing? Take note, the next time you are with a client and think about what you have discovered. Do you notice an emotional shift? How long does it take to return to your previous emotional state, the one you had prior to client engagement? On a day-to-day basis, begin to notice mimicry and empathy.

"Functional neuroimaging studies have demonstrated that there are areas of overlap between regions activated by watching others experiencing emotions or performing certain actions, and brain regions that activate ("light up") when we undergo those experiences ourselves. For example, part of the parietal lobe may light up both when we move, or when we watch someone else move."[228]

Boris C. Bernhardt and Tania Singer[229] provide a concrete understanding of empathy by pinpointing the parts of the brain involved in empathy through experiments in neuroscience using MRI imaging.

Empathy and sympathy tend to be used interchangeably. They are different. Sympathy is the understanding of distress or need in another living being. It does not necessarily involve a shared experience.

Compassion is an emotion that is sometimes intertwined with empathy and sympathy. Compassion is the understanding of another's distress and the desire to relieve that distress.

If you feel compassion toward another sentient being, it affects you, just as you affect them.

As you can see by this discussion of sympathy and related ideas, self-care is many things. It is not only proactive, it is reactive. The effects of mental health issues need to be a part of the overall picture of better self-care. We must not only respond when we notice symptoms of distress or mental health issues in ourselves and each other, we must be proactive and work to prevent or minimize the effects of these issues. As mentioned before, the number-one step is open communication, which allows for destigmatization for everyone, across all levels of status. As the effects of secondary trauma, stress,

---

[228] Pressman, Peter. "How Mirror Neurons May Explain Why You Feel Other's Pain or Emotion." Verywell Health, November 25, 2019. https://www.verywellhealth.com/mirror-neurons-2488711.

[229] Bernhardt, Boris C., and Tania Singer. 2012. "The Neural Basis of Empathy." *Annual Review of Neuroscience* 35:1: 1–23. https://www.annualreviews.org/doi/abs/10.1146/annurev-neuro-062111-150536

depression, anxiety, bullying and sexual harassment and even suicide are talked about more; individuals, institutions and organizations across the globe are beginning to respond openly.

## Section 3.2: Improving Self-Care at an Institutional Level

### *David Jaffe*

David Jaffe, Dean of Students, American University, Washington College of Law, has dedicated much of his work to law student wellness issues over the last decade, including involvement with the District of Columbia Bar Lawyer Assistance Program and the American Bar Association Commission on Lawyer Assistance Programs (CoLAP) Law School Assistance Committee. He was lead author for the Law School section of "The Path to Lawyer Well-Being: Practical Recommendations for Positive Change" released in August 2017. He also produced the video, "Getting Healthy, Staying Healthy" that is used as a resource in many Professional Responsibility Classes around the United States, and is responsible for modernizing the "Substance Abuse & Mental Health Toolkit for Law Students and Those Who Care About Them." Dean Jaffe says his best self-care is being in the moment as often as he can with his teenage daughters.

*How Law Schools Can Help Its Students Stay Strong and Resilient*

I am about to walk up to the microphone to welcome our next entering class of future lawyers. I have a million things I want to share about their strength and ability, and also about the grit and perseverance needed. I want them to think about the journey ahead and be prepared for the challenges they will encounter. How best to provide this without scaring them off? How can I position them to bring out their very best selves over the next three to four years and beyond, into their careers? How to I ensure that they do not lose themselves in the process of transformation to an attorney, an advocate, and a healthy individual?

Little had been studied of law school mental health and substance use challenges prior to 2014[230] when a survey conducted of more than 3500 law students across 15 schools provided significant data about the behavior of and help received around these issues.[231] Even for student-facing administrators, a number of the data points were staggering.[232] The results of this survey and a similar one simultaneously

---

[230] Organ, J., Jaffe, D., Bender, K., "Suffering in Silence: The Survey of Law Student Well-Being and the Reluctance of Law Students to Seek Help for Substance Use and Mental Health Concerns", vol. 66, *J. Legal Educ.* 116 (2016) ("Section II: Literature Review", pp.118-22).

[231] Id.

[232] The Survey yielded among many data points the following information:
-53 percent drank enough to get drunk in the prior 30 days to the survey (Id., at 129);
-43 percent binge drank at least once in the prior two weeks (Id.);
-14 percent used a prescription drug without a prescription in the prior 12 months (Id. at 134);
-17 percent screened positive for depression (Id. at 136);
-37 percent screened for anxiety (14% severe) (Id. at 137);
-4 percent reported having ever used a health professional for issues related to alcohol or drugs (Id.at 140);
-42 percent reported needing help with mental health issues in the prior year, but only half reported

conducted in the legal profession[233] resulted in additional, profound steps toward what is now viewed by some as a movement to begin to address these issues. A National Task Force on Lawyer Well-Being (lawyerwellbeing.net) was established to ensure that the survey results were not glossed over.[234] The Task Force in 2017 published a Report[235] of recommendations for all stakeholders in the legal profession to follow if they wished to support a change toward strengthening well-being in the profession. In September 2018, the American Bar Association announced a Well-Being Pledge,[236] inviting legal employers to commit to a series of actions to support and advocate change; as of publication of this chapter, 164 entities had added their names to the Pledge,[237] and assessments are being made to ensure "compliance" and sustainability to the actions to which each entity has committed.[238]

What does all of this mean for today's law student? Have things changed in the law school setting?[239] Are our students "better off" than even 5 years ago, as a result of the survey and have at least some advances been made? Allow me to take a step back and share a few anecdotes in an effort to suggest an answer.

I am fourteen years old. It is a Sunday morning, my parents are off somewhere, and I drift downstairs to the den for a lazy day of TV, joining my cousin Link, sixteen months my junior and a regular guest of our home, who is resting on the sofa. A few minutes in, I see Link point his arm to the ceiling and moan "OD." Panicked and unsure what to do, I run upstairs to find a bottle of opened sleeping pills in my parents' room. While the rest is a blur, I manage to locate my parents, who manage to get Link to a hospital and his stomach pumped. The end result is that my cousin winds up at a therapeutic private school hours away in another state—his goal all along, as he was desperate to join my older sister, who had previously been there for similar challenging behavior. That sister has been clinically depressed for as long as I knew what it meant and provides me incredible insight to the painful lows offset by the occasional highs of having to live with the disease.

Flash forward some thirty-eight years. I am working with a law student who the day prior assisted an unconscious classmate by propping up her head with a sweatshirt. The student who helped had lost her keys in the process but, in coming to grips with it, shared that for the first time she lost the keys "for the right reason"; she was, she reasoned, not drunk, not blacked out, and not waking up in a stranger's home. The student had been sober for some time, and this startling reflection was so very pure for her and for me.

---

receiving counseling (Id.);
-63 percent reported potential threat to bar admissions as reason not to get help for substance use (45% for mental health) (Id. at 141).

[233] Krill, P., Johnson, R., Albert, L., "The Prevalence of Substance Use and Other Mental Health Concerns Among American Attorneys", vol. 10, J. Addic. Med. 46 (2016)
[234] https://lawyerwellbeing.net/
[235] Id.
[236] https://www.americanbar.org/groups/lawyer_assistance/working-group_to_advance_well-being_in_legal_profession/
[237] Id.
[238] A plan was in place to gather the entities in Spring 2019 in Washington, DC.
[239] Jordana Confino summarized the results of a 2018 ABA CoLAP Law School Wellness Survey to assess well-being initiatives underway at law schools. See https://papers.ssrn.com/sol3/papers.cfm?abstract_id=3374976 (article forthcoming in the *Journal of Legal Education*)

Jump ahead another two years. We are holding a memorial service for a law student who lost his life through opioid addiction. With the mother's permission and encouragement, I share a few thoughts about classmates, faculty, and staff not assigning nor feeling blame for not seeing any signs or taking any steps, and about the incredible importance of talking to one another, about being open with one's feelings, moving past stigma, and allowing vulnerability to be okay and not so frightening.

At the conclusion of the service a student approaches and, amid tears, asks if we can meet. We return to my office, where the student shares that she is doing so well in many respects: she is a top academic student, has a coveted summer position with a major law firm, has friends, etc. She then states, "But I have been smoking pot for the last three years, almost nonstop. Peter's death and the memorial service hit me right between the eyes, and I have to stop." We then shared some tears, I expressed my admiration for her coming forward, and we started to chart a plan toward recovery. We shared a second set of tears when she stopped me in the hallway sometime later and just before the start of the summer, as she shared with me her sixty-day chip of sobriety. We maintained contact throughout an occasionally trying summer and continue to do so, as she experiences the triumphs and travails of recovery.

I have been a law school dean of students for twenty-three years. I have had my professional and personal share of highs and lows, but I draw on these experiences to reflect on today's law students who generally fall into three categories. How so? The first category of students is reflected in the initial story, where an individual is in pain, but does not know how to ask for help. The action taken is an obvious call for assistance, but of the potentially most dangerous kind. The second is the student who, having previously received assistance (likely through its own painful process), is well ensconced in her recovery and is able to provide meaning and aid to others. And the last is the student who was clearly feeling her own pain but in realizing it, had the desire and the ability to overcome enough of her qualms and fears to trust another to help and support. My experience with our law students is that most fall in the first of these categories: they are in need of some assistance, but do not know how or are too afraid to ask for it.

Our law school has had at least a part-time counselor on-site for several years. Although confidentiality laws prohibit counselors from sharing the identities of students who seek assistance, they can share the general trends they see in our students. Surprisingly, for some, the topics being discussed are not related to law school, at least not directly. To be sure, our students face significant stressors upon entering and throughout law school to include grades, networking, cost, acclimation and socialization. Law students are in "finishing school," so grades are ever-important, as are the networking opportunities, which are brand-new for many. Tuition can be backbreaking, as many students are already saddled with undergraduate debt and have placed their hopes on large law firm employment and an opportunity to pay down that debt while simultaneously building a nest egg for the future. Accompanying these practical necessities are the transition to a new city, and finding new friends, each of whom has been skimmed from the top graduating classes of universities around the country and across the globe, thus with their own aspirations of being atop the future graduating class. Many of these students are first generation, and they juggle the burdens of justifying their parents' and others' financial support for them to attend law school, and of not having the networks available to many of their classmates. In some instances, the language of the law is a third language for them, as law school also brings a new language, reflected both in the classroom and in hundreds of hours of reading, rereading, and hoping to understand, and the constant fear for some of being called on to face the professor in front of one's classmates. Finally, although perhaps not as present as decades ago, the Socratic method, grilling students with questions while not in all instances providing the answers, will add yet another level of anxiety to the uninitiated and to those not yet comfortable with public speaking.

In reviewing this noncomprehensive list of factors contributing both to a law student's success but also to potential mental health exhaustion, it may seem little wonder that drinking and substance use is pervasive in the law school community.

Yet as suggested above, most counselors working with law students say the issues brought to their office stem only indirectly from these factors. Students are seeking counsel on personal issues often borne years prior to law school, on family loss that is affecting their studies, on relationships that have ended badly or with which the student is struggling. For many of these students, the time prior to law school, typically their undergraduate studies, focused little on adjusting to adulthood and a lot on being away from home for the first time and all of the carefree experience's attendant to it. In law school, these students are simultaneously beginning to take stock of their lives and their futures, resulting in many of these issues being "brought home" for the first time. The ongoing separation from home calls for reliance on others, but only those students comfortable enough with themselves are going to find their way to the assistance needed. Law students are labelled in different ways, and one typical characteristic is "Type-A"—competitive, highly organized, and impatient, for which seeking assistance is anathema. Embedded within this inherent trait lies the perception that every other classmate is doing fine, that the students with the challenges is the only one undergoing them. It has been amazing to me the countless times that I have shared this with a student in my office, to see the exhalation of breath and the shoulders sag (in surprise and relief) that they are by no means alone. Because the default is that everyone is smart and therefore is doing well, the presenting student typically has been isolating and adding to his challenges through this faulty perception, falling in the process into a cycle of depression and or potential substance use.

Assigning responsibility for the stress felt by law students seems a useless errand. Genetics, one's upbringing, social media, one's peers, undergrad, law school, the legal profession—many factors can be ascribed to why a law student feels the way she does, or chooses to act (when choice is there) to move on one direction or another.

Prelaw advisors often play key roles in identifying and matching the best law school or schools for their students, based on one or more factors, including grades; cost, ability to pay, and scholarship possibilities; strengths of a law school; willingness to move away from home; anticipated post-law substantive interest, anticipated post-law geographic interest. What is often overlooked in providing this assistance, however, is the mental preparedness of their student in taking this next (and potentially last) critical academic step. Advisors are not to be blamed here; absent an incredibly profound relationship with each of their students, the advisors are typically working only with numbers and with what they know superficially. The students themselves, save for those who either have been blessed with incredible self-awareness or insightful parents or other mentors in the formative stages of their lives, or who have been unfortunately challenged with mental health issues at an earlier stage that brought these issues to light, are typically unaware of the many catalysts that may bring challenges to the fore. But I do believe that the more attentive (and brave) prelaw advisors can consider additional steps, checklists, and conversations with their students, assuming the student is both mature and willing enough to listen and follow the suggestions provided. Here are some examples:

* Ask the student about the mental health history of his family. If this type of information is unknown to the student, it is possible (if not likely) that the subject was considered taboo for conversation during the student's formative years; the student should speak to his closest relative, and probably should go back at least two generations, as genetics are a possible factor. I believe that a student's awareness in this area can later save significant time in lack of understanding, denial, fear, and lost time in seeking assistance, should the need arrive while in law school.

If a history of mental health is unearthed or shared, the student can probe more deeply into how the family member or members dealt with the issues, if they actually did. Was therapy used? Medication? A combination? The specific information gleaned or available may not be critical, as each individual would be subject to different levels of mental health issues and would respond differently to treatments. However, possessing the mere information may go a long way toward destigmatizing the notion that there is something wrong with the individual, that he is somehow responsible for the mental actions his body takes or may take in the future. As alluded to earlier, law students can have a really difficult time responding to personal issues beyond seeing them in the eyes of their classmates; this personalization then can bring home the possibility that the individual may later be affected, and that notwithstanding the upsetting, frustrating, challenging nature of it, that it is to a degree normal and has to be addressed as such.

* Much of the foregoing research should also be applied to substance use, particularly but not exclusively alcohol. Unfortunately, there are many who still suggest or believe that substance use is not a disease, but it is clear that a history of it can be traced through one's family. Owing in large part to leaving the family nest for the first time and engaging in the many experiences in college that were not allowed or did not occur previously, using and abusing alcohol is often viewed as normal in the undergraduate setting, masking for many the deeper hereditary underpinnings. I have lost count of the students with whom I have worked who discover, once ready to face the alcoholic demon, how pervasive its presence was in their family. While it is conceivable that the Thursday night "bar review" (not in preparation for the bar exam, the other one) may never go away, there is a difference between the casual, social drinker and the law student who is using alcohol to get through the day [see Organ survey, cited above, for CAGE assessment; CAGE may also be searched online]. While casual student's drinking may lead to a greater reliance if it occurs too frequently, the "get through the day" student often can be found drinking prior to the bar review to get a "head start," or to continue to drink when others have hit their limit, often alone, well into the evening. The downward spiral may be gradual, but the student is going to find himself isolated, and continuing to increase his drinking. The schoolwork and other law school obligations will quickly disappear.

Whoa. This is a lot for a pre-law advisor to take on. My advice is for the advisor to get the ball rolling by having the conversation and prompting the prospective law student to do a deeper analysis. If a history is discovered, one would hope that a family member or loved one will step up and provide the necessary and ongoing support for the student to begin to assess and address the issues before him.

The next most obvious point of contact for law students to connect to well-being is at orientation. Not much more than a handful of years ago, administrators were not expected to raise this early in a law student's education the possibility of student stress, anxiety, or falling prey to substance use: students were to be excited about getting started at x law school, and any notion of potential adverse effects was to be avoided at all costs—bad for morale, bad for admissions. Fortunately, the current tide has trended toward openness, which has included space to speak openly about these issues. Some schools employ upper-level students to speak to smaller groups of the entering class in breakout sessions; others hold plenary sessions and bring in local Lawyer Assistance Program (LAP) representatives, dietitians, and sleep experts to share tips and provide resources on combating the challenges that are surely to arise. Despite orientation being overwhelming and the belief that entering students only absorb a fraction of what they hear, they need to hear about this. You are setting the tone and indicating that you care by being open from the get-go. One law school has even gone so far as to mandate that every entering student meet the clinician for a check-in, to destigmatize the process and to ensure that the students know where to return[240] (Cerny and Tafuto 2019).

Once classes commence, everyone has a role to play. I ask our faculty to be diligent about attendance, not because we have an obligation to report or because I like metrics, but because a student who is missing class consistently has something going on that needs attention. The faculty do not have not get involved directly, but they need to be the law school's eye and ears and let the responsible administrator know. I also ask faculty to incorporate some level of well-being awareness into their classroom; time is precious, but 2 minutes of breathing exercises (which really works!) will not a lost semester make. Others have chosen to set aside time simply to ask how their students are doing; this step not only has the faculty member serve dual roles as the "sage on the stage" and the "guide on the side", but enhances incredibly the respect students have for such individuals.[241] Finally, faculty who want to understand better the mental health challenges their students may face can join their colleagues and staff in Mental Health First Aid training[242], a process that teaches individuals how to recognize certain behavior, how to de-escalate a conversation with an agitated student, and how to direct the student toward appropriate resources.

In addition to the foregoing training, student-facing administrators have to be ever-vigilant for the cues and clues offered up by their students. An occasional absence happens with the best of students, but tracking sequential absences, repeated requests for extensions, and nonresponses to emails are most typically indicators of a student headed for or already in a spiral. At my institution a student who does not reply to a second email or telephone call within a reasonable time frame is informed that he has one additional day to present, before a call to public safety triggers a welfare visit to the student's home. I never intend this as a threat, although it often has the effect of even the most challenged student popping

---

[240] Cerny, Jennifer, and Yvonne Tafuto. 2019. "73 Hours: What One Law School Learned from Taking an Untraditional Approach with their 1L Class." NALSAP Annual Conference, American University Washington College of Law, June 14, 2019.

[241] At American University Washington College of Law (and perhaps at other law schools as well), faculty are provided lunch passes to share with small groups of law students in an effort to get to know them better outside the law school setting.

[242] https://www.mentalhealthfirstaid.org/

his head up to indicate assistance is needed. Yes, our students are adults, but they are under a lot of developing pressures, are typically away from home or afraid to trouble their parents, and we have to step into this abyss.

A section here for students, our most important resource. Above all, you need to know how much we care. There are precious few of us relative to the community of you, and we are often charged with a lot more than meets the eye on a daily basis. But we are thinking about you, and about ways to strengthen your experience and to make you as comfortable as possible. Be our eyes and ears by letting us know when you need assistance, and not before things get out of control. Do not think that we have not seen your plight before in another student (the crippling stories we have heard . . .), or that we too old or out of touch, or too busy, for we are none of these things. For caring students: do not under any circumstance believe that you are aiding your classmate by not bringing to an administrator's attention your concerns. In most any instance (save for threat of imminent harm to self or another), the information can initially be relayed confidentially, and you can receive expert counsel from your dean of students on best next steps. My response to the student who says she doesn't want to lose a friend by telling on her is always the same: "I would rather you potentially lose a friend than all of us lose that person forever" (and, if she is truly in need of assistance, she will appreciate what you did, even if not in the moment).

For all students: you enter law school with ideas, goals, visions, and dreams. You carry baggage like all of us, some of which you may be able to carry through law school without having to open. If you are burdened with too much of that baggage, however, then you need to work with us, and us with you, to develop coping skills as the additional challenges and burdens begin to present themselves. You also come to us as human beings, and we want you not only to leave with those same human characteristics, but to employ them while here. At a relevant, closing point during each orientation, I lean into the microphone and offer my students the most important message I can: "This is just law school." Repeating it once, I suggest to my students that they earned their way here, and they will succeed if they take care of themselves—the rest is largely about what they do when they most need assistance. And it is.

Consistent sleep patterns, regular exercise, a decent diet. In addition, I encourage my students to practice mindfulness meditation, yoga, running, journaling, biking, hiking, sudoku—whatever productive release they had prior to law school should not be sacrificed while in it. And to engage in activity: it has been suggested that the opposite of depression is not happiness, but connection. When we are engaged with others and doing things in the community, we feel a sense of belonging, of giving, and of life. There is no reason to sacrifice these emotions and feeling while in school; if anything, one needs to identify with and embrace them even more so as not to fall prey to the challenges described herein. To those who believe that the time they give over to non-law activities is time they are losing to competing classmates who are studying, I suggest that said release time is exactly what they need to stay on even keel over the long haul.

A final word: make sure that you want to be in law school, and that you are here for the right reasons. Attending law school because you have been advised to go to graduate school is not in and of itself a good enough reason. Nor is "my parents offered to pay"; or "I didn't know what else to do"; etc.

I joke that my admissions office no longer invites me to travel to represent the school because if asked by a prospective student I share my belief that the individual best equipped to handle the rigors of law school is the one who has been out for a few years or has experienced trauma in their lives (a disproportionate few of each year's entering class). The commonality here is that these individuals have not only had to master the important skill of time management, but that they arrive at school with an enhanced sense of appreciation for the broader picture, and a relative calm about them and what needs to be accomplished ("Are you kidding? Try having walked in my shoes for the last year! I got this!").

While I do not for a second mean to suggest that recent undergraduates cannot be equally prepared for law school, I do feel that the resilience and grit necessary for many to work their way through law school is more readily discovered in these groups of individuals. Those students not in this group, or in a related cohort that has caused them to consider more profoundly their ultimate goals, need to make extra preparation for when they have to face and overcome the perceived adversity of a lower-than-expected grade, a paper marked up in red, a handful or more of employment rejections, and other unanticipated occurrences affecting them perhaps for the first time in their life.

I suggest to my students that they can be anything they want to be (within reason . . . ) and that with application, diligence, patience, a bit of entrepreneurship (and often a lot of networking), they will ultimately settle into the career of their dreams. Work put in will equal output achieved. I believe that students who follow the advice herein (aided by professionals who offer them the assistance suggested) will be well on their way to the well-being and happiness that they seek.

Through the words of David Jaffe, we have seen a number of variables contributing to the success and resiliency of law school students as well as ideas about how advisors and others may be able to contribute to well-being. David's own story, starting with adverse childhood experiences, reminds us that we come into law school with life experience, and life experiences may help us to persevere through law school.[243]

## **Section 3.3: Other Proposals to Help Students and Law Professionals**

There are several practical ways to help students with mental health issues. Mentors may be an approach, such as peer to peer mentors. Maybe pairing a first year with a second- or third-year student or even a faculty member who would be willing to take on an additional role could be helpful.

Of course, we cannot and should not expect faculty trained in law to provide psychological counseling or testing, nor should we expect peers to be trained in this way. However, volunteer faculty members or peers could be trained in solution-focused ways of approaching problems.

Professor Lawrence Krieger recommended health networks, as a way for attorneys as well as law students to discuss mental health and other concerns: "Potential benefits would include camaraderie of like-minded professionals; peer reinforcement to create a balanced and enjoyable life for one's self; an

---

[243] Jaffe, David. 2018. "The Key to Law Student Well-Being? We Have to Love Our Law Students," *PD Quarterly*, February 13, 2018. http://dx.doi.org/10.2139/ssrn.3123262.

environment that encourages one to notice and express personal feelings and beliefs; and an enforced opportunity to listen respectfully to the feelings and beliefs of others, all on a regular basis."[244]

Other ideas can be found in David Jaffe's article, "The Key to Law Student Well-Being? We Have to Love Our Law Students." He recommends that faculty invite students to share information about themselves and to consider having an open door of communication for students. Students could also attempt to reach out to faculty who seem to be more open. As Jaffe remarks however, this may be difficult for some students. He recommends that some faculty conduct mindfulness at the start each class or that the individual student take 2 minutes for mindfulness on their own.[245]

Dean Jaffe has also been advocating that faculty receive more training in "mental health first aid," which would educate them on the different types of mental health issues, how to deescalate these issues when they occur. The National Association of Law Student Affairs Professionals is attempting to look at these issues and receive the training that would enable more people to feel confident and be of help. Unfortunately, for many organizations and institutions the time required for the training, eight hours or more, is prohibitive.

## Section 3.4: The Trauma-Informed Lens- Being Kind to Each Other

The trauma-informed lens provides an important opportunity to acknowledge and then respond to the complicated process of emotional interaction with stress filled or trauma narratives. It is one way to orient an institution toward providing more self-care for its employees.[246] Katz and Haldar articulate four key characteristics of trauma-informed lawyering: identifying trauma, adjusting the attorney-client relationship, adapting litigation strategy, and preventing vicarious trauma. "Attorneys can learn how to identify trauma and adjust their methods of representation to incorporate an understanding of their clients' trauma history. Attorneys can also employ methods of self-care to prevent vicarious traumatization. When attorneys do this in systemic manner, their entire legal practice can become trauma-informed."[247]

A trauma-informed lens may seem at first glance as if it would only apply to family law and criminal law, but in fact its uses are broader. One attorney told me about his feelings of loss and sadness when a firm he represented went into bankruptcy, hurting many people, including his long-term clients, the owners of the firm, as well as hundreds of families. The same attorney noted that in such cases, children and families are often left without parental figures, spouses, or other support.

---

[244] Krieger, Lawrence S. 1998. "What We're Not Telling Law Students— and Lawyers  That They Really Need to Know: Some Thoughts-in-Action Toward Revitalizing the Profession From Its Roots." *Journal of Law and Health* 13 (1): 6–7.

[245] Jaffe, David. 2018. "The Key to Law Student Well-Being? We Have to Love Our Law Students," *PD Quarterly*, February 13, 2018. http://dx.doi.org/10.2139/ssrn.3123262.

[246] Katz, Sarah, and Deeya Haldar. 2016. "The Pedagogy of Trauma-Informed Lawyering." *Clinical Law Review* 22, number 2 (April 21, 2016): 353–393. Temple University Legal Studies Research Paper No. 2016-29. https://ssrn.com/abstract=2768218.

[247] Katz, Sarah, and Deeya Haldar. 2016. "The Pedagogy of Trauma-Informed Lawyering." *Clinical Law Review* 22, number 2 (April 21, 2016): 353–393. Temple University Legal Studies Research Paper No. 2016-29. https://ssrn.com/abstract=2768218.

As with all new concepts, there are challenges to accepting or adopting these ideas. Barriers to using a trauma-informed lens for better self-care include institutional cultures, stigma, ego, and judgmental attitudes. As one lawyer shared with me, "we look for the weak ones and if someone is judged 'weak,' we try to take them out because they are just competition." If this is the type of environment in which you interact, it will be very difficult to be vulnerable.

Better Care is exemplified by the work of Attorney Mary Digiglio of Australia, whom we will hear from as a Champion of Disclosure in Chapter 7, New Directions. During my interview with Attorney Digiglio, she explained the culture of her firm is one of openness where mental health is truly valued and thus, discussed. In Attorney DiGiglio's firm, posters and informational sheets are available and displayed and individuals are encouraged to share how they are feeling and if they are struggling. The environment that has been created is a supportive and compassionate place for people to work.

Attorney DiGiglio has created healthy ways for individuals and groups to function and ultimately, a healthy way for the entire organization to function as a collective group of relationships. When these relationships are healthy, the organization is more productive. When these relationships are adversarial, competitive, or full of conflict, the workplace becomes toxic, and the organization less productive.

Organizational function and health can be improved by providing a supportive and nurturing environment, according to Dr. Marilyn Kroplick, psychiatrist and Director of In Defense of Animals (IDA). She focuses her efforts on increasing staff productivity and (more surprisingly), increasing joyfulness. She believes that organizations can function in amazing ways when staff relationships are positive and respectful. Dr. Kroplick utilizes "morale boasting efforts," which focus on organizational dynamics as well as the emotional atmosphere of the group, especially when members undertake stress-filled work.

Dr. Kroplick confronts self-destructive behaviors. What kinds of self-destructive behaviors do we see in the legal profession? We have talked about the adversarial nature of the legal profession and the competition within schools and organizations. Self-destructive behaviors also include neglecting one's self through lack of sleep, skipping meals or poor nutrition, and lack of socialization both inside and outside of work or school.

Dr. Kroplick believes the responsibility for health and well-being is on everyone's shoulders and that verbal abuse and other distortions of power should not be tolerated. As she reminds us, "It's not easy to confront abusive, angry people who want to preserve their power and destroy the credibility of others." She encourages everyone to fostering compassion and solidarity, both within the organization and with the world at large. I would add that if we can activate our values, we will have more confidence move in this direction.

Self-care may also involve training about on nonviolent communication and mindfulness, which will help the organization and individuals beyond the walls of the institution or firm. Everyone must be on board. "It's everyone's responsibility to make this choice. First, decide to respect and help one another, then watch the transformation occur!"[248]

## Section 3.5: Trauma-Informed Language

Using a trauma-informed lens will help make questions and other communications more compassionate and respectful. Below are a few resources for trauma-informed communication.

According to The Information Access Group, using trauma sensitive language requires us to be aware of and remove from our communications our judgements, jargon, and labels.

Lakeside, a resource for therapeutic schools, as well as trauma training for educators and professionals, gives examples of non-trauma sensitive statements that we should avoid:

- "Oh, I don't think you should feel that way. You should be thankful for all that didn't happen; why do you always focus on the negative anyway?"
- "You're making this all about you instead of the person who was actually hurt."
- "If you don't get a handle on your feelings, you're going to lose all your friends."
- "You'll never succeed in life if you don't change these behaviors."
- "You must be getting something out of behaving this way."
- "I am sure if you tried a little harder, you could get better control over yourself."
- "This has gone on long enough. If you don't stop talking about this, I won't be spending much time with you."
- "I think most people would have resolved this by now. Clearly you aren't motivated enough to make the changes you need to make and move on with your life."
- "Come on, I'm sure if you just give this a little time, you'll feel better. After all, time heals all wounds."
- "I had an old friend who had the same thing happen to him and after a few sessions of therapy, he saw things in a whole different way and is back to his old self. You don't need more than one or two therapy sessions to fix what's wrong with you."
- "How often do you feel like this? I can't believe it's all you think about. When's the last time you thought about something happy?"[249]

---

[248] Kroplick, Marilyn. 2014. "Organizational Trauma." In Defense of Animals, July 2, 2014. https://www.idausa.org/organizational-trauma/.

[249] Vassar, Gerry. "How to Avoid Non-Trauma Sensitive Language." Lakeside, March 8, 2012. https://lakesidelink.com/blog/lakeside/how-to-avoid-non-trauma-sensitive-language/. *Copyright © 2020 by L. Diane Wagenhals and Lakeside Educational Network. All rights reserved. Printed in the United States of America. Reproduced with written permission. For information, address Lakeside, 1350 Welsh Road, Suite 400, North Wales, PA 19454.*

## **Section 3.6: Tools for Using a Trauma-Informed Lens**

We will be discussing more ways to encourage compassion and respect in the next chapter. However, here are a few simple ways to increase compassion and respect among colleagues.

**Group Stress Debriefings:** Learning about the law and practicing law is stressful and sometimes a negative experience. Group stress debriefings provide an easy route to get people involved after anyone is involved in or exposed to a traumatic event that overwhelms their ability to cope. It's an opportunity to process their thoughts and feelings about the event in a safe and supportive environment with peers. Before you begin, it's a good idea to review active listening skills.

A group stress debriefing allows for beginning conversations about stress and secondary trauma. It's meant to be nonstigmatizing. At its root, it's about stress, and everyone has stress. Making the meetings mandatory allows them to become routine and normalized. This will minimize later questions or discussions. If everyone is present and encouraged to participate, the environment becomes supportive and nonthreatening. It also sends the message that this is something important that must be integrated into the practice. Note, people who are still struggling should seek help from a professional.

**Compassionate Conversations:** This tool is similar to the previous one, but it's done on a peer-to-peer basis, so that those affected are heard, acknowledged, and supported by someone they know cares about them. The goal is to listen attentively and provide support through patience, kindness, and genuine caring.

Of course, not everyone is aware when they have been affected by trauma. This is an opportunity for colleagues, institutions, and organizations to play a role in helping to relieve suffering. However, this will not happen unless there is an understanding of secondary trauma and the importance of a trauma-informed lens.

We may think of these peer-to-peer sessions as alliances. Attorney Lee Moore is founder of the Association of Child Abuse Lawyers and a speaker, writer and trainer. She has stressed that one way to care for each other is through alliances.[250]

That's the challenge: radically changing attitudes and outdated beliefs. We can do this in a number of ways. We cannot underestimate the power of continuing legal education opportunities, which allows speakers to be brought in to emphasize, and normalize the discussion and acceptance of secondary trauma, stress, and other mental health issues among legal professionals. Bring to the table professionals in this area as well as colleagues and peers who are willing to talk about their experience and how they successfully overcame stigma and returned to physical and mental health. Students also can bring their own speakers and talk with each other. The Champions of Disclosure throughout this book have led the way as role-models in normalizing the discussion. Let's follow their lead, in a courageous and open-minded way.

---

[250] Moore, Lee. n.d. "Enhancing Well-Being & Confidence in Court." Lee Moore & Co. https://leemooreco.com/.

Normalizing the discussion of mental health is critical to removing the stigma surrounding these important issues. Through normalization we can start a discussion and create a solution-focused plan on how to move forward, void of judgement and stereotyped assumptions. As normalization continues it will become more common for schools and workplaces to discuss, teach, nurture and support self-care among students and legal professionals. Work by Andrew Levin can help us to normalize the conversation. He reminds us that secondary traumatic stress and compassion fatigue tend to be natural outcomes of the interactions with particular populations.[251]

Levin notes there has been a call for increased training for attorneys in interviewing techniques and self-care as well as a call for increased materials for law school training. If you are not comfortable with these techniques, please take another class to refresh or retrain.

---

[251] Levin, Andrew, Avi Besser, Linda Albert, Deborah Smith, and Yuval Neria. 2012. "The Effect of Attorneys' Work With Trauma-Exposed Clients on PTSD Symptoms, Depression, and Functional Impairment: A Cross-Lagged Longitudinal Study. Law and Human Behavior." *Law and Human Behavior,* 36(6), 538–547. https://doi.org/10.1037/h0093993.

## Discussion Questions

- What are your core values? Create a core values list. Are you living in a way that focuses on your core values? Try the worksheet by Professor Benjamin.
- What is the difference between intrinsic and extrinsic motivators? How can they change during legal education?
- How does talking about mental health issues destigmatize them?
- What do you think about the normalization of the concept of secondary trauma, so that colleagues are able to openly talk about their experience and receive help?
- What did Professors Kennon and Sheldon find as the most important factor for happiness in their study?
- What are the four myths Anneka Ferguson describes that relate to ethical behavior and well-being?
- What does the World Health Organization have to say about self-care?
- What roles do mimicry, empathy, sympathy, and compassion play in self-care?
- What is one action that you could take today that would demonstrate self-care?
- What is self-neglect? Provide examples of self-neglect.
- Why is the use of trauma-informed language important? What is one example of trauma-informed language that you could use today?
- What role does spirituality play in health and well-being?
- According to Mary Novak, how does secondary trauma exposure affect our worldview?
- What does David Jaffe state is the opposite of depression, and how do we achieve it?

# References

Benjamin, G. Andrew H., and Cynthia Alexander. 2011. "Civility is Good for Your Health." *Washington State Bar News*, April 1, 2011. https://ssrn.com/abstract=1803904 Reprinted with permission of the Washington State Bar Association from the April 2011 issue of the *Washington State Bar News*.

Bernhardt, Boris C., and Tania Singer. 2012. "The Neural Basis of Empathy." *Annual Review of Neuroscience* 35:1: 1–23. https://www.annualreviews.org/doi/abs/10.1146/annurev-neuro-062111-150536

Cerny, Jennifer, and Yvonne Tafuto. 2019. "73 Hours: What One Law School Learned from Taking an Untraditional Approach with their 1L Class." NALSAP Annual Conference, American University Washington College of Law, June 14, 2019.

Collaborative Law Institute. n.d. "Mission, Vision and Values." Collaborative Law Institute. Accessed January 1, 2020. https://www.collaborativelaw.org/mission-vision-and-values/.

Confino, Jordana Alter. 2019. "Where Are We on the Path to Law Student Well-Being?: Report on the ABA CoLAP Law Student Assistance Committee Law School Wellness Survey." Journal of Legal Education, April 19, 2019. (Summer 2019). https://ssrn.com/abstract=3374976.

Evans, Adrian. 2014. *The Good Lawyer*. Cambridge: Cambridge University Press.

Ferguson, Anneka. 2015. "Creating Practice Ready, Professional and Well Law Graduates." *Journal of Learning Design* 8 (2):22 This work is licensed under a Creative Commons Attribution 4.0 License.

Ferguson, Anneka, and Stephen Tang. 2019. "Chapter 5: The Value of Determination." In *Educating for Well-being in Law*, edited by Caroline Strevens and Rachael Field. New York: Routledge, 2019.

Figley, C. R. 1995. "Compassion fatigue: Toward a new understanding of the costs of caring." In *Secondary traumatic stress: Self-care issues for clinicians, researchers, and educators*, edited by B. Hudnall Stamm. Derwood, MD: Sidran Institute Press: 3–28.

Gabel, Peter. 2018. The Desire for Mutual Recognition: Social Movements and the Dissolution of the False Self. New York: Routledge.

Gabel, Peter. 2013. Another Way of Seeing: Essays on Transforming Law, Politics and Culture. New Orleans: Quid Pro Books.

Gentile, Mary. 2010. Giving Voice to Values: How to Speak Your Mind When You Know What's Right. New Haven: Yale University Press.

GoodTherapy. 2019. "Types of Guilt." GoodTherapy, November 21, 2019. https://www.goodtherapy.org/learn-about-therapy/issues/guilt.

Jaffe, David. 2018. "The Key to Law Student Well-Being? We Have to Love Our Law Students," *PD Quarterly*, February 13, 2018. http://dx.doi.org/10.2139/ssrn.3123262.

Katz, Sarah, and Deeya Haldar. 2016. "The Pedagogy of Trauma-Informed Lawyering." *Clinical Law Review* 22, number 2 (April 21, 2016): 353–393. Temple University Legal Studies Research Paper No. 2016-29. https://ssrn.com/abstract=2768218.

Kidder, Rushworth M. 2006. *Moral Courage*. New York: Harper.

Krieger, Lawrence S. 1998. "What We're Not Telling Law Students— and Lawyers—That They Really Need to Know: Some Thoughts-in-Action Toward Revitalizing the Profession From Its Roots." *Journal of Law and Health* 13 (1): 6–7.

Krieger, Lawrence S.. 2005. "The Inseparability of Professionalism and Personal Satisfaction: Perspectives on Values, Integrity and Happiness." *Clinical Law Review,* Spring 2005: 425–45. http://ir.law.fsu.edu/articles/97.

Krieger, Lawrence, and Kennon Sheldon. 2014. "What Makes Lawyers Happy? Transcending the Anecdotes with Data from 6200 Lawyers." SSRN Electronic Journal. 10.2139/ssrn.2398989.

Krieger, Lawrence, and Kennon Sheldon. 2015 "What Makes Lawyers Happy? A Data-Driven Prescription to Redefine Professional Success, 83 *George Washington Law Review* 83, number 2: 554-627.

Krill, Patrick, Ryan Johnson, and Linda Albert. 2016. "The Prevalence of Substance Use and Other Mental Health Concerns Among American Attorneys", *Journal of Addiction Medicine* 10, issue 1 (January/February 2016): 46–52. https://doi.org/10.1097/ADM.0000000000000182.

Kroplick, Marilyn. 2014. "Organizational Trauma." In Defense of Animals, July 2, 2014. https://www.idausa.org/organizational-trauma/.

Levin, Andrew, Avi Besser, Linda Albert, Deborah Smith, and Yuval Neria. 2012. "The Effect of Attorneys' Work With Trauma-Exposed Clients on PTSD Symptoms, Depression, and Functional Impairment: A Cross-Lagged Longitudinal Study. Law and Human Behavior." *Law and Human Behavior,* 36(6), 538–547. https://doi.org/10.1037/h0093993

Lipsky, Laura van Dernoot, with Connie Burk. 2009. *Trauma Stewardship: An Everyday Guide to Caring for Self While Caring for Others.* San Francisco: Berrett-Koehler.

Lucchetti, Giancarlo, Alessandra L. G. Lucchetti, and Harold G. Koenig. 2011. "Impact of spirituality/religiosity on mortality: Comparison with other health interventions." *EXPLORE: The Journal of Science and Healing* 7(4): 234–238. https://doi.org/10.1016/j.explore.2011.04.005

McAdams, D. P., and B. K. Jones. 2017. "Making Meaning in the Wake of Trauma: Resilience and Redemption." *Reconstructing Meaning After Trauma: Theory, Research, and Practice*, edited by Elizabeth M. Altmaier. London: Academic Press.

McGee, Teresa Rhode. 2005. *Transforming Trauma*. Maryknoll, NY: Orbis.

Mertz, Elizabeth. 2007. The Language of Law School: Learning to "Think Like A Lawyer" Oxford: Oxford University Press.

Moore, Jennifer, Donna Buckingham, and Kate Diesfeld. 2015. "Disciplinary Tribunal Cases Involving New Zealand Lawyers with Physical or Mental Impairment, 2009–2013." *Psychiatry, Psychology and Law* 22:5" 649–672. http://dx.doi.org/10.1080/13218719.2015.1055624.

Moore, Lee. n.d. "Enhancing Well-Being & Confidence in Court." Lee Moore & Co. https://leemooreco.com/.

Murdoch, Lynda L. 2000. "Psychological Consequences of Adopting a Therapeutic Lawyering Approach: Pitfalls and Protective Strategies." *Seattle University Law Review* 24: 494.

Organ, Jerome M., David B. Jaffe, and Katherine M. Bender. 2016. "Suffering in Silence: The Survey of Law Student Well-Being and the Reluctance of Law Students to Seek Help for Substance Use and Mental Health Concerns." *Journal of Legal Education* 66 at 1 (Autumn 2016):.118–22.

Park, C. L., and M. C. Kennedy. 2017. "Meaning Violation and Restoration Following Trauma." In *Reconstructing Meaning After Trauma: Theory, Research, and Practice*, edited by Elizabeth M. Altmaier. London: Academic Press, 2017.

Pressman, Peter. "How Mirror Neurons May Explain Why You Feel Other's Pain or Emotion." Verywell Health, November 25, 2019. https://www.verywellhealth.com/mirror-neurons-2488711.

Rowe, Margie, Stephen Tang, Tony Foley, Vivien Holmes, Colin James, and Ian Hickie. 2016. *Being Well in the Law: A Guide for Lawyers.* The Law Society of New South Wales, November 3, 2016. https://ssrn.com/abstract=2861586 This publication is licensed under the Creative Commons Attribution-NonCommercial-NoDerivatives 4.0 International License

Scott, Elizabeth. "Spirituality Can Improve Many Aspects of Your Life and Health." Verywell Mind. Verywell Mind, March 13, 2020. https://www.verywellmind.com/how-spirituality-can-benefit-mental-and-physical-health-3144807.

Shakespeare-Finch, J., and K. Adams. 2017. "Growth and Meaning From Negotiating the Complex Journey of Being an Emergency Medical Dispatcher." In *Reconstructing Meaning After Trauma: Theory, Research, and Practice*, edited by Elizabeth M. Altmaier. London: Academic Press.

Solomon, Andrew. 2014. "How the worst moments in our lives make us who we are." TED2014. https://www.ted.com/talks/andrew_solomon_how_the_worst_moments_in_our_lives_make_us_who_we_are?language=en.

Substance Abuse and Mental Health Services Administration (SAMHSA). n.d. "Talking About Spiritual and Religious Factors in Wellness." https://www.samhsa.gov/sites/default/files/programs_campaigns/wellness_initiative/spirituality-fact-sheet.pdf

Sheldon, Kennon M., and Lawrence S. Krieger. (2004). "Does Legal Education have Undermining Effects on Law Students? Evaluating Changes in Motivation, Values, and Well-Being." *Behavioral Sciences & the Law* 22, issue 2:261–86. https://doi.org/10.1002/bsl.582.

Tang, Stephen, and Anneka Ferguson. 2014. "The Possibility of Wellbeing: Preliminary results from surveys of Australian Professional Legal Education Students." QUT Law Review 14 (1):27. https://ssrn.com/abstract=2413269

"The Importance of Using Trauma Sensitive Language." The importance of using trauma sensitive language | Information Access Group. Accessed January 1, 2020. https://www.informationaccessgroup.com/news/trauma_sensitive_language.html.

Vassar, Gerry. "How to Avoid Non-Trauma Sensitive Language." Lakeside, March 8, 2012. https://lakesidelink.com/blog/lakeside/how-to-avoid-non-trauma-sensitive-language/. *Copyright © 2020 by L. Diane Wagenhals and Lakeside Educational Network. All rights reserved. Printed in the United States of America. Reproduced with written permission. For information, address Lakeside, 1350 Welsh Road, Suite 400, North Wales, PA 19454.*

Wade, N., J. M. Schultz, and M. Schenkenfelder. 2017. "Forgiveness Therapy in the Reconstruction of Meaning Following Interpersonal Trauma." In *Reconstructing Meaning After Trauma: Theory, Research, and Practice*, edited by Elizabeth M. Altmaier. London: Academic Press.

World Health Organization. 2014. *Self-Care for Health: A Handbook for Community Health Workers and Volunteers.* WHO Regional Office for South-East Asia. https://apps.who.int/iris/handle/10665/205887.

# Chapter 6 Abstract: Health and Resiliency Tools

In this chapter, we will be exploring tools which will help to better our health, maintain our health and become more resilient. The tools were created with time and simplicity in mind. Most require only a few minutes of time, some just a moment or two. They do not require a monetary outlay and most are green, and don't require electronics. It is important that you use these tools frequently; do not save them only for stress-filled times. They were developed from a strengths-based perspective, which focuses on the personal strength and self-determination of individuals. It is understood from this perspective that one inherently has self-determination and strengths. Sometimes these strengths must be remembered and practiced. If you use the tools frequently, you will better cope with stress and life in general.

We know the healthier we are, the better and the stronger we are, the better able we are to cope with the demands of our jobs and our lives. In this section, we will be exploring health and the different kinds of health. Some may automatically think of physical health and exercise, which is necessary and important. We will also be exploring tools that help with emotional health and well-being.

We all know the value of exercise, rest, and diet. But most of us do not practice these simple keys to basic health. Many people have an all-or-nothing attitude, if they cannot do the exact workout for the given amount of time or do the precise diet, they just stop trying with everything. In the tools section, we will gain some practical tools for trying to consistently implement basics for health and well-being in our lives.

# Chapter 6: Health and Resiliency Tools

Care enough about yourself to make room for sustaining your own health, well-being, and joy.

Why wouldn't we make room for joy in our lives? Indeed, isn't that truly part of the goal, to have a happy life?

## Section 1: Vicarious Resilience

We will begin by introducing some tools that others have created. I was introduced to vicarious resilience in the legal profession by the United Kingdom attorneys Joanna Fleck and Rachel Francis and their website, Claiming Space. Vicarious Resilience is the ability to obtain courage and comfort from clients.[252] The idea being that just as legal professionals can pick up vicarious trauma from their clients, they can also learn vicarious resilience. This is an interesting concept that needs further evaluation and study. We could, however, take it a step further and actively look for the positives in terms of how people are coping in health ways. What are they are doing right? How have they survived to this point?

This perspective is one that could be more frequently brought to our attention: what is going *right* for the client? For one thing, they were able to organize themselves to get to a legal professional. They want help. They are motivated. We could list a number of things that pertain to each individual case. However, this too takes time and there would need to be a pre-existing understanding that creating an informal list of positives can help the legal professional to cope. This also helps the client to understand they have done good things even in abhorrent situations.

Another example of how vicarious resilience can be transferred is through the work of Dr. Pilar Hernandez-Wolfe. She found in a comprehensive review of vicarious resilience that trauma therapists could be changed by their patient's own resilience in ways that were positive but not necessarily pain free. It was further found that vicarious resilience, like vicarious trauma or secondary trauma, occur naturally and together and include notions of resourcefulness and adaptation.[253] This can be applied to legal professionals as well.

---

[252] Vicarious Resilience: A Multilayered Model of Stress and Trauma Margaret Pack First Published November 11, 2013 Review Article https://doi.org/10.1177/0886109913510088 trauma Margaret Pack studied trauma therapists in New Zealand. As expected, the therapists were profoundly impacted by the trauma stories they encountered and as a result therapist searched for meanings which helped the therapists to create strategies and ways of being that promoted personal and professional resilience. The research showed that supervision, the use of support, humor and spirituality were variables that participants identified as helping to lessen the impact of vicarious trauma. This work of course was done using a different professional group however, I wonder what the implications could be for the use of these variables in the course of legal education and practice?

[253] Hernandez-Wolfe, Pilar. 2018. "Vicarious Resilience: A Comprehensive Review". *Revista de Estudios Sociales* 66: 9-17.https://doi.org/10.7440/res66.2018.02 The contents of the Social Studies Magazine are edited under the Creative Commons Attribution 4.0 International.

## <u>Section 1.1: What is Resilience?</u>

We can think of resilience as the ability to cope in healthy ways; enacting behaviors and ways of thinking that help us to get through difficult situations and return to our pre-incident state.

Resiliency can be grown. The Mayo Clinic provides tips to improve your resilience.

**"Get connected.** Building strong, positive relationships with loved ones and friends can provide you with needed support and acceptance in both good times and bad. Establish other important connections by volunteering or joining a faith or spiritual community.

**Make every day meaningful.** Do something that gives you a sense of accomplishment and purpose every day. Set goals to help you look toward the future with meaning.

**Learn from experience.** Think of how you've coped with hardships in the past. Consider the skills and strategies that helped you through rough times. You might even write about past experiences in a journal to help you identify positive and negative behavior patterns — and guide your future behavior.

**Remain hopeful.** You can't change the past, but you can always look toward the future. Accepting and even anticipating change makes it easier to adapt and view new challenges with less anxiety.

**Take care of yourself.** Tend to your own needs and feelings. Participate in activities and hobbies you enjoy. Include physical activity in your daily routine. Get plenty of sleep. Eat a healthy diet. Practice stress management and relaxation techniques, such as yoga, meditation, guided imagery, deep breathing or prayer.

**Be proactive.** Don't ignore your problems. Instead, figure out what needs to be done, make a plan, and take action. Although it can take time to recover from a major setback, traumatic event or loss, know that your situation can improve if you work at it."[254] (Mayo Clinic 2017).

---

[254] "How to Build Resiliency." Mayo Clinic. Mayo Foundation for Medical Education and Research, May 18, 2017. https://www.mayoclinic.org/tests-procedures/resilience-training/in-depth/resilience/art-20046311.

## Section 2: Emotional Intelligence for Strength and Resilience

Emotional intelligence is a much desirable social skill and is currently a hot topic area.

"Emotional Intelligence is a relatively recent term, being understood as the ability to perceive, value, and express emotions accurately; to access and/or generate feelings that facilitate thinking; to understand emotions and emotional knowledge; and to regulate emotions by promoting emotional and intellectual growth."[255]

Daniel Goleman has identified five components of emotional intelligence:

- Self-awareness is your ability to recognize moods and emotions and their effect on others.
- Self-regulation is how you control and manage your emotions.
- Internal motivation is what enables you to reach your goals and passion to do your work.
- Empathy is the ability to understand the emotional status of another.
- Social Skills is the ability to effectively communicate and interact through the recognition of your own feelings and the feelings of others.[256]
- Other suggestions for growing emotional intelligence:
- "Utilize an assertive style of communicating.
- Respond instead of reacting to conflict.
- Utilize active listening skills.
- Be motivated.
- Practice ways to maintain a positive attitude.
- Practice self-awareness.
- Take critique well.
- Empathize with others.
- Utilize leadership skills.
- Be approachable and sociable."[257] (Young Entrepreneur Council 2018).

---

[255] Trigueros R, Padilla AM, Aguilar-Parra JM, et al. The Influence of Emotional Intelligence on Resilience, Test Anxiety, Academic Stress and the Mediterranean Diet. A Study with University Students. International Journal of Environmental Research and Public Health. 2020 Mar;17(6) DOI: 10.3390/ijerph17062071. © 2020 by the authors. Licensee MDPI, Basel, Switzerland. This article is an open access article distributed under the terms and conditions of the Creative Commons Attribution (CC BY) license

[256] Cherry, Kendra. 2019. "5 Key Components of Emotional Intelligence." Verywell Mind, April 3, 2019. https://www.verywellmind.com/components-of-emotional-intelligence-2795438.

[257] Young Entrepreneur Council. 2018. "10 Ways to Increase Your Emotional Intelligence." *Inc.*, September 21, 2018. https://www.inc.com/young-entrepreneur-council/10-ways-to-increase-your-emotional-intelligence.html.

# Section 3: Victim Service Tools

We have heard from Will Meyerhofer and Orlando Da Silva that the practice of law can actually be traumatizing. They, as well as others, have experienced symptoms of secondary trauma through their work. Other lawyers have talked about secondary trauma and experienced symptoms or reactions that parallel post-traumatic stress disorder. Could it be possible that if legal professionals and law students are being exposed to trauma, be it primary or secondary, they could be victims?

It is not unusual as we have seen, and will see below, that many professional service providers identify as being victims at times. In fact, tools have been created for these victims, who are also professionals and are also moms, dads, brothers, and sisters. "Victim" is another highly stigmatized word in many cultures. We may have empathy for the victim, but we do not want to be labeled a victim. And many times, we will not seek out the help that is necessary to provide relief and support. We focus in so narrowly on a word and forget the other components of the person. It might be helpful to remember that one word is not our entire identity, just as "lawyer" or "law student" does not define your entire complex identity. It is striking how students and legal professionals advocate for victims and may dedicate their lives toward helping victims but are unwilling to ever consider that they themselves may be in need of victim assistance.

## Section 3.1: Victim Service Tools for and by Lawyers and Other Professionals

The following is based on my correspondence with Beth E. Molar, a professor at the Bouvé College of Health Sciences, Northeastern University.

The Vicarious Trauma Toolkit (VTT) was designed to encompass four disciplines: law enforcement, fire services, emergency medical services and victim services, as Professor Molar put it, "there are roles that legal professionals play in those fields . . . For example, the multi-disciplinary teams (MDT) that work in child advocacy centers to assist children who have experienced maltreatment include legal professionals on the teams. One of our partnering organizations, the National Child Advocacy Center (NCAC), has legal professionals within their membership, and thus they came to hear our presentations, responded to surveys and such . . . I do believe some of the victim services tools would be useful to [lawyers] in making their workplaces more vicarious trauma-informed and thus better equipped to prevent negative secondary traumatic stress symptoms."

## Section 4: Preventing Secondary Trauma

The late professor Amiram Elwork, the Director of the Law-Psychology Graduate Training Program at Widener University in Chester, Pennsylvania and the author of *Stress Management for Lawyers* made several recommendations for dealing with secondary trauma, including asking for help. He recognized that lawyers do not readily ask for help. He also recommended learning how perfectionism plays a role in daily life and stress levels.

Professor Elwork recommended keeping a daily log of thoughts and emotions and breaking them down into the four components: stimuli, thoughts, emotions, and behaviors. This does not have to be as tricky or time-consuming as it sounds. You can simply keep your log in your phone. In my own practice, sometimes people like to get very basic; the less time-consuming the better. I have created a quick check-in with basic emoticons: smiley face, frowny face, angry face, sad face. Then below it, clients boil down their thoughts into a single word or phrase, followed by one or two words describing the emotion and behavior. Over time, you will be able to see a pattern develop.

Elwork recommends keeping boundaries. Work should be kept at work and not in personal spaces. Finally, keeping a routine is necessary. Professor Elwork recommended making an effort to limit work at night. This may be difficult but try to maintain some blocks of time in the evening that are free for downtime, or personal and family time.[258]

Another factor in preventing secondary trauma is to understand your own background and environment. As Dr. G. Andrew H. Benjamin has found among his many clients; trauma is a pre-existing factor in many lives. If you have a personal connection with what you are seeing, for instance, if you were a victim of childhood molestation and you are reviewing a case where a child was molested, understand the ramifications for you. Your close connection to these issues may magnify or intensify secondary trauma.

Avenues for preventing secondary trauma can take place when you examine, watch, or work with raw graphic evidence, sometimes known as open-source investigation. In her powerful article, "How to Prevent, Identify and Address Vicarious Trauma — While Conducting Open Source Investigations in the Middle East," Hannah Ellis articulates a number of ways to stay healthy.

Hannah Ellis is currently an Associate at Business for Social Responsibility (BSR) and formerly the Team Lead for Syria Investigations at the Open Source Investigations Lab in the Human Rights Center at Boalt Law School.

Her guide, which was initially intended for individuals working with graphic videos related to the Middle East, can readily be adapted by legal professionals for their own needs. When working with a violent or otherwise disturbing video, for instance, Ellis recommends muting it, if possible. Research

---

[258] Elwork, Amiram. 2012. "A Lawyer's Guide To Dealing With Burnout: Does Burnout Mean I Should Leave My Job Or The Law Altogether." Lawyers With Depression, January 16, 2012. http://www.lawyerswithdepression.com/articles/a-lawyers-guide-to-dealing-with-burnout-does-burnout-mean-i-should-leave-my-job-or-the-law-altogether/.

shows that sounds of trauma are often more harmful than images. Also, you can pause the video and then, use your cursor to hover over the progress bar to preview the video in thumbnail form (this only works for YouTube and Facebook video and not for Twitter), allowing you to see if/when there is any content that might be traumatic. If a video includes something particularly explicit, or you are watching the video multiple times for a verification, consider using a sticky note or your hand to cover graphic images." Ellis also recommends disabling auto play, so that you aren't immediately exposed to another video that could be traumatic. Lastly, she recommends looking for keywords that signal explicit content, such as "child," "injury," "family," and "hospital."

"Over time, even with vigilance," she notes, "frequent exposure to graphic content can begin to affect the most resolute [investigator]."[259] She recognizes that we should not be pushing through or ignoring our feelings if we are noticing the effects of secondary trauma. Instead, we should take a break and work through those feelings. Take time to reflect with one another and support one another; this is part of the normalization efforts discussed earlier. Get professional help as needed and required. It always amazes me how often we allow ourselves to suffer when there are actions, we can take to better our situation.

Be aware of how you are interacting with the graphic materials you are handling. Any time you are exposed to explicit images and information, it is important to take direct measures to maintain health and well-being.

The following section provides tools divided into categories which describe the type of tool and how it is implemented.

# Section 5: Tools

## Section 5.1: Directional Tools

Directional tools are used to help us act on our core values and create short- and long-term goals.

*LifeMaps (hands-on)*

One of my favorite tools is LifeMaps, which helps us to define what we want out of life. We do this by evaluating how we are spending the 24 hours each day. It can help you look at where you are now, where you would like to be in the future, and (if you chose) where you were in the past.

You will find as you use this tool, that you are delving into your values in terms of what direction you want your life to take and what you want it to feel and look like. It can work particularly well in group settings, where colleagues can share and discuss.

---

[259] Ellis, Hannah. "How to Prevent, Identify and Address Vicarious Trauma — While Conducting Open Source Investigations in the Middle East." bellingcat, October 18, 2018. https://www.bellingcat.com/hashtags/vicarious-trauma/.

I recommend that people construct their LifeMaps at least twice a year, and more frequently if you are feeling particularly stuck or out of sync with where you want to be in your life.

The first time you work on LifeMaps it may feel a bit intimidating but keep moving with it. Do it quickly, follow your intuition or your gut, then analyse.

First, create a pie chart and accurately represent in each sector what you are doing with the time in your life. For example, I have seen charts where over 75% of the pie is represented by work.

Review the figures below and the different pieces of the pie. Your segments may be vastly different. Let us find out.

# LifeMaps

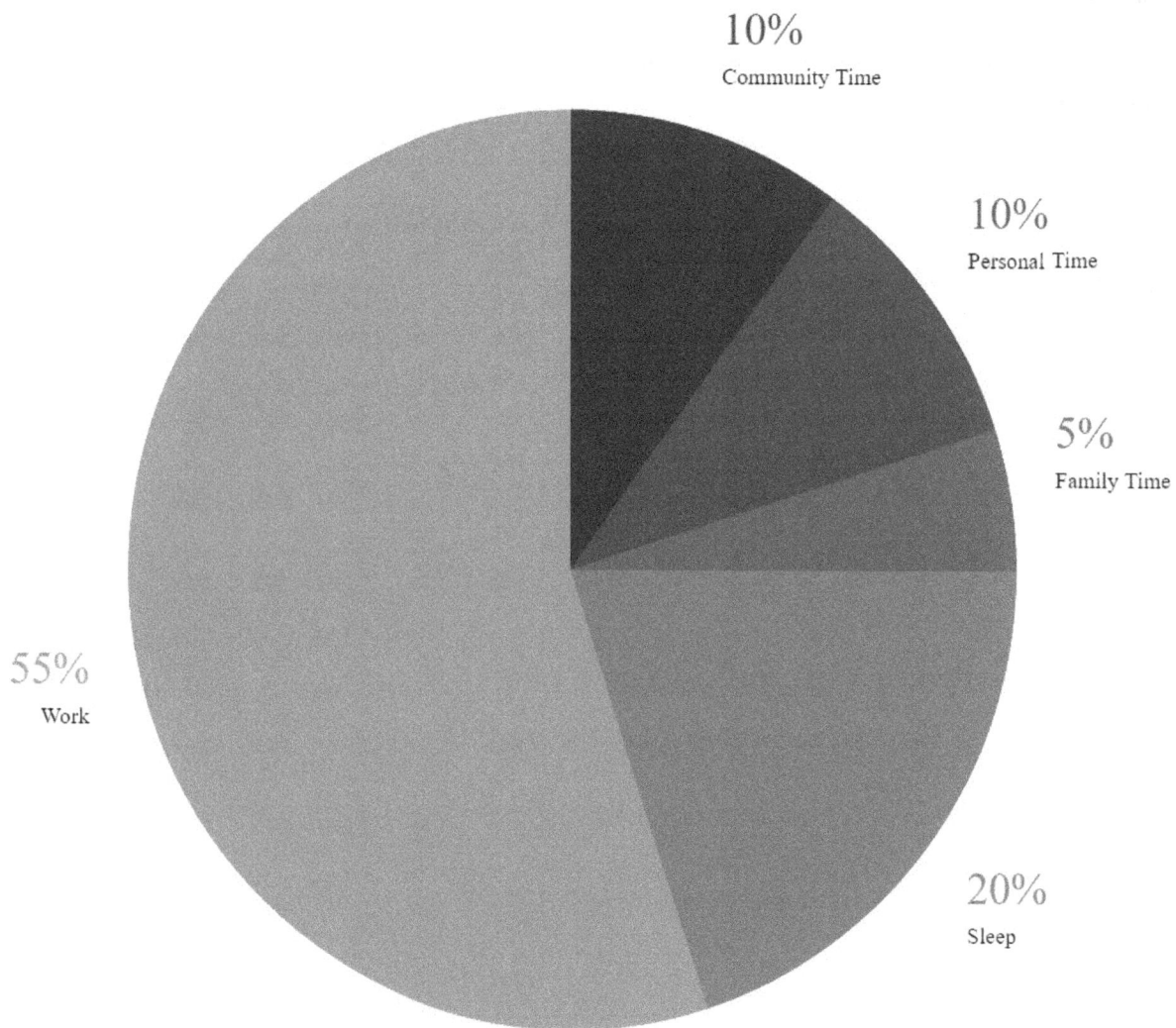

# LifeMaps

5%
Exercise

5%
Community Time

20%
Personal Time

40%
Work

5%
Family Time

25%
Sleep

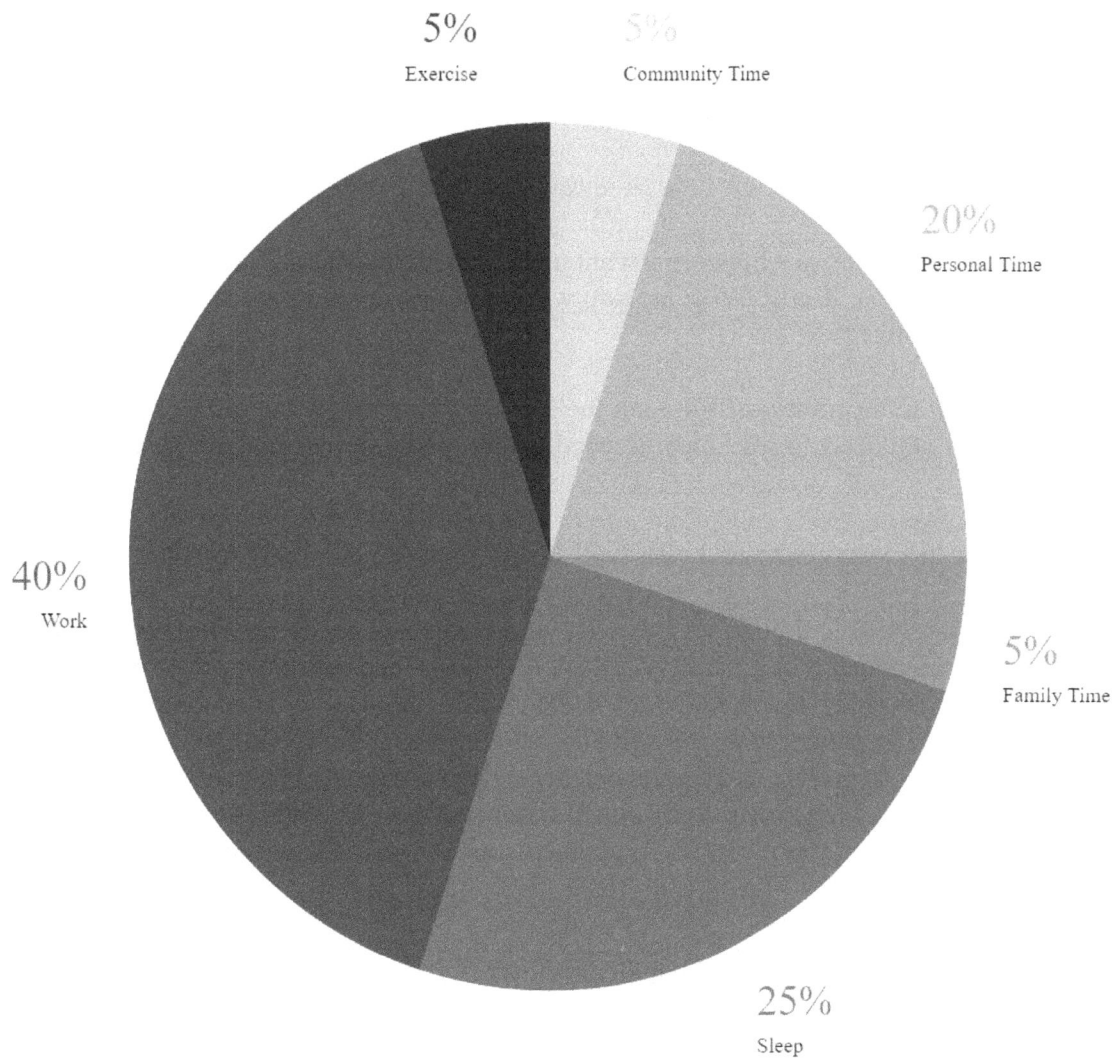

Now, create your own LifeMaps. What does it tell you about your life? When you think about your own LifeMap, it may seem lopsided. When you use this tool, you will find a simple and graphic way to make your life healthier and more balanced. LifeMaps helps us to be honest about ourselves and about what our life and time really look like.

Next, create a pie chart with sectors that you want or need to have in your life, sectors that you don't have right now, or sectors that you want to shrink or expand. I call this next step "waving the magic wand." At this point, place and space the sectors the way you would like your life to look. Don't worry about how to get there. Again, let analysis drop away and allow for your intuition to take over. I know that sounds odd, and it may be uncomfortable, but give it a try. What do you really want and need in your life? This may be a difficult question. So, let's break it down.

Create a T-chart, a two-column chart, with the headings of Wants and Needs. Set a timer for 10 minutes and fill in as much as you can without evaluating or analyzing. At this point, you are simply putting in subjects: for instance, physical exercise, family time, community service, spiritual pursuits, and hobbies.

*Take some time to review your Wants and Needs.*

Think about the difference between a want and a need? How far are you willing to go to get your wants met? How about your needs? What are you willing to give up in terms of one sector of your pie chart as opposed to another?

Now let's begin the process of filling in the sectors. I encourage you to complete this process over several days. If you become stuck or frustrated, put the work down and come back to it later, but do come back to it.

This is your life, your health and your well-being. Let's keep moving forward.

After you have had the time to review what your wants and needs are, start on a fresh LifeMaps. Work on creating sectors that will accurately reflect your wants and needs. Try to live it for one week and see how it feels. You may decide to redraw some of the sectors to better accommodate your wants and needs. That is OK; be patient with yourself and remember this is a tool to help you live a better life. Keep your LifeMaps, both present and future, where you can see them. They will help you motivate and navigate through this tricky territory called your life. Remember, LifeMaps can be used many times. I encourage you to utilize them frequently, to help keep yourself on track and centered with your goals and core values.

*Explode the Pie Chart (hands-on)*

You have created your LifeMaps pie chart and are working on it, dividing your life into different parts, finding balance, finding peace; wonderful. Now, I am asking you to explode the chart. Yes, that is right. Change it up.

Let us add to a segment or create a new segment in the chart. Maybe there is something that you have always wanted to do, like taking a mindfulness course, skydiving, etc. Figure out a way to add that activity to your chart and engage in it. Learning something different creates new neural pathways, which help us to stay out of old memory tracks, including tracks that might be filled with stress, anxiety, or unhealthy behaviors.

*Funnel (hands-on)*

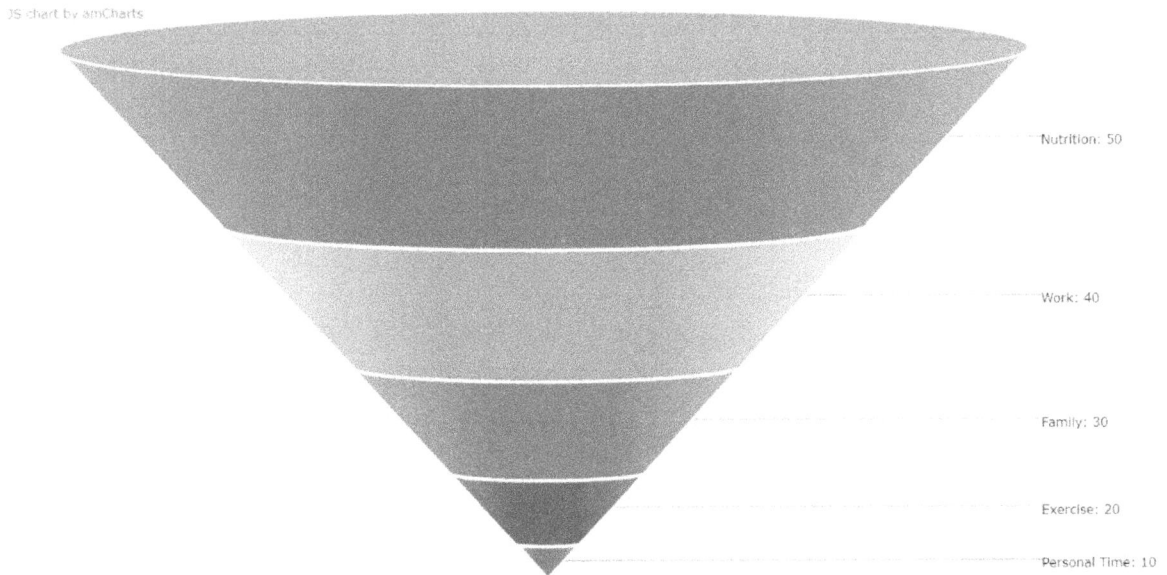

JS chart by amCharts

Nutrition: 50

Work: 40

Family: 30

Exercise: 20

Personal Time: 10

Draw the image of a funnel with 5 layers. As you work on the tool, you may decide to add layers or remove layers. Fill in the layers of the funnel with a word or words that represent what you put into your life on a daily basis.

You can start wherever you want.

Notice where you spend the most and least amounts of time.

Do you need to rethink the different layers? Everything you are putting in is contributing to who you are today. What you put in the most, is what you get out the most.

Change it if you need to, play with the funnel and the different layers: add more layers if you need to. Change them about and put them to a trial test for a couple of days. What does it feel like when you do the trial test?

*Mini Self-Assessment Toolkit (visual)*

This is a quick assessment of how well you are doing with your health globally. It forces you to actually see what is currently happening and how you are handling it. We need to evaluate our own global health now and then to make sure we continue to move toward well-being. The Mini Self-Assessment Toolkit allows us to make a quick assessment and then take action.

Take this Mini Self-Assessment Toolkit-Checklist. Use it in particular, when you are feeling rundown, out of sorts, or you have knowingly been exposed to difficult emotional narratives.

Check the physical signs below that apply to you:

- Diarrhea or constipation
- Soreness in back or neck
- Exhaustion
- Insomnia
- Nausea
- Heart palpitations
- Headaches
- Check the behavioral signs below that apply to you:
- Reoccurring thoughts or ruminating thoughts
- Racing thoughts
- Flashbacks
- Sadness
- Fear
- Increased irritability and anger
- Avoidance of social situations
- Increased use of alcohol or other drugs
- Emotional eating or loss of appetite
- Avoidance of clients
- Feelings of helplessness when hearing a client's narrative
- Imposture syndrome -feeling unskilled at your work
- Check the emotional signs below that apply to you:
- Depression
- Anxiety
- Emotional exhaustion
- Negative self-image
- Feeling of dissociation
- Reduced ability to feel empathy or sympathy
- Feelings of guilt
- Feelings of dread
- Hypersensitivity or hyperarousal
- Difficulty separating work life and personal life
- Lack of personal time or down time
- Suicidal thoughts (If you are having suicidal thoughts, get help immediately. Suicide hotlines are available 24/7, as are emergency services.)

If you have two or more checks in any category, take the time to find solutions. Now is the time to do some changing and add more healthy and balanced behaviors. It may also be time to get outside help. Always contact a physician or therapist if you are struggling.

*Self-Care Plan (hands-on)*

Self-care is what we do to take care of ourselves. These are the basic behaviors that keep us healthy. It is what we do on a daily basis that matters most. Create a plan that is actually doable. A plan that one can manage and enjoy, allows us to be consistent and feel the benefits of healthy living. As professionals, we may think of the things that we must do to look the part: well-cut suit, regular hair and nail appointments. But what about a regular visit to the dentist, physician, or therapist?

What other ways can we do basic self-care:

Eating properly: eating nutritiously dense meals, especially during times of stress, can really help. Taking the time to eat, instead of eating on the run or eating only finger foods.

Sleeping is another component of a self-care plan. Sleeping properly; going to sleep, staying asleep throughout the night and obtaining a healthy amount of sleep; not sleeping too little or too much. Use sleep hygiene techniques if you are struggling. Sleep hygiene is a way of creating healthy sleep. It includes going to bed at about the same time and waking up at the same time, having a darkened, cooler bedroom. Attempting to slow down before bed, perhaps with prayer or meditation, rather than alcohol, drugs, or food. Having a small snack or a cup of your favorite herbal tea before bed can be a part of your sleep hygiene ritual.

Getting Exercise: We all know that exercise helps us to combat stress, but intense physical exercise is also a stressor. Remember to have balance with your exercise. If you are doing intense aerobic exercise one day make sure to balance it with yoga, tai chi or something gentle the next day: perhaps a simple walk or stretching. The goal is to get some exercise every day, such as a gentle walk in nature.

Have regular uncomplicated fun and social interaction with friends, family and neighbors.

Maintain our environment in a way that is harmonious. If we are living in clutter and disorganization, we may feel internal chaos. Organize and declutter. And if you can't do it, get someone who can. Remember your pie chart. There are only so many hours in a day.

Create some down time to do whatever you want.

When self-care is not enough, it is time to visit a professional. If you are having difficulty with any part of the basic self-care framework and you have attempted to work on it to no avail, seek professional help. There are many caring and compassionate therapists and counselors who can help you find tools to navigate to better health.

*Agatha Petrulis Tool: Stencils (hands on)*

## Step 1

Confidence is key, but sometimes we can get lost when we second-guess ourselves. Something that you may have been 100% sure of, doesn't seem certain anymore. Over-thinking can create a rut in your creative mind and stencilling is the perfect way to regain that confidence. Acrylic paint works well or do it yourself by sectioning off shapes on your paper with painters' tape. You can even cut out shapes to use as stencils. When you do this drawing/painting, go with your first instinct. Ignore the background sound of doubt. You think that a triangle would look good next to that circle, then do it. Should green go next to blue? Paint it there. Should red overlap green? Overlap it. This project may seem messy and chaotic at first, but once it's done you will see that those first decisions are the best ones. They will come together to create something beautiful. If you don't have paint you can use different types of shading.

## Step 2

After you have completed your work- reflect. What were you thinking as you did this project? Was it hard to not second guess yourself? Or were you able to clear your mind of that nagging voice of doubt? If so, how did you successfully accomplish it? If not, why do you think it was hard to block it out? Did you slip up at all? When and why? What were you thinking when you slipped up, or did you not realize you had second-guessed until after the fact? Sometimes, we are so accustomed to second-guessing ourselves that it becomes like second nature and is done subconsciously? This is a great activity to remind yourself that usually, your first thought, is the best one. There is always time later to go back and review. Save those second guesses for where they belong, second. If you decide later that you still want to revise, you always can. Wait for the paint to dry and simply paint over it. When you are finished, make a pact with yourself to look at this piece when you are doubting yourself. It will remind you to go with your gut, and that you can always revise after. You can do this project over to remind yourself. If you're on the go, simply draw shapes without your home-made stencil and use different shading techniques with your pencil.

*New Beginnings (visual)*

Sometimes we hit a wall or a place in which we just get stuck. Sometimes we must reformulate or remake a story. As you know, we are constantly telling ourselves things about our environment, others, and ourselves. We are creating our story. The story may be real or have bits and fragments of reality or it could be completely made up. Remember, emotions are not necessarily reality.

It is important to check out the story occasionally. If we are finding ourselves in the same negative story over and over again, it is time to create another story. We can begin a new chapter in our life story any time we want to.

Tell yourself that you are creating something new and move the story in the direction that you want it to go. If you have been working and working on a particular relationship or idea, detach from it for a moment and move into a new place. Refocus on yourself, just for a moment in time. Do the next right best thing for you. Maybe the next right best thing is going back to basics, such as self-soothing.

Just doing something different can help us to get unstuck and moving in a new direction.

How would you like the next chapter to look? Instead of just thinking about it, actually do one thing to move in that direction. Perhaps it is getting up ten minutes early to enjoy the quiet or to do some prayer, mediation or stretching. You know what you need, try something.

### What Is Your Story? (hands-on)

Write down a brief description of your adult life. Highlight accomplishments as well as setbacks.

Now think about the next couple of chapters in your story. How would you like the story to continue? What and who would you include and exclude? How would you do it?

Keep the story somewhere you can review it from time to time; to keep you on track and remind you of where you have come from and where you are going. This kind of storytelling is like creative visualization. Creative visualization occurs when we create the story or the picture in our mind of the steps to achieving our goals. Professional athletes use this tool to achieve their goals.

### Vision (hands-on)

"Where there is no vision, the people perish."—Proverbs 29:18

Everyone lives according to some vision. Vision is what motivates us to behave in certain ways. It is important to articulate the vision. What is your vision for your life? Is your vision limiting? Does your vision include health and balance? Are you headed toward that vision? What is your vision beyond yourself? Do you have a vison beyond yourself? Is it important?

Explore these issues. Take some time to jot down your answers. Keep your vision statement nearby so you can look at it from time to time to help keep you on your path.

### A Future of Expanded Potential (cognitive)

How can we reclaim the parts of our lives that have been unlived, the parts that we still want to experience? Can we shift our focus from worry or fear or unending stress to that of potential for a different experience, be it of fun or joy or whatever you are looking for? Let us focus on how to expand without pushing and without pressure. Generate some thoughts and take the next, best step.

*Why Are You Not You? (cognitive)*

For many of us, since adolescence and even before, there has been a constant barrage from mass media, our peers, and our parents telling us what to strive for, what we should do with our lives, and how we should present ourselves to the world. This can become confusing; and we may lose are frame of reference about what is genuinely interesting and good for us in all of these areas.

We can become entangled in other peoples' wants, needs and perceptions. Are you genuinely able to be you, in all aspects of your life? If not, why not and what can you do to get back to the real you? If you are struggling, you may want to consider going back to the LifeMaps Tool for additional help. Remember to keep working; the answer will come.

*If Not Now, When? (hands-on)*

Answer this question, "if not now, when?" Write it down and keep it with you. Put it in your pocket for a day, touch the paper every now and then or maybe make it wallpaper on your phone. It can be a touchstone to remind you of what is important to you as you go through the hours in your day and make decisions on how to spend your life's time. Have fun, live your life, and don't delay. Put enjoyment into the work you are doing today.

## Section 5.2: Well-Being Tools

Well-being tools help us to create and maintain health and happiness in our lives on a daily basis.

*Agatha Petrulis Tool: A silhouette (hands on)*

## Step 1

Think of someone, or something, or even an animal that inspires you. Whatever you choose, should make you feel invincible. This should be something to remind you of your inner strength. Create a silhouette can be any color, faced any way. It can be of an object, a person, an animal or even a place. Make sure to think of what uplifts you, but still holds a calming feeling for you. Draw or paint any kind of background. Where do you imagine yourself as you draw your silhouette? Do you imagine being in a library, a coffee shop, or outside? Is it day or night? Fill this area with things that empower you.

## Step 2

Now write down what your silhouette is composed of. How does it inspire you? How does it make you feel? If you chose a person, what do you imagine they are thinking? What do you hear them saying when you are feeling discouraged? What is the background? Did you choose a location? Why? What would you do there? How does it inspire and uplift you? Did you choose to draw objects? What are they? Why did you choose them? How do they make you feel? When you're finished, make a pact with yourself to look at your drawing/painting when you need encouragement.

---

*Agatha Petrulis Tool: An Uncluttered and Peaceful Mind (hands on)*

### Step 1

Today you will be painting/drawing an uncluttered mind. A good metaphor for your mind can be portrayed by a three-dimensional shape. What comes to my mind, is a square. However, you can do any shape: circle, triangle, even a hexagon. Don't hesitate to google how to draw any of these 3-D shapes too. Your shape can have texture or be smooth. It can have bumps, or fur; however, you envision your mind when it's clear and calm. Make your background either a solid color that you find soothing or fill it with objects that give you peace of mind. You can leave your shape empty, or you can draw things in that help you focus.

### Step 2

Describe why you chose the shape you did, to represent your mind. What colors did you choose? How do they make you feel? Is anything inside your shape? Is anything inside your shape? What is it and why did you place it? Is your shape smooth or does it have texture? What does it resemble? How do you feel emotionally when your mind is at peace? What are some things you can do to achieve peace of mind? How is your energy level and sleep schedule when your mind is in sync with your body? When you are finished, make a pact with yourself to look at your 3-D shape when you're having trouble organizing your thoughts, or have too much on your mind. It will remind you of the things that help you to have a clear head and allow for better focus.

*Agatha Petrulis Tool: Abstract (hands on)*

### Step 1

Think of a pleasurable feeling. A feeling that is a great experience for you. A feeling that brings happiness, peacefulness, joy, serenity, peace, excitement, laughter, hope, and all things good. When you have that feeling in your head, just start painting. Allow your mind to open and create a visual representation of that feeling. Abstract art is non-representational; there is no right or wrong way to create it. Experience this feeling as it flows from your mind, through your hands, and onto the paper.

### Step 2

Now describe this feeling and what you were thinking. How long did it take to start this project? Did you have to think for a while about how to approach it? Did the feeling come before you began painting, during, after, or not at all? Did you experience the feeling, or just recall it? When you are finished, make a pact with yourself to look at this painting for creative inspiration.

*Illuminate (visual)*

Find things that light up your life; the things that make you glow from within. Now do them.

Think outside of the box. Maybe washing puppies at the local animal shelter is your thing, or reading to children, or writing your own book. Create pottery; take a class in anthropology, act in local theater. The list is endless. Embrace it and do it. Make your world interesting and rich.

By adding dimension to yourself as a human being, you are adding dimension to yourself as a student or legal professional. You will come back to your tasks refreshed and motivated in a healthy way, rather than feeling as if it's just another day you have to push through.

*Life Spring (visual)*

We are all like wells; deep and full or shallow and need to be filled. How do you replenish yourself? How do you re-motivate and get your drive back? Some people like to attend conventions where they meet others and get reenergized and learn new things. Some people read inspiring books or articles. Some people regularly meet with teachers or mentors to get motivated and filled with hope. The frequency with which we need to participate in these inspirational experiences varies from person to person; but we all need them.

How can you tell when your well is full or shallow or even drained? Check out your energy and your attitude towards life. What is it like? Does it need an injection of something to get it back on track or to maintain it?

*Negative and Positive Perspectives (cognitive)*

Take thirty seconds to glance around the room you are now in. View five objects. For every object that you gaze at, find something negative about it, just one aspect. This is a quick process. It shouldn't take you more than 30 seconds.

How do you feel? Frustrated, tired, or something else?

Now take thirty seconds and glance around the room at the same five objects, but now look at each of them in a positive light. What do you notice that is good about each object? Again, take only 30 seconds. Now come back to the room. How do you feel? Do you notice emotional and physical differences when you switched perspectives from negative to positive? We can become narrow in our thought processes, especially during stressful times. It is important to check ourselves to see if we are looking at the world through a grey, bleak, or dismal lens. Of course, we will not always be looking through rose-colored glasses. But we should make sure that we are moving in and out of cognitive and emotional states and not just sticking in a negative mode of thinking.

*HALTS (cognitive)*

HALT is a well-known tool that is used by the 12-step groups. It stands for Hungry, Angry, Lonely, and Tired. I have added the S for scared, worried, or nervous. When we are in any of these conditions we need to stop, pause or HALT(S), evaluate how we are feeling, and take action to take care of ourselves. Hunger, anger, loneliness, tiredness, and fear emotionally impact how we feel and how we communicate with others. These areas are vital to our well-being and the well-being of our relationships. When they get out of sync, do something about it: eat something healthy, look for a solution to your anger, socialize, get some rest, do some self-soothing.

*Don't Just Think It. Do It. (cognitive)*

Talking about an idea of getting healthier such as going to the gym or taking a yoga class is great. But do it. Put your words into action. Take one step at a time and see how it feels. Plan one goal that is doable.

This is not about all or nothing. This is about doing one step, even if we start out just once per week. We are progressing. Let us say your idea is to start eating healthier. What is one step that you could take? Maybe add an apple or salad to your day. Maybe you are thinking about quieting your mind. Again, think of a tiny step such as starting your day with a prayer or mediation.

*Joy (cognitive)*

What gives you great happiness, or pleasure? What amuses you? What do you find humorous? What delights you? What gives you joy?

Make a list, partake, and enjoy.

It can be as simple as finding a great joke every day. I like to look at comic blogs. All I have to do is press a button on my computer and there they are, anytime that I want a break and a laugh.

Jokes give physical and emotional breaks. Notice the difference after reading or looking at something funny; your body and your emotional state are more relaxed. When we are more relaxed, we can think clearly, and ultimately accomplish more of what we want.

Another resource can be a review of photos on your phone or in albums; we usually take photographs of what we like and what makes us happy. Find what makes you happy, laugh, and feel the joy.

## Solace (cognitive)

What gives you comfort? I can literally feel my tension ease when I visit the dog park. Visiting the dog park transports me to a place of peace. Going to a horse farm brings me solace, even if I don't ride. I still experience the smells, sounds, and feel of the horses. Sometimes just driving in the country relaxes me. I can feel my body and my emotional state shift.

What gives you solace? Maybe it is planning a day after school or work where you might have a special meal and a movie, or perhaps reading a book, or maybe simply sitting in the sunshine, or drinking a hot beverage watching the falling snow or rain.

If you don't know what gives you solace, start to experiment. Try a couple of things and see what is comforting and what brings you peace. Then regularly engage in that activity.

## Explore the New (cognitive)

Explore something new, such as a new cuisine or a new genre in books, movies, or music.

You might find great excitement in something new or it might be just OK. Either way you will find satisfaction in trying. Think out of the box. Many years ago, I was in East Africa and I loved every moment of it. I met colleagues I am still in contact with. I loved the music and energy and movement of the dance and the people. I hopped with a tribe while my daughter watched on, very embarrassed. Years later, I still longed for that energy and was fortunate enough to find an African Dance Class. I loved it. I could not keep up with the dance or the dancers, but I am quite sure that the music, the drums and what I could manage affected me at a cellular level. Find the new. You don't have to be good at it, just do it.

## Mini Cost-Benefit Analysis (cognitive)

It is time to revisit your day-to-day behaviors. Make a list of everything you did yesterday. How much time did you spend in each activity? Now go back to each activity and determine the cost and the benefit. Did you get to the gym? Yes, it took time away from work and family, but what was the benefit? Did you feel better, or calmer? Did that feeling transfer to your relations with your family or your work experience? Weigh each item: what was the cost and benefit of each action? Evaluate and make a stronger healthier plan for today.

## Spontaneity (cognitive)

How spontaneous are you? If a good, healthy opportunity comes up, such as seeing a concert or having dinner with friends who are passing through town, are you able to participate?

This tool allows us to look at past opportunities that we have participated in as well as opportunities that we have missed. When we were able to take a spontaneous opportunity, what was in place that allowed us to do so? How can we create more opportunities for ourselves to be spontaneous?

Most people, including myself, find spontaneity difficult. In the well-organized life of a busy professional person, how do we suddenly take that special opportunity that just came up?

I like to ask myself if, in the long run, would I regret turning it down or not participating in whatever popped up. Today as I write, the weather forecast was calling for clouds, rain, and cool weather, but right now it is sunny and 70 degrees Fahrenheit. Tomorrow the forecast is for rain. Though I am on a very tight schedule with this book, I am going to take a break and head outside. The sunshine and brightness are good for us all. This may have sounded like an easy decision, but it was not easy for me because I had committed this day to writing and this is not the only change that has occurred today in my schedule.

Check yourself and your own opportunities; will you regret it if you don't participate? Many times, this question gets to the heart of what we need to know. (Excuse me a moment, while I go enjoy my walk.)

## Enough (cognitive)

Are you ever "enough"? What is enough? How will you know when you have done enough at work, at home, with family, with friends, and most importantly, for yourself?

These are very important questions. Ultimately, they bring us back to the notion of work-life balance. You truly may have never considered these issues before. You may have just kept going until you were physically and or emotionally exhausted.

Think about it and write about it. You may have ignored an emotional state of exhaustion multiple times and now you face the physical symptoms of exhaustion, such as fatigue.

We must have boundaries. We must know what is enough, so that we can stop and have sufficient energy to do the things that create balance in our lives.

## Self-Compassion Assessment (hands-on)

How self-compassionate are you? Have you ever considered self-compassion? Perhaps, you are compassionate with others, but what about yourself? You are working on many things in a stress-filled profession, so how can you demonstrate some acts of compassion toward yourself?

Create a list of three things you could do to strengthen your self-compassion and try one a day for a week. See if you begin to notice a shift. Self-compassion feels good. Sometimes when we are going nonstop, we forget that we are supposed to enjoy ourselves, take breaks, and be compassionate.

Let's get you started with some examples:

A deliberate long soak in the tub instead of the frenzied shower that takes place every day.

When you are feeling weary of some subject, switch subjects just for 30 minutes and give yourself a break.

Make a nutritious hot meal and eat it with family or friends without any electronic devices being present.

Now you create the remainder of the list.

### *Balance Function (cognitive)*

What is a key for you to get balanced and remain balanced? Examples of balance might include downtime, alone time, exercise, meditation, or more sleep. What do you need? What's a practical way to include it in your everyday schedule?

Remember, we are looking for one key behavior. We can focus on that behavior, and once we get some reinforcement for continuing the behavior, we can try others.

### *Gentle Kindness (cognitive)*

Are you gentle and kind to yourself? Do an assessment of your daily living. For example, are you on a strict diet or strict exercise regimen? Maybe your work comes first, even before basic healthy living behaviors such as eating at least one hot a meal a day, exercising, and sleeping.

Do you find time to do gentle things for your body and your mind? Can you identify some gentle things that you could do for yourself? Have you ever thought about massaging your own hands, feet, or scalp? When we try these behaviors, we can get to know ourselves again. When you massage your feet or your hands, what do they look like? What condition are they in? When was the last time that you paid attention to them?

What do you do for yourself that is kind? Do you take time to eat? If you do, do you eat slowly and mindfully, or do you simply eat to get it done and move on? I know someone who will only eat finger foods because those are the fastest foods to consume. Is that kind and gentle?

If you get stuck, think about what you have done for others that is kind and gentle. Now try to apply it to yourself.

Remember, these simple and small behaviors can be done daily to help your overall well-being and create a more balanced life.

*Requesting Coursework or Continuing Legal Education (cognitive)*

Request the creation of classes and continuing legal education that target topics of health and well-being as ongoing and available courses. Ask that these courses become timely. Seek educators who are up-to-date and willing to present on current topics.

Remember, you are not asking for more work; you are simply asking for something different that may have an impact, not only on your legal practice, but on your long-term well-being.

*Let Go (cognitive)*

While sitting, allow yourself to occasionally attempt to let go of your tension. Notice your shoulders, your belly and your breath. If you are holding your shoulders up and your belly in and holding your breath or doing shallow breathing, let go. Let the weight of your shoulders release to your arms and let the weight of your arms be held up by the chair or your lap. Let your belly go, you do not have to hold it in. Give yourself a big deep breath in, hold it for a second, and let it go.

Repeat this tool every couple of hours while studying, working, or concentrating. You will become more aware of your body and your emotional state. You will also learn that you do not have to hold your body in certain ways, many of which you may not be conscious of. You will learn that you can encounter information in a more relaxed manner. This more relaxed manner is much better for your health.

If you find yourself continuing to return to a tense position, ask yourself why. Is it the material you are reading? The amount of material? A deadline?

Asking these questions allows you to get to know yourself and how you personally respond to different stressors. This knowledge is essential if you are attempting to learn how to best respond and take care of yourself.

*Take a Long View (cognitive)*

After an hour and a half or so of work, lift up your head and shift your gaze out the window or up to the ceiling, if you do not have a window available. Allow your eye muscles to focus on a distant object for a couple of moments. Then come back to your work. Long periods of time in front of the computer or case files lead not only to eye fatigue, but fatigue in general. Shift your gaze and come back a bit more relaxed and perhaps, a bit more focused.

*Coming Home to Oneself (cognitive)*

This tool helps individuals find what home means within themselves, that is, what they truly like to think about and participate in outside of work. These things may vary slightly from time to time. Coming home to one's true self is not only admitting what you love, but honoring it and yourself by participating in what you love. If you love poetry, are you actually taking the time to read a poem?

This tool is all about looking inside, admitting and honoring. It is not a far reach or a deep dig. We usually can recall that we loved to listen to music, but maybe we stopped for whatever reason. Or we knew that reading a cozy mystery was much more comfortable then reading what our own personal story told us was best for us to read, such as reading more legal articles. We became judgmental. We started to create a new narrative that did not allow for our personal time but focused on our work time almost exclusively.

Take time to honor yourself and do the healthy and enriching things that you like to do.

*Honor and Gratification (cognitive)*

When was the last time you paused and appreciated your life and the many wonderful things that you have accomplished thus far? Did you take the time to honor yourself and feel gratified for even one moment?

Start right now, where you are. You made it into law school, which is competitive and difficult to do. If you don't believe me, just google the statistics. And if you have already graduated or are established in your law career, that should be more gratification. Honor yourself and your accomplishments.

If you feel like you can't remember, or the accomplishments were so long ago, or you simply cannot get beyond the current stressors, create a short timeline of the year and the last five to ten years. Write down all of your positive accomplishments. Is healthy and balanced living one of them? If not, make it a goal.

Now sit with your list and really think about it. You don't need more than a couple of minutes; remember, focus only on the accomplishments. Be compassionate with yourself. Be gratified in this moment. Honor yourself.

*Stopping to Mark the Accomplishment (cognitive)*

So often, we move on from one feat to the next without even stopping to pause, reflect, or provide ourselves with reinforcement for the good things which we have completed. You made it into law school. Did you have a party, or do something for yourself? You completed a huge project at work or closed the contract, do you celebrate, or do you just move right onto the next job?

Have we stopped to give ourselves credit for what we have accomplished, such as landing the job, completing the difficult case, or getting admitted to law school to begin with? There will always be another achievement to be sought, so take the time to savor the victory, or the victory becomes hollow and we too become a bit hollow. Remember the children's song; *The Bear Climbed Over the Mountain*? The bear climbed over the mountain and what did he see? He saw another mountain and then what did he see? Another and yet another mountain, endless mountains. And what did he do? Endless, mindless, climbing. Is that you?

The bear never stopped to even look at the mountain he had just summited or even reflect on the mountains he had to climb to get to where he was. He just kept climbing.

Take time to celebrate your accomplishments. After all, why are you doing them if they don't make you happy?

Take time to reflect on your accomplishments and how they impact your life and the lives of those around you.

### Gifts, Part 1 (cognitive)

Are you thriving or are you just surviving? What gifts do you know you have, and yet you have been neglecting?

Listen, meditate, take time or pray. What is that inner calling?

You may have many gifts. Perhaps you are a great orator, reader, or singer. Listen closely, be still, and you will know. It is your decision, however, to take action on it. The goal is to enjoy living your life and not just enduring it.

### What I Would Do If I Had Time... (cognitive)

What is your authentic vision of the way you would like to live? What fun activity would you like to experience or learn?

Listen within, make a list, and do it. Do one thing at a time, over time. You don't have a deadline of when you must do these things as they are fun and interesting life experiences. You must make the time to participate in the experience.

### If Not, Why Not? (hands-on)

I love this simple question. First see how this question matches up with basic items like eating, sleeping, and exercising—all of them are gates to health and well-being.

For instance, if you are not eating one nutritious meal every day, why not? Truly, why not?

Keep going through your basic health list and answering the question, why not?

Then move on to other items in your list, such as something fun that you have been wanting or waiting to engage in for a while. It doesn't have to be something big. Maybe it is just going out to a movie. Apply the tool, then take an action.

Are you finding a theme as you answer the question why not? What is it? Examples could be, I am too busy, I am too tired, or I have other obligations. Go back to your notions of health and well-being and start there. Create at least one step that will bring you closer to doing, versus not doing today.

### Seasonal Changes (hands-on)

Mark the beginning of the change of seasons with a change in your environment. You change your clothes from something warm to something cool, so change your work environment too. Add something that reminds you of the season. For example, in Autumn maybe you'd like a small gourd or pumpkin on your desk or a card or photo to represent the season, or a pumpkin latte or spice tea. These simple additions can remind us of the bigger picture of our life.

During holidays, add something to your workspace to remind you of what you are celebrating and to provide cheer to you. It does not have to be big or flashy. It can just be something you are aware of. I like to use different candles that have scents to mark the season. On my birthday, I have a birthday cake candle. Though I am working, I am still marking seasons and special dates.

### Inspiration (hands-on)

What or whom do you find inspiring? Think about that person or place. What are the qualities that you admire? What qualities would you like to emulate?

Maybe the person or place is quiet, serene, and calm. Or maybe the person is bold, adventurous, and funny.

Print out a photo of the person or place and keep it somewhere that you can see it from time to time, to inspire you to keep moving forward in the direction of health and well-being.

### Live from the Heart (cognitive)

Most people do not consider their day-to-day work to be from the heart. Instead, they just muddle through it, or they have so much work that they plow through without feeling or really honoring what we have been given to do, or their unique capability to be logical and analytical.

Imagine your work and your life, if you lived from the heart. Take the time to remember as you enter into your work or study, where you spend eight to ten or more hours of your day, that you are following your calling or your passion. Something within you wanted to be a legal professional.

What was it? What inspired you? What made it interesting? Get back to that original thought or memory and let it vibrate through you.

Let it affect you and affect those around you. You do not have to tell others to affect them.

Systems Theory tells us that only one person needs to change in a group for the entire group to change. I think of Systems Theory like a pebble being dropped in the water. All of the water is affected not just where the pebble dropped.

Can you notice a difference? Keep trying and doing.

### *Compassion in Action for Ourselves (hands-on)*

We all have compassion. We are born with it and we may practice it frequently for others. Many of you may have gone into the profession of law to help those suffering in some way. Sometimes we get so entrenched in our work that we forget to have compassion for ourselves.

When was the last time you slept without alcohol or any other kind of sedative?

When was the last time you had a genuine good laugh or felt genuine peace?

Create your own compassion list: compassionate things that you can do for yourself on a daily basis. Every day pick at least one item. If you do this, you will be growing self-compassion.

### *The Starting Place (cognitive)*

Become sensitive to your natural rhythms and the rhythm of your environment. Sometimes we get stuck in our head questioning when to act, how to start, when to start. We are spinning in a cycle of analysis and we can become paralyzed. We get stuck in our story, our own creation. We may spend hours, days, and lifetimes in our heads.

Feel your own natural rhythms: do you problem solve best in the early morning, afternoon, or evening? What works well and where?

What feels natural? What is better? What makes you feel happy? Your head can be clear now. This is your starting place.

*Thinking Outside of a Monoculture (cognitive)*

Just because everyone does things one way, does not mean it is the best way for everyone. For example, if everyone skips lunch for efficiency's sake that is certainly not the best or most ideal for health and balance in our lives.

Monocultures may be efficient, but they are not resilient. Think of monocultures in nature, they are not resilient.

Start a trend; buck the system a bit, but in a healthy way, of course.

This is about how you behave in places where you spend the bulk of your day.

*Me Against Them (cognitive)*

What are you feeding your brain with? What is the story you are being told? Is it one of fear or one of peace? Negative influences may have a deeper impact on the human psyche than positive ones.

Be aware of what you intentionally expose yourself to. Make a log for a week or even a day of what you are exposed to at work and home. For example, at home, what are you watching on television, movies, and the phone? At work, what are you reading in case files, hearing from clients, etc.? Are these things you are exposed to calming or anxiety-producing?

What kind of human interaction do you have? Is it peaceful, adversarial, or something else?

Determine how you want to feel and how you engage with people and media.

Make conscious decisions about what to expose yourself to. It affects you.

*What Are You Saying? (cognitive)*

Watch your language. Is it full of negative words or positive words? Create a log for a day and see if you can challenge yourself to state everything in a positive light.

This sounds like such an easy activity. Most people find it to be a challenge to do for an hour. It requires real concentration and motivation to speak differently. You may have been trained to look for and highlight defects or deficiencies or speak in a manner that is adversarial or derogatory. Perhaps, this is helpful in some places in your life, but it will not be helpful or healthy in all places and with everyone.

Try this tool for an hour and then commit to an entire day, maybe at home or with friends. Your speech affects you and those around you.

*Living with Intentionality (cognitive)*

Sometimes it feels as though we are moving nonstop, from one event or drama to the next, like a ball in a pinball machine: like someone multitasking such as doing their homework or work while talking to a friend on the phone and making dinner.

How can we stop this nonstop ping-ponging, where we go from one thing to the next without stopping? The answer is we can live a life of intention.

Living with intention is creating, at this moment, now, a sustainable and comfortable life. A life that is deeply rooted in your passion and has a positive direction. What is your heart telling you that you need to do right now to live in this moment intentionally? Sometimes, it might be breathing or even eating with intention. Don't wait, do it now.

Living intentionally is a mindset and a commitment you make for yourself.

*Work, School, and Life Integration (cognitive)*

Technology has made us a 24-hour society. We are available for work all of the time. The distinction between personal and work life is blurred or no longer exists. How many times have you interrupted your family or personal time for business or school-related matters? Does it feel like it is really an interruption or is it more just a way of getting more done in the same amount of time?

The problem with this blur, even if family and friends do not mind, is that we really can't be in two places at the same time. If we are at a family dinner and we are texting or emailing for work or for school, we are not genuinely being present for the family at dinner. For some, this has become a normal part of the way they live their lives.

But the question remains, is it healthy and balanced?

This is a great time to go back to your LifeMaps and make adjustments. You have carved out sectors in your pie chart that are important to you. Remember, what you focus on, is what grows. If you are with your family or friends but you are not really present because you are busy doing homework or emailing, are you really getting that piece of the pie?

You created spaces in your life for the things that you want and need. Make sure to keep those spaces or sectors of the pie clear. If you look at the pie chart, each piece of the pie is distinct. You may need to consider creating personal boundaries to maintain this distinction. For example, in the above scenario, you may choose to ignore emails and phone calls. This allows you to be fully focused on the people that you are with. They get your full attention, and you get theirs. The relationships keep growing.

Create boundaries where they are needed. Boundaries are good. They allow for health and well-being.

*Glow (hands-on)*

Reflect on your life and think of occasions when you flowed with happiness, peace, pride, joy, and a sense of self-worth.

What did these events look like? What were you doing? Who were you with? What can you do to engage in these positive occasions more in your life?

Create a plan to reflect on these times and think of ways to create more healthy times in which you can feel a sense of self-worth, happiness, joy, peace, and pride. You may choose to make an event for each of those five categories and then engage in the events over time. Include other categories that reflect your personal "glow."

## **Section 5.3: Coping Tools**

Coping tools help us to deal with the stress we encounter in healthy and productive ways.

*Getting Unstuck 1*

Sometimes we get stuck on separating demands from wants and needs. It is very easy to do this. I became stuck in 2019, while I was writing this book. It was Spring in Wisconsin and the first warm day, almost 80 degrees Fahrenheit. I really want to be outside and yet I had to keep writing this book. I did some research and found a little tent that I could put my computer in. So, I am writing this from my backyard with my dogs at my feet and I am enjoying the sunshine and the fresh air as I write. Trust me, it took a little while to find this solution. Last year, I bought several different screen covers and a number of little tents before I found the right one. It is not perfect, but it will do. Now I can enjoy writing even more. I am meeting the demand and my personal goal and enjoying it at the same time.

In the Getting Unstuck Tool, we place ourselves in the middle of a bubble and then create a bunch of tiny bubble or spheres around us, a bubble chart.

In each bubble, write a demand. Brainstorm examples of demands, such as things that people are telling you that must be done, or stories you are telling yourself about what must be done. Some examples may include feeling pressured to attend community or committee meetings you are not particularly interested in. However, since you are a legal professional, people are pressuring you to participate, or you feel like you must participate. Other examples may include internal demands, also known as my demands, such as the idea that if you don't read from cover to cover every possible legal journal in your field, that you are going to fall behind or be less competitive.

After you have listed all of the demands, determine which are real and which are parts of the story you have created. Highlight the ones that are real and create first steps towards solutions for them.

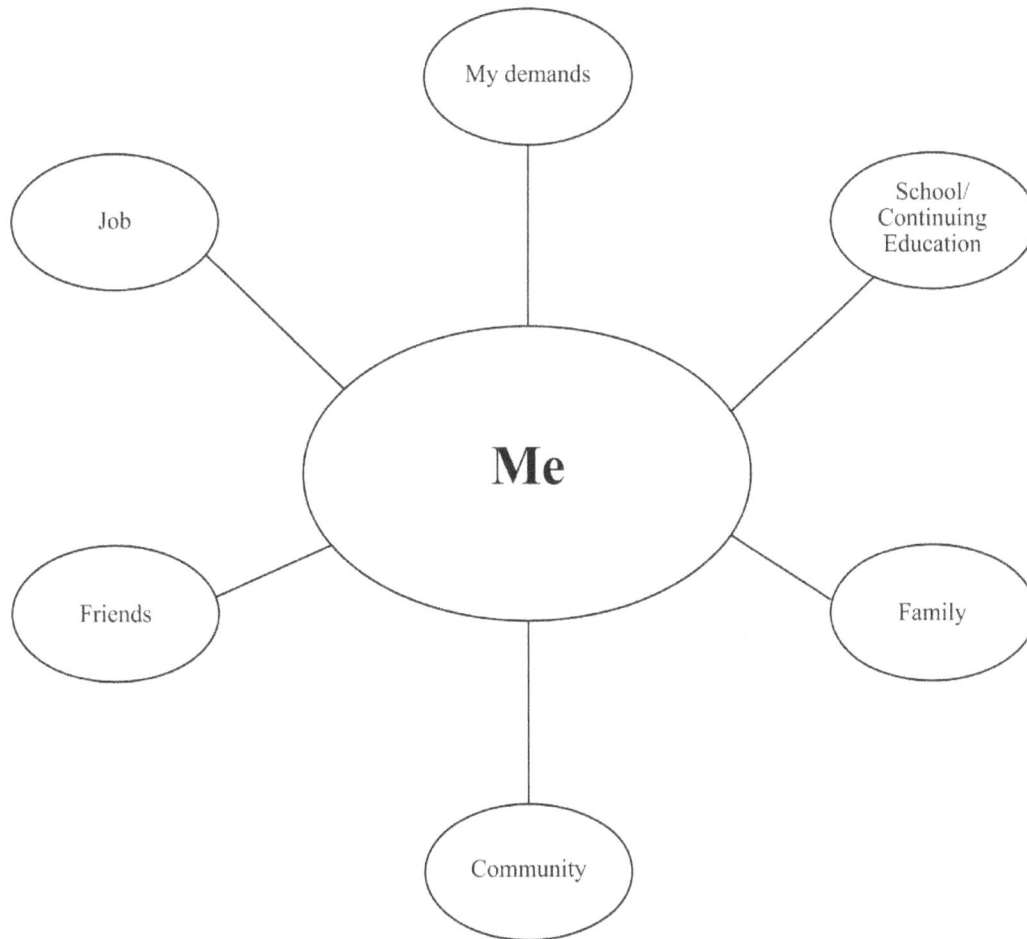

*Getting Unstuck 2: Dealing With Guilt (hands-on)*

Another area where people get stuck is with guilt. We can use the same format to create a tool to deal with guilt.

Guilt can be a strong source of motivation. We do a lot of storytelling surrounding guilt. Some examples may include, "I am not a good enough parent, spouse, friend, student, lawyer, barrister, judge." "I don't eat healthy foods." "I don't exercise.," etc. Create your bubble chart and then surround yourself with all of the stories of guilt that surround you. You can do this by simply writing a word which represents your guilt, such as "children" or "work."

Sometimes working on these bubble charts in a group setting can provide valuable insight and normalization, since it's likely your peers or colleagues are experiencing many of the same things.

One of the key questions to resolve, is what to do with the guilt. Sometimes we carry guilt with us on a day-to-day basis, and we may experience the negative physical and mental health outcomes such as headaches, nausea, anxiety, or sadness. Review what can you reasonably expect of yourself in your global life. And take action that is balanced and healthy. Review and brainstorm with peers. Open up the discussion and place ideas on a whiteboard, or other medium of how to take care of or resolve feelings of guilt. As we begin to analyze, reflect, and talk about feelings of demand and guilt, it is time to bring what we have learned to our LifeMaps.

Reflect on and determine what your story is and what is real. Then begin to reconfigure your LifeMaps. Maybe it means adding or taking away a small portion of a sector on your LifeMaps. Think about it.

You may also want to review LifeMaps with another individual or your group to learn how others manage their time. Working in a group setting also helps to deal with feelings of isolation or being the only person with the problem. As more people talk about the issues, the solutions become clearer and your LifeMaps become strengthened.

As you begin to review your completed future LifeMaps based on the findings from the bubble charts above, let's begin to compare what you currently have and what you have decided to place in your future LifeMaps. You may look at your map and be overwhelmed. Some people may have to shrink down some of the sectors and find what is critical for their well-being at this time.

Remember, you can go back whenever you want and change your LifeMaps. As you go through this process, your future LifeMaps will change as your life changes. As you integrate new sectors or expand or shrink existing sectors, you will be changing your life to accommodate more or different needs and wants. In the beginning, you may not know when it is necessary to review but as time goes by you will begin to notice when things are overwhelming, out of control, don't feel comfortable, or are just unbalanced.

At this time, some people like to review their LifeMaps and see how far they've come or how much has changed. We all come from a different place and our LifeMaps will reflect this. It will also reflect where in our life we chose to focus on. It is a good process to touch base from time to time, and in particular, to look for growth and strength rather than reviewing for weaknesses. Past LifeMaps are usually very inspirational. For many people, they can see how far they have come. They can see the progress they have made, and they also see their mistakes. And sometimes, we see a healthier life in the past than what we have in the present. We can use this information to create better and more fulfilling future LifeMaps. Remember, this is a strength-building exercise. You can get your wants and needs met and create a healthy and well-balanced life.

*Resiliency Toolkit (hands-on)*

Resiliency is the ability to bounce back or recover after a difficult life situation. Again, we are looking at resiliency from the standpoint of stressors and secondary trauma. How do we recover and get back to our previous state?

In our work, we must look at what health means to us. Generally, when people think of health, they think first of physical health. That's part of our overall health, but what about our emotional health and well-being? We must take emotional health and well-being into consideration as we think about resiliency.

A Resiliency Toolkit uses your senses to help you deal with problems and summon up your own resiliency. It should be small enough that you can keep it in a bag in your backpack or briefcase. In it you place what makes you stronger and what helps you to step out of a current damaging mindset. I recently had a client show me her resiliency toolkit. It included a funny-looking tiny plastic chicken that contained lip balm and smelled like candy. She said she never used it but loved the smell. She also had a small pocket-sized photo album of her family and a book of prayers.

Everyone's toolkit is unique. What you put in it makes sense for you. You only need a few simple items that help you to combat stress. I personally like to have a small meditation book or even a mini photo book of images that are healthy, such as those of nature.

An immediate tool to use for resiliency is self-soothing. This is a behavior that we engage in that provides an emotional calmness or release. Please take time to think about and jot down your own healthy self-soothing behaviors. This might be difficult, and of course not all self-soothing techniques are healthy, such as drinking too much alcohol or using other substances to quiet down or to forget our internal emotional state. Others use food as a way of comforting themselves, as with emotional eating or binge eating. There is nothing wrong with a nice home-cooked, comfort-food meal, and in fact that can be self-soothing, but emotional eating can occur when we purposefully consume foods to change our emotional state.

For example, a young professional I know eats eight slices of white bread with butter and a hot chocolate before she goes to bed as a way of coping with anxiety. At one time, she revealed to me she ate a whole loaf of bread. She feels that when she eats and drinks these types of foods before bed, she is able to calm down and try to sleep. Can you imagine the toll these behaviors will take if we are doing them on a daily basis?

Other unhealthy examples of self-soothing include binge watching television, or binge videogame playing. Both of these activities are attempts to change our current emotional state and to sometimes block thoughts or feelings. It is OK to watch your favorite television shows and play video games, but if every day you come home and you are not able to interact with others and isolate by watching or playing numerous movies or games, that is an issue.

Now let's look at some healthy ways of self-soothing. Create a list and do some brainstorming about things that you could do that would actually be soothing for you. For example, I love to walk in nature, hug my dog, be with family and friends, cook, and write.

Here are some other possibilities:

- Listening to music that you like or trying a new genre of music
- Cooking a healthy meal at leisure and eating it at leisure
- Going for a walk

- Gazing up at the stars
- Listening to nature
- Petting a companion animal
- Reading a book
- Breathing
- Stretching
- Practicing meditation
- Praying
- Practicing mindfulness
- Calling a friend or family member
- This is a jumping-off point for you. Create your own list and add it to your toolkit. Start using more and more healthy, self-soothing behaviors.
- As you use these new behaviors, you will be creating new neural pathways, which help us to have options and incorporate new healthy thinking and behaviors into our life.

### Self-Compassion Break (cognitive)

- Create a list of things that you can do for yourself that are self-compassionate.
- Create a small box that contains things that help to take care of or calm you. Some people may include in their box a positive statement, a funky pen, bags of herbal tea or hot chocolate, a good piece of chocolate, a yo-yo to remind them to play, Silly Putty or slime for different sensory stimulation, or essential oils or their favorite fragrance.
- Keep a box at your desk or in your bag so that you can have access to it when needed. Keep a separate box at home and use it.

### VentArt (hands-on)

VentArt is a creative, demonstrative, and bold way to express emotions. I initially created VentArt to provide a mechanism to help reduce violence and ease trauma in schools. This technique also helps reduce violence and ease trauma with adults.

You don't need any actual artistic ability to create VentArt, you just want to need to express emotion in a restorative way.

To do it, just get a pen and paper (or any other medium) to draw, color, or paint out your feelings. You can use different paints to create large swaths of color to help show an intensity of feeling. You can use stick people to re-create real life experiences that were disturbing. You can create yourself in scenes, for instance showing yourself slaying the dragon and being the hero. (One individual drew this after feeling like he was actually slaying a monster dragon when he was working on a particular case.) I have had other drawings in which nausea was depicted by creating a stick figure that was throwing up with the real-life scenario in the background.

VentArt's use of color and images can be provocative and powerful and can say more than we may be able to verbalize at any given moment in time. It is also a way to communicate our feelings with others, if we chose to share. Above all, it is a way for individuals to process difficult emotional experiences.

An example from my personal life, when I was in the middle of working on a blended family issue and I became quite frustrated and angry. I knew that I had release the feelings, so I drew them out. I created yellow swaths with a highlighter to represent hot anger and blue marker in circles and jagged lines to represent talking in circles and frustration. When I had completed the VentArt, I felt like I had just run a fast mile. I felt better and I was able to release the emotions. VentArt helped me to move past the emotions so that I could get back to more rational thinking processes and create a solution.

Another interesting example occurred when an individual used washable paint. She showed me her work. It was full of dark purples and blues, which were very heavy and somber. However, within a few days the colors had changed: they were much lighter and actually calming. It was full of dark purples and blues, which reflected her heavy and somber mood. As the client reflected on the feelings of letting go of the emotions on paper, her feeling state became lighter and calmer. She noted, as she had used washable paint, the colors on her painting changed over time to lighter and softer colors.

*Agatha Petrulis Tool: Put it into Action- Painting*
*or Drawing Ideas (Do one every day)-(Hands on)*

## Step 1

Draw or paint a calm, peaceful garden, or a soothing flower. This can be on a sunny day, or overcast, maybe even rainy. Whatever is a relaxing setting for you. Maybe it is snowing and there is a single flower that is withstanding the cold. Maybe your flower is detailed and takes up the whole page. Maybe it is a garden with many flowers with less detail. Make this your secret garden or special spot with your flower. You should feel calm and relaxed while letting your hand guide you. Don't worry about being perfect; if it was, there would be nothing unique. You can look back to your flower or garden when you are feeling overwhelmed. It will bring you to a place of peace and relaxation.

## Step 2

After, write about your place to escape, explore the weather. Describe how your flower(s) react. Is there dew? How does it look? How does it make you feel? Are all the flowers soaked in sun? Are there shadows? Where is the sun? Is it behind you, or is it warming your face? Maybe there is a light rain. How does it feel on your skin? How does it make you feel internally? Describe your flowers. What kind are they? Are they full grown? What colors? How many petals? How do they make you feel? It's okay if you didn't use color in your drawing, you will be able to fully envision the color as you describe it in your writing. When you are finished, make a pact with yourself to look at your garden/flower in times of stress or when you feel overwhelmed. This will be your sanctuary that will be with you always, just a grab away.

*Agatha Petrulis Tool: Control and Authority (hands-on)*

## Step 1

Think of something that stresses you out, (I know, so far this exercise seems contradictory) something that makes you feel out of control or overwhelms your mind. It could be driving, cooking, scheduling, phone calls, bills, etc. What is the first thing that popped into your head when you read the first sentence? For example, bills stress me out. I would either draw a bill held over a candle- not in the sense that the problem will go away, but in the sense that once they are complete, I no longer need to stress about it. Or I would draw a forest and a tent, because when it comes down to it, money isn't something that should be stressed over as long as I am happy and healthy. The bottom line is, whatever you decide to draw or paint, it doesn't control you. You control it. That is why you will be painting or drawing a still life of something that stresses you out. This will symbolize that you hold the power, not the stressor. This will not be the typical still life art, which is an arrangement of objects in front of you that you draw or paint, but rather this is the symbolic meaning of being in control of your stressors and not letting them take over. However, you are welcome to do a literal still life piece (as long as you have the objects needed). Otherwise, get creative. Think of unique ways in which you can conquer/overcome your stressor. Draw a battlefield, with you as the victor; or wrap your stressor in tinfoil, only to be taken out and dealt with in your own way. If you are unsure on how to portray your stressor, the tinfoil is a great way to overcome that. Take a sheet of tinfoil and crumple it, fold it, or throw it around. How do you imagine encasing your stressors? Once our tinfoil is secured with your symbolic stressors inside, set it on the table and begin to draw you still life. Be creative.

## Step 2

Describe how you feel about your stressor before and after drawing/painting your still life. What are some things that you thought of? How do they usually make you feel, and how do they make you feel now, knowing that you are the one who controls them? How did you choose to conquer your stressor and why? If you chose the tinfoil technique, describe how it feels to know that it is in control and wrapped up. How does it feel to know that you can unwrap it when you choose? Describe how you will go forward with handling your stressor? What frame of mind will you be in? Will you unwrap a little at a time, and deal with it step by step, or will you pre-game and tackle the whole thing at once? When you're finished, make a pact with yourself to look at your still life stressor when you are feeling overwhelmed, cluttered, or if you feel like you don't have control of your life. This drawing/painting will remind that you can stop these stressors, however you choose to; whether it is head on in a victorious battle, or by wrapping it up and putting it away while you clear your mind before you tackle it. That still life will be a reminder that you can stop these stressors and still them in your life. Look at this whenever you feel overwhelming stress, to remind yourself that you can handle anything.

*Open and Closed (hands-on)*

Open and closed is one of my favorite tools. It allows us to become aware of when we are physically and emotionally open or closed. We practice being aware of our body and changes we can make in our physical state that may impact our emotional state.

Lie down on the floor and pull your knees up to your chest. Now tuck your chin into your chest. Wrap your arms tightly around your legs and give yourself a good tight hug. Hold for a couple of seconds and then allow yourself to literally open up and unfold. Drop your legs to the floor and open your arms. Allow your neck to extend and gently drop your shoulders. You should now be completely, open, with your legs extended out and your arms up and open over your head. Make your body look like an X. Stretch and relax into the X position.

Notice the difference in your body. Do you feel more relaxed? We have muscle memory and if we have been clenching or tensing our muscles, we may continue these behaviors even after a stressful situation has resolved. We may not be aware that we are doing this. This clenching or tensing becomes the involuntary place our body moves into and our emotional state may then follow along.

Stretching, opening up the body from the closed position can help us to remember to return to healthier ways of holding our body. A more relaxed body affects our mental state, telling us we can relax emotionally and physically.

*Personal Debrief (hands-on)*

This tool to review your experience and feelings can be done by writing out your feelings of an event that has caused stress or a change from a state of well-being. With this tool, we take a brief overview of how we internalized the moment and set it down on paper. Write about the experience and the feelings it causes.

The second part of the tool is to determine what can you do, in this moment, to separate from the event and comfort yourself in a healthy way. Can you call a friend, family member, colleague, peer, or someone from your health group? Can you take it to a group meeting of colleagues or peers? Do you need to take it to a professional?

*When to Talk to a Professional: Various Avenues for Help (cognitive)*

Sometimes our thoughts and feelings become so overwhelming that even with our coping skills, we still struggle. If we are having reoccurring thoughts or images, racing thoughts, inability to sleep, changes in appetite or weight gain or loss, it may be time to seek professional help. There are so many options available for professional help.

Every country in this book has their own association for assistance. Within these associations are professional groups that serve legal professionals with mental health as well as drug and alcohol counseling. Many of the law schools also have in-house counseling available and referral resources.

There also exists international associations such as International Lawyers in Alcoholics Anonymous.

There is the traditional 12 Step Programs for Alcoholics Anonymous, Cocaine Anonymous, Narcotics Anonymous, Gambler's Anonymous, Co-dependents Anonymous, and Sex Addicts Anonymous. Many of these programs have internet presence and online groups available to participate in; which makes active membership quite easy and very accessible.

In addition, psychotherapists, professional counselors, and psychiatrists are private and provide confidential one on one treatment. Many of these professionals now provide services through ZOOM, Facetime or phone. Through such methods clients can maintain continuity of care, and be able to work on their issues regularly, regardless of where they are in the world.

### Taking It to the Street (cognitive)

Work through continuing education and professional meetings to start talking more about mental illness. Invite speakers who are known within the country and internationally to speak on these issues. The more we talk about these issues, the more normalized the issues become and the more opportunities we have for open discussions and ultimately to have action.

### Productivity and Balance (hands-on)

Every now and then touch base with yourself in writing. Create a T-chart, as we did in the beginning of this chapter, and list what you have produced in terms of work and how you are balancing your work life and your health. Remember, work and health should not be mutually exclusive.

Are you productive, not only productive in work but are you being productive in the areas of balance? Are you actually acting on and fulfilling the areas of your life that keep you healthy and provide you with a sense of well-being?

If not, why not? Re-evaluate and take action. If you are, congratulations. Keep going.

For my T-chart, I am doing wonderfully well, with production of work, my practice, and my two books. In terms of life balance right now, I am doing pretty well. I am exercising every day, playing with animals, visiting family and friends, and writing in nature. I occasionally watch a movie, which is always fun for me.

*Getting Quiet (cognitive)*

Find something that calms you, that quiets your central nervous system even for just a few minutes. Whatever you find has to be healthy and not a substance: no alcohol, drugs, or food.

Some possibilities: mindfulness, meditation, prayer, Tai Chi, meditative yoga, transcendental meditation, or just sitting, quietly petting an animal or observing a plant.

Look at details: with a plant you can look at the leaves, the texture of the leaves, and the way the veins of the plant run through the leaves. The purpose is to get a detailed look and give your mind a break from its ongoing chatter and noise. It only takes a few moments to notice things around us and get quiet. What a relief getting quiet can be.

*Candle Work (hands-on)*

Candle work is a tool that I created more than twenty years ago. Although it always amazes me how simple and effective it is, it can be difficult for some people in the beginning. People always tell me "Oh, I can do that," and then get disappointed or frustrated when they cannot. But it works if you keep trying. Here is what you do:

Get a candle, go into a darkened room, and light your candle. Set a timer for just one minute. (In my experience, people who are beginners in mindfulness or mediation cannot go beyond ten seconds without having to stop.) The goal is to simply observe the candle. Notice the flame, the color of the flame, the intensity of the flame, the smell of the candle, the heat of the candle, the candle wax dripping. As you are observing the candle, you will notice thoughts coming into your mind. Maybe thoughts like what am I having for dinner, what do I have to do next.

When the non-candle thought comes in, imagine the thought crossing over your forehead and literally falling away from your right or left temple. Choose the right or left temple based on if you are right- or left-handed, then bring your attention back to the candle. If a repeated thought comes in, acknowledge the thought. You could even say it out loud: "I recognize you, you are a reoccurring thought, and I will deal with you later." Go back to focusing on the candle. If the same thought comes back, blow out the candle and stop the exercise.

The goal is to be able to be with the candle for one minute. Be patient. If you are starting at 10 seconds, which is where most people start, it will take some time. Add time as you are able to and do candle work every day, it only takes one minute. The benefits are dramatic. You are actually creating a quiet space in your head, even if it is only for a couple of seconds in the beginning. One of my clients has moved his candle work from 10 seconds to one hour over time. Not all of us want to commit to that amount of time, although this individual's levels of anxiety and stress have dramatically decreased as he has practiced this technique. Remember, as with all things, be patient with yourself. You are worth the effort.

*Flexibility versus Rigidity (cognitive)*

Most successful people have plans and stick to their plans and have day to day schedules which they maintain to meet their goals.

The task now becomes, how do you manage change? Are you flexible, able to easily to move from one task area to another? Or are you so tightly scheduled that you have anxiety or panic if your schedule needs to flex?

Try to look at these changes as encouragement to learn flexibility. We are constantly in a learning process. We can all think of times when we have had to change quickly, how did we cope what did we do? What could we have done better or differently?

The more challenges that come into your schedule, the more flexible you become, so that when there is a change you are not panicking rather, you are moving fluidly. Keep in mind your must-dos to maintain health and well-being, and your to-do's; they are vastly different. We want to remain flexible, and that is part of the reason why we physically exercise: moving different muscle groups to keep us flexible. When we have to be flexible in our schedule, we are learning new ways of coping with the changes and ways to remain calm in our emotional state. We have all heard the old statement to remain flexible, otherwise you may break. Brainstorm some ways that help you cope with change. Sometimes just sitting for a minute comparing your to-do list with your must-do list can be enough to formulate a plan for change. Try it.

*Create a Positives Notebook (hands-on)*

Create a list of all of your positive attributes, the things that you like about yourself. The goal is to challenge yourself to create a hundred positive attributes. You can do it. You have them, maybe you just forgot. If you get stuck, think about compliments others have genuinely shared with you. Reflect on those compliments and see if you can accept them and include them in your list.

I can start your list for you:

- You are a good learner.
- People like you.
- You are a good conversationalist.
- You are a good friend, sister, brother, mother, father, pet owner, caretaker.
- Keep adding to the list.

*Poetry Process (hands-on)*

Write your own poem about your emotional state. No one has to see it but you. Seek out published poets. Read some classics, or poets' journals. Read about the different emotional states people experience, share and remember, we all have an emotional life. Some of the most renowned poets have suffered, survived, and thrived and their poetry lives on for generations. Many poets have processed their own feelings and experiences through their poetry. Your own poetry may not be as sophisticated, but think about it, it is only for you unless you chose to share it. Then head for the next open mic or poetry slam. In reading the poetry of children and adults, we can experience what they are feeling... Let your inhibitions go on paper.

If you don't believe that writing can reduce stress, look up Harvard's Stress Management Pamphlet, which encourages writing as a way to help to ease stress and trauma. (Health Harvard.edu)

### Commit (cognitive)

Commit yourself to using one tool of your choice every day for one week. Stay with the tool for the entire week. When we first start something new, we may feel nervous that we should be doing something else, like our work instead of taking care of ourselves. Push through, so that you can feel the benefit of the tool.

Notice how you feel physically and emotionally. What were you able to change in your schedule to accommodate the tool? Be aware that you were actually able to be flexible and allow for the new tool into your schedule.

### The Nonverbal Mirror (cognitive)

When you are feeling tense, stressed, or anxious, check your reflection in a mirror. Note where you may be holding the stress or tension in your face. Are your eyes crinkled, your brow furrowed? Are you frowning?

As you are looking in the mirror, attempt to release the muscles around your eyes and unfurrow your brow. Can you feel the difference? If you are frowning, bring your mouth into a neutral position and then try on a smile. Do you notice a difference when you smile?

Now take a breath and attempt to relax all of the muscles in your face. You may appear relatively expressionless, that is OK. The next time you notice these feelings of stress, tension, or anxiety arise, practice going back to the mirror and doing the exercise.

Eventually, you will be aware of the muscles in your face without looking in the mirror. Then you can work on changing the musculature and get back to a more neutral position, which can allow for a calmer state of mind. The benefits of a calmer state of mind, is clarity of thought.

### Smile (cognitive)

Yes, smile. While you are doing your work or any time you think of the word smile, do it. Scientists tell us that when we smile, real changes occur in our body, and we actually feel better. The muscles around the mouth are providing signals to the brain. I am smiling as I write this for you.

Test it. Try smiling. In addition to feeling better, even for the moment, you may notice that you had been frowning, scowling, or grimacing before. Perhaps one of these facial expressions is your usual expression and you are not even aware of it.

Try smiling during difficult times. We don't always need to bear down and tighten up to get things accomplished. Try to remember to break the old patterns and every once in a while, smile.

### *Beware Transference and Countertransference (cognitive)*

Students and practitioners alike should be aware of transference and countertransference. We all come to the table with our background, our personal history and stories, as do our clients.

Transference is when an individual transfers feelings and attitudes from an experience in their past onto a person or situation in the present. For example, a very negative or even traumatic experience with an influential person, such as a school principal, may be transferred, without your knowledge, onto other school principals. Transference is acted out by everyone, and often contributes to decision-making.

Countertransference is the professional's or the student's transference toward the client of their own emotional needs and feelings with personal involvement, to the detriment of the objective or the relationship.

Of course, none of us are judgment free. We all bring our background, personal history, and stories with us in whatever role we play. We may find ourselves reacting more positively or negatively toward a particular client. Checking ourselves and checking in with our peers can help us sort out our own bias, judgments, and feelings. If we recognize that we are struggling in a particular situation, we may consider passing the case to an individual who is not struggling with the particular issue.

Again, note your judgments and feelings and recognize that these issues may be interfering with the business of the case or causing emotional upset.

### *Storytelling, Part 1 (cognitive)*

Write a short story in the third person about a particularly emotionally challenging case. Describe what it looks like and feels like for the characters in the story. Describe ways in which the legal professionals in the story may be affected and what kinds of tools they could use to cope. Pass these anonymous stories around in groups and discuss further.

### *Storytelling, Part 2 (hands-on)*

Write a short story about a known case that may be referred to frequently. Follow the same steps as above, describing what it looks like and feels like for the characters in the case. Describe what it feels like for you encountering this information. (This may be the first time you have ever been asked what it feels like; food for thought.)

Describe ways in which the legal professionals in the story may be impacted and what kinds of tools they could use to cope. What about you, what tools could you use to cope?

You might want to have a sharing event with your group in which all members of the group share their story and use of coping tools.

### *Thresholds (cognitive)*

I give credit to my dear friend and colleague, Cathy Gawlick, for teaching me about thresholds, which I have adapted here. Thresholds are a place of pausing and assessing from where we are now to where we are going to. It is a place to pause and to decide how to act.

For example, I was recently reading an article discussing how new lawyers want to dig in and get going on a new project immediately. That makes sense, given the excitement and the adrenaline, but the article talked about needing a plan before getting started, so that you have the bigger picture of where this case is going. You can include many places for health, including learning from clients' resilience within this plan.

In this tool we pause to think about how we are going to move through this project. Are we going in a calm, healthy, balanced, and productive way? Or are we proceeding in a way that disregards our own basic health initiatives? How is this occurring? Create a journal entry and quietly reflect. Learn to stop and take the time to mark these places of entry, because they will, for the most part, determine how you move through the project, and ultimately your life.

For instance, before I crossed the threshold to start writing this book, I marked the moment by remembering my previous book and honoring myself by thanking God for giving me the intellect and the tenacity to move forward in this daunting project.

I also marked the threshold by actively surrounding myself with things that bring me comfort. I am sitting in my favorite writing spot in front of the French windows at my dining room table, with a maple-syrup candle burning, a dog at my feet, a cup of coffee and a bottle of water at my side. That's perfect for me. Now determine what's perfect for you and create it as you step through your threshold.

### *Journaling (cognitive)*

Journaling calms the hectic and sometimes nonstop conversation in our head. A great thing about journaling is that you can write what you need down and literally close the book on it. It will be there tomorrow or later for you. Journaling can help you remember, create, plan, record or just stop and feel. Some people like to take a couple of minutes to journal in the morning or in the evening. I like to do both. I especially like to journal during stressful periods of time. Journaling allows me to take care of my emotional self and intellectually process, so that I can "clear room" in my head to take on the next task or sometimes just to keep moving forward with the current task.

Another soothing journaling activity is to journal a few basic things that you are grateful for, such as coffee, family, friends, etc. Try journaling something new every day that you are grateful for. It does not have to big. This technique forces you to see what is currently going on in your life that is good and that we sometimes forget about. An example for me might be drinking out of a bright yellow mug that I picked up on a trip to my favorite Italian restaurant, or drinking hot tea on a rainy day. Think of simple things that we are already doing for ourselves.

### Compassion Break (cognitive)

Take a one-minute break. Stop everything and take a breath, stretch at your desk, and gaze at something in the distance to relax and strengthen your eye muscles. Have a drink of water.

It is also possible to create a compassion break in a group. It can be done at any time in the group meeting. It seems to be particularly useful at the end of the meeting, where a one-minute timer can be set and people can close their eyes to do some deep breathing, state an affirmation to the group, or offer a small prayer.

### Gifts, Part 2 (hands-on)

Give yourself permission while on your journey at work to give yourself small uplifting gifts every so often. A new, colorful, and fun pen, something that you can use during your day while working or studying that may lighten up your mood.

At my dining-room table at home, my new designated workspace, and at my conference table at work, I have a colored printout of my new mascot, Sydney, my friend's giant yellow Cockatoo with an attitude. I love his look; he is so serious he makes me laugh. Find special things that only you need to know about and enjoy them while you are working. This is about creative living and not just enduring.

### Ecopsychology (hands-on)

Ecopsychology is the science of letting nature nurture. When was the last time you walked outside and just listened, smelled, felt and looked around you?

How could you bring nature to you? Can you put out a bird feeder? Can you bring a plant inside? Can you bring a plant to work and watch it grow and nurture it? Take some time with the thought, perhaps a bonsai tree?

A number of years ago, I had a group of executives who were stressed, anxious, and stuck. I asked them to take care of a bonsai and bring it to work. They were required to take care of the bonsai for six months. Now the great thing about a bonsai is that the very concept of it requires slowing down. It is beautifully decorative, but it also required tending over time. The executives were overly prepared. They were supplied with miniature shears and a miniature watering can as well as a water spritzer and fertilizer. All of this was kept in a tiny box in some remote part of the desk. Everyone agreed to the task and were ready and waiting to get started.

The key word is waiting. With a bonsai, one must wait and watch. It grows slowly and on its own time, not ours. Some of the people hurt their plant by over-fertilizing or overwatering in an effort to get the plant to grow or even blossom. They were pushing the plant. Years later members of the group still had their bonsai. They were much more patient with the plant and had learned how to slowly and carefully groom it into the size and shape they wanted. I love the bonsai; it is a big-picture plant.

### Pop-Up Playtime (hands-on)

Call a local animal shelter and see if they provide any sort of playtime with puppies or kittens. Many shelters will bring the animals to your location for a fee, which supports the shelters and the animals they house. Playing with pets has been shown to reduce stress. Have fun, and who knows, maybe you will find a companion animal to adopt.

Companion animals provide a link outside of us; something other than us and our problems to focus on. Companion animals can be very therapeutic. But they also require a forever home and thus a commitment. Enjoy the fun that only puppies and kittens can provide. It is about fun and frolic, letting go and being care-free. Don't be surprised if you find yourself laughing out loud. When was the last time that happened?

### Animal Companions (hands-on)

Science has demonstrated again and again the physical and mental health benefits of companion animals. If you do not have a pet, maybe you could help a neighbor or friend. Or go to a dog park and spend time watching the dogs play. One or two dogs are sure to come up to you for a pet.

If you do not want to get so close and personal stop by the local humane society or pet store. Check out the fish or the lizards. I particularly enjoy gazing at the lizards, and from time to time and I have thought about adopting two for an office terrarium. I like the lizards because I have to slow down to see them. I have to look carefully in the foliage to find them. Then, interestingly, as I watch and they are so still, I suddenly see them blink. They are amazing little creatures, with their skills at camouflaging so well into their environments. When I am watching them and they are watching me, I find myself slowing down and almost giggling to myself about how hectic life can be at times. I also recognize that at this moment in my life, I do not have the time now to care for them, so I only visit. Find out which animal you would like to visit and enjoy.

### Handiwork (hands-on)

Handiwork can be quieting and meditative. It can be anything from beading, knitting, and carpentry to making fish lures. Handiwork is work that we do with our hands. It provides a steady focus which in turn allows our mind to quiet down.

Handiwork usually does not require intense concentration, and often one can listen to music or watch a movie while creating. You may also find that you are much less anxious in these activities if you do handiwork while participating in them.

### *Magic Carpet Ride (cognitive)*

We all remember the story, a magic carpet that can fly us to magical places. Let's get on it, in our minds. Let's imagine flying off, away from here. Feel the soft breeze on your face, feel your hair lift and fly away from your face, and feel your body weight sink into the carpet.

Where are you flying to? What do you see below you? What do you see above and all around you? What do you smell? What do you hear? What do you taste, if anything? Stay for a little while on your magic carpet, and if you choose, swoop in and out, up and down, through valleys or alleys, wherever your heart desires.

Now come back to today and where you were before the ride. Notice your body. Notice your emotional self. Take a deep breath and restart your work. You should feel more relaxed and focused. Enjoy your new concentration after your short break. Take short breaks and magic carpet rides occasionally; they help you to get back into focus.

### *Turquoise Praying Mantis (cognitive)*

Google a photo of a turquoise praying mantis. Look at this creature's beautiful color and detailed body. Can you see its eyes and antennae? It can be helpful to take a quick break from stress or concentrated events by simply gazing at another living being or an object. Find something you may have never considered before, like the turquois praying mantis.

These different images and thoughts create different emotional states and may give you a break from stress. It also is refreshing, and it only takes a minute or less. You will come back to your work more composed and with better concentration. Try another photo. How about a narwhal? Yes, they are real. Try to remember to take regular stress breaks.

### *Heart Out of Cage (cognitive)*

Take a moment and feel your body. Notice tension and notice if you are holding tension, particularly in your heart. Many of us have shielded our heart or put a cage around it at work and at home. We have been hurt or embarrassed or felt unloved or perhaps unlovable.

For just this moment, go inside and visualize your heart and open up the cage door. Feel yourself breathe and feel your heartbeat. Now take a breath. You can allow that space to close or stay open, whatever feels natural and OK for you. Move on in your day, remembering when your heart is open or caged. Try to open the cage door every so often.

*Express Raw Emotion (hands-on)*

Put it out there . . . your raw feelings. You may perceive these emotions as ugly or bad, but they are simply emotions. We do not have to judge or label our emotions. Having emotions provides us with the richness of human experience. We are allowed to experience the full breadth of our emotional range. It is OK; we just need to express ourselves in healthy, healing ways. Sometimes by just expressing emotions, they change. Put words on paper that you can crumple up and throw out.

*True You (hands-on)*

Write the truest sentence about you. Just write it and let's see what it says about you. Now what? Accept the positives and begin to unravel or change those things you are no longer comfortable with or simply do not like. Try this again tomorrow. Perhaps it will be different, as our emotional and cognitive states shift.

*Trust Yourself (cognitive)*

Sometime after age twelve, maybe even earlier, we start listening to all of the external communications, both verbal and nonverbal: our friends, our parents, our teachers, media, movie stars, models, etc. Sometimes within this cacophony, we have lost the ability to hear our own internal voice, the voice that guides us. I have asked clients simple questions, like what is their favorite food, or their favorite color. And they told me they no longer knew. They lost it in the middle of the cacophony. Or they remembered everyone else's preferences but not their own.

Turn back to your internal voice. It is not gone; it is muffled by all of the other communication. Usually our internal voice, if we really listen to it, is our truth. Trust it. It will help get you on a better, healthier, and more balanced path.

*Yield (cognitive)*

Do not judge yourself. Stop fighting with yourself. Yield. For most of us, this is a strange thought, not to wrestle with oneself. When was the last time you gave in and just did what you needed or wanted to do? The next time, in fact it might be at this moment, yield. Allow yourself to be yourself. Let go of the created demands for this moment in time. Take a much-needed breath and take the next step, easily and gently. Yielding in this context does not mean giving up, it means allowing.

*Success (cognitive)*

What is your definition of success? Remember that we are now looking at our life in a balanced way. Go back to your LifeMaps and refresh yourself, give yourself perspective again on balance.

In what sectors of your life are you healthy and balanced? Where do you need to focus more? The areas in which you place your time and attention are the areas that change and grow.

*Another Way (cognitive)*

In Japan, broken pottery is sometimes mended with lacquer and gold dust. The break is considered something unique and part of the beauty of the object. How can we apply this to our trials, setbacks, and perceived or real breaks or failures? Can we somehow weave the setback into our life and accept it and learn from it? It is part of the story, not the whole story. Try applying the Japanese philosophy about breaks or damage to your life and note any changes. Keep practicing, you will eventually be able to see it working and in turn, you may become kinder and gentler with yourself in the process.

*Games (hands-on)*

What are some of the games you remember from childhood which were comforting or soothing? Many board games have had a resurgence of popularity due to families and friends wanting to have physical time together. Call a friend or have a family game night with a game from your childhood. If you didn't do games in your family, get a game that looks interesting and enjoyable and try it out.

I still love playing Operation and KerPlunk with kids. It is a joy to hear them laugh. When I am with adults, card games are great, because they are easy and fun. Some people may prefer chess or something more complicated. If that is for you, great, do it. And remember, this tool is about fun not competition.

*The Power of Play and Puttering (hands-on)*

Play is not only for children. When we play or putter, we free up creative energy and create more energy. When was the last time you played? Playing can be anything from tinkering with an old car to creating a model-train set. Or playing an instrument or a game of golf. Playing can be a solitary event or with others. Within the next seven days, try to create a time to play or tinker. Notice how you feel when you have completed the activity.

*Learn through Joy, Not Struggle (cognitive)*

For many of us, there is a fierce competitive spirit. That's wonderful, it's a great attribute for success most of the time. Sometimes, however, when there is a competitive spirit, we forget balance. Balance includes not just a nose-to-the grindstone attitude and struggle-until-you-make-it philosophy. It also includes self-compassion and joy. Are you having any fun while you are learning, studying or working? If not, why not? Think about adding companionable conversations and light conversations with colleagues. Acknowledge the other individuals in the room. They will acknowledge you back, and it feels good. Have some compassion for yourself as you are working. Make sure to do the basics: drink water, rest, and take breaks.

### *Bird Out of the Cage (cognitive)*

The image of a bird sitting or standing on the outside of its cage has always been thought-provoking for me. It is free, not confined, not under anyone's control. I love the metaphor of being uncaged. I think of it frequently in my practice. It represents the essence of what I am trying to do in my professional life, which is attempting to help people find freedom from emotional suffering. Imagine yourself using the metaphor in your own life. Right now, at this moment write down on paper whatever is burdening you. Feel the physical weight in your body, and in your feeling state. Now for just a moment, fold up the paper and place it out of your line of vision. Set a timer for a minute and try to see what it feels like in your body and your feeling state to get it out and let go of it. Feel free and uncaged, or hemmed-in or confined. What do you notice in your body and emotionally? Do you feel your shoulders drop? Are you breathing differently? Do you feel calmer? Try adding on another minute. Are you able to relax even more?

Try this technique often. It allows your mind and body to have a break and it helps to break up muscle memory. Try this tool during difficult tasks or tasks which require great focus and concentration. It will improve your focus when you have completed it and you will feel refreshed.

### *Compression (cognitive)*

Place the palms of your hands together and exert pressure on both hands and feel the compression. Feel your muscles tensing as they go into this physical exertion. What do you notice about your body? Are you gritting your teeth, grimacing, tightening your arms and shoulders, holding your breath? Now think about when you are working on an intense project. Which of these physical behaviors do you think you repeat? What others might you notice that you engage in? When you let go of the pressure, what did you notice? Did you breathe differently? What else? Practice noticing yourself while you are entrenched in a stress-filled activity. Notice how you hold your body and your breath, notice your feeling state and attempt to realign yourself into a more relaxed physical and emotional space.

### *The Influence of Music (cognitive)*

Have you ever noticed how you are influenced by sound? Listening to upbeat music makes you feel more energized or happy. If you are listening to more somber music, perhaps you become tearful or quiet. Music influences us. With this being said, think about what you have on for background music or noise in your work area. How does it impact you? Think about when you are exposed to construction sounds and when you hear the sounds of nature: birds, whales, the wind, rain. Try listening to the sounds of nature. They are much different than music and other human-made sounds. Natural sounds contain microtones which are intervals smaller than a semitone. Microtones may be thought of as a note that falls between the keys of a piano. These kinds of sounds are not found frequently in western music. Humans and animals benefit from natural sounds. Natural sounds can be restorative and help lessen stress and attention fatigue. Studies have shown the sounds of a cat purring can cause positive physiological changes in blood pressure and respiration as well as reports of overall relaxation. Listen to the natural sounds, relax, and enjoy.

### Tapping (cognitive)

Have you ever noticed how you may be tapping your foot or your pen when you are in a stress-filled situation? The repetition of tapping allows for calming of the central nervous system. Many people find tapping to be self-soothing. Tapping is a rhymical way of self-soothing.

You can take a break at your desk and just gently tap a slow steady rhythm with your feet or your hands. No one will notice; it can be done discreetly under your desk, and just thirty seconds of tapping can make a difference in your stress state. Another method is to simply tap with one finger on the opposing hand. Try it.

### Unexpected Success (hands-on)

I know I am asking a lot of you, to live a balanced life. Most of the time culture applauds us if we are over-the-top in one area of our life, especially with work. The busier we are, the more successful we look and feel.

I found it interesting that Alexis Ohanian, the cofounder of Reddit, one of the most successful social news websites in the world, stated that social media can have a detrimental effect on work-life balance. He coined the term "hustle porn" to describe boasting on social media about how many hours they work.

Do you know how to be quiet or stand still and be calm? Do you have work-life balance? Do you brag about how many hours you work? Do you apply pressure to others to work long hours? Try something different. Try recording how many hours you put into the other aspects of your life. Do it for just one week. At the end of the week, evaluate what you see. Is this how you want to live? If not, make some changes.

### Creative Visualization, Part 1 (cognitive)

This technique has been used successfully for years by athletes, actors, and many others attempting to reach a goal. Creative visualization asks you to imagine, in detail, exactly what you want, and how it would look and feel.

Today, I am asking you to visualize what peace of mind looks like for you. Maybe for you, peace of mind is sitting on a beach watching the waves move in and out, feeling the sun on your body, hearing the waves, tasting the salt of the ocean, feeling the sand between your toes. Pick a scene. It might be somewhere where you have felt peace of mind. If you can't think of one, then create one. Perhaps, you could imagine the dark forest and the smell of the earth, the sound of the leaves in the trees, the feel of the wind. You create it. It's your state of peace. If you practice enough, eventually you can have peace of mind throughout your day. Can you imagine what a day would look like if you were in a peaceful mindset?

### *Creative Visualization, Part 2 (cognitive)*

Next, I would like you to imagine what a balanced life would look like. Everyone's balanced life will look a little different. For example, visualize what a morning could look like. My ultimate balanced life morning is waking up, mediating, and praying, writing and having a hot cup of strong coffee, then taking the dogs for a walk, exercising, showering, mediating again and off to work. I can actually visualize myself doing this. The second half of the day would look like coming home for dinner between patients, feeding the animals, eating a hot meal, going back to work for a few hours, and then home to relax with a book or a movie.

I have given you a lot of detail. You need to use detail too. In my creative visualizations, I might even think about what the hot meal is that I am eating. Try visualizing your day the way you want it to look in your healthy balanced life.

### *Hope in a Jar (hands-on)*

Fill a small jar with hopeful images and words. Cut words and images out of magazines or newspapers or create your own. Place them inside of the jar. These are images and words that give you hope or remind you of hopeful things and times. After you have filled the jar, pick one piece of paper as you are heading out the door to your workday. Keep it with you. Try to remember it throughout the day. The images and words that we surround ourselves with help us with the state of mind we are trying to maintain.

### *Enjoy Now (cognitive)*

It's great to finish things, but some jobs take more time than others. You may sometimes think that you can only enjoy your life once you complete a particular project. If you can't complete the task today, is there still a way to enjoy it along the way?

As I am writing this book, I am sitting with a cup of tea and an Irish Wolfhound mixed rescue dog at my feet. My room is not cluttered; it is a beautiful study I created. I have candles, books, and dogs and cats coming in and out. It is quiet and peaceful, and it allows me to create. I feel good when I am in this room, and even during the difficult times of writing it has always been easier here, in the sanctuary that I have created. What can you put in your office, or study space that makes it more comfortable, peaceful, and maybe even joyful? Keep it simple, you know what you like. Maybe a child's drawing, plants, a scent diffuser, photos of family and friends. Do some brainstorming and then create it.

*Breaking it Down (hands-on)*

"Breaking it down" means taking a big task and breaking it apart into doable steps. I often go one step further. After starting the first step, I break that down too. By doing this, I have more of a sense of control on the project and I can see the end is doable. By implementing this tool, the project suddenly no longer feels overwhelming or as stress filled. One template you could use is the form below. This plan should be stated simply, and it should not take hours to develop. Leave out the details and any extras so that you can focus on the big steps and get going. You can look at it every day and have a clear easy way to get to your goal; completion.

| The Project | |
|---|---|
| The Deadline | |
| My Plan to Finish: | |
| List Any Resources You Still Need: | |

*Practicing Mindfulness, Part 1 (cognitive)*

Remember, mindfulness is being present in the moment. We can be present in everything we do by staying focused and using our senses, as opposed to what we probably do on a daily basis, which is to race through the task while we are talking on the phone while listening to the radio and planning what we'll do next. Doing all of this at once, means we are not giving focused attention to any one thing.

As we continue on with this mindless flow, we feel the anxiety and stress associated with it. For many, it has simply become a way of doing, a day-to-day juggling act for all of our demands. If one could try to be mindful with just one event, such as conversation with a friend or preparing a meal, just one time, you'll feel better. You'll feel calmer, and you'll feel more in touch with yourself, and better able to face the next task.

Mindfulness allows you to be what is known as an observer. As an observer you are simply watching your thoughts behaviors and beliefs. You do not judge or criticize. You do not block them. You just allow them to float by and not attach.

*Practicing Mindfulness, Part 2 (cognitive)*

Mindfulness is not jumping ahead or creating what I call "a scare story" which is a projected narrative about an event that is frightening, creates stress and anxiety, and for the most part is unlikely to happen. Some of us learn to create scare stories as a form of motivation, and some of us create scare stories to control all possible negative outcomes. For some, this controlling feels like it reduces stress or anxiety, but it actually creates more stress. Mindfulness allows us to stop creating scare stories. It allows us to stay on task and remain focused.

I know this is hard. As I was writing this book, there were many occasions where I felt like I would not meet the deadline. I would create scare stories in my mind that would make me anxious and keep me up at night. When I brought myself back to staying focused, I was less anxious, and I could generally enjoy myself as I worked.

Staying focused and mindful on what we are doing, and at times actually being OK with doing nothing could be a goal. What, do nothing? Here's one possible scare story that you might have in response: "I can't, I don't have enough time, I will be scrutinized, I will fail."

Here is your next challenge: take one minute a day to do nothing. What will one-minute do? It will teach you to slow down and know that everything is OK, even though you are not in constant action and continual production.

Set a timer and go. Take a deep breath, close your eyes, and just be. It might feel weird at first, but try to listen to your breath, feel your heart beating, maybe even feel your heart beating in your fingertips or toes. You might notice your shoulders dropping or the weight of your arms coming down and releasing. You also might notice that you can't let go, or you feel even more stressed. Your mind races with all of the things you have to do, and you can't stop the racing.

Don't give up. Keep trying. Every time you do your one-minute mindfulness practice it will become easier and your body and your mind will relax. You will eventually come out of your one-minute mindfulness mediation feeling refreshed.

### Daily Meditation (cognitive)

Chose a daily meditation book or phone meditation application and use it. Start your day with a good mindset and see how long you can keep that mindset with you throughout the day. Challenge yourself to practice it all day. See how far you can go and keep practicing.

### Happiness Is a Living Emotion, Part 1 (cognitive)

We don't have to wait for an event like a promotion, graduation, or completion of a difficult project to be happy. Happiness can be regular state of being. We can become happier immediately by thinking of everything in our life that we are grateful for. Try to create a list of at least twenty items that you are grateful for and notice how easy it is to fill this list. You can make the list as long as you like, but at least list the twenty items.

As you work through the list, notice how your mood shifts to a place of peace and happiness as you recall these people, places, animals, and events. Keep your list in a place where you can refer to it occasionally, and feel free to add to it as often as you would like.

### Happiness Is a Living Emotion, Part 2 (cognitive)

Surround yourself with happiness. Gather photos, music, a seashell, or other mementos that bring back great memories from a trip or other times or events in your life that make you happy. Be with them. Memories can elicit positive emotions.

### Respite from Stress (cognitive)

It is important during times in our lives where we don't see an end to the stress, to have a respite.

Respite is a term commonly used with caregivers. It is a time away from day-to-day demands. It does not have to be a long time away, but it is essential, due to stress and the unrelenting nature of demands. Where you are at this present moment may be a chronic place of stress. It is essential for you to take a respite.

Respite does not have to be complicated; it is simply a break. Get away from your work. Go to a movie, concert, dinner, or coffee shop; be with a friend. When you return from your outing you will feel refreshed and more at ease.

## Section 5.4: Community Building Tools

Communities are groups of people with shared ideals who work towards building relationships rather than using each other for business purposes. Community building can work in a professional legal setting where individuals with shared experiences of long hours, intense work, stress, and similar backgrounds in terms of education, income, and lifestyle come together. Community building is a prime opportunity to fix what is wrong by connecting around common experiences. The more we can work on community building within the legal profession, the more general health and well-being will prevail.

My ideas surrounding beginning community building are quite simple. There is a need for better care and focus on well-being with that being said, you can start with the following tools and expand from there:

*Creating a trauma informed work or school environment:*

- Evaluate what is available to individuals within the institutional and/or organizational environment that is supportive and capable of providing ongoing education, feedback, resources, and training. Talk with other students and or employees and ask them to identify areas of need including areas not addressed or underserved.
- Create collaboration between other students and professionals; consider outsourcing education, training, or additional resources.
- Create easy access to these professionals and other outsourced groups.
- Create a plan to survey or re-evaluate measures on a regular basis.
- Create an organizational or institutional plan identifying key individuals who are sources for policies, procedures, and operations within a trauma-informed environment. If this is not available at your institution or organization, create it using health groups (which are discussed in the next tool).
- Create opportunities for individuals directly impacted by trauma to be part of the key organization plan.
- Gain momentum and continue the momentum throughout the process and proclaim the importance of creating a trauma informed environment.
- Create a healthy work/study environment.
- Locate mentors, which can include peers. Students may seek out 2nd year or 3rd year students, faculty members, or professionals. Legal professionals may seek out mentors within in or outside of their organization.

*Creating a Health Group:*

Teams and groups get things done. One of the primary functions of a support group or team is to destigmatize problems through openly addressing issues, and further addressing healthy coping mechanisms.

Creating a health group, which provides support and coping for group members and real, in the moment, regular feedback, can have a tremendous impact on well-being. The health group that you create will be different than traditional support groups from the perspective that group members are able to provide feedback, also known as cross talk. Members of the group share issues they have experienced and how they have positively and negatively coped, as well as outcomes associated with the different coping methods. Group members should acknowledge privacy and not talk about others and their situations outside of the group. Remember, it only takes one member to open up and start the conversation to get the ball rolling. Maybe you could be that person.

Creating a group and drawing colleagues and/or peers in can be done by sending invitations for a monthly breakfast, lunch, or dinner, or any other time where individuals are able to attend regularly, to continue the conversation. Some groups may find it helpful to meet on a weekly basis, if time is available.

Be flexible and start where you and your colleagues and/or are. After the group has determined how they will function and what the privacy rules are, get creative. You may want to invite guest speakers, listen to podcasts, or share new ways of coping.

Create solid interventions and plans, such as active discussion occurring after potentially traumatic situations and events. Create avenues for access for individual group members to share and receive support during times when the group is not meeting.

Enjoy the comradery, friendship, food, and warmth.

*Bridge Building (cognitive)*

Create student and work alliances with outside professionals and professional organizations. Bridge building seeks to include others interested in mental health and wellness as special agents to work with you or within groups such as the health group. In addition to providing a service, these individuals and groups may provide guidance, mentorship, and potentially leadership.

Bridge building can include reaching out to known professional resources for lawyers in your country. Regular workshops and events can be created that are committed to continued strategy building for coping, and health and wellness for legal professionals.

Bridge building can also include links to individual practitioners, such as dieticians or mental health providers. Group members may suggest or recommend speakers or special interest practitioners.

Sometimes just being around these individuals and groups are good reminders of healthy living and may provide role model opportunities.

### Community Workshops (cognitive)

Community workshops further extend communication and topics of coping and health into provinces, regions, and other designated areas. For example, I might consider developing the Southeastern Wisconsin Student Lawyers Association for Health and Wellness Workshops.

Such workshops can allow for the distribution of health and wellness information among members as well as pulling in more creative thoughts from people that students and lawyers may not encounter on a regular basis.

### Mentoring (cognitive)

Mentoring allows individuals to give and receive knowledge. One can be a mentor and be a mentee. Mentoring reinforces in us the healthy and good decisions that we have made. It affirms choices and helps to sustain healthy lifestyles. It also affords the opportunity to form additional, close relationships with people we care about, trust, and want to see succeed.

Being mentored is a wonderful way to gain information and to learn how to negotiate difficult times and achieve day-to-day health and balance. It also provides yet another valuable and close relationship. As a mentee, you can learn countless lessons. You will have an additional person in your life who wants to see you have a healthy and balanced experience, as well as a successful career.

Of course, not all mentors need be in the legal profession. Sometimes having a mentor who is simply a healthy well-balanced individual can give us a great perspective too. Look around you and take the opportunities of mentoring or being mentored.

### Food Clubs (hands-on)

Food clubs, or coffee and tea clubs are a great way to create informal and sustainable get-togethers to provide support, affirmation, and comradery. Over meals or coffee and tea, take time to get to know your colleagues. Are they working on a particularly difficult challenge? When was the last time you asked colleagues how they are and then genuinely listened to their response?

Give everyone a chance to check in with the group. The group is informal, and some people may only attend for a short period of time but are still attending, so be affirming. This is about building healthy and supportive relationships with each other.

### Role playing (hands-on)

Practice how you will help someone respond to secondary trauma. Think of what you would actually say and do. Use common language. Create practice scenarios with your health group, colleagues, or peers to be prepared. Remember to switch roles so that everyone has an chance to participate. The goal is to be prepared for a real-life opportunity, to help each other in these scenarios.

### Group Debriefing (hands-on)

Group debriefing is a wonderful tool. It can be less formal than healthy group meetings. It can be scheduled one time per month where group members just briefly talk about the stressful situation and share how they coped. The group can decide if they would like to have cross talk or feedback from other group members. If the group chooses not to use cross talk, the meeting can sometimes move very swiftly. Group members learn from each other by hearing and/or by sharing what ways of coping have or have not worked for them.

### Half-Day Retreat (hands-on)

This is not your typical retreat. It is not about business agendas, bottom lines, or billing. It is not mandated continuing education. It is about taking a half-day to reinvigorate individuals as well as the group. Hire someone who can lead a retreat or have someone from your group lead. You may follow a similar outline to below. Everyone will need to bring a blanket, a pillow, a notebook, and a pencil. Everyone should wear comfortable clothing.

Here's the agenda:

### Hour One

Take 10 minutes of personal time to reflect on what you need to get out of the retreat. Simplify what you need from the retreat in terms of one or two words such as clarification, peace, renewal, or whatever you may need.

20-minute discussion of needs in small groups

30-minute discussion in a larger group about commonality of needs from the small group discussion

### Hour Two

Take 20 minutes to learn about mindfulness and practice it by taking a walk or being in nature

10 minutes to write down what you experienced in your walk. What did you notice?

30 minutes to learn about and utilize guided imagery to help the group to relax

### Hour Three

Take a 15-minute coffee or tea break or refill your water bottle and stretch.

10 minutes to listen to a particular piece of music, such as The Flower Duet.

10 minutes to write or draw in your journal or just relax on your blanket.

5 minutes to listen to the sounds of nature. Introduce information about nature sounds.

### Closing:

Take 20 minutes to write or talk about what you have learned and what you would like to do differently.

*Best Practices for Office and Institutional Environments: The Eight Steps*

Finally, the community can also utilize Best Practices for Office and Institutional Environments

As you use this tool, you will be establishing trust and building a community around true needs. Everyone in the community grows stronger and the community becomes attractive to others who have been on the periphery.

**Step 1:** Assess the environment. What is it like? Everyone should have regular access to natural light and living things such as plants or fish in an aquarium. These things do make a difference. Recent research has shown that the simple addition of plants to the work environment can decrease stress. Think outside the box to change the environment occasionally, such as having a visiting therapy dog or a group of puppies or kittens.

Does the environment provide access to plenty of good water, healthy, ready-made foods, and snacks, and time to obtain these items? People need breaks, not only bathroom breaks, but breaks to stretch, give a break to their eyes from screen usage, and refocus.

We may recognize these as simple requirements, however, many people do not have access to these items. Think about yourself and what you can do to optimize your environment. Bring in a plant, obtain and use full-spectrum lighting for your desk, and bring healthy snacks for yourself and perhaps the group occasionally. You are ultimately in control, so do something healthy. Once these basic environmental factors are in place, you are ready for the next step.

**Step 2:** Implement Mental Health First Aid Training or an alternative speaker(s). As Nigel Jones, lawyer and Executive Director of London's City Mental Health Alliance, told me, "we have a social responsibility to create health versus sickness." Mental Health First Aid teaches about mental health issues and how to react to them.

The draw back for some, is the eight-hour time commitment. Alternately, have a speaker come in to talk about mental health. Do it over a lunch period so that people can relax and learn.

**Step 3:** Teach mindfulness and create a mindfulness charter. Creating a mindfulness charter helps to create a culture of well-being. A charter gives institutions an opportunity to support individuals in changing the way they work and managing the risks of work-related stress. All of the signatories commit to a set of principles centered on improved communication, respect for working hours, and considerate delegation of tasks. Performance against these principles is monitored as part of a review process. Healthy Cities London also created a Mindfulness Business Charter, which was historic as it was the first-time banks and their legal services providers came together to reach a shared agenda for mental health and well-being.

**Step 4:** Learn and post signs about mental health and well-being around the environment. With workplace reminders, we can help to move the culture towards openness and transparency of these issues. Create a free lending library where people can donate and borrow books on mental health and well-being.

**Step 5**: Enact IMPACT and CARE and post these tools throughout the office. These are quick and easy memory tools to help react to mental health situations. These programs were inspired by my conversations with Judge John Broderick, Jr.

**IMPACT**- If something doesn't look right or you suspect a mental health concern...

Include yourself; let your colleague know that you are with them

Make a difference; tell your colleague you want to help

Pause/breath-both of you

Assess the situation- does this person need emergency care

Create an agreed-upon plan

Take action together on the plan

**CARE**

Create an environment of open communication about mental health and wellness

Act out and practice narratives of destressing

Respect each other's thoughts and feelings

Embrace this new culture of empathy

**Step 6:** Build resiliency with the help of the 3Rs:

- RESTORE Values
- REGAIN Perspective and Control
- REBALANCE Again

Restore Values means going back to, remembering, or rediscovering your values. This can be done in a number of ways, including utilizing the Values Worksheet created by Professor Benjamin, reading Giving Voice to Values or attending a Giving Voice to Values Workshop. Contemplate, clarify, and restore your values.

Regain Control and Perspective means that you reorganize your life, so that you are living from a values-based perspective and not just any values, your values. When you are living from your values-based perspective you start to regain your sense of control.

Rebalance Again means that you keep coming back to these issues and readjusting your life, to improve health and well-being.

In this chapter, we have discussed many different tools to help you tend to your health. These tools were meant to be light-hearted and help you cope with the difficulties of your work. They are meant to be efficient and effective. The only thing that will stop you from using them is your decision not to. I hope that you indeed, will try many tools, if not all of them. You may experience more freedom, fun, and lightness. From time to time, come back to this chapter. As you change and your coping skills advance or your stressors change, you may want to explore using different tools. I wish you the best.

## Discussion Questions

- Complete your present and future LifeMaps. How do the two maps compare? What is one small step that you could take immediately to help you move in the direction of your future LifeMaps?
- What is resilience? What is vicarious resilience? What is an action that you could take to become more resilient?
- What are the five components of emotional intelligence outlined by Daniel Goleman?
- What do you think about the notion of victim service tools as it might apply to the legal profession?
- Name two of Ellis's recommendations for lessening the possibility of secondary trauma when working with open source documents.
- What is a self-care plan? Create your own self-care plan.

# References

Cherry, Kendra. 2019. "5 Key Components of Emotional Intelligence." Verywell Mind, April 3, 2019. https://www.verywellmind.com/components-of-emotional-intelligence-2795438.

Ellis, Hannah. "How to Prevent, Identify and Address Vicarious Trauma — While Conducting Open Source Investigations in the Middle East." bellingcat, October 18, 2018. https://www.bellingcat.com/hashtags/vicarious-trauma/.

Elwork, Amiram. 2012. "A Lawyer's Guide To Dealing With Burnout: Does Burnout Mean I Should Leave My Job Or The Law Altogether." Lawyers With Depression, January 16, 2012. http://www.lawyerswithdepression.com/articles/a-lawyers-guide-to-dealing-with-burnout-does-burnout-mean-i-should-leave-my-job-or-the-law-altogether/.

Hernandez-Wolfe, Pilar. 2018. "Vicarious Resilience: A Comprehensive Review". *Revista de Estudios Sociales* 66: 9-17.https://doi.org/10.7440/res66.2018.02 The contents of the Social Studies Magazine are edited under the Creative Commons Attribution 4.0 International.

"How to Build Resiliency." Mayo Clinic. Mayo Foundation for Medical Education and Research, May 18, 2017. https://www.mayoclinic.org/tests-procedures/resilience-training/in-depth/resilience/art-20046311.

Trigueros R, Padilla AM, Aguilar-Parra JM, et al. The Influence of Emotional Intelligence on Resilience, Test Anxiety, Academic Stress and the Mediterranean Diet. A Study with University Students. International Journal of Environmental Research and Public Health. 2020 Mar;17(6) DOI: 10.3390/ijerph17062071. © 2020 by the authors. Licensee MDPI, Basel, Switzerland. This article is an open access article distributed under the terms and conditions of the Creative Commons Attribution (CC BY) license

Young Entrepreneur Council. 2018. "10 Ways to Increase Your Emotional Intelligence." *Inc.*, September 21, 2018. https://www.inc.com/young-entrepreneur-council/10-ways-to-increase-your-emotional-intelligence.html.

# Chapter 7 Abstract: New Directions of Well-Being

In our final chapter, we will examine additional facets of well-being. We will explore five definitions of well-being and we will learn to create our own definition of well-being, one that's consistent with what we have learned about ourselves throughout the journey in this book. We will contemplate examples of philosophies of life and different ways of viewing life and mental health issues from our Champion of Disclosure. We will learn to think about and integrate elements of living that are essential to our own personal well-being while taking into consideration the well-being of those around us. Finally, we will look to well-being as a goal to be worked on daily. We will learn to be consistent in our work toward the maintenance of this goal to achieve a happy, healthy, and personally fulfilling life.

# Chapter 7: New Directions of Well-Being

Let us remove the criticism and harshness and be open to something different, perhaps a truly kinder and healthier path.

## Section 1: Well-Being

Like so many of the concepts in this book, there is no single definition of well-being; rather, well-being is deeply personal. What works for me may be vastly different then what works for you. However, as living beings we all have the need for the basics like fresh air, water, food, sleep, social interaction, and exercise. How we do these things is uniquely ours. We will end our journey together with Tchiki Davis, Ph.D., founder of the Berkeley Well-Being Institute, who states that "Well-being is the experience of health, happiness, and prosperity. It includes having good mental health, high life satisfaction, and a sense of meaning or purpose."[260]

Davis also notes five major types of well-being:

"Emotional Well-Being. The ability to practice stress-management techniques, be resilient, and generate the emotions that lead to good feelings." (Some of the skills that can be used, according to Davis, include positive thinking, emotion regulation, and mindfulness.)

"Physical Well-Being. The ability to improve the functioning of your body through healthy eating and good exercise habits." (Davis recommends eating for health, detoxing your body, correcting nutritional deficiencies, removing plastic from your home.)

"Social Well-Being. The ability to communicate, develop meaningful relationships with others, and maintain a support network that helps you overcome loneliness." (Davis recommends practicing gratitude, building meaningful social connections, and managing your relationship with technology).

"Workplace Well-Being. The ability to pursue your interests, values, and purpose to gain meaning, happiness, and enrichment professionally." (Davis recommends maintaining work-life balance and finding your purpose).

"Societal Well-Being. The ability to actively participate in a thriving community, culture, and environment." (Davis recommends living your values, and making positive impacts in other people's lives through kindness).

---

[260] Davis, Tchiki. "What Is Well-Being? Definition, Types, and Well-Being Skills." *Psychology Today*, January 2, 2018. https://www.psychologytoday.com/us/blog/click-here-happiness/201901/what-is-well-being-definition-types-and-well-being-skills.

---

## The Wheel of Wellness

I have created the Wheel of Wellness to help you easily remember simple categories of health and well-being. Chose a different category within the Wheel and work on it every day for a week. Move around the circle and land on each section and practice one or more of the activities for wellness in the section. Some sections you may not be familiar with, but give them a try, and create your own interpretation of how to participate in each section. As you practice using the Wheel of Wellness, you may find yourself adding sections. By all means be creative, so that you will continue to use it.

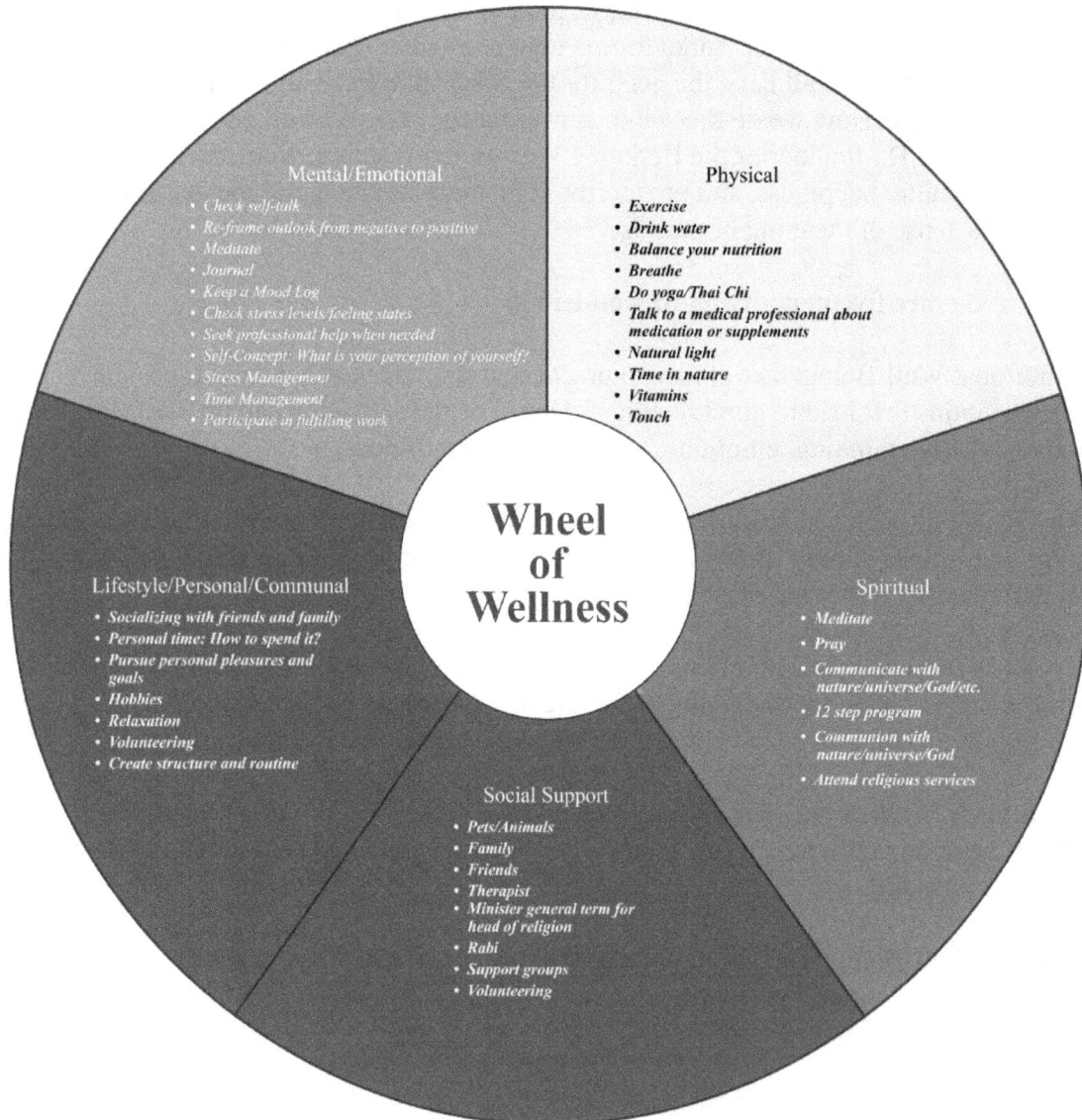

**Mental/Emotional**
- *Check self-talk*
- *Re-frame outlook from negative to positive*
- *Meditate*
- *Journal*
- *Keep a Mood Log*
- *Check stress levels/feeling states*
- *Seek professional help when needed*
- *Self-Concept: What is your perception of yourself?*
- *Stress Management*
- *Time Management*
- *Participate in fulfilling work*

**Physical**
- *Exercise*
- *Drink water*
- *Balance your nutrition*
- *Breathe*
- *Do yoga/Thai Chi*
- *Talk to a medical professional about medication or supplements*
- *Natural light*
- *Time in nature*
- *Vitamins*
- *Touch*

**Lifestyle/Personal/Communal**
- *Socializing with friends and family*
- *Personal time: How to spend it?*
- *Pursue personal pleasures and goals*
- *Hobbies*
- *Relaxation*
- *Volunteering*
- *Create structure and routine*

**Spiritual**
- *Meditate*
- *Pray*
- *Communicate with nature/universe/God/etc.*
- *12 step program*
- *Communion with nature/universe/God*
- *Attend religious services*

**Social Support**
- *Pets/Animals*
- *Family*
- *Friends*
- *Therapist*
- *Minister general term for head of religion*
- *Rabi*
- *Support groups*
- *Volunteering*

**Wheel of Wellness**

We have learned so much about what to change and what to do differently. As you now know, there are numerous solutions. There is so much to be done, dear reader. Yet, this is not as daunting of a task as it may seem. There are many individuals and groups who are working diligently to create change. The goal of health and well-being should be universal. We should not be waiting for sickness or even death to be wake-up calls. We need action now.

I hope the studies and personal stories you have read from around the globe, motivate you to action. For many individuals that I have had the opportunity to speak with during the creation of this book, the day to day work is exhausting physically, mentally, and emotionally. There is not a lot of reprieve or break from the constant work. Therefore, there is not as much balanced living as we would like.

I would like to propose that we all work to make joy a component of everyday living. Not a celebration, party, or moment in time, rather a day-to-day way of being. Let us look at the bigger picture of our lives and those around us. Let us examine our inner world and be openly brave and truthful to ourselves about how we want to live. As one wise person said, how we live in the moment is how we live.

Let us look at our lives in wholeness, joy and gratitude for our incredible abilities, strengths, and supports.

This may seem like an impossible task, as joy seems to come from performance and achievement, making the next grade, in school or at work. The kinder and healthier path is the joy of living, doing the hard work, feeling great about it, and living life in its fullness. It is being with our families, our partners, our friends, and our companion animals and noticing how much we appreciate them. Spending an hour with our face raised up to the sun, rather than down at a computer screen. One way to achieve this joy is by asking ourselves what is good about the day, ourselves, our families, partners, friends, companion animals. A gentle shift in our worldview from time to time makes a difference. Notice how your body reacts when you look for what is good or right in people and things. Remind yourself from time to time to take this viewpoint.

In addition, joy happens when we spend time helping and being supportive of each other as though it really mattered, not just for appearance's sake but because it does truly matter. Think of nature; why do thousands of zebras and wildebeest travel miles and miles together during the Great Migration? They help each other. They work together on the long journey to find water. They are aware of each other's strengths and depend on each other for survival. One doesn't see well, and one doesn't have a distinct sense of smell. One looks for predators and one smells for predators. Together, they have a better chance of making it safely and successful on their journey.

We have choices on how we behave with each other. Seagulls peck at each other and compete for food while geese work together, they honk to encourage each other while flying. If a goose is grounded, another will stay with it until it can fly again.

How you live on a day-to-day basis is the reality of how you live your life. It is possible to create an environment where we hold each other up vs stepping upon each other to rise up? Would you rather be a seagull or a goose?

As discussed, one organization that I had the pleasure of interviewing early on in the writing of this book is the City Mental Health Alliance of London and Attorney Nigel Jones. The City Mental Health Alliance of London is working to provide mentally healthy workplaces. They work on many initiatives including Mental Health First Aid Training to employees, creating healthy business charters, and promotion of open communication and discussion of stigma as it relates to mental health issues. It is a membership organization which helps business to create leadership strategies and stories of collaboration vs competition. The Alliance wants people to thrive at work. If people are thriving in health in one aspect of their lives it can become contagious and cross over to other areas in their life and to other people. The City Mental Health Initiative has member organizations around the world, all trying to create better and mentally healthier workplaces.

Amazing and historical things are occurring. The City Mental Health Alliance of London worked with the World Economic Forum, and for the first time, mental health was on the agenda. The goal was to invigorate business leaders to create mentally healthy workplaces. Leaders from around the globe came to the table to openly talk about their organization's approaches to mental health initiatives as well sharing their own mental health experiences. This is historic work.

Important figures, such as Jacinda Ardern, Prime Minister of New Zealand, recognized publicly that nearly everyone has been affected by mental health issues in some way or another. New Zealand has one of the highest suicide rates in the Organization for Economic Co-operation. Support and a sense of community are crucial aspects for coping with these issues. Your peers and colleagues may be able to understand and relate to your stress or traumatization in ways that others may not. Create that pathway of communication and help to keep it open.

As a greater openness to talking about mental health occurs, we see more interest and discussion in secondary trauma, depression, anxiety, and suicide. There appears to be a beginning awareness in particular of secondary trauma with a sprinkling of articles and discussion, but there is much more to do. This beginning interest and discussion is occurring in all of the countries which we are examining, as well as other countries. Pioneer Attorney Manel Atserias Luque of Spain created a mental health initiative, the Mental Health Institute of European Legal Professions, a historic move for the legal professionals in Spain and Europe.

As these articles and agencies appear, increased organizational awareness of the need to address these issues grows and ultimately, impacts health and well-being. In-country resources and distribution of information has become better over the years though, at the same time, individual workplace stigma seems to continue to be of issue.

Can you imagine working in unison with others toward a common goal in a way that is meaningful and supportive for every person involved? It is possible. Can you imagine a serene day at the office? This, too, is possible. We will see how, as our Champion of Disclosure, Attorney Mary Digiglio discusses ways in which she created a supportive and open atmosphere within the legal practice.

## Section 2: Case Studies

### *Mary Digiglio*

Mary Digiglio is managing partner at Swaab, a Sydney-based mid-tier commercial law firm. She works as a commercial practitioner with an accreditation specialization in property law. Since becoming a managing partner in 2014, Mary has led by example, with a focus on improving education and awareness of mental health and well-being in the legal profession. In 2019, she was named Wellness Advocate of the Year (2019), at the Lawyers Weekly Partner of the Year Awards. Her community work includes membership on the board of Minds Count Foundation, which focuses on promoting well-being in the legal profession.

Mary, you know that I admire the way you have been able to educate the entire office in your organization on mental health issues. How did this effort begin?

My effort in promoting the education of mental health issues began in 2014 when I attended my first Minds Count Lecture (formerly known as Tristan Jepson Memorial Foundation). Minds Count is a charity which was established in 2008 by George and Marie Jepson, who tragically lost their son, Tristan, to suicide. Minds Count's objective is to decease work related psychological ill-health in the legal community and to promote workplace psychological health and safety. The foundation has been at the forefront of building greater awareness of depression and anxiety across all areas of the legal fraternity. Back in 2014, at the lecture, I learned that the majority of the foundation's funding came from law students, and very little funding came from commercial law firms.

I wanted to do my bit to change this, particularly given the majority of the attendees to the annual lecture where in fact employees from commercial law firms. From that point until today, Swaab (the law firm I manage) has been a regular donor to and supporter of the foundation. In 2015 I was invited to become a director of Minds Count, and my affiliation with the foundation and my personal commitment to the well-being has grown from there. Over the last five years, Swaab has focussed on weaving well-being into the culture of our firm, and I am pleased that through the support and passion of many people at Swaab, the well-being of our people and our clients is a fundamental consideration in every decision we make and action we take.

How did the office initially react? Were people open to the discussion?

There will always be the naysayers, those who won't open their minds beyond their own sphere of belief and influence. I believe this is the case for any issue which is new, different or challenges the comfort zone. However, largely my partners responded positively and with support. The fact that back in 2014 the partnership unanimously voted to financially support Minds Count, and this position has been endorsed every year since, reflects the firm's reaction. This does not mean that we have not been challenged by how we ought to react to "real life" incidents of the onset of a mental health condition. This is why we decided that education was key to the success of our commitment.

Our awareness and learnings have been supported by appropriate firm-wide education provided by the Black-Dog Institute, a not-for-profit facility for diagnosis, treatment and prevention of mood disorders such as depression, anxiety and bipolar disorder, and Mental Health First Aid Australia . . . Personally, I have complemented these learnings by enrolling in a Diploma of Counselling with the Australia Institute of Professional Counsellors.

In 2020, the promotion of well-being and mental health awareness is woven into our culture. It is a constant discussion in our firm. It doesn't come and go—it is always present in our working environment. Our younger people have been tremendous in supporting me in advocating well-being, [and] our firm is a leader in the promotion of well-being and awareness of mental health conditions.

Mary, you have shared that you have educational wall hangings or posters and brochures providing mental health information located around the office, and not just hiding in the corner of a lunchroom or lavatory. How did you create an environment where this was welcomed?

Authenticity has been key to achieving buy-in from people across the firm. Whilst I do not have any diagnosed mental health condition, like every person I know, I have experienced some trying times in my life, whether as a result of unfortunate personal experiences, health challenges of loved ones, substance abuse by a loved one, or the stressors that come with managing a law firm and maintaining a large commercial client base and practice of my own. I speak to the firm about my own challenges [and] I have revealed my own vulnerability because in my opinion, this assists people in accepting that everyone is challenged emotionally from time to time and for some people, resilience gets them through these challenges. However, for other people, obstacles are created, and more support and assistance are needed to get out the other end.

In addition to authenticity, education about mental health conditions and permission to discuss mental health issues is vital to creating a constructive and supportive working environment. This is why visual aids become so important. It is one thing to promote well-being by the odd lecture invitation and it is another thing to "walk the talk" by ensuring the issue is a part of our firm's general daily conversation. All of our new starters are given two well-being publications and a copy of the Minds Count best practice guidelines as part of our induction program. The visual aids serve as a constant reminder about our firm's values and the expectation of everyone at our firm.

As we have discussed, stigma is one of the biggest challenges we face when we are trying to do simple things surrounding mental health, such as trying to have a basic conversation. How do you address the issue of stigma so that people can feel safe and ultimately take care of themselves, if they are facing mental health issues?

Here is a list of practical ways we address stigma and the challenge of de-stigmatising:

- Constant conversations, regular external presentations, and continued education for all of our people.
- Commitment from the leaders in the firm to creating an environmental to speak openly about mental health issues and to feel safe to do so.
- Our leaders and managers responding to incidents of mental health within our firm appropriately with kindness, care and compassion—and providing support for recovery.
- Making mental health awareness part of our induction process by providing relevant resources and aids.
- Expecting our people to become and remain educated by (at the very least) attending the mandatory education sessions we facilitate as a firm.
- Promoting mental health month and participating in country wide mental health initiatives during October.
- Continuing our affiliation and support (both financial and non-financial) with Minds Count.
- Participating in (and promoting) our employee assistance program.

What would your advice be to individuals, both professionals and students, who are struggling with these issues?

Identify a colleague you trust and whom you know is an advocate for mental health awareness, talk to them and ask them to help you facilitate appropriate support. Identifying an individual who is going to respond in a constructive manner is important, so it is worth giving this consideration. If you can't identify a colleague, identify a leader in your industry who has a profile in the area and reach out to them for some guidance. It is important to remember that advocates (like me) are not properly trained to deal with mental health issues. We are just a conduit to getting appropriate help and responsible for creating a platform for open and non-judgemental conversation.

Mary Digiglio has shared how her firm has created an open environment that not only acknowledges mental health issues and stigma but openly discusses and shares mental health resources; it's so important to "walk the talk."

## Section 3: New Directions

"Walking the talk" is critical. We can talk about these issues for a long time without taking action. We need a global acceptance followed by global action. You have the opportunity as legal professionals and students to change culture, not just the legal culture but culture in general. People look up to you as leaders and role models. You can continue to perpetuate a dog-eat-dog mentality, or you can create a world where taking care of our health, mental and physical is as readily accepted as taking care of a broken leg. We can create an atmosphere where looking at ourselves and our world in a gentle, joyful manner is acceptable. Can you imagine a day where your body is not bursting with stress or adrenaline? Can you imagine what it feels like to be tranquil and content?

As Professor Adrian Evans states in his book *The Good Lawyer*, "The negatives of life as a lawyer are not intended to dampen your enthusiasm. The reality of legal practice as a moral mixture of good and bad and there is no intrinsic reason why the good should not prevail, if we each recognize that a choice must be made. 'Forewarned is forearmed' could almost be the subtitle, but once you are prepared, there's every reason why your own lawyering can and will be both emotionally satisfying, morally sustaining, and powerfully enabling inside your law firm. You have a tremendous opportunity to improve the culture of your law firm: by showing collegiality, by being fair and honest in your work relationships, and by understanding that the quality of these human relationships can transform the 'culture.' We may be a product of our culture, but we are also contributors to it. Cultural leadership by those at the top is naturally important but being optimistic about your contribution as a lawyer is part of being a 'good' lawyer."[261]

Please take to heart the idea of accountability and your own contribution to shaping "the way things are." Help each other to be brave and speak out. I know you have the courage to make change, or you would not have been attracted to the field of law. You are a fighter. You fight for the law, and families and individuals, please fight for health and well-being. We have a window of opportunity, do not be stagnant and wait for another generation to come through. Use the tools in this book, check in with yourself and your peers, and open discussions on these topics and keep coming back to them. "Educate" and "implement" are good keywords for the journey forward.

Remember, there is quiet beauty everywhere, look around as you are traveling on this planet earth so fast. Do what you need to do in a way that brings health and well-being to you and those around you. There are many of us striving towards this goal. Seek us out and join us.

---

[261] Evans, Adrian. 2014. *The Good Lawyer*. Cambridge: Cambridge University Press, 2014. Reproduced with permission of Cambridge University Press through PLSClear

## Discussion Questions

- What are the five types of well-being? Which ones do you feel are a strength for you and which ones need improvement?
- What components from the Wheel of Wellness can you apply to your life?
- How could you further remove your personal criticism and harshness?
- What do you think of the notion of collaboration versus competition?
- What did you learn from Mary Digiglio?
- What is one step that you could take today, to contribute to your personal health and well-being?
- What is one step that you could take today, to contribute to the health and well-being of your peers?

# References

Davis, Tchiki. "What Is Well-Being? Definition, Types, and Well-Being Skills." *Psychology Today*, January 2, 2018. https://www.psychologytoday.com/us/blog/click-here-happiness/201901/what-is-well-being-definition-types-and-well-being-skills.

Evans, Adrian. 2014. *The Good Lawyer*. Cambridge: Cambridge University Press, 2014. Reproduced with permission of Cambridge University Press through PLSClear